THE IRWIN SERIES IN ECONOMICS

CONSULTING EDITOR

LLOYD G. REYNOLDS
YALE UNIVERSITY

BOOKS IN THE IRWIN SERIES IN ECONOMICS

ECONOMIC POLICY

Readings in Political Economy

. . . the ideas of economists and political philosophers, both when they are right and when they are wrong, are more powerful than is commonly understood. Indeed the world is ruled by little else. Practical men, who believe themselves to be quite exempt from any intellectual influences, are usually the slaves of some defunct economist. Madmen in authority, who hear voices in the air, are distilling their frenzy from some academic scribbler of a few years back. I am sure the power of vested interests is vastly exaggerated compared with the gradual encroachment of ideas. Not, indeed, immediately, but after a certain interval; for in the field of economic and political philosophy there are not many who are influenced by new theories after they are twenty-five or thirty years of age, so that the ideas which civil servants and politicians and even agitators apply to current events are not likely to be the newest. But, soon or late, it is ideas, not vested interests, which are dangerous for good or evil.

J. M. KEYNES, *The General Theory of Employment, Interest, and Money* (1936)

ECONOMIC POLICY

Readings in Political Economy

Edited by

WILLIAM D. GRAMPP
University of Illinois, Chicago

and

EMANUEL T. WEILER
Purdue University

THIRD EDITION

1961

RICHARD D. IRWIN, INC.
HOMEWOOD, ILLINOIS

To the writers whose ideas have made this book possible.

PREFACE

This is a book of readings on economic policy. The first four sections are about the problems of a mixed economy: (1) instability, growth, and their relationship; (2) the market power of firms and unions; (3) the inequality of income and wealth; (4) international trade and economic development. The fifth section is about policy in a planned economy: what its principal features are, how they differ from policies in a mixed economy, and how they are similar.

For each of the first four sections we have looked for readings that (1) state what the problem is that policy must try to solve; (2) present the economic theory that applies to the problem, (3) describe the facts of the problem, (4) indicate the ethical issues that direct policy, and (5) propose some ways by which the problem might be solved. It is not suggested that the readings correspond completely to this preconceived pattern, but in their entirety in each section they remark on all of the aspects of policy as they are outlined above: definition, fact, analysis, value, and action. Together they constitute political economy and give the book its subtitle.

The book is meant for supplementary use in principles of economics, and it can be used in the same way in other courses in which policy figures, such as employment theory, applied economics, government and business, and comparative economic systems. Economists agree that policy has an important place in the study of economics, and some believe it is only in order to solve problems that economics is studied at all. We believe it is well to introduce policy in the principles' course. It engages the student's interest, helps him to understand economic analysis, and dispels the illusion of unreality about it. Even more, it gives him an opportunity to think about public issues under guidance and so can help him later to think about them more effectively on his own. In this field it is not true that a little learning is a dangerous thing—if indeed a year's study of economics is a little thing. Whether it is or not, it is all that most students ever will spend. Yet later they will have to make quite important decisions about economic policies.

In order to introduce students to economic writing of a more substantial kind than they usually encounter, we have provided some editorial assistance. Each section is meant to be a fairly complete statement of the topic it is about. It opens with an editorial introduction that defines the topic and explains how each reading is related to it. Each reading is preceded by a synopsis that summarizes the central ideas in the order presented by the author and directs the students to them. Occasional footnotes have been added, and brackets distinguish them from the author's own footnotes. At the end of each section is an editorial summary that restates the topic in greater detail, defines the goals of policy, and summarizes what each reading contributes to them. The editorial material is not a restatement of the readings, a condensation, or in any other way a substitute for them. Its sole purpose is to introduce students to what in our opinion is a part of the best that has been written on economic policy. It is the thinking of adults, expressed in an adult way, for the adult world of which the students soon will be a part.

Students are not always treated this way. They often are protected from what is difficult. Our experience has been that they usually can manage the difficult if they have a modest amount of help. At the time of the first edition of this book, we expected that some teachers would think it was too formidable for sophomores, even though our own, remarkably typical, sophomores did not find it so when they used it in a preliminary edition. We since have been pleased to learn there are many others who manage quite as well, and we expect that students will find this, the third edition, just as manageable. Economic policy is not a simple thing. Simplicity however is not as appealing as it often is made out to be. There seem to be many who think of it as Santayana did of one of his contemporaries. He said of him, "It was rather simplicity that perhaps he had carried a little too far; so far, that the moral comfort of not apprehending too much had passed into the practical inconvenience of apprehending too little." The contemporary ended his days in an institution for the simple-minded.

The editorial arrangement of this edition is the same as that of the first two, and its purpose is the same. But in other ways it is much different. Of the twenty-six chapters here, only seven were in the second edition and four in the first. The content of the first four sections is more extensive. For example, the first is about growth as well as stability, and the fourth contains more on development than was in the last edition. That on planning contains some of the major changes of recent years in democratic socialism as well as in communism. There is a closer relationship than before between the sections. For example, Schultz's study of investment in human capital (in the section on inequality) has a clear connection with growth, and Galbraith's study could have been placed in the section on market power instead of in that on stability.

We wish to thank our colleagues who have provided comments and suggestions about the content of the previous editions (and also some astonishing differences of opinion). We are grateful again to the librarians who have helped us in many ways, and we wish to thank the publishers who have permitted us to reprint material they have copyrighted. Especially we want to thank the writers whose work is republished here. The value of the book is theirs, and it again is inscribed to them.

WILLIAM D. GRAMPP

EMANUEL T. WEILER

August, 1961

TABLE OF CONTENTS

PART 1. STABILITY AND GROWTH

PART 2. MARKET POWER

PART 1

Stability and Growth

1. BURNS
2. MUSGRAVE
3. BROWNLEE
4. GALBRAITH
5. SMITHIES

Editorial Introduction

THE PROBLEM OF STABILITY AND GROWTH

The last thirty years have witnessed some of the most acute problems in the history of economic policy. They have been the years of a great depression and numerous small recessions, of a world war, of small wars, and of unremitting international tension; and the last twenty have been years of inflation. Economic stability once was defined as the attainment of full employment and a stable price level. Today its objectives are more modest, and most economists would be content with measures that prevented prolonged and substantial unemployment and prevented the small but steady upward movement of prices that constitutes creeping inflation. Growth once meant the gradual improvement of the economic condition of the people, but now it means something more specific and self-conscious: a continuing increase in the real value of the gross national product at a pre-determined rate and by measures that simultaneously promote stability.

The problems that confront the economist are more difficult, because the economies of the world and the world itself have changed. The measures for stability in the United States must contend with the nagging recurrence of minor recessions, a persistent upward drift in the price level, and a structure of markets that may produce cost inflation. The measures must also take into account their international effects in a way that never had to be done in the past. Those that promote growth must be consistent with those taken to secure stability, but must operate in a wider area and over a longer time, taking into account both the limits of stabilization policy and those distinctive to growth itself, such as long run saving and investment, the long run effect of taxes and public expenditure, and the changes in the structure of the economy.

The structural changes are the subject of the paper by Arthur F. Burns, who relates them to the problem of stability and explains how they make the American economy less vulnerable to a massive depression, although not to minor recessions. The government may deal with them in a discretionary way, using measures of different sorts as it believes they will be effective. Or it may commit itself to the use of particular measures made explicit and announced in advance, and act in a rule-abiding and predictable manner. The former is discretionary policy, and how it can best be employed is explained by Richard A. Musgrave. The

3

latter is non-discretionary policy, and is explained by O. H. Brownlee, who proposes rules for stability and growth. Both forms must contend with monopoly in product and labor markets. The relation between monopoly and stability is a fairly new area of policy. J. K. Galbraith explains how competitive industries and oligopolies react differently to fiscal and monetary measures. What the government's fiscal policy is depends very much on what its budget policy is. Economists almost always have said that fiscal measures which promote stability should not be sacrificed to balancing the budget annually. Yet they have not convinced those in authority. In a longer view that takes growth into account, the conventional notions about the balanced budget may have some merit. Its relationship to stability and growth are examined by Arthur Smithies.

1. PROGRESS TOWARD ECONOMIC STABILITY*

Arthur F. Burns

SYNOPSIS

1. Changes in the structure of the economy have promoted growth and moderated the business cycle, the recent downswings being the mildest in one hundred years.

2. In the downswing of the cycle, personal income does not fall as much as production, because dividends vary less than corporate profits and because changes in taxes and government expenditure partly offset changes in private income and spending.

3. There has been a relatively greater increase in employment in the service industries and others where it is more stable than in manufacturing, and the change will become more important as white-collar jobs increase.

4. Consumption has become less sensitive to cyclical changes and is a larger part of aggregate income. It now retards recessions and hastens recoveries.

5. Financial institutions now lessen the danger of liquidity crises, and neither the government nor the private sector any longer believes the cure for the downswing is to let it run its course.

6. The most important contribution of the government has been to lower interest rates in the downswing, and that of business firms to prevent large changes in the ratio of inventories to sales.

7. The structural changes probably will continue and cycles become still milder; but there is no assurance of either because the future will not necessarily repeat the past.

8. Potentially unstabilizing influences are continued price and wage increases, the growing consumer and mortgage debt, the excess of imports over exports, and mistaken ideas of economic policy.

9. The nation must decide whether its policy for the cycle and other problems shall be made after they have presented themselves or whether it shall be made in advance and coordinated by a federal economic policy board.

The American people have of late been more conscious of the business cycle, more sensitive to every wrinkle of economic curves, more alert to the possible need for contra-cyclical action on the part of

* Reprinted by permission from *The American Economic Review*, March 1960, pp. 1–19.

government, than ever before in our history. Minor changes of employment or of productivity or of the price level, which in an earlier generation would have gone unnoticed, are nowadays followed closely by laymen as well as experts. This sensitivity to the phenomena of recession and inflation is a symptom of an increased public awareness of both the need for and the attainability of economic progress. It is precisely because so much of current industrial and governmental practice can be better in the future that our meetings this year are focused on the broad problem of improving the performance of the American economy. However, as we go about the task of appraisal and criticism, it will be well to discipline our impatience for reform. In the measure that we avoid exaggerating our nation's failures or understanding its successes, we shall make it easier for ourselves as well as for economists in other countries to see current needs and developments in a just perspective.

It is a fact of the highest importance, I think, that although our economy continues to be swayed by the business cycle, its impact on the lives and fortunes of individuals has been substantially reduced in our generation. More than twenty-five years have elapsed since we last experienced a financial panic or a deep depression of production and employment. Over twenty years have elapsed since we last had a severe business recession. Between the end of the second world war and the present, we have experienced four recessions, but each was a relatively mild setback. Since 1937 we have had five recessions, the longest of which lasted only thirteen months. There is no parallel for such a sequence of mild—or such a sequence of brief—contractions, at least during the past hundred years in our own country.

Nor is this all. The character of the business cycle itself appears to have changed, apart from the intensity of its over-all movement. We usually think of the business cycle as a sustained advance of production, employment, incomes, consumption, and prices, followed by a sustained contraction, which in time gives way to a renewed advance of aggregate activity beyond the highest levels previously reached. We realize that changes in the price level occasionally outrun changes in production, that employment is apt to fluctuate less than production, and that consumption will fluctuate still less; but we nevertheless think of their movements as being roughly parallel. This concept of the business cycle has always been something of a simplification. For example, during the early decades of the nineteenth century, when agriculture dominated our national economy, occasional declines in the physical volume of production, whether large or small, had little effect on the number of jobs and sometimes had slight influence even on the flow of money incomes. As agriculture diminished in importance, the nation's production, employment, personal income, consumption, and price level fell more closely into step with one another and thus justified our thinking of them as moving in a rough parallelism. In recent years, however, and especially since the second world war, the relations among these movements have become much looser.

The structure of an economy inevitably leaves its stamp on the character of its fluctuations. In our generation the structure of the American economy has changed profoundly, partly as a result of deliberate economic policies, partly as a result of unplanned developments. In considering problems of the future, we can proceed more surely by recognizing the changes in economic organization which already appear to have done much to blunt the impact of business cycles.

I

In the early decades of the nineteenth century the typical American worker operated his own farm or found scope for his energy on the family farm. Governmental activities were very limited. What there was of industry and commerce was largely conducted through small firms run by capitalist-employers. Corporations were rare and virtually confined to banking and transportation. As the population grew and capital became more abundant, individual enterprise expanded vigorously, but corporate enterprise expanded still more. An increasing part of the nation's business therefore came under the rule of corporations. By 1929 the output of corporate businesses was already almost twice as large as the output of individual proprietorships and partnerships. The gap has widened appreciably since then. Corporate profits have therefore tended to increase faster than the incomes earned by proprietors, who still remain very numerous in farming, retail trade, and the professions. Fifty years ago the total income of proprietors was perhaps two and a half times as large as the combined sum of corporate profits and the compensation of corporate officers. By 1957 this corporate aggregate exceeded by a fourth the income of all proprietors and by two thirds the income of proprietors outside of farming.

The great growth of corporations in recent decades has occurred preponderantly in industries where the firm must operate on a large scale to be efficient and therefore must assemble capital from many sources. But a corporation whose stock is held publicly and widely has a life of its own, apart from that of its owners, and will rarely distribute profits at the same rate as they are being earned. While profits normally respond quickly and sharply to a change in sales and production, the behavior of dividends is tempered by business judgment. In practice, dividends tend to move sluggishly and over a much narrower range than profits. Corporations have therefore come to function increasingly as a buffer between the fluctuations of production and the flow of income to individuals. In earlier times the lag of dividends was largely a result of the time-consuming character of corporate procedures. More recently, the advantages of a stable dividend—especially its bearing on a firm's financial reputation—have gained increasing recognition from business managers. Meanwhile, modern trends of taxation have stimulated corporations to rely more heavily on retained profits and less on new stock issues for their equity funds, and this development in turn has facilitated the pursuit of stable dividend policies. Thus the evolution of corporate practice, as well as the growth of corporate enterprise itself, has served to reduce the influence of a cyclical decline of production and profits on the flow of income to individuals.

The expansion and the means of financing of governmental enterprise, especially since the 1930's, have had a similar effect. The increasing complexity of modern life, a larger concept of the proper function of government, and the mounting requirements of national defense have resulted in sharp increases of governmental spending. Fifty years ago the combined expenditure of federal, state, and local governments was about 7 per cent of the dollar volume of the nation's total output. Governmental expenditures rose to 10 per cent of total output in 1929 and to 26 per cent in 1957. This huge expansion of governmental enterprise naturally led to increases in tax rates and to an energetic search for new sources of revenue. In time, taxes came to be imposed on estates, gifts, employment, sales, and—most important of all—on the incomes of both corporations and individuals. Fifty years ago, customs duties still yielded about half of the total revenue of the federal government, and none of our governmental units as yet collected any tax on incomes. Twenty years later, personal and corporate income taxes were already the mainstay of federal finance. Subsequently, the activities of the federal government increased much faster than local activities, and taxes followed suit. By 1957 the income tax accounted for nearly 70 per cent of federal revenue, 8 per cent of state and local revenue, and a little over half of the combined revenue of our various governmental units.

This dominance of the income tax in current governmental finance, together with the recent shift of tax collection toward a pay-as-you-go basis, has enlarged the government's participation in the shifting fortunes of the private economy. During the nineteenth century, taxes were not only a much smaller factor, but such short run elasticity as there was in tax revenues derived almost entirely from customs duties. Hence, when production fell off and private incomes diminished, the accompanying change in governmental revenues was usually small. In recent years, however, governmental revenues have become very sensitive to fluctuations of business conditions. When corporate profits decline by, say, a billion dollars, the federal government will collect under existing law about a half billion less. When individual incomes decline by a billion, the federal government may be expected to collect about $150 million less. State income taxes accentuate these effects. In short, when a recession occurs, our current tax system requires the government to reduce rather promptly and substantially the amount of money it withdraws from the private economy for its own use. The result is that the income from production which corporations and individuals have at their disposal declines much less than does the national income.

Moreover, the operations of government are now so organized that the flow of personal income from production is bolstered during a recession by increased payments of unemployment insurance benefits. Unemployment insurance was established on a national basis in 1935, and the protection of workers against the hazards of unemployment has increased since then. Not all employees are as yet covered; and the benefits, besides, are often inadequate to provide for essentials. Nevertheless, there has been a gradual improvement in the ability of families to get along decently even when the main breadwinner is temporarily unemployed. At present, over 80 per cent of those who work for a wage or salary are covered by unemployment insurance, in contrast to 70 per cent in 1940. The period over which benefits can be paid to an unemployed worker has become longer, and the typical weekly benefit has risen in greater proportion than the cost of living. Furthermore, arrangements have recently been concluded in several major industries whereby benefits to the unemployed are supplemented from private sources.

Other parts of the vast system of social security that we have devised since the 1930's have also served to support the flow of personal income at times when business activity is declining. Payments made to retired workers kept increasing during each recession of the post-war period. The reason is partly that workers handicapped by old age or physical disability experience greater difficulty at such times in keeping their jobs or finding new ones and therefore apply for pensions in somewhat larger numbers. Another factor has been the intermittent liberalization of statutory benefits. But the most important reason is the maturing of the social security system. In 1940, only 7 per cent of people 65 and over were eligible for old-age insurance, in contrast to 23 per cent in 1948 and 69 per cent in 1958. The trend of other public pension programs and the various public assistance programs has also been upward. Between 1929 and 1957 the social security and related benefits paid out by government rose from 1 per cent of personal income to 6 per cent. In 1933, with the economy at a catastrophically low level, these benefit payments were merely $548 million larger than in 1929. On the other hand, in 1958—when business activity was only slightly depressed —they were $4.4 billion above the level of 1957. Even these figures understate the difference between current conditions and those of a quarter century ago, for they leave out of account the private pensions which are beginning to supplement public pensions on a significant scale.

As a result of these major developments, the movement of aggregate personal income is no longer closely linked to the movement of aggregate production. During the post-war period, we have had several brief but sizable setbacks in production. For example, in the course of the recession of 1957–58, the physical output of factories and mines fell 14 per cent, the physical output of commodities and services in the aggregate fell 5.4 per cent, and the dollar volume of total output fell 4.3 per cent. In earlier times, personal incomes would have responded decisively to such a decline in production. This time the government absorbed a substantial part of the drop in the dollar volume of production by putting up with a sharp decline of its revenues despite the need to raise expenditures. Corporations absorbed another part of the decline by maintaining dividends while their undistributed profits slumped. In the end, personal incomes, after taxes, declined less than 1 per cent, and the decline was over before the recession ended.

Although the details have varied from one case to the next, a marked divergence between the movements of personal income and production has occurred in each of the post-war recessions. Indeed, during 1953–54 the total income at the disposal of individuals defied the recession by continuing to increase. This unique achievement was due to the tax reduction that became effective soon after the onset of the recession as well as to the structural changes that have reduced the dependence of personal income on the short run movements of production.

II

When we turn from personal income to employment, we find that the imprint of the business cycle is still strong. During each recession since 1948, unemployment reached a level which, while decidedly low in comparison with the experience of the thirties, was sufficient to cause serious concern. But although the fluctuations of employment have continued to synchronize closely with the movements of production, the relation between the two has been changing in ways which favor greater stability of employment in the future.

As the industrialization of our economy proceeded during the nineteenth century, an increasing part of the population became exposed to the hazards of the business cycle. Manufacturing, mining, construction, freight transportation—these are the strategic industries of a developing economy, and they are also the industries in which both production and jobs have been notoriously unstable. Shortly after the Civil War, the employees attached to this cyclical group of industries already constituted 23 per cent of the labor force. Employees of industries that have remained relatively free from cyclical unemployment—that is, agriculture, merchandising, public utilities, financial enterprises, the personal service trades, and the government—accounted for another 32 per cent. The self-employed in farming, business, and the professions, whose jobs are especially steady, made up the rest, or 45 per cent of the work force. This was the situation in 1869. Fifty years later the proportion of workers engaged in farming, whether as operators or hired hands, had shrunk drastically, and this shrinkage was offset only in part by the relative gain of other stable sources of employment. Consequently, the proportion of employees in the cyclical industries kept rising, decade after decade, and reached 36 per cent in 1919.

Clearly, the broad effect of economic evolution until about 1920 was to increase the concentration of jobs in the cyclically volatile industries, and this was a major force tending to intensify declines of employment during business contractions. Since then, the continued progress of technology, the very factor which originally was mainly responsible for the concentration in the cyclical industries, has served to arrest this tendency. The upward trend of production in manufacturing and the other highly cyclical industries has remained rapid in recent decades. However, advances of technology have come so swiftly in these industries as well as in agriculture that an increasing part of the nation's labor could turn to the multitude of tasks in which the effectiveness of human effort improves only slowly, where it improves at all. Thus the employees of "service" industries constituted 24 per cent of the labor force in 1919, but as much as 44 per cent in 1957. The proportion of self-employed workers in business and the professions, which was 9.4 per cent in the earlier year, became 10.6 per cent in the later year. True, these gains in types of employment that are relatively stable during business cycles were largely canceled by the countervailing trend in agriculture. Nevertheless, the proportion of employees attached to the cyclically volatile industries has not risen since 1919. Or to express this entire development in another way, the proportion of workers having rather steady jobs, either because they work for themselves or because they are employed in industries that are relatively free from the influence of business cycles, kept declining from the beginning of our industrial revolution until about 1920, and since then has moved slightly but irregularly upward.

Thus, the changing structure of industry, which previously had exercised a powerful destabilizing influence on employment and output, particularly the former, has ceased to do so. The new stabilizing tendency is as yet weak, but it is being gradually reinforced by the spread of "white-collar" occupations throughout the range of industry. For many years now, the proportion of people who work as managers, engineers, scientists, draftsmen, accountants, clerks, secretaries, salesmen, or in kindred occupations has been increasing. The white-collar group, which constituted only 28 per cent of the labor force outside of agriculture in 1900, rose to 38 per cent in 1940 and to 44 per cent in 1957. Workers of this category are commonly said to hold a "position" rather than a "job" and to be paid a "salary" rather than a "wage." Hence, they are often sheltered by a professional code which frowns upon frequent firing and hiring. Moreover, much of this type of employment is by its nature of an overhead character and therefore less responsive to the business cycle than are the jobs of machine operators, craftsmen, assembly line workers, truck drivers, laborers, and others in the "blue-collar" category. For example, during the recession of 1957–58, the number of "production workers" employed in manufacturing, who approximate the blue-collar group, declined 12 per cent, while the employment of "nonproduction workers," who approximate the white-collar group, declined only 3 per cent. This sort of difference has been characteristic of recessions generally, not only the most recent episode; and on a smaller scale it has also been characteristic of industry generally, not only of manufacturing.

It appears, therefore, that changes in the occupational structure of the labor force, if not also in the industrial structure, have been tending of late to loosen the links which, over a considerable part of our economic history, tied the short run movement of total employment rather firmly to the cyclical movement of total production, and especially to the cyclical movement of its most unstable parts—that is, the activities of manufacturing, mining, construction, and freight transportation. This stabilizing tendency promises well for the future, although up to the present it has not left a mark on records of aggregate employment that is comparable with the imprint that the stabilizing influences we discussed previously have left on personal income. In the post-war period, as over a longer past, the number of men and women at work, and even more the aggregate of hours worked by them, has continued to move in fairly close sympathy with the fluctuations of production.

We can no longer justifiably suppose, however, when employment falls 2 million during a recession, as it did between July 1957 and July 1958, that the number of people who receive an income has declined by any such figure. In fact, the number of workers drawing unemployment insurance under the several regular plans rose about 1.3 million during these twelve months, while the number of retired workers on public pensions rose another million. Hence, it may be conservatively estimated that the number of income recipients increased over 300 thousand despite the recession. In the other post-war recessions, our experience was fairly similar. In other words, as a result of some of the structural changes on which I dwelt earlier, the size of the income-receiving population has grown steadily and escaped cyclical fluctuations entirely.[1]

III

Turning next to consumer spending, we must try once again to see recent developments in historical perspective. The fact that stands out is

[1] This upward trend would appear steeper than I have suggested if recipients of property income and of public assistance were included in the count. In the present context, however, it has seemed best to restrict the income-receiving population to the working class, or, more precisely, to members of the labor force or those recently in the labor force who receive an income as a matter of right and on some regular basis.

that the impact of business cycles on consumption has recently diminished, while the effects of consumption on the business cycle have become more decisive.

In the classical business cycle, as we came to know it in this country, once business investment began declining appreciably, a reduction of consumer spending soon followed. Sometimes the expansion of investment culminated because the firms of one or more key industries, finding that their markets were growing less rapidly than had been anticipated, made an effort to bring their productive capacity or inventories into better adjustment with sales. Sometimes the expansion culminated because the belief grew that construction and financing costs had been pushed to unduly high levels by the advance of prosperity. Sometimes it culminated for all these or still other reasons. But whatever the cause or causes of the decline in investment, it made its influence felt over an increasing area of the economy. For a while, consumer spending was maintained at a peak level or even kept rising. But since businessmen were now buying on a smaller scale from one another, more and more workers lost their jobs or their overtime pay, financial embarrassments and business failures became more frequent, and uncertainty about the business outlook spread to parts of the economy in which sales and profits were still flourishing. If some consumers reacted to these developments by curtailing their spending in the interest of caution, others did so as a matter of necessity. Before long, these curtailments proved sufficient to bring on some decline in the aggregate spending of consumers. The impulses for reducing business investments therefore quickened and the entire round of events was repeated, with both investment and consumption declining in a cumulative process.

As the contraction continued, it tried men's patience, yet in time worked its own cure. Driven by hard necessity, business firms moved with energy to reduce costs and increase efficiency. Consumers whose incomes were declining often saved less or dissaved in order not to disrupt their customary living standards. Hence, even if sales and prices were still falling, profit margins improved here and there. In the meantime, bank credit became more readily available, costs of building and terms of borrowing became more favorable, the bond market revived, business failures diminished, and the investment plans of innovators and others began expanding again. When recovery finally came, it was likely to be led by a reduced rate of disinvestment in inventories or by a new rush to make investments in fixed capital. At this stage of the business cycle, consumer spending was at its very lowest level, if not still declining.

Many of these features of earlier business cycles have carried over to the present. However, the behavior of consumers in the post-war recessions has departed from the traditional pattern in two respects. In the first place, consumers maintained their spending at a high level even after business activity had been declining for some months, so that the tendency of recessions to cumulate was severely checked. During the recession of 1945, consumer spending actually kept increasing. In each of the later recessions it fell somewhat; but the decline at no time exceeded 1 per cent and lasted only a quarter or two. In the second place, instead of lagging at the recovery stage, as it had in earlier times, consumer spending turned upward before production or employment resumed its expansion. This shift in cyclical behavior appears clearly in department store sales, which have been recorded on a substantially uniform basis for several decades and are widely accepted as a tolerably good indicator of consumer spending. In the recoveries of 1921, 1924, 1927, and 1938, these sales lagged by intervals ranging from two to four months. In 1933 their upturn came at the same time as in production and employment. It thus appears that, during the 1920's and 1930's, consumer spending in no instance led the economy out of a slump. In the post-war period, on the other hand, department store sales have led successive recoveries by intervals stretching from two to five months. Of course, department store sales cover only a small fraction of consumer expenditure, and correction for price changes would alter their historical record somewhat. But the main features of the cyclical behavior of dollar sales by department stores are broadly confirmed by other evidence on consumer spending, which is extensive for recent years. We may therefore conclude with considerable assurance that consumer spending has played a more dynamic role in recent times. Not only have consumers managed their spending during recessions so that the cumulative process of deflation has been curbed, but consumer spending has emerged as one of the active factors in arresting recession and hastening recovery.

This new role of the consumer in the business cycle reflects some of the developments of the post-war period that we considered earlier, particularly the greatly enhanced stability in the flow of personal income, the steady expansion in the number of income recipients, and the relative increase in the number of steady jobs. It reflects also the improvements of financial organization and other structural changes which have strengthened the confidence of people, whether acting as consumers or investors, in their own and the nation's economic future. Whatever may have been true of the past, it can no longer be held that consumers are passive creatures who lack the power or the habit of initiating changes in economic activities. There is no harm in thinking of consumer spending as being largely "determined" by past and current incomes, provided we also recognize that the level of current incomes is itself shaped to a significant degree by the willingness of people to work hard to earn what they need to live as they feel they should. The evidence of rising expectations and increased initiative on the part of consumers is all around us. It appears directly in the rapidly rising proportion of women in the labor force, in the sizable and increasing proportion of men who hold down more than one job, in the slackening of the long term decline of the average work week in manufacturing despite the increased power of trade-unions, as well as indirectly in the improvement of living standards and the great upsurge of population. Indeed, the expansive forces on the side of consumption have been so powerful that we must not be misled by the cyclical responses of consumer spending, small though they were, to which I referred earlier. There are no continuous records of inventories in the hands of consumers; but if such statistics were available, we would almost certainly find that consumption proper, in contrast to consumer spending, did not decline at all during any of the post-war recessions.

In view of these developments in the realm of the consumer, it is evident that the force of any cyclical decline of production has in recent years been reduced or broken as its influence spread through the economy. Production has remained unstable, but the structure of our economy has changed in ways which have limited the effects of recessions on the lives of individuals—on the numbers who receive an income, the aggregate of personal incomes, consumer spending, actual consumption, and to some degree even the numbers employed. It is, therefore, hardly an exaggeration to assert that a good part of the personal security which in an earlier age derived from living on farms and in closely knit family units, after having been disrupted by the onrush of industrialization and urbanization, has of late been restored through the new institutions that have developed in both the private and public branches of our economy.

IV

In concentrating, as I have thus far, on the changes of economic organization which have lately served to reduce the impact of business cycles on the lives of individuals, I have provisionally taken the cyclical movement of production for granted. Of course, if the fluctuations of production had been larger, the impact on people would have been greater. On the other hand, the stabilized tendency of personal income and consumption has itself been a major reason why recent recessions of production have been brief and of only moderate intensity. Many other factors have contributed to this development. Among them are the deliberate efforts made in our generation to control the business cycle, of which I have as yet said little.

In earlier generations there was a tendency for the focus of business thinking to shift from the pursuit of profits to the maintenance of financial solvency whenever confidence in the continuance of prosperity began to wane. At such times, experienced businessmen were prone to reason that it would shortly become more difficult to collect from their customers or to raise funds by borrowing, while they in turn were being pressed by their creditors. Under the circumstances, it seemed only prudent to conserve cash on hand, if not also to reduce inventories or accounts receivable. Such efforts by some led to similar efforts by others, in a widening circle. As pressure on commodity markets, security markets, and on the banking system mounted, the decline of business activity was speeded, and the readjustment of interest rates, particularly on the longer maturities, was delayed. More often than not, the scramble for liquidity ran its course without reaching crisis proportions. Sometimes, however, as in 1873, 1893, and 1907, events took a sinister turn. Financial pressures then became so acute that doubts arose about the ability of banks to meet their outstanding obligations; and as people rushed to convert their deposits into currency, even the soundest banks were forced to restrict the outflow of cash. With the nation's system for making monetary payments disrupted, panic ruled for a time over the economy, and production inevitably slumped badly.

It was this dramatic phase of the business cycle that first attracted wide notice and stimulated students of public affairs to seek ways and means of improving our financial organization. The Federal Reserve Act, which became law under the shadow of the crisis of 1907, required the pooling of bank reserves and established facilities for temporary borrowing by banks. The hope that this financial reform would ease the transition from the expanding to the contracting phase of business cycles has been amply justified by experience. But the Federal Reserve System could not prevent the cumulation of financial trouble during business expansions. Nor could it prevent runs on banks or massive bank failures, as the Great Depression demonstrated. The need to overhaul and strengthen the financial system became increasingly clear during the thirties and led to numerous reforms, among them the insurance of mortgages, the creation of a secondary market for mortgages, the insurance of savings and loan accounts, and—most important of all—the insurance of bank deposits. These financial reforms have served powerfully to limit the propagation of fear, which in the past had been a major factor in intensifying slumps of production.

But more basic than the financial innovations or any other specific measures of policy has been the change in economic and political attitudes which took root during the thirties. The economic theory that depressions promote industrial efficiency and economic progress lost adherents as evidence accumulated of the wreckage caused by unemployment and business failures. The political belief that it was best to leave business storms to blow themselves out lost its grip on men's minds as the depression stretched out. In increasing numbers, citizens in all walks of life came around to the view that mass unemployment was intolerable under modern conditions and that the federal government had a continuing responsibility to foster competitive enterprise, to prevent or moderate general economic declines, and to promote a high and rising level of employment and production. This new philosophy of intervention was articulated by the Congress in the Employment Act of 1946, which solemnly expressed what had by then become a national consensus.

In recent times, therefore, the business cycle has no longer run a free course, and this fact has figured prominently in the plans of businessmen as well as consumers. During the 1930's, when the objectives of social reform and economic recovery were sometimes badly confused, many investors suspected that contra-cyclical policies would result in narrowing the scope of private enterprise and reducing the profitability of investment. These fears diminished after the war as the government showed more understanding of the need to foster a mood of confidence so that enterprise, innovation, and investment may flourish. In investing circles, as elsewhere, the general expectation of the post-war period has been that the government would move with some vigor to check any recession that developed, that its actions would by and large contribute to this objective, and that they would do so in a manner that is broadly consistent with our national traditions. This expectation gradually became stronger, and it has played a significant role in extending the horizons of business thinking about the markets and opportunities of the future. The upsurge of population, the eagerness of consumers to live better, the resurgence of western Europe, the revolutionary discoveries of science, and the steady flow of new products, new materials, and new processes have added impetus to the willingness of investors to expend huge sums of capital on research and on the improvement and expansion of industrial plant and equipment. Some of these influences have also been effective in augmenting public investment. The fundamental trend of investment has therefore been decidedly upward. The private part of investment has continued to move cyclically; but it is now a smaller fraction of total national output, and it has displayed a capacity to rebound energetically from the setbacks that come during recessions.

The specific measures adopted by the government in dealing with the recessions of the post-war period have varied from one case to the next. In all of them, monetary, fiscal, and housekeeping policies played some part, with agricultural price-support programs assuming special prominence in one recession, tax reductions in another, and increases of public expenditure in still another. Taking a long view, the most nearly consistent part of contra-cyclical policy has been in the monetary sphere. Since the early 1920's, when the Federal Reserve authorities first learned how to influence credit conditions through open market operations, long term interest rates have tended to move down as soon as the cyclical peak of economic activity was reached, in contrast to the long lags that were characteristic of earlier times. Since 1948 the decline of long term interest rates in the early stages of a recession has also become more rapid. This change in the cyclical behavior of capital markets reflects the increased vigor and effectiveness of recent monetary policies. Inasmuch as optimism, as a rule, is still widespread during the initial stages of an economic decline, a substantial easing of credit, provided it comes early enough, can appreciably hasten economic recovery. This influence is exerted only in part through lower interest rates. Of greater consequence is the fact that credit becomes more readily available, that the money supply is increased or kept from falling, that the liquidity of financial assets is improved, and that financial markets are generally stimulated. The effects of easier credit are apt to be felt most promptly by smaller businesses and the home-building industry, but they tend to work their way through the entire economy. There can be little doubt that the rather prompt easing of credit conditions, which occurred during recent setbacks of production, was of some significance in keeping their duration so short.

Business firms have also been paying closer attention to the cycle, and not a few of them have even tried to do something about it. These efforts have been expressed in a variety of ways—through the adoption of long range capital budgets, closer control of inventories, and more energetic selling or some relaxation of credit standards in times of recession. I do not know enough to assess either the extent or the success of some of these policies. Surely, investment in fixed capital has remained a highly volatile activity—a fact that is sometimes overlooked by concentrating attention on years instead of months and on actual expenditures instead of new commitments. There is, however, strong evidence that the businessmen of our generation manage inventories better than did their predecessors. The inventory-sales ratio of manufacturing firms has lately averaged about a fourth less than during the 1920's, despite the increased importance of the durable goods sector, where inventories are especially heavy. The trend of the inventory-sales ratio has also moved down substantially in the case of distributive firms. This success in economizing on inventories has tended to reduce the fluctuations of inventory investment relative to the scale of business operations, and this in turn has helped to moderate the cyclical swings in production. Not only that, but it appears that the cyclical downturns of both inventories and inventory investment have tended to come at an earlier stage of the business cycle in the post-war period than they did previously, so that any imbalance between inventories and sales could be corrected sooner. Since consumer outlays—and often also other expenditures—were well maintained during the recent recessions of production, the rising phase of inventory disinvestment ceased rather early, and this naturally favored a fairly prompt recovery of production.

Thus, numerous changes in the structure of our economy have combined to stimulate over-all expansion during the post-war period and to keep within moderate limits the cyclical declines that occurred in production. Indeed, there are cogent grounds for believing that these declines were even more moderate than our familiar statistical records suggest. The line of division between production for sale and production for direct use does not stand still in a dynamic economy. In the early decades of the industrial revolution an increasing part of our production was, in effect, transferred from the home to the shop and factory. This trend has continued in the preparation of foods, but in other activities it appears on balance to have been reversed. The great expansion of home ownership, the invention of all sorts of mechanical contrivances for the home, longer vacations, the general eagerness for improvement, if not also the income tax, have stimulated many people to do more and more things for themselves. Consumers have become equipped to an increasing degree with the capital goods they need for transportation, for the refrigeration of food, for the laundering of clothes, as well as for entertainment and instruction. They have also been doing, on an increasing scale, much of the carpentry, painting, plumbing, and landscaping around their homes. Such activities of production are less subject to the business cycle than the commercial activities which enter statistical reports. Yet these domestic activities have undoubtedly been expanding rapidly, and perhaps expanding even more during the declining than during the rising phase of the business cycle. Hence, it is entirely probable that the cyclical swings of production have of late been smaller, while the average rate of growth of production has been higher, than is commonly supposed.

V

It is the nature of an economic vocabulary to change slowly, when it changes at all. We keep speaking of the price system, the business cycle, capitalism, socialism, communism, and sometimes we even refer to the "inherent instability" of capitalism or of communism; but the reality that these terms and phrases are intended to denote or sum up does not remain fixed. I have tried to show how a conjuncture of structural changes in our economy has served to modify the business cycle of our times. Some of these changes were planned, while others were unplanned. Some resulted from efforts to control the business cycle, while others originated in policies aimed at different ends. Some arose from private and others from public activities. Some are of very recent origin and others of long standing. The net result has been that the intensity of cyclical swings of production has become smaller. The links that previously tied together the cyclical movements of production, employment, personal income, and consumption have become looser. And, as everyone knows, the once familiar parallelism of the short term movements in the physical volume of total production, on the one hand, and the average level of wholesale or consumer prices, on the other, has become somewhat elusive.

To be sure, special factors of an episodic character played their part in recent business cycles, as they always have. For example, a pent-up demand for civilian goods was highly significant in checking the recession of 1945. The tax reduction legislated in April 1948 helped to moderate the recession which began toward the end of that year. The tax cuts announced soon after business activity began receding in 1953 merely required executive acquiescence in legislation that had been passed before any recession was in sight. Again, the sputniks spurred the government's response to the recession of 1957–58. Special circumstances such as these undoubtedly weakened the forces of economic contraction at certain times; but they also strengthened them at other times. In particular, governmental purchases from private firms have not infrequently been an unsettling influence rather than a stabilizing force. We need only recall the drop of federal expenditure on commodities and services from an annual rate of $91 billion in the early months of 1945 to $16 billion two years later, or the fall from $59 billion to $44 billion soon after the Korean hostilities came to a close. The ability of our economy to adjust to such major disturbances without experiencing a severe or protracted slump testifies not only to our good luck; it testifies also to the stabilizing power of the structural changes that I have emphasized.

It seems reasonable to expect that the structural changes in our economy, which have recently served to moderate and humanize the business cycle, will continue to do so. The growth of corporations is not likely to be checked, nor is the tendency to pay fairly stable dividends likely to be modified. The scale of governmental activities will remain very extensive, and so it would be even if the communist threat to our nation security were somehow banished. Our methods of taxation might change materially, but the income tax will remain a major source of governmental revenue. Governmental expenditures might fluctuate sharply, but they are not likely to decline during a recession merely because governmental revenues are then declining. The social security system is more likely to grow than to remain stationary or contract. Private pension arrangements will multiply, and so also may private supplements to unemployment insurance. Our population will continue to grow. The restlessness and eagerness of consumers to live better is likely to remain a dynamic force. Research and development activities will continue to enlarge opportunities for investment. Governmental efforts to promote a high and expanding level of economic activity are not likely to weaken. Private businesses will continue to seek ways to economize on inventories and otherwise minimize the risk of cyclical fluctuations in their operations. Employment in agriculture is already so low that its further decline can no longer offset future gains of the service industries on the scale experienced in the past. The spread of white-collar occupations through-out the range of industry will continue and may even accelerate. For all these reasons, the business cycle is unlikely to be as disturbing or trouble-some to our children as it once was to us or our fathers.

This is surely a reasonable expectation as we look to the future. Yet it is well to remember that projections of human experience remain de-scriptions of a limited past, no matter how alluringly they are expressed in language of the future. A lesson of history, which keeps resounding through the ages, is that the most reasonable of expectations sometimes lead nations astray. If my analysis is sound, it supports the judgment that the recessions or depressions of the future are likely to be appreciably milder on the average than they were before the 1940's. It supports no more than this. In view of the inherent variability of business cycles and our still somewhat haphazard ways of dealing with them, there can be no assurance that episodic factors will not make a future recession both longer and deeper than any we experienced in the post-war period.

Nor can there be any assurance that the conjuncture of structural changes on which I have dwelt will not be succeeded by another which will prove less favorable to economic stability. For example, although the stabilizing influence of the rising trend of white-collar employment in manufacturing has been more than sufficient to offset the cyclically in-tensifying influence of a greater concentration of employment in the durable goods sector, the balance of forces might be tipped the other way in the future. This could happen all the more readily if, as white-collar work continues to grow, the need to cut costs during a recession should make this type of employment less stable than it has been. Again, our exports in recent decades have tended to intensify the business cycle somewhat, and this factor may become of larger significance. Also, it still remains to be seen whether the rising trend of prices—to say nothing of the rapidly growing consumer and mortgage debt—may not serve to complicate future recessions.

A generation ago, many economists, having become persuaded that our economy had reached maturity, spoke grimly of a future of secular stagnation. Parts of their analysis were faulty, and their predictions have proved wrong; yet their warning helped to mobilize thought and energy to avert the danger of chronic unemployment. Of late, many economists have been speaking just as persuasively, though not always as grimly, of a future of secular inflation. The warning is timely. During the post-war recessions the average level of prices in wholesale and con-sumer markets has declined little or not at all. The advances in prices that customarily occur during periods of business expansion have there-fore become cumulative. It is true that in the last few years the federal government has made some progress in dealing with inflation. Neverthe-less, wages and prices rose appreciably even during the recent reces-sion, the general public has been speculating on a larger scale in common stocks, long term interest rates have risen very sharply since mid-1958, and the yield on stocks relative to bonds has become abnormally low. All these appear to be symptoms of a continuation of inflationary expectations or pressures.

Such developments have often led to economic trouble. They could do so again even if our balance of payments on international account remained favorable. That, however, has not been the case for some time. The "dollar shortage" which influenced much of our economic thinking and practice during the past generation seems to have ended. The economies of many areas of the free world, especially of western Europe and Japan, have lately been rebuilt, and their competitive power has been restored. This re-establishment of competitive and monetary links between our country and others may cause us some inconvenience, but it is basically a promising development for the future. It should stimulate our economic growth as well as contribute to the economic progress and political stability of other nations of the free world. Our financial policies, however, will gradually need to be adjusted to the changed international environment. Although our gold stocks are still abundant and the dollar is still the strongest currency in the world, we can no longer conduct our economic affairs without being mindful of gold, or of the short term balances that foreign governments and citizens have accumulated here, or of the levels of labor costs, interest rates, and prices in our country relative to those in other nations. Unless the deficit in our balance of payments is soon brought under better control, our nation's ability to pursue contra-cyclical policies during a business recession may be seriously hampered.

We are living in extraordinarily creative but also deeply troubled times. One of the triumphs of this generation is the progress that our nation has made in reducing economic instability. In the years ahead, no matter what we do as a people, our economy will continue to undergo changes, many of which were neither planned nor anticipated. However, the course of events, both domestic and international, will also depend— and to a large degree—on our resourcefulness and courage in deliberately modifying the structure of our economy so as to strengthen the forces of growth and yet restrain instability.

Great opportunities as well as difficult problems face our nation. Monopoly power, which is still being freely exercised despite all the exhortation of recent years, can be curbed by moving toward price and wage controls or, as many economists still hope, by regenerating competition. Higher protective tariffs, import quotas, and "Buy American" schemes can be embraced or, as many economists hope, avoided. A tax structure that inhibits private investment and directs people's energy into activities that contribute little to the nation's economic strength can be retained or reformed. Costly farm surpluses can be further encouraged by government or discontinued. The problems posed by the slums and the inefficient transportation of many of our cities can be neglected or attacked with some zeal. The inadequacy of our unemployment insurance system can be ignored until the next recession or corrected while there is opportunity for a judicious overhauling. In general, our governmental authorities can deal with recessions by trusting to improvisations of public spending, which often will not become effective until economic recovery is already under way, or by providing in advance of any recession for fairly prompt and automatic adjustment of income tax rates to a temporarily lower level of economic activity. The coordination of governmental policies, which may make the difference between success and failure in promoting our national objectives, can be left largely to accidents of personal force and ingenuity, or it can be made systematic through an economic policy board under the chairmanship of the President. These and other choices will have to be made by the people of the United States; and economists—far more than any other group—will in the end help to make them.

2. THE OPTIMAL MIX OF STABILIZATION POLICIES*

Richard A. Musgrave

SYNOPSIS

1. Stabilization policies are related to growth policies. But while full employment and price level stability are the accepted goals of stabilization, the appropriate growth rate is more difficult to determine.

2. The choice of stabilization policies is determined by whether instability is caused by (a) an excess or deficiency of aggregate demand or (b) monopoly power in setting prices and wages.

3. Independent decisions must be made about the amount of resources to be devoted to the public sector and the type of tax structure which is best for accomplishing this. Counter-cyclical adjustments should be made in the level of taxation and not in (a) the level of government expenditure or (b) the structure of taxes.

4. Monetary policies are more effective in restricting than in expanding aggregate demand.

5. Monetary policies are not as neutral as believed in their effect on the structure of the economy. By restricting local government spending during tight-money periods, for example, monetary policies may affect the structure as much as tax changes.

6. Built-in stability is not adequate to prevent instability, and discretionary fiscal and monetary policies are necessary.

7. When monopolistic sellers initiate price increases, full employment and price stability become inconsistent goals. Even small annual price increases add up to a great deal over a lifetime. But sustained unemployment is an excessive cost for price stability.

8. Fiscal and monetary policies cannot prevent cost-push inflation, and the only remedy may be a public review of wage and price decisions in key industries.

9. The methods used to stabilize the economy will have an effect on its rate of growth and on social values.

10. The limiting of savings and investment restricts growth; tax policies that promote it can be inconsistent with equity; and suitable fiscal policies may produce large deficits.

11. Stabilization policy is consistent with a number of different growth rates, and the choice of the rate must be made on non-economic as well as economic grounds.

*Reprinted from *The Relationship of Prices to Economic Stability and Growth*, prepared for the Joint Economic Committee (Washington, D.C.: U.S. Government Printing Office, 1958), pp. 597–609.

It is the function of stabilization policy to maintain a high level of resource utilization, especially the full employment of labor, and to provide for a stable level of prices or value of money. The achievement of these objectives is related closely to economic growth. A high level of investment is needed to maintain full employment; but a high level of investment raises economic capacity, and this requires that an ever-growing demand be forthcoming to take the rising full-employment output of the market. The economy, if it is not to collapse, must keep growing. Economic growth, therefore, is essential to the maintenance of full employment and price level stability.

But growth is more than a means to full employment and a stable price level. It is also a policy objective in its own right. If the appropriate policies are pursued, full employment and price level stability may be compatible with a wide variety of growth rates, and the choice of policy measures by which full employment and price level stability are secured may have considerable bearing on the resulting rate of growth.[1] Thus, public policy is confronted with the further problem of selecting the appropriate rate of growth. While the objectives of full employment and price level stability are readily agreed upon, the choice of an optimal rate of growth is a difficult matter.

Public policy must intervene when the economy fails to provide for full employment or price level stability, and when the prevailing rate of growth falls short of (or conceivably exceeds) the optimal rate. There are many reasons why unemployment or inflation may arise, and the appropriate choice of stabilization policies differs, depending on the underlying causes of instability. Without attempting to explore these causes, I shall merely distinguish between two types of situations:

1. In the first group, I include all those instances where a departure from the objectives of full employment and price level stability is caused by a deficiency or an excess in aggregate demand. Costs and prices are assumed to follow the level of demand, at least in the upward direction, but they do not make for an initial change. In this case the remedy for deflation or inflation must be found in restoring demand to the proper level. Aggregate demand is deficient if planned saving at the full-employment level of income exceeds investment plus government deficit, and vice versa for an excess in demand. This is the situation to which most of the traditional discussion of stabilization, both fiscal and monetary, addresses itself.

2. In the second group, I include those instances where instability originates not from the demand but from the sellers' side of the market. This is the more recent case of "push inflation," and the currently experienced phenomenon of recession with price rise. Here the remedy points to direct action in the sellers' market, be it on prices and/or wages.

---

[1] In connection with this entire topic, see the discussion of similar problems in Secs. I, II, and V of *Federal Tax Policy for Economic Growth and Stability*, Joint Committee on the Economic Report (Washington, D.C.: U.S. Government Printing Office, 1959).

As we look at various situations of instability, we find that the government may choose between various fiscal, monetary, and direct control devices. The purpose of this paper is to examine the considerations which should underlie the choice. We shall find that the answer does not lie in considerations of stabilization policy alone, but that it depends also upon the effects of various measures on the allocation of resources, the distribution of income, and the rate of growth. Stabilization policy, therefore, cannot be divorced from other objectives of public policy.

STABILIZING THE LEVEL OF DEMAND

We begin with conditions of potential deflation or inflation, caused by a deficiency or excess in the level of aggregate demand, with costs and prices a passive factor. The problem is one of raising or restricting the level of demand, and for this purpose various fiscal or monetary devices may be used. For the time being, I shall look at the matter from a short run point of view, so that effects of investment upon capacity may be disregarded. Those effects and the resulting problem of growth are taken up in the next section.

Alternative Fiscal Measures

Consider first the choice between various fiscal approaches to stabilization. In particular, consider (*a*) the choice between adjustments in the level of goods and service expenditures of government, and adjustments in the level of tax rates; and (*b*) the choice between adjustments in the general level of tax rates and adjustments in the structure of the tax system.

Expenditure Adjustment versus Tax Adjustment. The earlier thinking in compensatory finance was concerned primarily with depression and ran in terms of deficit spending. That is to say, the remedy was seen in an increase in the goods and services expenditures of government, be it in the form of public works or other outlays. In recent years, writers have emphasized the possibility of reducing tax rates, thus raising disposable income and thereby the level of private expenditures. In comparing these two approaches, a number of considerations arise.

To begin with, we may compare the amounts of tax reduction and expenditure increase which are required to obtain a given leverage on income. If we disregard possible incentive effects of changes in tax rates on investment, it may be shown easily that per dollar of change, an increase in goods and services expenditures of government is more effective than a decrease in tax yield.[2] This is so because the initial increase in de-

---

[2] The case of increase in transfer payments is similar in principle to that of tax reduction. However, transfer recipients, if unemployed, are likely to spend the entire amount of the transfer. Therefore, dole payments will be as effective as goods and services expenditures of government.

mand is a full dollar in the first case, whereas part of the tax reduction may be lost in the second as consumers increase saving as well as spending. In both cases, the initial gain in spending is subject to a multiplier effect. Since the multiplicand is less in the second case, the total effect will be less as well. Thus, it appears that anti-depression policy by tax reduction requires a larger deficit than anti-depression policy by expenditure increase. If it was our objective to minimize deficit, this would be a reason for choosing the expenditure approach. By the same logic, anti-inflation policy would rely on tax increase, as this would require a larger surplus and hence permit greater debt reduction.

Most economists agree that this is not the proper basis of choice. Changes in the public debt have some significance because they affect the state of liquidity, but they are not that important a factor. Turning now to a set of practical considerations, the choice between tax and expenditure changes may be made to hinge on such factors as the speed with which they can be introduced, the speed with which they become effective in changing demand after they are introduced, the rate at which action in any one direction may be reversed, and so forth. I shall not consider these points in detail, except to note that the introduction or abandonment of public works projects is not a highly flexible matter. For this reason, public works policy is more applicable in a situation where expansionary or restrictive action is required on a sustained basis. This basic difficulty does not apply to changes in tax rates which, in principle at least, may be introduced and discontinued promptly, as economic conditions require. The difficulty here is one of speeding up the legislative and administrative machinery by which such changes are made.

In this connection I should like to repeat my recent suggestion to the Ways and Means Committee that Congress, in its annual concern with revenue legislation, deal with two types of measures.[3] The first would be the traditional task of providing for an equitable tax structure, and for setting tax rates so as to provide the yield called for in view of expenditure requirements and the likely economic outlook for the coming year. In addition, Congress would authorize the President to apply changes in tax rates or exemptions within prescribed limits and forms, provided that such changes are necessary to meet his responsibilities under the Employment Act. Thus the President may be authorized to raise or lower income tax exemptions by $100, or to raise or lower the first bracket rate by two percentage points. Such a policy would add greatly to the President's ability to meet his responsibilities under the Employment Act, and I am confident that the arrangement could be made without weakening congressional control over tax policy.

Leaving aside these matters of flexibility, there is a further and perhaps more basic consideration in the choice between adjusting expendi-

[3] Hearings on Tax Revision, Committee on Ways and Means, U.S. Congress, January 9, 1958.

tures and tax rates. This is the question whether the change in expenditures should be in the form of public expenditures for public purposes, or private expenditure for private purposes. It is a sound principle that we should not undertake public expenditures and provide public services merely to raise employment, and that we should not curtail public expenditures and public services merely to check inflation. Putting the matter more positively, we should decide in any given situation how much resources we wish to devote to supplying public services, and how much we wish to devote to supplying private services; and we should then provide for full employment and price level stability without interference with this requirement of efficient resource use.

This principle leaves room for some degree of counter-cyclical fluctuation in the level of public expenditures, but it suggests that the main burden should be borne by the tax adjustment.[4] Once this principle is accepted, public services must always be justified on their own merits, never in terms of a make-work project. Similarly, a curtailment of public services must be justified on its own merits, not merely as a means to check inflation. While expenditure adjustments may be in order within certain limits, and to meet special situations such as localized unemployment, it is most important to understand that compensatory adjustments cannot be made without interfering with an efficient allocation of resources between public and private uses. Lest my position be misinterpreted, let me hasten to add that my personal preferences speak in favor of a liberal allocation of resources to public use, but this is not the issue here. The issue is that such allocation as is made should be made on its own merits; it should not be swollen as an anti-deflation or shrunk as an anti-inflation device.

Change in Tax Level versus Change in Tax Structure. I now turn to a second choice in fiscal policy, referring this time to various types of tax adjustment. The question here is whether tax adjustments to check deflation or inflation should be essentially through a change in the general level of tax rates, while leaving the tax structure more or less unchanged, or whether they should be selective.

The selective approach is frequently justified by the argument that we should change those taxes which give us the greatest possible leverage effect per dollar of yield change.[5] Thus, it is argued that tax reduction to check depression should be concentrated at the lower end of the income scale, it being assumed that investment cannot be stimulated anyhow, and that the consumption response of low income groups

---

[4] Under conditions of potential depression, people devote a smaller part of their resources to capital formation than under conditions of potential boom. Therefore, they will devote more to other uses, including those of a public and private sort. Such may be expected to be the case even though a full-employment level of income is provided by tax and transfer policy. See P. A. Samuelson in *Federal Tax Policy for Economic Growth and Stability.*

[5] See my paper in *Federal Tax Policy for Economic Growth and Stability.*

will be stronger than that of high income groups. Similarly, it is argued that a tax increase to check inflation should again be concentrated at the lower end, since investment is needed to secure additional capacity, and consumption is checked more effectively by taxing low incomes. This gives us a tax structure, the progressivity of which fluctuates in a counter-cyclical manner. Other results might be obtained if other objectives are set. However this may be, such is not the correct view of tax adjustments.

My reasoning is similar to the case of expenditure policy. The use of fiscal policy for compensatory purposes is important and essential, but it can and should be performed without interference with other and no less important objectives of budget policy. The other objective, in the present case, is that of equity in taxation. Equity is a complex subject which cannot be dealt with here. As I see it, there are two aspects to it. First, taxes ought to be distributed so that people pay for public services in accordance with their desire to have such services performed and their ability to pay for them. Second, taxes (along with transfer payments) have the function of securing adjustments in the distribution of income. This is the primary reason why most people agree that the tax structure should be progressive. However one feels about equality or inequality, people should be permitted to form their views as to what constitutes a desirable distribution of income and a fair distribution of the tax bill independent of the need for anti-inflationary or anti-deflationary action. If a certain degree of progression is held desirable, then we should not be forced to deviate from it for compensatory reasons; and quite similar considerations apply to what I like to think of as the principle of "horizontal equity," the rule that people in equal positions should pay equal amounts of tax.

We thus arrive at the basic principle: that compensatory adjustments should be in the level rather than the structure of the tax system. Let me note here the current discussion with regard to tax reduction. If taxes are to be reduced at the lower end of the income scale, I would prefer this reduction to be made by way of splitting the first bracket and cutting the rate on the initial $1,000 rather than by way of raising exemptions. I feel this way because, from the longer run point of view, it is more equitable to tax the lower income groups by way of income taxes rather than by way of sales taxes. Due to the effects of exemptions, the former are highly progressive at the lower end of the scale, whereas the latter are highly regressive.

As before, there are certain exceptions to the general rule. Selective tax adjustments may be desirable where the deficiency in demand is not general but originates in a particular point in the income flow, such as the hoarding of retained earnings as a cause of depression. Where such is the case, differential taxation of retained earnings may be desirable, even though it may not be justifiable on equity grounds. Or differential adjustments, such as a reduction of excises in a recession, may be desirable on grounds of equity as well as economic policy. Students of taxation are not entitled to demand that the tax tool be left alone so that the tax structure remain beautiful, thus falling in line with the overly devoted librarian who does not wish his books to be used. At the same time, students of taxation are justified in applying the equity test to proposed tax changes, and in supporting inequitable changes only where the underlying policy objectives are of overriding importance and cannot be met as effectively by other means.

Monetary versus Fiscal Measures

It remains to consider the balance between fiscal and monetary policy. While this has to be discussed primarily in the longer run context, some comments may be made with regard to its shorter run aspects.

While there can be little question regarding the potential effectiveness of fiscal policy in meeting a recession or depression, this is not the case with monetary policy. Federal Reserve policies to ease credit—be it in the form of open market purchases or reduction in reserve requirements—will be effective only if borrowers are inclined to avail themselves of this credit at eased terms. If they are not inclined to do so, easing credit is like pushing on a string, and there will be little or no effect on aggregate demand. If conditions are sufficiently depressed, such will tend to be the case. Here the choice between fiscal and monetary approaches will be decided by the much superior effectiveness of the former. But this applies to the case of a severe depression only. In a moderate recession a policy of monetary ease may not be without effectiveness, and may present an alternative to—or at least, render important support to—the fiscal approach. Monetary policy fares better when it comes to restriction. If sufficiently aggressive, monetary restriction will check demand inflation. At a time when people wish to use funds to excess, a reduction in the available supply of funds is not likely to be offset wholly by an increased use of remaining funds. There is now a pull on the string; and by pulling back, monetary policy has a better chance to be effective.

Also, it must be noted that the monetary approach has the advantage of flexibility in policy initiation. Open market policies may be varied on a day-to-day basis and thus retain greater short run flexibility than could be provided by even my proposal for flexible tax adjustments. At the same time, we have tended to exaggerate the flexibility of monetary policy. As money is eased or tightened, it takes time for the changed conditions in the money market to transmit themselves, and borrowers may be affected with considerable delay. Relatively little is known about this, but recent experience suggests that monetary policy is not as flexible in its final impact on the credit market as it is in policy initiation.

There is still much debate among economists regarding the precise mechanism by which restrictive monetary policy is effective, and regarding the degree of effectiveness which will be associated with a given rise in interest rates. The voluminous hearings and documents on monetary policy which have been forthcoming in recent years have shed little light on these basic questions. Proponents of a new monetary doctrine have argued that emphasis should be shifted from the reaction of borrowers to the reaction of lenders, and that relatively slight measures of restriction may have substantial effects on the willingness of lenders to part with funds. As a result of changes in market structure, so they hold, the supply of available funds to borrowers may be restricted sharply, and this may be the case even though there is but a slight increase in the cost of funds. Critics of the new doctrine have pointed out, and I believe with good reason, that not all the structural changes in the market have been favorable to monetary policy; that the so-called locked-in effect, which is said to restrain the lender, is not easily reconciled with intelligent lender behavior; and that a policy of restricting credit availability without raising the cost of credit involves an increasing degree of imperfection in the credit market, a phenomenon which is hardly compatible with the traditional claim that one of the merits of monetary policy may be found in its alleged neutrality in the market place.

However this may be, the potential effectiveness of monetary restriction cannot be denied. The more interesting question, to my mind, is how this restriction operates. By and large, monetary restriction works by restricting capital formation. Fiscal restriction may be designed to work in this direction, but it may also be aimed at restricting current consumption. Clearly, fiscal restriction is more flexible in this respect, as will be noted again when considering the longer run aspects of growth. Moreover, monetary restriction may have a quite different impact as between types of capital formation than does fiscal restriction. The impact of monetary restriction falls with particular emphasis upon investments which must be financed by borrowing in the market, and upon investments which have a long pay-off period so that interest constitutes a substantial part of the total cost. It falls severely upon borrowers who, for some reason or another, are inflexible in adjusting the rate of return which they can pay on their debts.

For these and other reasons, we find that monetary restriction falls severely upon capital formation by municipal governments. Similarly, there seems good ground for suspecting—although this remains to be verified by the current investigation of the Federal Reserve into this matter—that monetary restriction falls particularly severely upon the weaker competitor and small enterprise. More basically, there is the question whether the kind of credit curtailment that results from the preferences of the lender leads to the proper allocation of the restricted credit resources. Clearly, the answer to this question is the more negative, the more weight one wishes to place on the new monetary theory and its emphasis on credit rationing.

In all, the traditional view of monetary policy as benign and neutral in its impact on markets appears to have been based on lack of information regarding discriminatory effects, rather than on positive evidence to the contrary. There is no a priori argument on these grounds in favor of monetary as against fiscal policy. The same applies with regard to the problem of incidence. When it is decided to raise or lower taxes—be it for budgetary or compensatory reasons—there arises (and properly so) the question of who is going to pay the bill. Where taxes are raised to check inflation, this would seem to be a crucial question, since the main reason for checking inflation is to avoid its inequities. No such question is raised when the problem is one of monetary restriction. Yet there is a problem of incidence, interpreting this term to mean effects on income distribution, in monetary no less than in fiscal policy.

This question may be pointed up by comparing the distributional effects of restriction by monetary action with those of restriction by a proportional income tax. Will monetary policy fall on the progressive or on the regressive side of the latter? There is no ready answer to this question. The problem involves not only such redistribution as may result from increased tax payments and interest payments on public debt, but one must consider as well the distributional effects of increased interest payments in the private sector of the economy. Finally, a change in the rate of interest has repercussions on the yield of equity capital and, in its longer run effects, on the rate of growth and hence on the distribution of the national income between wage and capital earnings. While the distributional effects of these long run changes defy prediction, it appears that the short run changes are on the regressive side of the proportional income tax. Moreover, the comparison with a proportional income tax may not be the proper one. More precisely, we should compare the incidence of monetary policy with that of such marginal change in the tax structure as will be made in lieu of monetary restriction. If this marginal change is progressive, the preceding result is strengthened, and monetary restriction tends to be more favorable to higher incomes than fiscal restriction. If the marginal tax adjustment is regressive, the result may be reversed.

All this is highly speculative and presents an almost entirely new area for investigation. However, it suggests that monetary policy is no more neutral on a priori grounds than is fiscal policy, and that monetary policy, alas, may not be as different from tax policy as we have been accustomed to think.

Discretionary Policy versus Built-in Flexibility

Before turning to the problem of growth, a word should be added regarding the choice between discretionary action and reliance on built-in flexibility. There has been much said in recent years about the virtues of built-in flexibility and the fact, or hypothesis, that the built-in flexibility of our system has been increased so greatly as to make our economy pretty much depression-proof.

Now, it is true that the existence of a large budget adds a core of stable (public) expenditures, expenditures which are not sensitive to changes in income. Also, it is true that a high rate of taxation such as goes with the large budget, plus transfer programs, cushions the changes in disposable income which result with a given change in national income. All this is to the good, at least as long as the economy is at a high level of activity to begin with. At the same time, I think it important not to overestimate the effectiveness of built-in flexibility. Such estimates as have been made suggest that it will be of some help, but that it will fall far short of what needs be done to maintain stability if a serious disturbance should arise. Dreaming about the beauties of built-in flexibility, therefore, must not lead us to neglect the more realistic task of perfecting our tools of discretionary action, tools which most likely will have to remain our primary reliance. It is precisely this line of thought which leads me to urge a provision for flexibility in tax policy, thereby giving us in tax policy some degree of freedom for prompt discretionary action, such as has been available traditionally in monetary policy.

STABILIZING THE LEVEL OF COSTS

We now turn to our second type of disturbance, where instability results from the cost and price side of the market. Suppose we begin with a situation of full employment and price level stability. Now some powerful group in the economy decides that it wishes to have its income raised, without there being a corresponding gain in productivity. This may take the form of unions insisting on higher money wage rates which will be transmitted in turn into higher prices; of producers insisting on a higher profit margin, or of accentuating increases in wage costs by adding a percentage markup; or of farmers insisting on an increase in their respective share. For these or other reasons, wages may be raised without a gain in productivity, and prices may be increased without an initial gain in demand.

The Dilemma

Confronted with this situation, the government finds itself in a dilemma. If a full-employment output is to be maintained at the higher level of prices, money incomes must be permitted to rise accordingly. This requires expansionary fiscal or monetary measures of the type described in the preceding section. But if this is done, the very policy which maintains full employment also serves to verify the rise in prices. What is worse, it demonstrates to various parties in the economy that an increase in earnings (money earnings, in any case) can be obtained without endangering the level of employment, thus inviting a new round of increases, and so forth. In the process of upward adjustment, *rentiers* get squeezed out; as a result, other groups which have gained may come to be satisfied with their winnings, and stop further pressures on prices and costs. But we cannot be sure of this. It is equally possible, or indeed more likely, that appetites will be whetted. In this case the push will continue, and the maintenance of full employment will be accompanied by a continued and perhaps increasingly rapid price rise.

If the government chooses price level stability as its first objective, it will refuse to provide the increase in money income which is needed to maintain full employment at the increased level of prices. In this case, unemployment will result, which in turn may discourage the insistence on further increases in costs and prices. Or the government may go further and insist on a reduction in money income, hoping thereby to reduce costs and prices to their old level. If it turns out that costs and prices are sticky in the downward direction, this will result in an even greater degree of unemployment.

Under such conditions, controls over the level of demand can serve no longer to obtain the twofold objective of full employment and price level stability. This holds equally for both general monetary and general fiscal devices. Another solution must be found.

Solutions

To begin with, there is the possibility of discarding one or the other stabilization objective. Thus, full employment may be maintained, together with rising prices. How troublesome this would be depends upon the rate of price increase that would result. Economists have argued for a long time that some moderate rate of price advance may be a wholesome thing. It provides for a bullish economic climate, gives everyone a feeling of rising incomes and well-being, and permits union leaders to demonstrate success in raising money wage rates. However, even a slow rate of price advance adds up to a great deal over a lifetime, and resulting inequities may be substantial. I have little confidence in the proposition that these will disappear as everyone learns to adjust himself to the rising prices. Therefore, I am hesitant to accept this solution.

The other possibility is to insist on price level stability, while letting employment drop to whatever level it may. This approach is not only absurdly inefficient and unjust, but it is altogether unrealistic. Sustained unemployment is incompatible with social stability in our society. Nor do I have much sympathy for a qualified version of this argument—that we should have just enough unemployment to introduce the necessary discipline into wage-price behavior. For one thing, I am not certain that discipline will be increased by "some" administered unemployment; for another, I doubt whether unemployment will accrue to just those sectors of the economy which are most in need of disciplining. To my mind, these either-or solutions must both be discarded. We must find a way in which the economy can be made to function adequately on both objectives.

The economist's natural answer is that we should establish **market** conditions in which no groups are in a position to exert autonomous pressures on wages and prices. The problem will vanish if only sufficiently competitive conditions are established in both factor and product markets. If we consider the industries which are of primary concern in this connection, we find that firms tend to be larger than is needed on grounds of efficiency; and no matter how furious competition may be in fins and headlights, price competition leaves much to be desired. Surely, price competition might be improved by increasing the number of firms. If this was done, producers would be more hesitant to grant wage increases in excess of productivity gains, wage increases which in the present setting afford a nice opportunity and excuse for corresponding (or more than corresponding) markups in profits. Something might be done in this direction, but vigorous action seems unlikely.

Moreover, even if it was taken, there remains the union side of the picture. Simple changes in union structure are not the solution. A reduction in the size and increase in the number of unions, all of which would operate on an industry-wide basis, may lead to inter-union competition for the highest wage demand, rather than to a more moderate policy. This is suggested by foreign experience. A breakup of unions so as to limit any one union to any one company might do the job of curtailing wage demands, but unions would be pretty much wrecked in the process. Neither of these solutions is acceptable. Thinking in the other direction, it may be argued that union leadership will be more statesmanlike if unions are made bigger, but this also poses the danger of greater power and possible abuse. This solution, therefore, must be excluded as well.

Since there is no simple solution in terms of changing union structure, other restraints are called for. Union power, as an originating factor in cost-push inflation, is exaggerated by the fact that the parties with whom the effective bargain occurs—namely, consumers and other wage earners—are absent from the bargaining table. These other parties might be introduced through adherence to certain rules of the game, e.g., that wage increases should be limited to productivity gains, that price increases should be forbidden as long as there is excess capacity, that prices should be reduced where there is unemployment, and so forth.

Such an approach would accept the present division of monopoly gains between capital and labor as the base from which to make future adjustments, which is a dubious point of departure; and there is the further question whether such rules can be administered short of a national wage-price policy, a step which most people hope can be avoided. A more moderate proposal is to submit wage-price decisions in key industries (note that I say wage-price decisions, because I do not see how the one group can be called upon to submit to control without the other) to a public board including consumers in its representation. As proposed by various people, the opinions of such a board would be advisory rather than mandatory; yet the publicity involved would encourage both parties to seek vindication before the court of public opinion. The public in turn would be supplied with an impartial view, and be spared its present fate of being bombarded by two sets of data, apparently proving the precisely opposite point.

Whatever the precise solution, it is evident that the problem of cost-push inflation is quite a different animal, and requires quite different treatment from that called for in dealing with our old and more pliant friends of demand inflation or deflation. Whereas the latter may be approached by more or less general fiscal and monetary controls, the former requires structural intervention into the functioning, or better, non-functioning, of the market. Such intervention might be accomplished conceivably by fiscal devices, such as taxes on excess profits and on wage gains in excess of productivity; but even where this is done, the fiscal tool merely serves as a means of wage or price control. The problem of stabilization policy in this case is inherently one of market structure.

STABILIZATION POLICY AND GROWTH

I now turn to my final topic, the relationship of stabilization policy to economic growth. As noted at the outset, we are concerned here with two aspects of the problem. To begin with, growth has an important bearing on the maintenance of full employment and price level stability, and different approaches thereto give rise to different rates of growth. Beyond this, there remains the more difficult question as to what particular rate of growth we should aim to accomplish.

Effects of Stabilization on Growth

Suppose we are in a situation where the level of demand is inadequate to purchase the full-employment output at the given capacity of the economy. As shown before, measures must be taken to raise demand to the appropriate level. This may be done by increasing expenditures on current consumption, or by raising capital formation. From a quite short run point of view, the result will be the same in both cases; but it will differ in the longer run. In the former case, the economy's capacity will be unaffected; in the latter case, it will be increased. If capacity is increased, future output at full employment (including labor and capital) will be increased accordingly. The economy will grow at a faster rate, and a higher level of expenditures will be needed in the future to maintain full employment. Precisely the same holds for the case of restrictive measures. Curtailment in consumption or capital formation both serve to reduce current demand, and to prevent a current rise in prices. At the same time, the latter will result in a lower level of capacity, a slower rate of growth, and a lower level of required expenditures for the future. A stabilization policy aimed at encouraging growth must thus meet several tasks. It must see to it that a large share of the economy's resources must flow into capital formation, and it must do its best to stimulate technological progress. At the same time, it must assure that there is sufficient demand to take the product off the market when the new capital is put to work in producing final output.

All this involves public expenditure no less than revenue policies. Expenditures on education may be more important than any other factor, including tax policy. Public expenditures on research and development, similarly, are of crucial importance. Indeed, economic growth would be a dreary affair if it had to rely on increasing the capital stock only. The crucial factor in economic growth, in the setting of our economy at least, is technological progress. It is this progress which permits us to grow at a rapid rate and with relatively little cost in "waiting"; and it is this progress which offers the inducement for a high rate of private investment. Sad though it may be, public outlays for research, made in conjunction with military objectives, have been the greatest contributor to economic growth in our age, and chances are that they will continue to play this role. There is every reason, for peaceful purposes as well, to pursue such expenditure policies.

Turning now to the revenue side, it is evident that a tax policy aimed at maximum economic growth would avoid restraints on capital formation and would not interfere with inducement to innovation. Subsidies might be given to investment, and restraints on expenditures would be placed on consumption, especially current consumption. This would require a tax structure which goes easy on progression and, if carried to its logical conclusion, more or less exempts investment income and/or income which is invested. By the same token, it suggests a combination of easy money with tax restraint, the reason being that the restrictive effect of monetary policy is primarily on capital formation.[6] Some devices such as accelerated depreciation may accomplish these tax objectives with less damage to equity than others, such as the exemption of investment income. Nevertheless, it appears that a tax structure designed to maximize growth tends to be one which runs counter to widely accepted notions of equity and distributional adjustment in tax policy. This appears to be a situation where we cannot have the best of all worlds all at once: A policy designed to maximize growth may require a degree of inequality in income distribution which is unacceptable on other grounds. Techniques might be considered which could soften this conflict, such as tax incentives to investment which are limited to investors

[6] The argument is clear-cut where effects on plant and equipment expenditures are concerned. The case of mortgage credit and other credit for the purchase of durable consumer goods is less clear-cut. Such expenditures constitute capital formation in that they add to the stock of available goods, but they do not add to productive capacity, as does expenditure on plant. In terms of the Domar-type growth model, they are not included in the investment expenditure to which a stigma is attached.

with small incomes, but this could not be done readily on a large scale.

However this may be, a tax policy to encourage investment cannot be successful unless the basic market conditions are such as to render investment profitable. Such at least is the case if we disregard the possibility of taxes on hoarding or investment subsidies. These market conditions will not be favorable unless there is sufficient demand to take the product off the market. In other words, tax restraints upon consumption must be sufficiently light to permit this demand to be forthcoming. Or, as may well be the case, a deficit may be required to assure the necessary demand. A fiscal policy aimed at a rapid rate of growth, to be successful, may require a higher degree of public deficit than one which is satisfied with a lesser rate of growth. This point should be emphasized, because we have become accustomed to think of the deficit as a means of maintaining full employment in an otherwise stagnant economy. Such is not necessarily the case. It may also be a means of maintaining a rapid rate of stable growth.

The Optimal Rate of Growth

There remains the basic question of what constitutes the optimal rate of growth in the economy. In the present setting, this may be answered more or less easily by reference to Russia: Whatever we do, the Russian rate of growth is likely to exceed ours, simply because they are at a much earlier stage of the game; therefore, if we want to maintain our relative advantage, we had better grow as fast as we can. Moreover, the potential scope for aid to development in other parts of the world is almost unlimited; and the faster we grow, the more we can help others to grow as well.[7] This approach has considerable merit, but it leaves open the question of what the answer would be in a somewhat happier world, where a greater freedom of choice was permitted. And even in the present setting, we cannot determine the desirable rate of growth without considering the changes in our social and economic institutions which might be required in order to accelerate growth beyond certain limitations.

Conceivably, we could operate an economy in which such enormous subsidies were paid to investment incomes that capital formation would absorb well-nigh all the economy's resources. Such a system is conceivable, but it would be absurd, since the ultimate objective of economic activity is consumption. The basic question of growth policy —apart from the more or less technical considerations of stability—is simply this: By how much should society postpone present consumption so that more can be had in the future, and what is the rate at which future consumption may be substituted for present consumption? Investment in innovation raises this rate, and may provide for increased future

---

[7] By "help" I do not mean out-compete in world markets, but supply long term loans and technical aid while lowering tariffs.

consumption (including leisure) with little cost in present consumption. Growth by increased capital formation with existing techniques is a more costly process, especially if the postponement of consumption extends from one generation to another. The decision to undertake this cost should be made by the consumer; or, if the market cannot give the answer, it should be decided upon through the political process, along with the determination of other social wants.

In making this decision, the social implications of various rates of growth cannot be disregarded. It seems likely to me that a higher rate of growth tends to require a higher degree of income inequality. To be sure, as the rate of growth is increased, those who lose in relative position may still gain in absolute terms; and such being the case, they may have little reason to complain. Moreover, a higher rate of growth tends to imply a higher degree of social mobility, and this may be more important than the state of distribution at any one time. For instance, many people will agree that one of the most important steps in the solution of our race problem is that of raising the absolute economic standard of the Negro population. Still, these distributional implications of various rates of growth cannot be overlooked, and it is easy to see that higher growth is more attractive to those who stand to gain in relative as well as in absolute terms.

However this may be, the problem of economic growth goes much beyond that of stabilization. Stabilization policy can do with a number of different growth rates, so that the choice among these rates must be made on other and not only economic grounds.

3. AN ECONOMIC POLICY FOR ECONOMIC GROWTH AND STABILITY*

O. H. Brownlee

SYNOPSIS

1. The federal government should set taxes and expenditures at amounts that will balance the budget at some desired gross national product. When the gross national product falls short of this amount, the resulting deficit should be financed by the creation of money. When it exceeds this amount, the resulting surpluses should be used to reduce the money supply.

2. It follows that the Federal Reserve cannot be permitted to change the money supply at its discretion.

3. The government should invest only when the prospective rate of return on its investment is larger than that on private investment. It should not change its investment expenditures in response to a change in employment. The government should finance its investment expenditures by selling securities in competition with privately issued securities.

4. The government should supply more goods and services only when their marginal values exceed those of private output.

5. The government should not control individual prices to keep them from rising. If wages rise more than productivity and thus make full employment more difficult to achieve, the solution should be to remove restrictions on entry to the labor market, and should not be to control wages.

6. Economists know little about the short run effect of discretionary stabilization measures, such as increases in government expenditures, tax reductions, and open market operations.

7. Because of time lags, about which economists know little, some of the discretionary measures used since the war may actually have destabilized the economy.

8. Given the rule in (3), above, government investment will be larger when interest rates are low than when they are high. Hence, even though government investment is not meant to be a stabilizing device, it will vary inversely with private investment.

I shall present my beliefs with respect to the general outlines of economic policies which will best promote economic stability and at

* Reprinted from *The Relationship of Prices to Economic Stability and Growth*, prepared for the Joint Economic Committee (Washington, D.C.: U.S. Government Printing Office, 1958), pp. 575–82.

the same time permit the amount and composition of capital investment (including that in factors giving rise to technological improvement) to be determined in somewhat the same manner as are other resource allocation decisions in a free economy. I shall not rationalize adequately my assertions by presenting a detailed picture of how I believe the economy operates, since the earlier presentations before the committee have been devoted to this subject. Furthermore, my prescriptions are suited to a fairly wide variety of diagnoses.

My proposals are not original, and have been drawn from numerous sources. Briefly stated, they are as follows:

1. There should not be direct control of product prices, wages, or interest rates. Direct controls make it impossible to obtain information that otherwise would be available with respect to peoples' preferences for various goods and services and their willingness to sacrifice current consumption for potential future consumption. Such information is vital for determining how much growth should take place and for achieving any given amount of growth at minimum cost.

2. The primary stabilizing mechanism should be a "stabilizing budget" such as has been proposed by the Committee for Economic Development and by Professor Milton Friedman.[1] The schedules of government payments to the public and receipts from the public should be established so that these two quantities are equal at a desired level of gross national product and so that receipts exceed payments for values of gross national product above the desired level whereas payments exceed receipts for values of gross national product below the desired level. An excess of payments over receipts should lead to an increase in the amount of money in the hands of the public as a result of monetary issue to fill the deficit. Symmetrically, an excess of receipts over payments should lead to a decrease in the quantity of money in the hands of the public. These automatic changes in the money supply can act as a stabilizer in that they will tend to push the level of gross national product toward the pre-determined desired value. This desired value will move upward through time as a result of economic growth, and the payments and receipts schedules must be revised periodically in accordance with this growth.

It should be noted that if such a proposal were to be put into practice, an independent monetary policy designed to influence the over-all level of spending could not be pursued. For example, if the monetary authority were to purchase securities in order to increase the money supply during a period in which gross national product was at or above

---

[1] *Taxes and the Budget: A Program for Prosperity in a Free Economy*. A statement on national policy by the Research and Policy Committee of the Committee for Economic Development, November 1947; and Milton Friedman, "A Monetary and Fiscal Framework for Economic Stability," *The American Economic Review*, June 1948, pp. 245–64.

the desired level, this money automatically would be withdrawn by the Treasury. The monetary authority might possibly influence the rate of interest and hence the rate of growth, but not the current aggregate money income level.

3. The amount of government investment should be such that its marginal rate of return is the same as that of private investment. I am aware that this statement is largely an exhortation to "do good" without specifying how marginal rates of return on government investment should be computed; and I am aware that I cannot, for lack of both time and competence, deal adequately with this problem. However, it is my contention that regardless of the procedures employed in determining rates of return on governmental investment, an improvement over existing procedures would result from following my proposal.[2] In particular, it would avoid wide variations in government expenditure for capital investment as a stabilization device. It is uneconomic to expand and contract expenditures on such items as roads, schools, and dams simply because total expenditure is temporarily below or above desired levels.

To finance governmental investment, the government should sell securities to the public, paying such interest rates as are necessary to clear the market. Expansions in government investment will thus compete more directly with private investment and will be judged more upon their effects upon economic growth—the criterion most applicable for making such decisions. In effect, the government will be trading securities for goods and services to be used for investment purposes, as does a business when it issues bonds or stocks to finance expansion.

4. Government provision of current goods and services which are essentially in the nature of consumer goods and services should be at a level such that the marginal values of these goods and services are the same as those of privately produced goods and services. This statement also is another exhortation to "do good," but it can be made into a more definite criterion for action if markets for such goods and services are more widely employed or if market conditions are more widely simulated in making such expenditure decisions.

In effect, I am proposing that government establish a capital budget, the level of which would be determined by expected returns from government investment in comparison with private investment. This budget is not to be used for stabilization purposes, although it will, in general, exert some stabilizing influence. Expenditures on capital items will be financed by long-term government debt. Payments and receipts in the current budget will balance at a desired level of gross national product, receipts consisting of tax collections and payments consisting of expendi-

[2] See Arnold C. Harberger, "The Interest Rate in Cost-Benefit Analysis," *Federal Expenditure Policy for Economic Growth and Stability*, Joint Economic Committee (85th Cong., 1st sess.) (Washington, D.C.: U.S. Government Printing Office, 1959).

tures for government consumption plus transfer payments plus debt repayment. Monetary policy would no longer be concerned with economic stability.

In the sections that follow, I shall elaborate upon these proposals and indicate how they will contribute to stability and growth.

THE ABSENCE OF DIRECT CONTROLS

Most economists profess a belief in the efficiency of a free market as a device for allocating goods and services among various potential users and for allocating productive resources among various alternative producers. Consequently, I may be whipping a dead horse in accenting the absence of direct controls upon prices, wages, and interest rates as a part of a proposed policy for growth and stability. However, since there is persistent talk of administered prices, the need of wage controls if we are to have both a stable price level and full employment, and qualitative controls upon borrowing to prevent inflation, I hope that I am justified in devoting a few words to my reasons for not employing direct controls.

I have mentioned, in summarizing my proposals, the importance of the information provided by the price system. Such information shows those goods whose output should be expanded, where labor is most productive, and the areas of investment in which investors expect to make the greatest returns. If upper limits are placed upon prices and these upper limits are effective, there are shortages of all of the goods and services whose prices are limited. There is no easy way of determining the relative importance of the various shortages. Furthermore, some other criteria—such as "first come, first served" or "friends and relatives served first"—must be worked out to ration available supplies. I must confess that I have never fully understood the significance of the term "administered price." It is true that some producers may pursue a price policy, i.e., they may choose to establish a price at which they will sell their product. However, if they make such a choice, they cannot also choose the quantity to be sold. A monopolist who chooses to maintain price unchanged and let only the quantity sold decrease during a period of declining demand is not acting in his own self-interest—if profit maximization is his objective.

Monopoly imposes a cost upon the entire economy—through less production of monopoly-produced and more of competitively produced goods and services than is optimal. If monopoly is important in our economy, the source of monopoly power should be uprooted through assuring freedom of entry into any line of production to those who can obtain the required resources. Price control is not the answer.

Many statements have been made during the past decade about the incompatibility of arbitrarily determined money wage levels, full employment, and a stable general level of prices. These statements are true. One cannot have money wages rising more rapidly than the productivity of labor without having either a rise in the price level or less than full employment. In my estimation, however, the price level has determined money wages, rather than money wages having determined the price level. In the event that my belief is incorrect, the cure, again, is not wage controls but the establishment of conditions whereby entry into trade-unions is without restrictions.

Frequently, interest rates have been viewed in a different light from prices, and some persons unwilling to accept price and wage controls have advocated controls on interest rates with the objective of increasing or diminishing demand for particular types of capital goods. The same kinds of objections that were raised to direct controls on the prices of individual goods and services or wage rates apply also to qualitative controls on interest rates. They can lead to a distortion in the price pattern of capital assets and to over-investment in certain types of capital assets and under-investment in others. Thus, whatever capital formation takes place is not of the best composition.

The objection is not that prices or wages should be uncontrolled in a general sense. Economic stability implies stability in the general level of prices and a rising level of real wages. But broad controls—those over a general price index or a representative interest rate—rather than specific controls are urged. Relative prices, wages, and interest rates should be free to adjust to changes in supply and demand conditions if currently available resources are to be efficiently utilized and the growth that is to occur is at rates desired by the society.

THE STABILIZING BUDGET

As potential stabilizing devices, changes in government expenditure, changes in net tax collections (tax collections minus transfer payments), and the purchase or sale of securities by an agency of the government (such as the Federal Reserve banks) have been advocated by economists. Any of these devices or any combination of them could be instrumental in establishing some given equilibrium level of total spending in the economy. For example, a tax reduction, an increase in government spending, or the purchase of securities from the public could raise the equilibrium level of gross national product. However, even though they may be equally effective in influencing this equilibrium level, they need not bring about the desired adjustment with equal speeds, nor will their effects upon economic growth be the same.

Relatively little is known about the speeds at which the desired eventual adjustments might be reached as a result of the various fiscal or monetary changes that could be made. Some recent investigations indicate that substantial amounts of time have elapsed between the peaks in the rate of increase in the supply of money and the peaks in the general level of economic activity during a period dating from soon after the Civil War to the present. Such evidence suggests that the lags between changes in the quantity of money brought about by open market operations and changes in the general level of economic activity have been on the average a little more than a year. No comparable direct evidence is available with respect to tax changes and changes in government expenditure, but one investigator claims that there has been no noticeable lag between changes in income and changes in consumer expenditure.[3] Tax collections directly affect disposable income; and government expenditure for goods and services—unless it changes only inventories—increases wage payments and profits, both of which are income components. It is my guess that fiscal changes have speedier effects than do monetary ones, particularly insofar as monetary changes first influence the level of investment—business plant and equipment, housing, and some consumer durable goods.

Variation in net tax collections (taxes minus transfer payments) rather than in government expenditure for goods and services has been chosen as a means for damping fluctuations in gross national product because it is believed that the resulting resource allocation would be superior. If one could diagnose accurately the reason for an increase or decrease in aggregate demand for goods and services, a combination of a change in government expenditure and in taxation might be still better than a change in net tax collections alone. However, it usually is difficult to determine the structure of the change in demand until some time after it has taken place. Furthermore, if it can be ascertained that a long term shift such as a decline in demand for private investment and consumption relative to government investment has occurred, an upward adjustment in government spending can be made.

The Stabilizing Budget and Economic Growth

Because net tax collections are directly related to gross national product, a fall in gross national product is accompanied by a decline in net tax collections. With government expenditure constant, and assuming that a balanced budget existed initially, a deficit occurs. This is filled by monetary issue. A rise in consumption expenditure as well as private investment occurs. In general, one would expect the interest rate to fall. The deficit is of course wiped out as soon as gross national product returns to the value from which it fell initially. And if a change in preferences accounted for the initial decline in aggregate demand, the structure of gross national product will be changed in accordance with these preferences.

Suppose that there is a decline in the willingness to undertake

[3] Lloyd A. Metzler, "Three Lags in the Circular Flow of Income," in Lloyd A. Metzler et al., Income, Employment, and Public Policy (New York: Norton, 1948).

private investment—as apparently has occurred during the current [1957–58] recession. This is reflected in less willingness to borrow for plant and equipment purchases and a decline in the rate of interest. The impact of the stabilizing budget is to push gross national product toward a value equal to the initial one but in which consumption relative to investment is larger. And if government investment is guided by interest rates in the private sector, an upward adjustment in this category of investment also would be warranted at the earliest periodic budgetary review. The decline in private investment denoted (1) an increase in the desire for present rather than future goods, that is, a decline in the desired rate of capital accumulation and economic growth, and (2) a desire for less private investment relative to government investment. And a move toward fulfillment of these desires has been made as a result of the stabilizing budget.

Economic growth, defined in many different ways, depends upon the rate and composition of capital accumulation and improvements in technology. The very high rate of capital formation in Russia during recent years has been, in part, responsible for what appears to be a relatively rapid economic growth in that country, just as low rates of capital formation in Egypt, India, and some Latin American countries relative to the fairly high rates of population increase have meant low rates of increase in per capita income. However, a given amount of capital can be used in different ways, some of which will lead to larger amounts of output than others, so that the composition of net capital formation, as well as its absolute amount, is important. The construction of plant and equipment in certain Latin American countries for the manufacture of items in which these countries have no comparative advantage in international trade has resulted in less rapid growth than would have been possible had the capital been used in other ways. Using production techniques which permit more of a given product to be produced from a given amount of resources—such as has occurred in agriculture from the use of hybrid seeds and meat animals—obviously increases per capita output. Just how important capital formation has been relative to technological improvement in accounting for economic growth in any country is difficult to determine. Generally, the use of a new technique requires a different machine or other capital item than previously was used, and hence also requires additional capital. Our procedures for valuing capital do not permit us to separate accurately the contribution of the discovery from that of the capital. Furthermore, the development of improved technology might be considered as capital formation, particularly insofar as it is the result of research requiring investment in training and equipment. Investing in research is an economic problem comparable to that of investing in machines or drilling for petroleum, so that one need not separate technological improvement, as a kind of capital formation, from the other varieties.

A country could channel a very large proportion of its current income into investment in plant and equipment and research—as the Russians apparently have been doing—and its potential productive capacity would grow more rapidly than if the proportion of its current income invested in this way were small. However, a larger growth rate obtained in this way is not necessarily better than a smaller one. A larger proportion of income used currently to expand productive capacity and improve technology means that more consumption could take place in the future but less in the present.

In deciding how much of each good to produce, one can compare (*a*) what people are *willing* to give up of one commodity to get another with (*b*) what they *have* to give up. Similarly, one can decide how much of current income should be sunk into plant, equipment, and research by comparing (*a*) what people are willing to give up of goods and services in the future with (*b*) what they have to give up. Those who trade current for future consumption, the "lenders" or "savers," whether they be persons building up savings deposits or their holdings of equities in corporations, or persons using their own labor and materials to make additions to their houses—such persons are willing to save more of a given income at higher rates of return than at lower rates. Those who use resources currently for production in the future, the "borrowers," whether they be persons building houses, school boards constructing schools, "wildcatters" drilling wells that may or may not produce petroleum, or corporation presidents deciding whether to expand research activities—such persons are willing to use more of current income for these investment purposes at lower rates of interest than at higher ones.

The amount of capital formation that makes what investors are willing to invest equal to what savers are willing to save depends upon the amount of government expenditures. But the amount that should take place is not arbitrary—if the amount of government expenditure is determined in accordance with the criteria suggested as a part of this policy package. One would expect it to vary over time. Once productive capacity has been built up so that excess capacity exists or would exist if the previous rate of accumulation were maintained, continued accumulation at the previous rate would be uneconomic. Similarly, if productive capacity has been destroyed or kept from growing—by a war, for example—a rapid build-up generally would be desired. Achieving variation in the desired rate of capital accumulation as expressed in the market is compatible with the stabilizing budget.

How Much Stability Can We Have?

If a stabilization program such as has been outlined here were to be put into effect, how much stability could be achieved? A precise answer to this question probably cannot be supplied, since the reason for the fluctuations affects the amount that will occur. However, I believe that stability would be greater than that which has been experienced during the past decade, which—with the exception of the period July 1950 to March 1951—has been one of the most stable in our history.

During the past decade, our fiscal system has contained a considerable degree of built-in flexibility. For example, current net tax collections have been rather closely geared to current income payments. In the private sector, stock dividends have varied much less than corporate profits. However, built-in flexibility in the fiscal system and a stabilizing budget are not the same things. Under built-in flexibility a deficit or surplus need not be treated in the same manner as in a stabilizing budget. There are not the provisions for changing the money supply as have been proposed here. Those persons who contend that we have had an adequate test of automatic stabilization procedures are incorrect, for such a procedure is not a part of our current policy.

Furthermore, the government itself probably has been a source of instability. There have been fairly substantial variations in expenditures, at a given level of income, not matched by variations in receipts and not designed for stabilization purposes. Open market operations may have contributed to instability, because of the time lags in their effects. Budget policy—while an improvement over that of thirty years ago—still is not pointed toward achievement of a balance at a desired level of gross national product. In fact, data regarding the prospective receipts and expenditures of the federal government have been extremely difficult to interpret so that one does not know at what income level the budget would balance.

The introduction of forces that automatically push the income level back toward its equilibrium value (as does the stabilizing budget) rather than merely reducing the change in the equilibrium value (as does built-in flexibility), making the budget balance at a pre-determined income level, and the elimination of open market operations as an instrument of stabilization policy would lead to greater stability than we have had.

GOVERNMENT INVESTMENT

The role of government investment as a factor in economic growth already has been stressed in this paper. If government investment is at a level such that its marginal rate of return exceeds that of private investment, there is too little government investment in the bundle comprising the total of capital formation. Similarly, if the marginal rate of return on government investment is less than that on private investment, there is too much government capital formation relative to private capital formation. I am aware that there are many ways of estimating rates of return on governmental projects and that each may yield a different answer. However, as a beginning, whatever the procedure employed to estimate returns, an investment should not be made unless these returns are at least as large as would be obtained if one, for example, purchased a bundle of stocks selected at random.

The fact that government may be able to borrow at more favorable terms than private borrowers should have little to do with the determination of investment policy. The differential between rates at which government may borrow and those at which private businesses may obtain funds do not reflect lenders' estimates of the productivities of the investments. They result from lenders' knowledge that government does not have to rely on earnings to repay loans.

In general, government investment should grow as national income grows, because of productivity considerations. However, like private investment, the growth rate need not be a constant. From a given set of prospective governmental investments with their corresponding expected rates of return, more should be undertaken at lower rates of interest than at higher ones. A fall in the productivity of private investment should lead to a rise in government investment. Thus, although government investment should not be considered as a stabilization device, it would tend to vary inversely with private investment in situations where private investment opportunities varied. Similarly, if there were shifts in governmental investment opportunities and government borrowed from the public to finance its investment, private investment would increase in response to a fall in government investment. Some additional stability could result from a policy designed to influence growth.

* * *

I have attempted to sketch the bare outlines of a package of proposals which I believe should form the backbone of government action for economic stability and growth. To obtain at least cost a growth rate which is desired by the population, the level of government expenditure for goods and services should be determined by productivity criteria rather than by its effect upon economic stability. Fluctuations in economic activity should be damped by means of a stabilizing budget. How much stability this would bring cannot be estimated accurately but would exceed what we have had during the past decade.

The kind of stabilization action proposed is largely automatic. If accurate forecasts could be made, discretionary action could achieve greater stability. However, until greater forecasting accuracy than has been thus far demonstrated is achieved, discretionary action is unlikely to achieve the degree of stability that can be provided by the programs proposed here.

Anti-competitive Effects of Stabilization Policy

4. MARKET STRUCTURE AND STABILIZATION POLICY*

J. K. Galbraith

SYNOPSIS

1. In competitive industries like agriculture, bituminous coal mining, and textiles, increases in aggregate demand result in immediate price increases.

2. In oligopolistic industries, increases in demand result in increased order backlogs. Because prices are slow to rise, "unliquidated monopoly gains" appear. These gains persist for some time.

3. In many oligopolistic industries, increases in wage rates resulting from union negotiations are a signal to producers to increase product prices. Because of the possible loss of bargaining advantage, management in oligopolistic industries is reluctant to increase prices until wage rates have been negotiated.

4. Because of unliquidated gains, prices in the oligopolistic sectors may continue to rise during recession periods when competitive prices are falling.

5. Monetary policies leading to higher interest rates curtail investment in the competitive industries, but unliquidated gains in the oligopolistic sector offset an increase in interest rates and prevent it from curtailing investment there.

6. Tight-money policies lead to "credit rationing" by the banks reducing loans to the weakest borrowers and the poorest credit risks, thereby reducing the credit available to the competitive sectors relative to the oligopolistic.

7. Fiscal policies may reduce prices in the competitive sector, but in the oligopolistic sector only reduce the size of the backlogs at first, while prices there may even continue to rise.

8. By discriminating against competitive enterprise, fiscal and especially monetary policies conflict with a major American value, and it may not be politically feasible to use them to their full extent to secure the goals of stabilization.

9. Economists should recognize the discriminatory effect and develop alternative stabilization policies. Otherwise, the economy will have to choose between inflation and a weakening of competition.

Any explanation of the relation of market structure to inflation and its control implies, first of all, a view of such structure. I propose to as-

* Reprinted by permission and shortened from *The Review of Economics and Statistics*, May 1957, pp. 126–38.

sume only that the economy is distributed between different structural forms and that an analytically significant part approximates the pure competitive model where no individual producer has power to influence prices and that in another significant part prices are subject to monopoly power. The latter I identify more specifically with small numbers or oligopoly: Price making there reflects the somewhat varied patterns which we identify with oligopolistic rationality. My assumption amounts to saying that an important part of the economy is like or approaches the organization of agriculture and that another important part approximates the organization of the steel industry. My conclusions are not altered in kind, although they will be quantitatively changed, by the distribution of industries in between. This should be acceptable even to those (if such there be) who are practiced in subordinating their observation of markets to their preference system.

The central clue to the problem is in the differential rate of adaptation of different market structures to changes in demand. This is a matter of prime importance: The solution it yields is also generally consistent with present conclusions as to the behavior of competitive and imperfect markets.

Inflation, either before or subsequent to the point of what Keynes called "true inflation,"[1] presents itself to the individual firm in the form of an increase in demand both for its product and for the factors which it employs. In the case of the purely competitive market—archetypically, the market for an agricultural product—the process is commonplace. The increase in demand brings an increase in price for the currently available supply. The adaptation of prices to the increase in demand is automatic: In the nature of the competitive market, no individual has the power to halt the adaptation. The price adaptation proceeds *pari passu* with the increase in demand; it is completed *pari passu* with the completion of the movement in demand.

If it is a general inflationary movement, factor prices will also be rising. However, an increase in a factor price in these markets does not of itself cause an increase in price. Prices will only rise as the result of the adjustment by firms of their production to the new marginal cost-price relationship, this in turn bringing a new price equilibrium.

In sum, in these markets, price adaptation to changing demand is contemporaneous and hence always complete. Price adaptation to changes in costs requires time, depending on the period of production and the capital transformation period. In all cases the rate of adaptation is market-controlled; none of the aggregate industry effect is subject to the discretion of the individual firm.

[1] "When an increase in the quantity of effective demand produces no further increase in output and entirely spends itself on an increase in effective demand we have . . . true inflation. . . . Every previous increase in the quantity of money is likely so far as it increases effective demand, to spend itself partly in increasing the cost-unit and partly in increasing output." J. M. Keynes, *General Theory of Employment, Interest and Money* (New York, 1936), p. 303.

None of the foregoing requires lengthy elucidation; it is the ancient and familiar model of price and supply responses in the competitive market and with no adornments. But neither does it depart from the broad reality of agriculture, bituminous coal mining, forest products, the staple branches of the cotton textile industry—wherever, in short, producers are numerous in the same market and each firm (or even most firms, as measured by aggregate volume) is too small to have a determining influence in the common market.

In the opposite case, that of the oligopolistic market, the response pattern is very different. Since it is also subject to alteration by individual entrepreneurial decision, the outcome is less predictable. However, the regularities are more than sufficient for the solution of the present problem.

The first regularity is that the inflationary shift in demand presents itself to the oligopolistic firm in the form of an increase in orders or sales rather than in the form of an increase in prices. This is inherent in all but the most exceptional oligopolistic solutions; the convention requires group adherence to given prices or price structure and differentials to which all are interdependently subject. To this end there must be a reasonably definite price, subject to reasonably deliberate change. The immediate effect of the increase in demand will be to move the firm nearer capacity production. If it is already producing at capacity, the effect will be to increase its backlog.

These are the first effects. The price adaptation must always come later and as a result of specific entrepreneurial decision. This adaptation is not automatic, as in the competitive market; again, in all but the most exceptional cases, there will be some time interval. During this interval, profits are not maximized. The point can hardly be disputed: If prices were at a level to maximize returns before the shift in demand, they cannot be afterward. And if they did not maximize returns before, they will not, except by accident, do so afterward.

I come now to a central point. With inflation, the demand curves of the firm and industry are moving persistently to the right. Under these circumstances, there will normally be an incomplete adaptation of oligopoly prices. Prices will not be at profit-maximizing levels in any given situation, for the situation is continually changing, while the adaptation is by deliberate and discrete steps. This means that at any given time, there will ordinarily be a quantum of what may be called unliquidated monopoly gains in the inflationary context. The shift in demand calls for a price increase for maximization; since the adaptation is currently incomplete, prices can at any time be raised and profits thereby enhanced. Absolute generality cannot be claimed for this proposition. There is an obvious, although I think outside, possibility that although adaptation is by discrete steps, there will be anticipatory adaptation at each move. The full case also requires consideration of the factor markets, which will also be under inflationary pressure and to which I turn presently. I should like to argue that under quite commonplace conditions the lag in adaptation will be considerable, and the unliquidated short run monopoly gains substantial.

First, there are commonplace features of the oligopoly solution which are relevant here. One is what Professor Bain has termed the inevitable imperfection of collusion—the fact that any change under conditions of interdependence takes time.[2] In the context of inflationary demand, it is true, the time may be reduced. The individual firm can raise prices without short run loss of customers. But the habit of awaiting leadership or the formation of a tacit consensus can be assumed to continue. The use of average cost pricing is recognized as a restraining influence.

A much more important factor making for incomplete adaptation is the conflict between short and longer run maximization and the high probability that prices which would keep profits at a maximum at any given time will defeat the goal of maximizing profits over time. Effective merchandising and good commercial relations ordinarily require a measure of price stability and hence the sacrifice of short run opportunities. So, frequently, does the maintenance of the oligopolistic convention. To take all that the short run demand situation permits may be itself to induce adverse movements in demand for the individual firm in the somewhat longer run. Customers will remember and, in the longer run, take steps to protect themselves. Potential competitors will observe and, in the longer run, appear. Finally, there will ordinarily be some consideration of the adverse long run effects of public ill will.

Under conditions of inflationary increases in demand, there will almost certainly be increased divergence between the prices that maximize in the short and longer run. Then price increases are watched with anxiety by the public.[3] Any firm which undertakes to exploit fully and promptly its short run position will probably be more than usually sensitive to the public and official displeasure that it is incurring. Taxation also acts to lower the marginal utility of large short run increments of return. A final reason for restraint comes from the factor markets. Wages, the most important factor cost, are not determined independently of the profit position of the industry. On the contrary, it is commonplace that high profits invite the attention of unions. This means that some of the gains from maximization will have to be surrendered in higher labor costs. Further, in ordinary business calculation, wage-cost increases are regarded as irreversible; as a general rule, price changes are not. Short run price maximization thus may invite inconvenient or even what may be

[2] Joe S. Bain, *Price Theory* (New York, 1952), p. 340.

[3] A case in point was the popular and congressional reaction in late 1956 and early 1957 to the increased oil prices which followed upon the Suez crisis and which concluded with widespread fears of inflation.

regarded as dangerous cost movements. Under all these circumstances, we can say with considerable confidence that, in an inflationary context, the prices indicated by considerations of long run maximization will always be below those which would maximize current return.

The effect of the foregoing can, moreover, be prices well below levels which permit of short run maximization. Under conditions such as those obtaining in late 1955 or early 1956, this seems likely to have been the case. A commonplace feature of a firm under inflationary demand is a backlog; in the inflationary movement of the mid-fifties, these were taken for granted over a large area of industrial production, especially in the field of producers' durables. A backlog means that demand is in excess of what can be supplied at the going price. Instead of rationing thus by queue, there could be rationing by higher prices. The higher price forgone measures the short run gain sacrificed.

One final point must be carefully emphasized. Under conditions in which demand exceeds capacity at current prices, the industry will ordinarily be seeking to expand plant and output. Should this expansion at some stage outrun the increase in demand—should backlogs disappear and firms begin to operate at less than capacity—this does not mean that prices will then be at or above the point of short run maximization. Depending on the shape of the cost and demand functions, there may still be unliquidated monopoly gains. Especially if these functions are inelastic as they are presumed to be in the case of producers' durables, firms may still be able to increase profits by increasing prices.[4]

* * *

The foregoing analysis is, I believe, essential for a satisfactory explanation of price movements in recent years. It also provides, I venture to suggest, the first wholly satisfactory integration of the wage-price spiral with aggregative demand and price analysis. This has long been a troublesome point. The wage-price spiral (except in transmitting demand effects) is the poor relation of the inflation problem. It has never had any real standing in the analysis; at the same time, as with the poor, it has been omnipresent.

The rapid adaptation of competitive prices to the rapid increase in demand in the World War II period and in the Korean period accords with expectations. In 1948–49 and again in 1953–54, when the increase in demand was interrupted, these prices promptly subsided. At the other extreme, the prices of steel, machinery, and other products of the con-

---

[4] In reflecting on the chance for getting agreement on my case for non-maximization, I have been struck, though hardly encouraged, by Mr. Harrod's estimate of the probable reaction ("Profiteering: An Ethical Study," in *Economic Essays*, by R. F. Harrod [New York, 1952]). "Is it possible that some monopolists . . . have endeavored to provide goods at prices related to their costs? At this suggestion loud howls will arise from certain intellectuals. It is absolutely ludicrous, it will be said, the apotheosis of nonsense."

centrated sector, after adapting much more slowly to the wartime increases in demand, continued to rise when the rate of increase in the latter subsided. These price advances were not interrupted by the appearance of some excess capacity in the steel industry in 1949 and 1953. In this period there were still unliquidated short run monopoly gains. Prices thus could rise in response to these in the oligopolistic sector while falling in the competitive sector. With moderate movements in demand in recent years the divergent behavior has persisted.

We may now consider the relation of these price increases to wage increases resulting from collective bargaining contracts. It is assumed in many industries that product price increases will be announced following the conclusion of new wage contracts. This is so nearly taken for granted in, say, the steel industry that we now fairly successfully conceal our sense of its inconsistency with the accepted economic analysis. For the inconsistency is plain. Capacity operations are commonplace, as noted. The meaning of "capacity" is that supply is inelastic because the firm is nearing the output where marginal costs approach infinity. If marginal costs are approaching infinity, they are not increased by the wage increase. Thus, nothing in the cost situation as it relates to the equilibrium of the firm is changed by the wage increase. Since demand in accordance with usual (and valid) special equilibrium assumptions is also substantially unaffected, the conclusion is inescapable. If the increase is profitable after the wage increase, it would have been just as profitable before. More briefly, if the firm can sell its capacity output after the wage increase at a higher price, then it could have sold the capacity output before the wage increase at this price and with a proportionately increased average and total return.

Plainly, the firm was not maximizing returns before. The answer— the only answer—is that it had an unliquidated margin of monopoly revenue.

But we must ask what *was* changed by the wage increase—why do price advances occur following the negotiation of contracts? Again the explanation is wholly consistent with the model. A price increase prior to the wage increase would have encouraged the latter. It would have invoked, as noted, the problem of the irreversibility of these costs. Once wages have advanced, these considerations disappear; the higher costs are a *fait accompli*. Meanwhile, this sequence accords with the requirements of public relations which, as noted, are important in the question of short run maximization. The public related the price increases at such time to the pay increases and thus attributes the advance to the unions. The latter provide what Professor Mason has termed "an excellent rationalization" for simultaneous industry-wide price increases.[5] In recent years in numerous industries, including steel, it has been customary to use the oc-

---

[5] *Economic Concentration and the Monopoly Problem*, p. 218.

casion of the price advance, following wage increases, to get substantial additional revenues for the company. This is further evidence of the presence of unliquidated gains.[6]

Some lesser problems may now be disposed of. It will be argued by some that in citing the case of agriculture or cotton textile manufacturing, on the one hand, and steel and the large metal-using and engineering industries, on the other, I am dealing with special cases. Even should these be special cases, they are highly important ones. If my argument is applicable to these industries, this would go far to validate my conclusions on the relation between controls and market structures. However, I do not think that these are special cases; they represent at most the boundary positions in market structures.

A more serious contention is that much more can be attributed than I have conceded to differential increases in demand. In recent years we have had an investment boom. As a result, the prices of capital goods have been strong, those of manufactured goods less so, while foods, reflecting in general a low income elasticity, have been weakest of all.[7]

This argument obviously cannot be used to explain the slower rate of increase in the capital goods industries during the earlier inflations. Then, particularly perhaps in the post-World War II period, the metal-using industries were under great pressure of demand. There is also the interesting difference in price behavior already alluded to between farm products and the food-processing industries. Here the demand influences are common, at least for domestically consumed products.

However, I do not wish to exclude demand effects from this analysis. On the contrary, they are necessary for it. The effect of an increase in demand—a rightward shift in the function—in competitive industries is to increase prices. Its immediate effect, under conditions of oligopoly, is to increase output or, if the industry is at capacity, the backlog of firms. Increasing the latter, as I have shown, amounts to increasing the range in which prices and therewith profits may be increased for the given supply. It seems to increase the amount of unliquidated monopoly gain. As these gains are realized over time, price increases result. These will reflect the differential movement in demand. Such an effect is not inconsistent with the present analysis.

*   *   *

I come now to the consequences for policy. These are considerable. The analysis means that both monetary and fiscal policy must have

[6] I note that, at least by implication, Professor Chandler's view of post-war price-wage relationships accord with the foregoing. He attributes increases in wage rates to "a large and price-inelastic demand for output" which, in turn, made price increases possible. This is to say that firms enjoyed a high degree of monopoly and were not maximizing prior to the wage advances." Lester V. Chandler, *Inflation in the United States, 1940–1948* (New York, 1951), pp. 35–36.

[7] I am grateful to Alvin Hansen for pressing this point.

a markedly differing impact on different parts of the economy, and this will be different at different times, depending on the state of adaptation. This is especially true of monetary policy.

We may think of monetary policy as having two types of effects on individual firms: what may for convenience be called the *impact* effects and what may be called the *demand* effects. By impact effect, I mean the effect of changes in interest rates, and under appropriate circumstances in the supply of loanable funds at given rates, on the operations of firms and specifically on their short and long term investment. If the policy is successful, this investment is reduced or slowed down. By the demand effect, I mean the effect of the resultant reduction or less rapid increase in aggregate demand on the demand curves of all firms.

The impact effect of monetary policy will be almost diametrically different for competitive firms and non-maximizing oligopolies. In the case of the first the initial incidence of an increase in interest charges must be on the firm—it cannot advance its prices to offset the advance in costs, no more than the wheat farmer of real life can increase the price of wheat when his interest charges go up. The increased cost will be passed on only after the higher marginal cost of capital has forced a curtailment (which may be relative) of investment and output. In other words, the incidence is on the firm until after the policy has accomplished the result that it is supposed to accomplish.

In the case of non-maximizing oligopoly, by contrast, the higher interest cost can be absorbed or passed on as the firms prefer or circumstances suggest. Within a wide range, investment that was profitable before the rate increase will be, or can be made, profitable after the increase. Since profits are not being maximized, prices and profits are not being determined by marginal cost-revenue relationships, and hence the increase in costs will not affect investment or output at least so long as the precondition of increasing demand holds. This is the equivalent of saying that the impact effect of higher interest rates will not be fully felt in the oligopolistic sector of the economy until it has made itself effective via the competitive sector on demand.[8]

The other impact effect of monetary policy consists in the limitation of rationing of bank loans at given rates. Here, too, there must be sharp differences, depending on market structure.

We may assume that when loans are rationed, the excluded borrowers will be those with the least creditworthiness, the lowest profitability as clients, or, conceivably, the lowest capacity to resort to a competitive supply. These seemingly obvious points must be pressed, for some commercial bankers, in arguing that there is no adverse effect from monetary policy on any particular class of borrowers, have come close to argu-

---

[8] I do not say it will not be felt by all. Even though higher costs of funds can be readily absorbed or passed along, there may, as in the case of wages, be reluctance based on the irreversibility of these charges or other precautionary tendencies.

ing that in their lending operations there is no discrimination between good customers and bad.

Some preference for the large customer is all but inevitable when credit is being rationed. Other things equal, such firms are more economically served. Their size accords them a greater chance of resorting to non-bank sources, or they may have multiple banking connections. All this reduces the chance that they will be denied credit and very much reduces the chance that they will ultimately be deprived by all sources.

An association between size of firm and oligopoly structure, though pragmatically likely, is not inevitable. However, a more precise and definite relationship between credit rationing and market structure is inherent in the present analysis. As noted, rationing must be expected to discriminate against the least competent borrowers; it proceeds in the context of an active monetary policy which will include advancing interest rates. Obviously, the least creditworthy borrowers will be those who are vulnerable to rate advances—who cannot pass them on—and whose prices are vulnerable to any reduction in aggregate demand. But the firms so affected are, we see, those of the competitive sector. They are *pro tanto* the weakest borrowers and the poorest credit risks. In other words, an active monetary policy acts to make the competitive sector of the economy the least creditworthy and the oligopolistic sector the most creditworthy part of the economy.

Finally, firms in the oligopolistic sector have the opportunity of offsetting any credit restriction to which they are subject by increasing their prices and their earned resources and devoting these to investment. In a non-maximizing context any firm can, in effect, contract out of the effects of monetary policy. This, again, is an opportunity that is not open to the competitive sector; it cannot be done where prices and profits are given. As everyone is aware, the reinvestment of earned income has become a central source of capital formation, and there is plainly a supposition among firms in the oligopolistic sector that prices should be set (and depreciation allowances granted) with a view to realizing the revenues necessary for capital requirements.[9]

Coming now to demand effects, it is possible to expand the argument to treat also the consequences of fiscal policy. (Concern is with the effect of a curtailment of demand, and it is a matter of indifference whether this is the result of a curtailment of private investment, or of public expenditures, or of an increase in taxes.)[10] That there will be a differential effect is already clear. In the competitive sector there will be immediate adaptation through reduced prices. Thereafter, there will be

---

[9] Cf., for example, "Inflation as a Way of Life," by Roger M. Blough, Chairman of the Board, United States Steel Corporation (address before National Editorial Association, November 9, 1956).

[10] In the case of some business taxes, there is a possibility of a differential impact effect. However, their practical likelihood is not great.

reduced investment and output in accordance with the elasticities and transformation period of the particular industry. In the case of the oligopoly there will be no initial effect on prices; a frequent initial effect will be only a shortening of the backlog. Under appropriate stimulation —i.e., a new wage agreement—prices may still rise, and they may continue to do so even after the backlog has been worked off. The critical factor is the unliquidated monopoly gain. Investment that was profitable before will still be profitable, since marginal revenue is (or can be) above long run marginal cost. There may be a curtailment of investment, but it will be the result not of a calculation of marginal cost and price relationships, but of a revision of long term expectations. Clearly, these are portentous differences. In the one case the policy works directly on prices, profits, and therewith on investment. In the other case it leaves prices and profits unaffected and may be consistent with an increase in both. Investment is not forcibly curtailed; at most, a revision is suggested.

Finally, we should notice that all of these effects will vary with the state of adaptation, which means that to measure the consequences of these policies is a far more complex exercise than has commonly been supposed. At the beginning of an inflationary movement, as for example in the autumn of 1950, strong monetary and fiscal measures would be following a period of very rapid adaptation in the competitive sector. Oligopolistic prices, including factor prices of the competitive sector, would not have adapted. A strong monetary and fiscal policy at such a time, reversing the recent adaptation, might be imagined to have relatively mild effects on market structure. (It is to be observed that, as a result of the movement in demand, unliquidated monopoly gains would be large in the oligopolistic sector.) At a later stage, after factor cost adjustment had proceeded, it is easy to imagine that the same policy would be much more severe and painful in the competitive sector. The lesson is that generalization on both the effectiveness and the consequences of macro-economic policy can only proceed with a close regard for a changing context.

* * *

This analysis does not disprove the efficacy of monetary or fiscal policy. Nothing here casts doubt on their restrictive impact on the competitive sector of the economy. And if this is sufficiently severe, the oligopolistic sector will also be affected. How severe it must be will depend, among other things, on the way economic activity is distributed between the competitive and the oligopolistic sectors.

The important thing is that the impact of these policies is unequally distributed. Especially in the case of monetary policy the discrimination can be profound. Inflation is controlled by denying credit to what are, in a general way, the least powerful firms. At the same time, more powerful firms are effectively exempted from the policy. This being so, it is quite possible that they will absorb some or all of the funds denied to the smaller firms. For a considerable period (as this is written in late 1956), there has been a serious and growing volume of complaint from farmers and smaller businessmen over the growing pressure of the credit squeeze. As earlier noted, so far as observation suffices for judgment, there has been no similar complaint from larger firms. The available data on the distribution of bank loans between firms of different size is far from conclusive, for they compare a sampling of member bank loans for 1946 with another for the autumn of 1955. At the latter date the current credit squeeze was still in a fairly early stage; numerous influences, including the general increase in the value of corporation assets and shifts to non-bank sources of funds, impair the value of the comparison. For their limited worth, the figures show that where firms with assets of less than $50,000 had 9.2 per cent of member bank business loans in 1946, by 1955 they had only 5.5 per cent. Firms with assets of from $50,000 to $250,000 had 16.4 per cent in 1946 and 14.5 per cent in 1955. Firms with assets of from $250,000 to $5 million increased their share of the total from 29.0 to 34.3 per cent, and firms with assets in excess of $5 million, which have the best access to non-bank funds, increased their share slightly.[11] During 1956 there was a continuing rise in bank loans. There was also a record investment in producers' durable goods. At the same time, farmers and smaller firms complained bitterly of their deprivation. Accordingly, while the case cannot be proved, there is a strong probability that in the last couple of years the effect of monetary policy has been to ration credit from all sources away from smaller firms in the competitive sector and to larger firms in the oligopolistic sector. This would be in accordance with the present analysis.

Apart from the question of technical effectiveness, there is the question of the political feasibility of a severe application of measures which are discriminatory in their effect. In the past the willingness of the community to tolerate unemployment has been thought one of the conditioning factors in the use of monetary and fiscal restraints; the policy was recognized as falling with discriminatory force on those who were thrown out of their jobs. This we now see is only part of a more general problem. There is also the question of how much pressure can be applied to the competitive part of the economy, and *pari passu* to the smaller and more numerous firms, at a time when far less restraint is being applied to larger firms.

[11] *Federal Reserve Bulletin*, April 1956, p. 331. A very large proportion of all loans—nearly half—are to firms with assets of less than $50,000. This has been seized upon by at least one leading banker to prove that the banks are caring adequately for small firms (J. Stewart Baker, President, The Chase Manhattan Bank, "Changing Times for Banking," speech before the National Association of Supervisors of State Banks, October 19, 1956). As will be immediately evident, the figure proves only that small borrowers are individually numerous. All public-relations-conscious men should be warned on the strategic unwisdom of such usage. Those who are persuaded by the figures soon forget. Those who observe the misuse remember forever.

Finally, there is the question of the wisdom of such discrimination. On this we are plagued by the evident gap between what is professed and what is believed. The small businessman and the competitive sector of the economy are deeply beloved in principle; their fate, however, inspires no particular concern in practice except, perhaps, as it may be tied to historic symbols such as the anti-trust laws. In considerable measure the liturgy in praise of small business serves as a substitute for action.

Still, the policy should be understood. By monetary policy we seek to control inflation by denying to the small business *cum* competition sector the credit on which growth depends. By sufficiently repressing growth in this sector, we may eventually hope to limit growth in the big business *cum* oligopoly sector. By both monetary and fiscal policy we reduce prices and profits in the competitive sector by methods which leave them unaffected in the oligopolistic sector. As a centralizing influence in the economy it is possible to imagine that an active and continuing monetary policy is not less effective than, say, the repeal of the anti-trust laws.

*   *   *

I would not suppose that the analysis here offered will be completely palatable. Monetary policy is profoundly popular with larger business firms and appropriately so. It represents an intelligent manifestation of self-interest; it merits the defense of any large firm that reacts to its own competitive interest.

I would imagine that there would also be some resistance by economists to these ideas. Apart from such objection as may be merited, we need to recognize that, as economists, we have a deep vested interest in monetary and fiscal policy. The conviction, or rather the assumption, that these controls are effective is vital for the present comfortably uncontroversial state of economic policy. Both are widely accepted; the assumption that they work bars the need to explore new or uncomfortable remedies over which passions might easily be aroused. Under these circumstances, any questioning of our present rites can hardly be welcome.

Yet, if it be assumed that the goal of the economist, unlike the monopolist, is not merely a comfortable life, then some questioning is evidently in order. To doubt the efficacy of our present weapons for attacking inflation is not to predict continued inflation. Public policy is not the only determinant of aggregate demand, and this can still be subject to large autonomous movement. But if the future, immediately or later, is like the recent past, we shall be increasingly faced with the choice between inflation or highly discriminatory (and perhaps socially unacceptable) measures for contending with it. Events, as on occasion before, may reveal a most unsanguine nakedness in our profession, all the worse for its contrast with the present confidence.

The Balanced Budget Re-examined

5.   THE BALANCED BUDGET*

Arthur Smithies

SYNOPSIS

1. Despite the long opposition of economists to the annually balanced budget, it still is an objective of public officials, and they are willing to sacrifice essential defense spending to it. Centuries ago, it was a means of preventing government extravagance, and it still disciplines the financial operations of government.

2. But to balance the budget annually is to make difficult the proper allocation of resources between the private and public sectors.

3. When lower tax receipts require reductions in expenditures, new programs of merit are likely to be reduced as much as or more than programs which, because they are old, have political support.

4. It may be necessary to use expenditure, tax, and monetary policies independently of each other in order to achieve separate goals; if expenditures and revenues must always match, the achievement may be more difficult.

5. Expenditure and taxation should be based on long run needs. Once expenditures are increased to combat a recession, it is difficult to reduce them. Similarly, once taxes have been reduced, it is difficult to raise them.

6. Thus, short run stability should be achieved as far as possible by the built-in flexibility of the budget and by monetary measures which can be readily reversed.

7. But these methods probably would be insufficient in a severe recession. Under certain specified signs of recession, there should be an automatic reduction in the first bracket of the income tax, to be restored automatically when recovery reaches a certain point. Such a policy would allay the fears of those who believe that the balanced budget is necessary for financial restraint.

8. The saving needed for growth may be obtainable only by budget surpluses; and in the past, it has been unintentional. It may be made more certain by a balanced budget, and so the doctrine may have long run merit.

I

For over a quarter of a century, economists, or the majority of them, have been protesting against the dogma that the annually balanced budget

*Reprinted by permission from *The American Economic Review*, May 1960, pp. 301–9.

is the path of financial virtue. I regret to have to report that we have made remarkably little headway at the high political levels. Despite the economists, or perhaps because of them, every President has clung tenaciously to the dogma. President Roosevelt's papers clearly reveal that he regarded budget deficits as an evil that had to be tolerated in order to achieve a greater good. The published views of President Truman make his views on the subject abundantly clear. The spoken utterances of President Eisenhower leave no doubt about where he stands on the matter. But despite our failure to demolish this pillar of the financial temple, there seems to be general acceptance of the view that deficits, though evil, are inevitable during depressions. The $12 billion deficit in 1958 does not seem to have been grist for anyone's political mill—perhaps because everyone participated in creating it. But 1959 and 1960 have seen desperate if not ruthless efforts not only to achieve a balanced budget but to achieve balance at the pre-existing level of taxation. I can easily visualize the tortured sessions in the Budget Bureau and the Treasury that produced a surplus of $100 million in the President's budget for fiscal 1960. I imagine similar sessions are going on this minute with respect to fiscal 1961.

Adherence to the dogma is so strong that we are prepared to delay vital defense programs in order to pay lip service to it. The government is also willing to impair the budgetary process itself in order to preserve the semblance of balance. As one spectacular example, I can find no indication of the capital cost of post office construction in the President's 1959 budget. Even though the government has decided to buy its post offices on time, surely the public is entitled to know how many post offices are being bought. If rationality rather than dogma dictated attitudes toward the budget, there might be less incentive for deception.

The survival of the balanced budget rule, however, is not entirely a matter of dogma. Individuals and groups with no dogmatic convictions have a strong interest in keeping the dogma alive. The classical objection to government debt was a natural reaction to the consequences of government extravagance during the seventeenth and eighteenth centuries.[1]

The requirement of a balanced budget was and still is the simplest and clearest rule to impose "fiscal discipline" and to hold government functions and expenditure to a minimum. Those who still entertain this desire as an overriding objective may be well advised not to retreat from the general rule until they are reasonably sure that the retreat will not become a rout.

The advocates of unbalanced budgets have not been reassuring from the conservative point of view. The unbalanced budget usually means fiscal freedom, borrowing, and deficits, and not deficits or surpluses as the occasion demands. The New Deal deficits were associated

---

[1] For an admirable survey of the history of the balanced budget doctrine, see Jesse V. Burkhead, "The Balanced Budget," reprinted in *Readings in Fiscal Policy* (1955).

not simply with recovery but with recovery and reform; and when the New Deal was in full flower, the President took pains to insist that recovery was inseparable from reform.

Even an avowedly counter-cyclical fiscal policy is believed to give rise to an upward trend in expenditures that might not otherwise occur. The expenditures undertaken to counteract a depression are unlikely to be discontinued in the succeeding boom. If the boom is countered at all, the measures taken will be credit restriction or increased taxation; and then further expenditure programs will be taken to offset the next depression. The increased expenditures hastily undertaken to meet the 1958 recession indicate that this possibility is by no means academic.

The discipline of the balanced budget is not necessarily the right degree of discipline. It is generally agreed that in time of war the unwilling taxpayer should not be allowed to hamper the defense of the country. The taxpayer is supposed to come into his own in times of peace. But the present situation is neither peace nor war. Despite amiable conversations among heads of state, a permanent state of military readiness for the indefinite future will be imperative. Organized groups of taxpayers have not shown a clear appreciation of the situation. The President and the leaders of Congress must have some freedom to act even though they cannot pay the bills from current revenue. But if all notions of fiscal discipline and budget balance were removed and no alternative was provided, there can be no doubt that expenditures would increase to a level that was economically undesirable and politically demoralizing. However rich we become, public and private wants are likely to increase more rapidly than the means of satisfying them; and in our complex political system, some rules of financial conduct that are simple enough to survive in a political context seem to me to be desirable.

II

Nevertheless, the rule that the budget should be balanced annually is inadequate to secure the proper allocation of resources between the public and the private sectors. The objections to it have been stated time and again. I shall therefore confine myself to a brief summary of those I consider the most important.

First, to attempt to balance the budget on an annual basis is inconsistent with the long range character of many government programs. Research, development, and procurement for defense purposes inevitably involve activities extending over a number of years. If the programs are well conceived in the first place, waste and inefficiency will result from disrupting them in order to achieve particular budget results. I remember that on one occasion during the Korean war the government deferred payments to contractors for the sake of the appearance of the budget and naturally had to pay a high rate of interest to them as compensation for waiting for their money. Again, it is wasteful to suspend work on a battleship for the sake of avoiding disbursements at a particular time. Perhaps the battleship should not have been started, but to leave it half-finished for a time simply adds to its cost.

Another case where the requirement of annual balance is disruptive is the foreign aid program. This program is the favorite target for indignant charges of waste and inefficiency. But there is no surer way to waste and ineffectiveness than to expose our own program to such vicissitudes and uncertainties that the receiving countries are unable to mesh their own activities with it. Everyone who has examined the problem with understanding and sympathy has stressed the need for continuity.

With respect to the question of "annuality," the economists and the accountants are in league against effective government operations. The accountants like to clean up their books every year and hence stress the need for annual control. The economists take the same point of view because they want a flexible fiscal system whose impact on the economy can be varied from year to year as a contribution to general economic stability. Some compromise between the programming and the annual points of view is clearly needed. Neither can be ignored. But a satisfactory compromise, in my opinion, requires less strict adherence than we now attempt to the annual point of view.

A second objection to the balanced budget rule is that stress on the balanced budget as a criterion tends to give the misleading impression that the government is well managed if the budget is balanced. The examples I have just given illustrate this point; but more generally, there is no indication that some over-all rule will secure efficiency down the line. When budget requests are cut to conform to the rule, the programs most likely to suffer are the new ones designed to meet new situations; and those most likely to survive are those that have acquired the support of powerful vested interests inside or outside the government. Not all new activities are necessarily more meritorious than the old, but some of them are. The way we now seem to be placidly accepting the Russian lead in space exploration—presumably for budgetary reasons—is a vivid illustration of my point.

Government efficiency cannot be achieved by budget ceilings imposed at the behest of hardheaded budget directors and appropriations committees. While some discipline of this kind is probably inevitable, the solution must lie in application of the economics of choice, subject to budget constraints, at every level of government. Public administrators traditionally do not learn economics, and vested interests have a strong interest in avoiding the application of economic principles.

The third objection related to the effect of the balanced budget on economic fluctuations. Surely it is now agreed by economists that attempts, especially successful ones, to balance the budget every year worsen economic fluctuations. If governments curtail their expenditures when they are short of revenues and expand them when yields rise as a result of economic prosperity, their activities will be cyclical rather than counter-cyclical. It may be argued that I am stressing income effects and ignoring the monetary consequences of the balanced budget. The pre-Keynesian view was that depression cuts of expenditures released funds for the private economy. But the decisive objection to this point of view is that a central bank can do the same thing, so that the country can have the benefit of both income and monetary effects.

My final objection is that the balanced budget will not necessarily be the policy needed for achieving desired rates of economic growth. One of the unhappy ironies of the present time is that although the country is richer than it has ever been, further growth is becoming an explicit objective of policy—at a time when we should be enjoying the euphoria of John Stuart Mill's stationary state. We are not prepared to get the additional resources needed for national security and social welfare by cutting back on consumption. That would mean higher taxes. We must therefore grow in order to obtain more resources. Some eminent authorities maintain that the American economy must grow at 5 per cent a year instead of its traditional 3 per cent. If accelerated growth is required, it seems to me very likely that the total rate of national saving must be increased, and the only practicable way to increase total saving is through the generation of budget surpluses. Budgetary doctrine in this country has hardly begun to contemplate this possibility.

III

A more general objection to the balanced budget or any other budgetary rule is that it places unnecessary restrictions on ability to achieve a variety of economic policy objectives. In terms of Tinbergen's now famous proposition, the requirement of balance may leave the government with fewer instruments than it has targets, and consequently may mean that objectives more important than balance must be ignored or that new instruments must be discovered.

The point can be illustrated very simply. Let us ignore for the moment pressing issues such as inflation and the balance of payments and assume that the government has only three policy objectives: First, it must spend enough to give effect to foreign and domestic policy objectives; second, it must maintain full employment; and, third, it must ensure that private investment will, in each year, be carried out at the rate required to maintain a given rate of growth for the economy as a whole. Thus, every year it has three fixed targets: national income or output, private investment, and government expenditures. With present institutional arrangements, convictions, and predilections, it is virtually restricted to three instruments, namely, expenditures, taxation, and general credit expansion or contraction.

If the government has freedom to use these three instruments, it can attain the three objectives. If, in addition, it must balance the budget or maintain any prescribed relationship between expenditures and revenues, it has set for itself a fourth objective and is consequently one instrument short.

So long as it possesses only the three instruments, some other must give way: growth, full employment, or the government's own programs. As a matter of fact, during the last few years the government has placed even more severe restrictions on itself. It has attempted not only to balance the budget but to balance it at existing levels of taxation. This means that it has denied itself the use of one instrument. The expenditure objective necessarily gives way to this requirement (insofar as the requirement is met), and the government is left with general credit policy to achieve both full employment and a satisfactory rate of growth—a task that it is logically and practically impossible for the harassed monetary authorities to perform. Their difficulties are compounded when, in addition, they are expected to help correct the balance of payments and to prevent inflation.

If the government is short of instruments, it must acquire new instruments if it is to attain its objectives. Such new instruments could be selective credit controls, selective tax measures, and various kinds of direct controls. It would take me too far afield to discuss these possibilities in detail. Suffice it to say that many of them are pure anathema to those who must vehemently support the balanced budget doctrine. They are likely to be required to pay a high price for the dogma.

IV

We are unlikely to achieve full coherence in the formation of fiscal and budget policy. Some incoherence is likely to remain so long as there is separation of powers between the President and Congress and between the powerful committees of the Congress. Nevertheless, considerable improvement is possible and feasible. To be optimistic about that, one only has to reflect on the extent to which economic thinking has penetrated the government since World War II, largely as an outcome of the Employment Act of 1946 and the institutions set up under it. I therefore consider it worth while to offer some suggestions concerning the directions that improvement might take.

First of all, the President should transmit his budget to Congress as part of a comprehensive economic program. This is not done at the present time. The present Budget Message is notable for its lack of economic analysis. The President's Economic Report, on the other hand, is equally notable for its lack of an analysis of the economic impact of the budget. However much they may consort in private, the Budget Bureau and the Council of Economic Advisers do not embrace in public. The

President's program would analyze economic policy as a whole in terms of the variety of objectives to be attained and the instruments to be employed.

With respect to the budget itself, the President would recommend a surplus, balance, or a deficit, depending on economic conditions. If a deficit were proposed, this should be proposed as a positive recommendation, not as a confession of failure to balance the budget combined with a wistful hope that balance will be achieved next year.

This approach could have the same disciplinary value as the balanced budget. If the President were prepared to give the weight of his authority to the need for a surplus or a deficit of a certain amount, that should have the same disciplinary value as balance from the point of view of the Congress and the executive departments.

For this suggestion to be as effective as possible, the Congress would have to cooperate. In particular, the Joint Economic Committee should join with the Appropriations Committee and the Ways and Means Committee in considering the President's program and in formulating congressional economic and budgetary policy. But such a change in congressional procedure is unlikely to come about unless the President takes the lead.

Second, the President's economic program should distinguish between long run economic policy and the policy needed to counteract particular episodes of boom and recession. The long run policy should contemplate continuity in government operations and continued growth of the economy. Budgetary policy in particular should be designed to conform with the requirements of long run growth.

Of course, long run policy would be revised from year to year, to take account of changing circumstances and to correct errors in diagnosis. But in the absence of violent changes, say in defense requirements, it seems unlikely that abrupt changes in the relation of government expenditures to revenues would be required. Consequently, some simple budgetary rule that should apply in normal circumstances may be feasible. In times of full employment without inflation, it could be said that the budget should have a surplus or a deficit of some known order of magnitude.

It follows that the basic revenue and expenditure estimates should be made and published with reference to a full-employment situation rather than to the situation actually predicted. This is the stabilizing budget approach that has long been advocated by the Committee for Economic Development, but which has made very little headway in official circles.

I suggest, also, that if the government's policy is to keep a stable price level, the expenditure and revenue estimates should be made in stable prices. This procedure provides an automatic check on inflation. It would tend to prevent inflationary increase in revenues from being regarded as a substitute for taxation. It would also put some pressure on the spending agencies in the event of inflation. They should make some contribution by attempting to curtail their activities. But if they consider that impossible, they should demonstrate the fact in requests for supplemental appropriations.

Thirdly, the question of counter-cyclical policy should be dealt with in a separate chapter of the President's program. This would include a discussion of the effects of recessions or booms on the budget and recommendations concerning the budgetary measures needed as correctives.

In view of what I said above, long range government procurement programs should be interfered with as little as possible for cyclical policies. Nor should new programs that will last for a number of years be be hastily adopted merely for the sake of relieving a single recession. This, however, does not mean that all public works should be continued at the same rate regardless of booms and depressions. Highway construction and many items authorized by the Rivers and Harbors Bill can be adjusted to short term economic needs.

However, if the main emphasis were placed on changes in taxation and transfer payments for purposes of short run stability, the inefficiencies connected with abrupt alterations in expenditure programs could be avoided. The 1958 recession furnishes a good example. The government refused to use tax reduction as its fiscal weapon, and consequently got large and ill-considered increases in expenditures which will continue long after the anti-depression need for them has passed. Nevertheless, I believed at the time and still believe that the tax route would have been wrong. Taxes once reduced are notoriously hard to restore. In fact, it is hard to think of any tax increases during the last thirty years that were not undertaken in response to emergency situations. Even the tax increases of the New Deal come under that category. If the existing tax rates are likely to be needed for long run purposes, it is of questionable wisdom to reduce them for short run reasons, unless the reduction can be of an explicitly temporary character.

This leads me, and has led many others, to the conclusion that short run stability should be achieved as far as possible through "built-in flexibility" of the budget and through monetary measures that can be readily reversed.

Built-in flexibility has increased appreciably as a result of social security, unemployment compensation, and agricultural support on the expenditure side and through the automatic operation of the tax system. But such measures—even in conjunction with vigorous credit measures —are unlikely to meet the requirements of a severe recession. There is need for further automatic measures. Consequently, I venture to repeat a proposal in which I participated some years ago.[2] Under certain specified

[2] See the United Nations Report, *National and International Measures for Full Employment* (1950).

signs of recession, there should be an automatic reduction in the first bracket of the income tax. The reduction should be restored automatically when recovery has reached a prescribed point. To guard against inappropriate use of the remedy, its application should be subject to veto by the President. Devices such as this could give reasonable assurance that anything but the deepest depression would be corrected and would help materially to avoid the psychological conditions that might produce depressions of the catastrophic kind.

Our proposal was considered in the chancelleries of the world and was unanimously rejected by respectable opinion. Had it been in effect, it would have been very serviceable in 1958. Automatic reversible devices are the most effective way to avoid the radical political consequences of a flexible fiscal policy, and thus to allay the fears of those who cling to the balanced budget rule on rational rather than superstitious grounds.

To return finally to the long run question: I have suggested that surpluses rather than deficits may be needed in the future—if the government pursues an economic policy that is consonant with national and international needs. But surpluses are hard to achieve. Senator Taft once remarked that in his long experience, surpluses and debt retirement occurred only through inadvertence. If that is true, perhaps the balanced budget doctrine has some long run merit, after all.

MEASURES FOR STABILITY AND GROWTH

Most economists believe that fiscal and monetary measures are among those that should be used to promote stability and growth. Other measures may also be essential; but fiscal and monetary measures, nearly everyone believes, certainly should be. That is because they have an important effect, although not necessarily an adequate one, on total employment, the price level, and the rate of economic growth. There is substantial agreement also about the way fiscal and monetary measures should be used. When employment and the price level are falling, the government should increase its expenditures and reduce its net taxes (total taxes minus transfer payments); and the Federal Reserve System should increase the money supply by reducing the discount rate, lowering the reserve requirements of the member banks, and providing them with greater reserves by buying government securities on the open market. When there is full employment and prices are rising, each of these measures should be reversed.

There is, however, disagreement about other aspects of stabilization and growth. Before explaining them, we wish to remark that disagreement does not necessarily mean economics is ineffective. It means that economics is not as effective as it could be. Its policies therefore must be provisional, must be undertaken with more than the customary prudence, and applied in a way that makes them easy to revoke, if they are mistaken, and easy for others to be put in their place. The world would of course be a more serene place if stabilization, growth, and other matters could be put aside until economic opinion about them was clear and certain. But they cannot be. Economists must use the knowledge they have so long as they think it is more likely than not to be helpful. Their disagreement, which so often confuses and exasperates the public, means more than that there are unsettled questions of policy. It means that a continuing effort is being made to answer them.

There are differences over whether fiscal or monetary policy is the more effective in particular circumstances, over which particular measures of each policy are the more suitable, over whether government should use its powers according to its best judgment or according to announced rules. There are differences over the definition of the goals of stability and growth and over whether the goals of the one are compatible with those of the other.

71

If full employment means that the unemployed are mainly people who are changing jobs, there is a question of whether it is compatible with long run price stability. Contrariwise, if price stability means that changes in the price level over a decade are within the small range of 3 or 4 per cent, it is doubtful that price stability is compatible with full employment and proper economic growth. Or if the major goal is a high growth rate, it is doubtful that price stability can be achieved.

There are unsettled questions about the structure of the economy. Given the institutions of a mixed economy, can it operate to attain some tolerable combination of the three goals? Is the stabilization problem that of moderating the effects of recurrent business cycles—of smoothing the peaks and filling in the valleys of the gross national product curve? Or is the economy prone to persistent unemployment, so that more drastic measures are needed? Or do prices tend to rise continuously, so that stabilization measures must be especially adapted to prevent creeping inflation?

There are difficulties in predicting short run changes in business conditions, and perhaps even more in determining the time lags between stabilization measures and their effects, e.g., the time that will elapse between a change of tax rates and the consequent change of income and employment.

There is a growing recognition that stabilization measures which would be appropriate for a society of the civic-minded may not be appropriate for one in which there are special interest groups with their blocs in Congress. How far the stabilization measures should be tailored to political realities is an unsettled question. A specific example is how far they can limit credit for small businessmen and farmers during inflationary periods without provoking political opposition that would imperil the entire stabilization program.

In summary, there is widespread agreement among economists about how to combat massive unemployment and declining price levels, such as characterized the thirties. There is also agreement (although probably not quite as extensive) about how to combat rapid inflation such as occurred immediately after the second world war. There is much disagreement over how to achieve full employment, long run price stability, and an optimum rate of economic growth in economy characterized by recurrent business cycles, creeping inflation, and congressional sensitivity to pressure groups.

Structural Changes Moderating the Cycle

Arthur F. Burns argues that significant institutional changes have cut the close tie between production and income. This means the economy is much less responsive to swift changes in investment spending than it was before the second world war. There are a number of reasons for the change. Corporate dividends do not vary as much as corporate income, largely because of the increased importance of undistributed profits. Most federal taxes are progressive and tend to decline sharply when business declines. At the same time, government expenditures tend to remain high and indeed to rise during recession periods as a result of additional spending on farm subsidies and of larger transfer payments. Large private transfer payments, in addition to those made by government, also account for the divorce of production and income. The number of people employed in the service industries, in white-collar jobs, and in other overhead operations has increased significantly. The employment of these people is not closely connected to total output.

Another factor of importance is that consumption spending has become less sensitive to business cycle developments than it was during the twenties and thirties. Indeed, consumption has developed into a major force that leads us out of recessions. It appears from Burns's argument that the newer practices of business and government have made the economy more stable. Associated with these changes is the development of new financial institutions: the Federal Reserve System, the Federal Deposit Insurance Corporation, and the modifications in them. Coupled with a willingness on the part of the government to use discretionary measures, such as tax reductions, these institutions have limited the spread of recessions.

As a result of these and other developments, Burns ventures the guess that recessions in the future are likely to be milder than in the past. Although it is true that rising prices and greater consumer credit could intensify cyclical movements, he believes that on balance the problem we now face is mainly one of dampening them.

In dealing with instability in the future, we should, Burns states, continue to make such institutional changes as will promote stability rather than depend on our ability to predict recessions and to adjust public spending and/or taxes quickly enough to promote recovery. His is essentially an optimistic view of the problem we face.

Discretionary Policy for Stability and Growth

Richard A. Musgrave acknowledges the difficulties of using fiscal policy to combat relatively small cyclical variations around the long term trend of total output. He also notes the complexities that come from trying to attain a number of different stabilization goals simultaneously. Because of these and other problems, he argues that the government's decisions about how much to spend on goods and services should be determined by the long run needs of the public sector and that the tax structure should reflect the public's beliefs about equity. Neither government expenditures nor the tax structure should be altered simply to combat cyclical developments. The two remaining important stabilization measures are changes in the amount of taxes (the structure being unchanged) and monetary policy. But even if they were used promptly in combatting inflations and recessions, there would still be many un-solved problems. Monetary policies are more useful in limiting than in expanding aggregate demand. They also fall heavily on certain sectors of the economy, notably local governments. Hence, monetary policies should be used carefully in order to avoid serious dislocation problems. In Musgrave's opinion, automatic stabilizers are not adequate to cope with instability. He would supplement them by giving the fiscal and mone-tary authorities the power to employ discretionary measures, such as tax reductions and changes in the money supply.

Non-discretionary Policy for Stability and Growth

In contrast, O. H. Brownlee would rely on pre-determined rules of policy instead of on discretionary policy. Like Musgrave, he would not have the government increase or decrease its expenditures in response to cyclical changes. He would, however, have it develop a capital expend-iture budget in which the rate of return is computed for each project according to the social benefits it produces. Then, when the govern-ment is able to sell its securities at an interest rate smaller than the ex-pected rate of return, he would have the government increase its invest-ment spending. In this way the government would invest more heavily during recessions, when the interest rate is low, than during prosperity, when the interest rate is high. But, he points out, this result would be an unintended gain from a rational public investment policy rather than from the application of counter-cyclical stabilization measures.

Essentially, Brownlee's argument stems from his conviction that economists know little about the short run effect of discretionary stabili-zation measures, and that it is better to accept whatever instability is as-sociated with the application of rules rather than to risk the destabilizing effects of discretionary measures. Specifically, Brownlee would have the government determine a target amount of the gross national product in current dollars for each year. It then would establish taxes and expendi-tures that would balance the budget at that gross national product. Should it fall short of the target, the resulting deficit would be financed by the creation of money; and should it exceed the target, the resulting surplus would be used to reduce the money supply. Brownlee, therefore, would not leave any discretionary authority with the Federal Reserve or the Treasury.

Both Musgrave and Brownlee are concerned about the possibility of sellers initiating increases in prices before full employment is reached. Musgrave suggests that the only way to combat such cost-push inflation may be a public review of all price increases, particularly in key indus-tries. On the other hand, Brownlee is categorically opposed to any form of price control and would try to solve the problem by the fragmenting of national unions and other means that would limit the monopoly power of sellers. The proper method of managing cost-push inflation is one of the major unsettled questions of stabilization policy and of growth policy also.

Anti-competitive Effects of Stabilization Policy

One of the puzzles of the post-war period has been the tendency of industrial prices to rise even during recessions. Cost-push inflation complicates the task of achieving full employment and an optimum rate of growth at stable prices. Many economists wonder whether the three goals are mutually consistent. J. K. Galbraith, in his study, divides the economy into the competitive and the oligopolistic sectors. When aggregate demand changes, competitive prices react immediately—either rising or falling as aggregate demand changes. But in the oligopolistic sector, changes in aggregate demand are reflected in the size of the backlogs of orders. "Unliquidated monopoly gains" appear when aggregate demand increases. Industrial firms are reluctant to increase prices because that may induce a demand for higher wages from the unions. However, once a union contract is negotiated, managers of oligopolistic industries tend to use the settlement as a signal to increase prices. They can do this during recessions because, many times, unliquidated monopoly gains are still available from the preceding prosperity. This explains, Galbraith says, the continuous rise of industrial prices through periods of recession as well as of full employment.

His analysis seems to call for limiting the growth of aggregate demand during prosperous periods by monetary and fiscal means. But the realities of politics make Galbraith pessimistic about their long term acceptability. Restrictive monetary measures cause banks to reduce credit, but the reduction falls more on risky competitive forms than on oligopolies with their large backlogs of orders. Thus, the oligopolistic sector is permitted to grow relative to the competitive sector. And since restrictive fiscal policies reduce prices in the competitive sector more than in the oligopolistic, those policies too are likely to be unpopular with the voters.

The Balanced Budget Re-examined

Arthur Smithies is also concerned with the political feasibility of fiscal policies as a means of achieving stability. The requirement that the budget be balanced can lead to a misallocation of resources. If some public projects are curtailed in order to balance the budget, there will be a waste of resources. The balanced budget rule also makes it more difficult to achieve the multiple goals of full employment, growth, and price stability, since it imposes an additional restraint on government. However, Smithies argues, the political goals of democracy have also to be considered in making economic policy. If the proper balance between the private and public sectors is to be secured, expenditures and tax policies should be based on long run rather than on cyclical conditions. Expenditure programs that are started in order to combat a recession are likely to continue after it has ended. And in the long run the only widely accepted rule for controlling expenditures is the balanced budget rule. This would mean that short run stability should be achieved as far as possible by flexibility built into the budget and through monetary policies that can be reversed by administrative rather than legislative decision.

Measures for Stability and Growth: A Summary Statement

In the light of the post-war experience, economists are now convinced that the task of achieving both full employment and price stability within the context of economic growth is immensely more complicated than it appeared to be at the end of the war. Lack of knowledge about the relevant time lags, the difficulties of making short run predictions, the conflict of social goals, the differential effect of monetary and fiscal policies on various parts of the economy, the growth of unions and oligopolistic pricing, pressure-group voting in Congress, and the administrative problems involved in making small adjustments to taxes and expenditures—all combine to make the achievement of a stable economy very difficult. Possibly the most that can be hoped for is that the institutional changes which have been made and may continue to be made will create a framework within which the economy will achieve a tolerable amount of stability and growth. To attempt more could make "the best the enemy of the good."

PART 2

Market Power

THE PROBLEM OF MARKET POWER

Market power is the ability to influence prices or wages. It is synonymous with monopoly when that word is used to mean price or wage power but not in its literal sense of one seller. Market power has its origin in many circumstances, it discloses itself in many ways, it may be weak or strong or an unknown quantity; and a firm may use all it has, some of it, or none at all, and may use it to change prices or wages or to keep them from changing.

It is a problem because it has an effect on the efficiency with which resources are used at any particular time; that is, it affects the size of aggregate income. It also has an effect on investment and innovation, and so influences the growth of income. Because it has an effect on particular prices, it will influence the way they change when there are inflationary or deflationary movements operating on all prices. Finally, market power is a problem because it affects the distribution of wealth and income.

To formulate a policy for controlling market power requires, first, that we understand what it is and how it affects efficiency, growth, price stability, and distribution; second, that we decide which of all these desirable things we want and in what proportion; and third, what means are suitable for obtaining them.

J. M. Clark explains the meaning of competition and the values it is expected to produce; he shows how some market power is consistent with it; and he submits that, for policy purposes, it is most helpful to think of competition as neutralizing behavior. James S. Duesenberry examines competition and concentration for their effect on investment, innovation, and price stability, and concludes that no one market structure achieves all three, although the one that is most generally useful is a concentrated industry with a competitive fringe. When market power is viewed over a long period of time, it shows less concentration and more competitive consequences than in the short run. Joseph A. Schumpeter explains this in his analysis of the relationship between monopoly, innovation, and competition.

Given an understanding of market power, we then must know which courses of action are open to us for controlling it. Harold M. Levinson and Otto Eckstein submit that the government can enforce competition or persuade firms and unions to use their power in the public interest, or can force them to.

About the market power of unions, there is less agreement than about that of firms. Two views are presented here. Henry C. Simons states that unions are no different from firms with market power except in their greater power for harm. Edward S. Mason takes a different view of the structure and effects of union power, examines the alternative standards by which unionism may be controlled, and proposes a political reconciliation of them.

6. COMPETITION AND THE OBJECTIVES OF GOVERNMENT POLICY*

J. M. Clark

SYNOPSIS

1. Most American economists favor inter-firm competition in large scale manufacturing, lumbering, and metal mining, in securities markets, and oil drilling, and inter-industry competition in transportation and anthracite coal; they oppose competition in bituminous coal and agriculture and are ambiguous about it in merchandising.

2. They do not believe there should be as much competition in labor markets as in product markets, but they believe there should be more competition in labor markets than there now is.

3. What economists want from competition is cheapness and quality in products; social values like opportunity, mobility, and freedom; incentives for improvement and growth; and certain values implied by the theory of competition.

4. The theories they and anti-trust authorities hold are too simple to explain competitive behavior or to guide its enforcement.

5. It is more helpful to think of competition as neutralizing behavior in which one firm initiates action to increase its profits and its rivals respond to avoid losses. The action consists of offering price, quality, and other inducements to buyers. There usually is a lag before rivals respond with similar inducements, and during the lag the initiator has a temporary monopoly.

6. If neutralization were instantaneous, there would be no incentive to the initiator. The theory of competition is deficient in the matter of neutralization.

7. In actual competition the costs of some firms are below price and of others above it. The differences are necessary for growth, and promote competitive behavior even where there are only a few firms.

8. A competitive economy removes the necessity of choosing between concentrations of private or of public power.

9. It assists policies for aggregate stability by providing them a flexible setting within which to operate.

10. Competitive impulses are deeply rooted in human behavior, and the economy should permit their expression; but it must also satisfy the need for group solidarity, the latter placing a limit to the scope of competition.

* Reprinted by permission and shortened from *Monopoly and Competition and Their Regulations*, ed. E. H. Chamberlin (London: Macmillan, 1954), pp. 317–37.

11. A policy for market power should try to impose competitive incentives within the framework of institutions that provide solidarity and security.

It seems that American economists have been taking the desirability of competition for granted while things have been happening, in the realms of theory and practice, which have changed the perspective in which we see a number of our objectives; and it may be worth while to re-examine our position.

Briefly, Americans do believe that competition has an important place in the economic system while some other countries lean more to cartelization or centrally organized rationalization, and this indicates a difference of some importance. But having said this, one has merely begun the task of defining what the place of competition is, as judged by practices which Americans in general explicitly or tacitly approve. Any idea that Americans adhere to competition as a universal principle would be grossly misleading. Actually, Americans believe competition needs to be restrained in various large sectors of the economy, and our attitude differs as between different aspects of competitive action—on price, output, quality, etc.

The most obvious and simple attitude is to approve of the fullest competition for others and of shelters from its more severe rigors for oneself. If the test of genuine belief in competition were: "Do you believe you yourself should be exposed to unmitigated competitive pressures?" I wonder how many people would qualify. Not the academic profession—witness the importance they attach to tenure for professors. Logically, this attitude of "competition for you, security for me" should mean that, in each particular case, a majority favors competition. Actually, it is likely to be transformed by "log-rolling" into mutual toleration by each group for the protections desired by the other groups, so long as they reciprocate.

This tends to vitiate the simplest test of genuine belief in restraining competition, namely, whether members of one group approve of shelters from competition for other groups. At any rate, in what follows, I shall consider only cases in which the approval (of restraining competition) is fairly general, or is expressed in policies presumably in the public interest, or where the rationalization is fairly convincing. In short, I shall be trying to confine myself to reasonably genuine departures from competitive theory, including those expressed in policy.

HOW MUCH COMPETITION DO THE AMERICAN PEOPLE WANT?

Production and Sale of Goods and Services by Business Units

Broadly speaking, the sector in which Americans most unqualifiedly approve of competition is in the production and sale of goods and services by "big business." Even here, one must make exception of naturally monopolistic industries of the sorts treated as "public utilities"—telephone, telegraph, electricity, and railroads to a less thorough-going extent. And we shall see that there are other exceptions. The primary field in which competition is most clearly and unqualifiedly desired seems to be that of manufacturing, lumbering, and metal mining.

As to merchandising, the ambiguous state of opinion is highlighted by the recent legal contest over the status of the "fair-trade laws" which give a manufacturer power to fix prices at which dealers shall resell his product; and the price war that was precipitated in June 1951, by a court decision to the effect that dealers who have not agreed to maintain a manufacturer's resale price could not be compelled to observe the resale prices on which others had agreed. Small local merchants want protection against the competition of chain stores and super-markets, and allege that these large scale merchandisers enjoy unfair advantages in buying; while some small merchants organize to buy cooperatively, in order to reduce their disadvantage on this score. The public attitude on this issue, as expressed politically, is not clearly defined. Consumers are not willing to forgo the low prices that modern large scale distribution brings them, or to subsidize small scale methods where large scale ones can be really more efficient. But they tolerate guild-like behavior in many areas of small trade, especially the service trades.

The business of lending money and floating securities must, on the whole, also be classed as one in which competition is desired, despite the large measure of control exercised by the Federal Reserve System. The rate of interest is a managed rate, but not managed on private monopoly principles. And the selection of credit risks is left to the independent action of multiple credit institutions.

In agriculture, the case is clear; we approve of protections against the rigors of competition, in the shape of restrictions on output and supports for prices. This policy was defended by former Secretary Wallace as merely giving agriculture an equivalent for the protections given industry and trade, since it appeared hopeless to bring about equalization by making industry and trade as competitive as unregulated agriculture. Behind this over-simplified conception lie some knotty questions; suffice it for the present that non-competitive policies are approved in agriculture.

As to coal, anthracite is so closely held that one must expect the main active competition there to be that of other fuels. In bituminous coal, there are many producers, of all sizes, down to what used to be called "wagon mines," many of which were worked only when the price was good. And this has long been a "sick industry." For some years before our rearmament drive of 1941, a federal commission had been preparing a comprehensive system of minimum prices for bituminous coal; and the system was ready to go into effect at just the time when ample demand and rising prices made the minima needless and ineffective. This policy is likely to be revived when demand falls slack for any considerable period. It appears to record the judgment that competition in bituminous coal is tolerable only when demand is strong, and becomes unendurably severe when the industry has to adjust to a shrinkage of demand.[1] The effective competition for bituminous and anthracite includes oil and natural gas.

Drilling for crude oil is naturally competitive, but actual extraction is subject to various restrictions. There are restrictions on drilling wells too close together, and on production, partly to maintain gas pressure and partly to sustain price. There are also controls over transportation of oil from distant fields. The state of Texas produces enough oil to enable its state commission to exert a strong influence in the national price structure. Crude-oil production is clearly a case of approved restriction of competition. This may be thought of partly as action by a producing state in the interest of its own residents. Why does the federal government uphold the policy? The rationale of this may be a mixture of "log-rolling," conservation, and the kind of attitude that supports agricultural price maintenance.

In transportation there is powerful competition between air carriers, railroads, and different kinds of motor carriers—common carriers, contract carriers, and private carriers. Such competition has shown a strong tendency to go to destructive lengths except in times of pronouncedly strong demand. This occurs in spite of—or perhaps because of—differences in quality, and the sloping individual demand schedules that result. In such situations, minimum rates have been set by the Interstate Commerce Commission and by some state authorities, on the theory that the carriers were in danger of ruin, against which no automatic safeguard appeared. There was sometimes added the view that rate reductions would not create added business for the whole system in the way in which they might increase the business of one carrier, but would merely mean carrying approximately the same volume of business at rates below total cost.

If one searches for a simple summary of the competitive picture so far presented, perhaps the most promising first approximation would be: Americans, in general, favor more competition than we have, in those parts of the economy where it works weakly or is interfered with or threatened; and they seem to want to dilute it where it naturally comes full strength. This, however, is too simple, and one must differentiate between different effects of competition: on price, on quality, and on growth in efficiency. I will attempt to do so in the second part of this

---

[1] This is, of course, to be taken in connection with the high wages which John L. Lewis has gained for coal miners.

paper, after looking at some further areas where unrestricted competition is not desired.

Attitudes toward Competition in the Sale of Labor

The prevailing consensus in the United States favors trade-unions. While it does not favor everything they do, and there is no consensus as to where the line should be drawn, bargaining methods are permitted which would be clearly contrary to the anti-trust laws if corresponding things were done by business. The principle that "labor is not a commodity," enacted into law long ago, means in practice that labor should not be exposed to the rigors of unmitigated competition, and wages should not be at the mercy of "supply and demand." Probably few economists believe that wages should be fixed by competitive bargaining of individual workers, or that they should be reduced whenever demand for labor falls short of supply—however these may be defined—with the implication that there is always some reduction in the level of wages that will cause the whole supply of workers to be absorbed. But the majority probably think that methods of determining wages have departed too far from this standard.

Starting with the conception that bargaining with individual workers gives the employer an undue advantage, economists of a generation or more ago seem typically to have thought that collective bargaining might do no more than equalize this difference, provided it did not control supply or insulate wages from the pressure of an excess supply. That is, collective bargaining in itself was not regarded as necessarily "monopolistic." Under it, the employer, in utilizing the competition of workers available in the market, would have to replace all or most of his working force, just as the worker who utilizes the competition of employers is likely to have to abandon his job and seek another. But if the employer had this option of mass replacement of workers, and especially if unions were local, so that there was some competition between workers-and-employers in one locality, and workers-and-employers in the same industry in other localities, the labor market would still be fairly competitive.

The realities of collective bargaining have, of course, gone far beyond this. Unions may be able to control the supply of eligible workers, or merely fix wages and prevent them from being broken down by the unemployed. Striking workers maintain tenure of their jobs, and employers rarely try to replace them. As to the underlying economics, most economists doubt whether, in a country like the United States, a general reduction of wages is an effective way of restoring employment, let alone whether it is a desirable one. They do, however, think particular wages may be high enough to generate particular unemployment; and features of the relative structure of wages may make some workers less profitable to employ than others, by departing too widely from the competitive principle of differentiating pay according to the value of the worker to the employer. The market has considerable tolerance for such departures—a plant will employ at the same wage workers of different value—but this tolerance is not unlimited.

To sum up, wide departures from the competitive principle are sanctioned in the labor field, and wider ones are in practice acquiesced in, even if not approved by most economists. Some officials might wish to make limited application of the anti-trust laws to the tactics of organized labor; but if so, they are presumably deterred by fear that this would forfeit too much political support for anti-trust policies in general.

Over the whole economic field there are notable differences among economists, and between economists, anti-trust officials, and other authorities in contact with the actual problems of competition. In general, while economic theorists tend to the view (expressly or by the implication of their theories) that competition cannot be too strong (except in the labor market), those in contact with the actual problems obviously hold by their policies that it can be too strong, as well as too weak.[2]

Competition in Selling Political Promises to Voters in Exchange for Votes

Political competition is so different from industrial that analogies are not dependable guides; but they may be of some interest. In the United States and Britain, a form of duopoly is approved: the two-party system. The reasons lie partly in things not applicable to industrial competition—chiefly the fact that one governmental policy must (at least in theory) be furnished to all the consumers. More instructive is the fact that we have here what seems to be an unmistakable case of competition in quality, in which the only meaning such competition can have consists in the differences between the offerings of the rival parties. There may be too little difference, more often than too much. This reinforces the point for which I shall contend in the following section, that quality competition is one of the major important forms.

WHAT DO WE WANT COMPETITION TO DO FOR US, AND TO US?

Introduction

What we want competition to do makes a long list, but leading objectives may be grouped under four headings. First, as to the product, we want cheapness and cognate benefits, and we want quality.[3] Sec-

---

[2] In the light of subsequent discussion, I would add that while I agree with the latter view, I recognize that policies based on it are often dubious, or raise at least as many problems as they solve.

[3] For the economy as a whole, real cheapness is a compound of efficient use of productive resources, including their correct allocation between different uses and, impliedly, defensible distribution—wide and not too unequal. But these latter may deserve the status of coordinate main heads.

ondly, we want competition to help us toward certain more general social and political conditions concerned with opportunity, mobility, and absence of concentrated power. Thirdly, there are the effects of competition on the individuals exposed to its pressures: effects both desirable and undesirable. We want the best balance we can get. Finally, there are certain qualities or objectives that seem to be desirable. They are found less in actual competition than in theories about it. Yet the theories may affect what people think they want from actual competition. There are pitfalls in these derived objectives—objectives found in economists' theories and in theories used to prosecute or defend anti-trust cases. These objectives may be examined first, because their pervasive influence is largely unconscious.

Objectives Residing in the Realm of Theory Itself

Besides wanting to make the world better, or to describe it as it is, theorists as theorists start with a desire for assumptions simple enough to yield definite conclusions, and they go on to a craving for more and more precise formulations, requiring increasing precision in the over-simplified assumptions. Thus, reality is made subservient to theory instead of theory serving as an approach to reality. Alfred Marshall steadily combatted this temptation; E. Ronald Walker has devoted a chapter to it under the heading of "The Theoretical Blight."[4] Theories about competition exhibit this characteristic quite plainly.

It all starts quite commendably. Competition standardizes human behavior to an extent that is, on the whole, useful. We need some standardization of behavior, or else the world would be chaos. We can manage our lives to the extent that we know, in general terms, what to expect of others. Competition forces most businessmen to try to make as much profit as they can, because under competitive conditions there is plenty of difficulty and uncertainty about being able to make any profit at all. Even so, the formula of "maximizing profit" does not in itself tell enough to enable one to predict just what a businessman will do in many particular situations, especially a low cost producer or a near-monopolist, whose position gives him considerable security and range of choice in acting for a distant future, often beyond the term of his own probable connection with the business he represents.

Economists have two reasons for being allergic to such a range of discretionary choice. It means power, and economists do not like the situation in which the businessman is free to choose how he will use his power and whether he will furnish a good commodity at the lowest price he can afford. Further, it is difficult for an economist to satisfy his desire for precise "economic laws," if a businessman's personal wishes can determine the outcome. The economist wants to produce theoretical models

---

[4] [*From Economic Theory to Policy* (Chicago, 1943).]

whose operation is precisely determinate. The most available models are those that reach a static equilibrium. The outcome is the theory of "perfect competition," a model whose characteristics are dictated by the requirement that price shall equal cost and all profits be eliminated.

Actual competition is not like that; and the model may lead us to deplore this fact, but this is uncalled-for. A world in which conduct is absolutely standardized would be arid, deadly, and intolerable. It would even be destructive of ethics and morality as we understand them. For while they are incompatible with utterly irresponsible pursuit of individual self-interest, they also presuppose some margin of discretion and choice in conduct. If precise laws conflict with this feature of the human materials with which they deal, it is the precision of the laws that should give way.

The theories that guide anti-trust authorities could probably be helpful in this matter, if the more significant ones were available for critical examination, meaning by this the theories by which it is decided what cases involve sufficiently serious evils to call for public action. Unfortunately, what is publicly available consists of the briefs and arguments of lawyers prosecuting and defending cases. For the prosecution, there is obvious use in an unattainable standard, such as "perfect competition," where industries can be attacked for not attaining some particular feature of it. On the other side, a theory explaining how rigid prices can come about without collusion can be equally useful. Both are over-simplifications; the economist's concept of "*a* price" is a sadly inadequate first approximation, doing less than justice to the resourcefulness of businessmen in manipulating the features of an actual price structure.

A Unifying Framework for a Broader Theory: Competition as a Sequence of Initiatory Moves and Counteracting Responses

If "perfect competition" is defined by one objective only—the equating of price and cost—it seems that there is a real need for a concept of competition which will relate it to as many as possible of the other objectives here indicated, and which will make room for more of the complexities of reality while still putting them in a unifying framework. Such a framework needs to be clearly applicable to the quoted-price type of selling, characteristic of manufacturing and most merchandising; whereas "perfect" competition is of doubtful relevance to anything other than the produce-exchange type of selling, characteristic of wholesale markets for staple agricultural products. The materials of which this framework is built are not new, though the pattern as a whole may contain some element of novelty.

Business competition is a form of independent action by business units in pursuit of increased profits, or avoidance of reduced profits, by offering those with whom each unit deals inducements to deal with it, the customers being free to accept the alternative inducements offered by rival business units. Active competition consists of a combination of (1) initiatory actions by a business unit and (2) a complex of responses by its customers and by its rivals.[5] All these elements are necessary to it, and a desirable outcome depends on the relative timing and speed of the different movements in the pattern. The more aggressive form of competition consists in giving the buyer more inducement, either in lower prices or more attractive quality or more selling effort, the advantage to the initiator consisting in increased volume of sales, wholly or partly at the expense of rivals. Defensive competition by the rivals acts on the same dimensions, aiming to prevent or minimize a loss of volume of sales. Competition includes the sale of goods at inducements so determined—one should avoid the implication that competition exists only at the moment when price is moving down or quality moving up or selling effort being increased. If the initial move consists merely in a reduction of costs, rivals may feel no direct pressure until reduced costs are passed on to the buyer.

A rival's response may seek to neutralize the initiator's advantage by offering the buyers something equally effective, or he may go further and try to offer something more effective, establishing a positive sales-increasing advantage for himself. In poker parlance, he may "see" the initial move or "raise" it. Or there may be uncertainty about what the initiator is doing and disagreement over whether a given difference in quality or service needs a price differential to equalize it. Such disagreement can lead to "cut-throat competition," where A repeatedly creates a price differential which B repeatedly neutralizes. The sloping individual demand curve associated with quality differences is also accompanied by uncertainty, which may invite price reductions more effectively than in case of few producers of homogeneous products, though price remains above short run marginal cost and does not clearly tend in the short run to any precise relation to total cost. The producer in question may cover less than his total cost, or more.

In terms of this framework, the current theory of competitive *price* tends to emphasize the neutralizing process—the meeting of price reductions completely and instantaneously. Corresponding conceptions of *productive techniques* do not envisage the neutralizing process as a process, merely its completed result—all producers' cost curves equal at the lowest level afforded by existing techniques. But with respect to *quality*, the same theory emphasizes the initiating action (establishing of a quality differential) and neglects the neutralizing process, treating the initiating process as establishing a limited monopoly. The treatment of these different cases is not symmetrical.

---

[5] For brevity, customers will be taken to typify those with whom it deals, though workers and suppliers of other means of production are included.

The neglected factor is that of velocity and time. The outcome hinges on the relative speeds, or expected speeds, of the initiator's gain, in the form of added business or otherwise, and the speed of the neutralizing process whereby rivals follow the initiator's lead and destroy his differential advantage as his action becomes standard practice. In the case of new productive methods or products, both initiation and neutralization generally take a substantial time. If a potential innovator expects neutralization to be complete before he has recovered the costs of innovation, his incentive vanishes. Fortunately, such pessimistic expectations are not common enough among American entrepreneurs to be a serious obstacle to innovation. Most innovators probably expect some enduring residue of advantage. On the other hand, if neutralizing action were permanently blocked, the initiator would have a limited monopoly, in the sense of a permanent differential advantage. Actual cases may approximate this to a harmful extent chiefly where there is undue extension of patent rights in products or processes, or of secret processes.

Instantaneous neutralization is approximated in practice only for reductions of openly quoted prices of homogeneous or very closely competitive products, with few sellers. But even here the initiator can shade list prices, make forward contracts, or benefit from other "market imperfections," so that competitive action seldom is complete unless marketing practices are strongly standardized.

The desirable case lies somewhere between too prompt and too slow neutralization. I will not call it an "optimum," because that term suggests a precision which no actual system could attain. Neutralization needs to take time enough to leave the innovator incentive that is adequate, but not more, and then to diffuse the gains as promptly as is consistent with there being ample gains to diffuse. It may take away the gains the innovator has made in his relative volume of sales, or may merely stop further gains, or it may stop further gains quickly and encroach more gradually on gains already made, so that a residue of these gains may last a fairly long time. If such a residue is expected, it is the innovator's chief incentive, since small but long-lasting gains outweigh large temporary ones.

Cheapness of Products, Monetary and Real

For the economy as a whole, cheapness means production at a minimum expenditure of real factors of production. And here, as throughout this study, the principle holds that a small rate of progressive gain outweighs a large but once-for-all gain. Considerable "wastes," or departures from static optima, are worth incurring if they are the costs of progress that could not be had without them. There is, of course, the question whether technical progress goes faster than society can adapt itself to the results, and whether we might be better off with a slower rate of technical progress and more attention to social adaptation. But at present, rapid technical progress is probably one of the foremost among the necessary conditions for survival of our kind of civilization. So, in this study, I shall be looking for the conditions of progress, not for those of static equilibrium. We shall see that this carries with it considerable changes in the customary theoretical models of competition.

To return to real cheapness: It implies production at an efficient scale—once more I avoid the implication of a precise optimum—let us say a scale within the range that permits maximum economy. This range is likely to be fairly wide; and even if it were not, so long as demand is growing and fluctuating, no precise adjustment is possible. Progress in efficiency implies leaders and followers; hence, differences in efficiency and cost in different enterprises are not a mere random imperfection, but are of the essence of a progressive state. This in turn has its effect on the theory of the adjustment of price to cost.

The idea that competition reduces price to the level of cost may belong in the category of ideas adopted to simplify theoretical analysis and exposition. If the buying prices of the factors of production are provisionally assumed to be constant, reduced prices can stand as a shorthand symbol for the equating of prices and costs, though the actual process may involve either reduced or increased prices to those furnishing productive factors, chiefly workers. Price will normally be above the costs of low cost producers, and below the costs of high cost producers. The low cost producers are receiving the rewards of past increases in efficiency: rewards which are bound to be temporary, except as further improvements keep these producers ahead of the procession. In times of expanding demand, nearly all producers may be making profits, while in times of contracting demand, nearly all may be making losses.

All this contrasts with the concept of "perfect" competition, which focuses on an impossibly precise equating of prices and costs. For our purposes the question is: Do the conditions of the perfectly competitive model describe something we should like to reproduce in industry and trade if we could? I shall contend that they do not. They define a model from which competitive progress would be ruled out; progress could come only by governmental fiat. Either no producer is allowed to make improvements that reduce his costs below those of his rivals, or else the rivals imitate him instantly and eliminate his differential profit. In the terms we have been using, competitive neutralization is so perfect that there could not be anything to neutralize. It represents perfection in one half of the competitive process, at the sacrifice of the other, equally necessary, half. This appears to be, to say the least, a misleading concept of "perfection."

Perhaps the most unfortunate thing about this concept is its effect in making people needlessly despondent about actual competition, which is, actually, better than the one-sidedly "perfect" model, because it manages, somehow, to facilitate progress. The theory of perfect competition teaches, among other things, that effective price competition requires an impossibly large number of competitors. But actual competition does not require this. It was a mathematical necessity because the model, assuming costs equal, required that a producer should have an incentive to reduce prices until they reached *his own costs*. It needs no such enormous numbers to give a low cost producer an incentive to expand his output and reduce prices below other producers' costs, while they are still substantially above his own.[6]

Furthermore, in a world where demand fluctuates and where there usually is more capacity than can be fully utilized at prices covering full costs, short term marginal cost is substantially below average cost, so that producers may have chances to make competitive gains by cutting prices below their own average costs, though prices may remain well above their marginal costs. A producer may cut prices below his own average costs, even if his demand curve slopes downward. Probably, in a mature industry, low cost producers do not often indulge in this dangerous form of rivalry; and it is somewhat less dangerous to the general solvency of the trade if only high cost producers do it. But trades sometimes get demoralized. And if they secure protections, as under the fair-trade laws, they probably tend to over-reach themselves.

We want competition to eliminate the less efficient, but not to demoralize whole trades. Progress probably is best promoted if industry and trade are subjected to recurring "challenges," more formidable than the trades themselves would like, but less serious than if price wars became chronic. The lack of any automatic assurance of striking such a happy medium may be the main substance behind theorists' uneasiness at the non-existence of perfect competition. The chief saving fact is probably that the long run neutralizing factors—including "potential competition"—are stronger than appears on the surface. Whether they are strong enough remains a problem, to be examined case by case.

Quality of Products

In terms of quality, what the customer wants from competition is an adequate variety to choose from (once more I avoid speaking of an optimum number and range of qualities). He wants enough variety so that he can know what the economy is capable of producing. From that, he can set up a selective process. He can then exert effective pressure toward progressive improvement of quality and toward adapting quality to the price he is willing to pay. A departure in quality may in part be an attempt to bring in buyers who have not been sufficiently tempted by the previous offerings, and in part an attempt to divert existing buyers by

[6] It is significant that J. B. Clark's competitive concept, which assumed only moderate numbers necessary, assumed progress and differences in costs. See *Essentials of Economic Theory* (New York, 1907), pp. 262–64, 286–87.

offering them something they will like better, or to induce them to buy more.

We also want continued development of new products, and expect it to be promoted by free rivalry in the search for them. The United States is accustomed to an annual increase of 2 per cent or more in its real productive power per person, which represents, in peacetime, a corresponding increase in power to consume, roughly doubling in thirty-five years or less. This means either enlarged consumption or enlarged leisure or mass unemployment. Part of it is taken in shorter hours, but not at the rate of halving the working week every thirty-five years. The rest of the gain—the majority of it—depends on the development of new products, in order that it may be converted into increased consumption rather than too largely into unemployment. This increased consuming power may be regarded as a fund of potential consumers' dollars; and the designers of new products are engaged in rivalry to tap it.

At present, of course, this rivalry in the search for new products is being largely absorbed into the search for new and more deadly weapons of war. The competitive nature of this rivalry is too obvious to need proof, and this really includes the brief monopoly of the atomic bomb by the United States. If the world ever succeeds in escaping from this incubus of military preparedness, there will be an enormous release of consuming power, calling for new products in which to embody it.

Incentives to quality change may be impaired where the chief competing producers are all known to be ready to install a given improvement if required, with the result that an initiator may expect to see his move neutralized with extreme promptness. In such a case, the improvement may hang fire; but if it is sound, it is not likely to be permanently shelved.

Another type of improvement that may be delayed consists of improvements which at one step bring a large increase in the durability of products of not very elastic demand, so that total demand will be reduced as a result of the improvement; and unless the initiator can increase his proportionate share a great deal, before his move is neutralized, his own demand will be decreased by his improvement. Yet improvements of this sort do get made—witness the increased durability of automobile tires.

In connection with the selection of products, and especially of new ones, the customer wants to know what quality and service value he is getting; and to that end he wants a system of customer guidance, including salesmanship, advertising, and other agencies, which does not cost him an inordinate amount, and from which, if he is reasonably sensible, he may have a fair chance of getting such information as he has time and capacity to assimilate. He wants checks on the partisan character of competitive guidance; and a good economic system needs to include such checks or supplements. It is perhaps too much to ask commercial guidance to elevate standards of taste and morals; but peoples surely have an interest to ask that these standards shall not be exposed to degenerative influences for private gain. Public regulation can attend to a few of these evils; for the rest, competition needs to be disciplined by an effective moral sense, in which business is exposed to leadership and pressure from appropriate social groups, religious, educational, or other.

Escape from Concentrated Power, via Diffused Opportunity

To many who favor competition, the opportunity to be an entrepreneur is a desirable thing in itself, aside from its results in the shape of plenty, cheapness, and quality of products. As between two systems of equal efficiency in terms of end products turned out, they would prefer the one in which more people participate in the independence and the responsibilities of entrepreneurship. They are inclined to give the small entrepreneur the benefit of the doubt in cases that raise the question of whether he has been discriminated against, or whether his larger competitors have advantages that are unfair or do not represent actual productive efficiency. And some would go further; they simply do not like bigness of the sort that seems to overwhelm the individual who has to deal with it or to find his place in it somehow. One may note that Adam Smith clearly had the same feeling, though he did not have the painful task of adjusting it to the inevitable features of a mass production economy.

Some dislike massed private power, but do not seem to object to massed power in the hands of government, assuming that it will be exercised in the general interest, under a representative system. Others dislike concentrated power about equally, whether it is public or private. Actually, the first attitude seems to over-rate the contrast between the two types of power. Both are subject to various sorts of "checks and balances," very imperfect in both cases, working differently, but with differences that seem to be diminishing. To such persons, massed private power carries with it the necessity of massed governmental power to keep it in check, perhaps via direct controls of wages and prices in time of peace, or via a "regimented" economy. And competition, so far as it can be maintained, affords a partial escape from both horns of this dilemma.

Employment Opportunity

If opportunity for entrepreneurship is important, opportunity to get a job as an employee is not less so. And competition can play a part in a system that looks to assuring high and stable employment, though there are few who still maintain that it could perform the whole task itself. Harking back to the period between the first and second world wars, there can be little doubt that a more thoroughly competitive system would have made a better record than the American system did in terms of high and stable employment, and better than a system thoroughly controlled by non-competitive organizations, unions or cartels or both. But it would not have prevented ups and downs. And it would be an obstacle to the type of proposal for stabilization that hinges on planned regularization of private capital outlays.

On this there is one qualification. If competition extended to bringing about cyclically flexible wages and prices in the capital goods industries (preferably not in other industries), it would give private employers a financial incentive which might be utilized by a skillful planning organization to induce them to make their capital expansions in dull times, when they could do it cheapest. But mere cyclical flexibility of wages and prices would not bring about stabilization automatically. Producers would still hold off while prices went down, not wanting to commit themselves earlier than necessary, because among other things, they would want to minimize the risk that their equipment would begin to be out of date before it was used. Tax incentives have been proposed by Dr. Morris A. Copeland.

It seems that the real place of competition in this matter of employment is to furnish an economy sufficiently mobile and flexible to respond to the policies necessary to stabilize total demand. It would respond better if free from undue rigidities of particular prices and wages, from non-competitive features of the wage structure that tend to produce what Professor Slichter has called "wage-distortion unemployment," and from obstacles to movement and to entry into particular trades or professions. Then, if a reduction of demand of one sort is countered by increasing demand of a somewhat different sort, the economy would respond, and "pools of unemployment" would be minimized. We would like to have this kind of competitive flexibility—but it would be overly optimistic to consider that we are very likely to get it. At best, one can hope for slow progress; and in the meantime, stabilization policies will work under greater handicaps than should ideally be necessary.

Competition and Human Nature

Perhaps the deepest difficulties about a competitive system stem from the fact that human nature is a compound of different kinds of characteristics. Among these, competitive impulses are very deeply rooted; but along with them, and perhaps even more deeply rooted, are impulses of group solidarity—the need of "belonging," or some sort of underlying status and security (there are various sorts), or integration of self with something larger and more meaningful. For such an individual, a desirable and tolerable system must involve some kind of working balance between these types of impulse, not an inexorably logical embodiment of any one principle. To throw the individual into a world in which he must make his place in an unmitigated competitive struggle with all other individuals would be catastrophic. But to put him in a world that denies any place to these competitive impulses would stultify a vital part of his nature, and deprive him of stimuli which he may need to prod him into developing his capacities sufficiently for his own good.

The problem is to superimpose competitive incentives and fluidities on an underlying structure of group solidarity and security. For furnishing the individual a basis for security, the private family is basic, but it is too small and weak to do all that is needed in the economic realm. People seek other groups, intermediate between the family and the "great society," which is too large, impersonal, and overwhelming. Some of these intermediate groups do not interfere with competition, others do; and it is here that some of the greatest difficulties arise. These groups will retain power—especially labor unions with their exemption from the anti-trust laws. And in some cases it seems likely that some of the useful features of competitive adjustments will not be realized in practice unless they are identified, distinguished from harmful restrictions, and deliberately allowed to come to pass, by organizations which have power enough, if they choose, to restrain them and to bring about non-competitive results.

For example, high level employment would benefit from a differential structure of wage rates more like that which competition would bring about, and which the non-union shop used to exemplify. And the dilemma of unemployment or inflation would be eased by a general level of union wages more nearly in keeping with the general advance of productivity in the economy as a whole. Voluntary adoption of such policies is not a remedy likely to be quickly or easily brought about; neither is any remedy requiring substantial weakening of the powers of labor unions.

A structure meeting these multiple requirements, and also adapted to promote progress in technical methods and in competitive differentiation of products, presents plenty of problems. But they are different from the problems suggested by the current formal theory of competitive price.

CONCLUSIONS

The orientation and emphasis of this paper were influenced by a desire to counteract three tendencies: (1) a tendency to over-stress the differences between American and European views on competition and monopoly; (2) influence on policy stemming from theories too abstract to be dependable guides for the purpose; and (3) the pessimistic view of competition embodied in the title of Mrs. Robinson's paper,[7] this title having been available to the other participants in the writing of their papers, and constituting a challenge to any who believe that effective

[7] ["The Impossibility of Competition," *Monopoly and Competition and Their Regulation*, pp. 245–54.]

competition, while not universally feasible, and bristling with perplexing problems, is not so generally impossible as this title suggests, at least not under American conditions with a large and expanding economy, a tradition of anti-trust policy, and an energetic and resourceful body of entrepreneurs. I believe this challenge influenced the various American participants to combat the idea of "impossibility"; and if they succeeded too well, conveying an impression that they think all is rosy and "there is no problem," I hope that a re-reading of their actual statements, plus the informal discussions that ensued, may by now have dispelled much of that impression. Mrs. Robinson's contention that policy in this matter must be a choice of evils is one with which I think the American participants would fully agree, together with much of her able analysis of the actual problems.

Her most telling thesis concerns conditions in which marginal cost is less than average cost, resulting in a tendency to collusion as an escape from destructive degrees of competition. With regard to this, active anti-trust policy appears capable of dealing with most outright collusion. Differentiation of products, instead of compounding this difficulty, may, under favorable conditions, serve to mitigate it, as may some of the other hybrid conditions lumped under the head of "competition of the few," without necessarily leading to the evils associated with the term "monopoly," competitive forces being more manifold and pervasive than sometimes conceived, especially in formal theory, or even by anti-trust officials. Whether the remaining rivalry is sufficiently effective appears to be a problem to be attacked case by case, possibly with some help from a more comprehensive framework of theory, toward which a small contribution is attempted in this paper.

The papers and discussion have strengthened the present writer in his belief in the need for distinguishing two types of factors nowadays lumped under the head of "monopoly": namely, restrictive practices on the one hand, and on the other departures from "perfect competition," including temporary differential advantages which are open to competitive neutralization and which are inseparable from the processes of progress. These appear to have opposite effects on the ends which competition is generally desired to serve.

Market Power, Growth, and Price Stability

7. STATEMENT*

James S. Duesenberry

SYNOPSIS

1. There can be inducements to cut costs and improve products even in industries with only a few firms, but the inducements are not as strong or as steady as in competitive industries.

2. The inducements are weakened by collusion, by the fear of retaliation by rivals, and by a strong financial position that makes imitation instead of innovation profitable.

3. But the inducements can be strengthened by fringe competition which is the presence of small but sound and aggressive firms that reduce costs and improve products, thereby forcing the large firms to do the same.

4. Large firms have a research advantage. Being able to support more projects, they are more likely to find one that pays off. They can afford the large outlays needed to conduct research on an efficient scale. And their diversification enables them to use more of its results.

5. But smaller firms can also conduct research. Not all is expensive and risky, nor are all important forms done by large firms.

6. The effect of market power on price level movements depends on whether they are caused by rising aggregate demand that pulls up prices or rising costs that push them up.

7. An increase of aggregate demand will not in the short run cause as much of a price increase in a concentrated as in a competitive industry, because in the former, firms want price stability and do not want to offend customers or invite government attention or give unions a reason to ask for higher wages.

8. But in a competitive industry operating at capacity, price will rise as aggregate demand rises, and the same will occur in a concentrated industry with a competitive fringe.

9. Although in the upswing of the cycle, competitive prices rise more than those in concentrated industries, in the downswing they also fall more, and hence competition does not directly contribute to secular inflation.

10. But it may contribute indirectly in the upswing by raising the prices of consumer goods and of goods bought by concentrated industries.

* Before the Joint Economic Committee Hearings on Employment, Growth, and Price Levels, Part 7: *The Effect of Monopolistic and Quasi-monopolistic Practices upon Prices, Profits, Production, and Employment* (Washington, D.C.: U.S. Government Printing Office, 1959), pp. 2324–33.

The former price increase causes wage increases that are not revoked in the following downswing, and the latter causes a non-reversible increase of prices in concentrated industries.

11. A wage increase is more likely to push up prices in a concentrated than in a competitive industry. In the former, it is likely to affect all firms, and they usually believe the industry demand for their product is inelastic. In the latter, some firms may not have to raise wages, and the demand is elastic for the product of each.

12. No single market structure provides incentives to invest and is favorable to research and promotes price stability; but a concentrated industry with a competitive fringe may provide as much of all three as it is possible to get from any one structure.

The committee has asked us to discuss the effects of market power on economic growth and price stability. Each of these is in itself a very large subject so that in a short paper one can do no more than sketch some of the more important considerations.

In discussing the growth problem, I shall confine myself to some observations on the effects of market power on investment incentives and on the effects of market power on costs and returns in research and innovational activity.

In this connection I shall put the emphasis on the effect of size of firm on investment and research.

Market power is not the same thing as size, but it is generally true that large firms do have market power. There are many other ways of acquiring market power, but I cannot discuss them in a short paper.

In discussing price stability, I shall try to bring out differences in the reaction of industries with different competitive structures to changes in demand and to union-generated wage pressures.

Concentration and Investment Incentives

Competition is supposed to provide business concerns with especially strong incentives to invest in new equipment in order to reduce costs, improve old products, or introduce new ones.

Even without competition, managements are prepared to invest to reduce costs or to improve products in order to widen profit margins or expand their sales.

But a firm faced with competition has stronger investment incentives. If it reduces costs or improves product, it can not only expand the market for its products, but it can take business from its rivals. Moreover, even if a concern's management were content with its profit position, it would have an incentive to reduce costs and improve product to avoid losing its markets to its rivals, or being forced to accept low profit margins to maintain its sales.

In principle, even a very small number of rivals may provide one another with strong incentives for cost reduction, product improvement, and development of new products.

In practice, it is easy to observe many industries dominated by a small number of large firms who are engaged in intense rivalry in terms of cost cutting and product improvement.

However, the tendency for oligopolies to generate competitive cost cutting may be frustrated in a number of ways. Formal or informal market-sharing agreements obviously weaken the drive for cost cutting.

Cost reporting and standardization of cost accounting reduce the chances of concealing cost reductions and, therefore, the risk that a rival is stealing a march. Any firm which controls key patents or resources can protect itself against price cutting by rivals by withholding licenses or resources. Its fear of aggressive action is reduced, and the possible gains from aggressive action are reduced for the others.

Industries dominated by a small number of large firms may be as progressive as others, but that is not necessarily the case.

We noted above that the incentive for cost reduction in such industries depends in part on each firm's fear that its rivals will gain a cost advantage and force it to choose between low—or even negative—profit margins and a loss of market share.

In industries with very few firms the resources of each firm are generally large. One which wishes to pursue a conservative investment policy is in a position to refuse to take the risks involved in investing for relatively low pay-offs. If its rivals should gain a cost advantage, its resources are large enough to permit it to take losses or low margins for a time and still catch up.

It is possible that all the firms in the industry would take the same conservative attitude, with the result that the industry would make relatively slow progress in cost reduction. That possibility is reinforced by the fact that market-sharing agreements are more easily maintained when only a few firms are involved.

The possibility that all firms will be prepared to accept a conservative investment policy and an attitude of mutual non-aggression becomes smaller as the number of firms grows larger. Even when a few large firms produce a high proportion of the output in an industry, the presence of a number of aggressive small firms prevents the large firms from resting on their laurels.

Thus, the small and medium sized firms may make a much more important indirect contribution to progress than their size or direct contribution to development of new techniques would indicate.

The role played by Sylvania in speeding up the development of the fluorescent lamp and the role of several small companies in the introduction of small radios are only two of a number of examples of the contribution of small firms.

But even when they do not succeed in taking business from the large firms, the small firms provide incentives to the large ones by trying to increase their market shares.

It is important to note, however, that fringe competitors contribute to progress in that way only when they are strong competitors. They will not be effective unless their scale of operations is large enough for reasonable efficiency and unless their financial resources are adequate to permit them to take some risks.

Research and Innovation

Our economy's capacity to produce goods and services at any one moment depends on the amount of resources and the technical knowledge available and the efficiency with which those resources and techniques are utilized.

But the rate of increase in our capacity to produce depends on the rate at which we accumulate resources and on the rate of development and application of new techniques of production.

The rate at which new techniques are developed and applied depends on many factors, but it can be influenced to an important degree by the size distribution of business firms.

In this section, we shall consider the influence of firm size on the ability of firms to undertake research activities and to apply the results in practice.

It appears to be the case that large firms are in a distinctly better position to support systematic research activities than small firms. That is true for a number of reasons.

The strongest of these reasons is the effect of size on the pooling of risks. There are many calls on the financial resources of firms to justify the allocation of additional funds to research, and the management must suppose that the prospective returns from additional research will be greater than those available from other types of investment.

As the proportion of resources devoted to research increases, the return required to justify additional research expenditures will increase.

Even if there were no risks, small firms would not find it profitable to spend a much larger proportion of investable resources on research than large firms. If a large firm and a small firm both spend the same proportion of resources on research, the large firm can support more projects than the small firm.

Since results of research are very uncertain, the small firm with a small absolute research budget takes a greater risk about the outcome of research than a large firm with a large budget.

When a sufficient number of projects can be undertaken, some are bound to succeed and pay off enough to compensate for the failures; when only a few projects are under way, there is a chance that the firm will get nothing for its efforts.

Of course, some firms with small budgets will be successful and obtain a very high return on their investment since the success is not affected by failures in other projects, but most firms have an aversion to making long-shot investments. As a result, small firms are likely to hold down their research budgets because investment in research is too risky. In addition, most small firms are in a riskier position than large firms on other grounds. In general, they have lower profits and less access to outside funds. Moreover, they are more dependent on demand in particular localities or for a small number of products than large firms operating over a wider range of locations and products.

The general risk position of small firms makes them still less able to gamble on research. A second factor working against small firms is the existence of economies of scale in research itself. Laboratories require complex equipment which will not be fully utilized unless large numbers of research workers share its use.

In addition, there is an interaction between research workers in different fields or in different projects which cannot be exploited in a small laboratory. This is not to suggest, of course, that much useful work cannot be done in small laboratories, but there are some reasons for thinking that large laboratories have an advantage over small ones. These disadvantages can be overcome to a considerable extent by contracting out research to universities or to firms specializing in research work.

A third advantage for large firms arises from the diffuse nature of the benefits of research. The outcome of scientific research is, in the nature of the case, unpredictable. Investigations aimed at the improvement of a particular product or process may produce results with applications to quite different areas. A large firm with a diversified line of products can view that situation with equanimity. It has a good chance of finding an application for whatever turns up. A small one can use only a small part of the knowledge gained from research. This advantage is, of course, of much greater importance in basic research than in engineering work with a narrow focus.

The advantage of large firms in research activities is reflected in the results of the 1953–54 study of industrial research and development activities. The survey showed that the percentage of companies conducting research and development programs rose steadily with company size. Only 8 per cent of manufacturing firms with less than 100 employees had them, while 94 per cent of those with over 5,000 employees had research and development programs. Manufacturing companies with over 5,000 employees paid for 66 per cent of research and development work but employed only 40 per cent of the workers in manufacturing.

In contrast, firms with less than 500 employees accounted for only 14 per cent of the research and development cost, though they employed 35 per cent of all workers in manufacturing.

Government-financed research is even more highly concentrated among the large firms.

It is clear enough that large firms have a distinct advantage in carrying out industrial research and development, but that is not the whole story. Industry does relatively little basic research. To a large extent, industrial research exploits scientific principles developed elsewhere.

The existing stock of scientific knowledge at any one moment contains an enormous reservoir of potential industrial applications. Any single research organization works on a limited number of these possibilities, the ones chosen depending on the interests and vision of the firm's management and research directors.

Certain possibilities will be ruled out by a particular firm as impractical, outside the range of the firm's interests, as having insufficient potential markets.

In pursuing a given line of research and development, any one individual or any small group is likely to make very serious errors in judgment as to the practicality or market potential of a given research proposal.

Large research organizations may be more efficient than small ones; but from another point of view, a good deal may be lost by having a heavy concentration of research and development activity in the hands of a relatively small number of firms. Of course, it is possible for a large firm to decentralize its research and development activities and allow a great deal of independence to research directors, and even to encourage internal competition, but that is not always done.

The research activities of small and medium sized firms may make an important contribution to our total resources by insuring that the development possibilities overlooked or neglected by larger organizations are tried out and exploited.

Finally, it is important to note that much progress in industry takes place without formal research. Many useful developments in technology are worked out by production personnel with relatively little formal research expenditure.

Similarly, new applications of existing knowledge may sometimes be made without much formal research. In some cases, foreign patents may be applied in this country with relatively little further work.

Finally, minor modifications in products may make them cheaper and open out new market possibilities.

In all these cases the very large firms have relatively little advantage over small or medium sized firms, provided that resources are adequate for the necessary investment.

Market Power and Price Stability

In analyzing the effects of market power on prices, it is necessary to draw a distinction between price movements induced by changes in aggregate demand—relative to industrial capacity and labor supply—and those induced by increase in wage costs resulting from trade-union action and other forces affecting costs.

Such a distinction is somewhat artificial. The extent of the influence of trade-unions on wages is influenced by the level of unemployment and capacity utilization in the economy.

We cannot ordinarily say whether any particular price increase is due to cost push or demand pull. In most cases, we have to suppose that actual price increases are due to the interaction of both factors. Nonetheless, the two factors are distinct from one another, and different sectors of the economy react differently to the movements of demand and the pressures on wages exerted by trade-unions.

Let us first compare the effect of changes in demand on price movements in industries with many small firms with the effect of demand changes on prices in highly concentrated industries.

It seems fairly safe to say that prices of goods produced in industries in which many small firms compete in the same market, for example, textiles and apparel, are more volatile than the prices of goods in more highly concentrated industries.

At any one moment the producers in a competitive industry are producing as much as is profitable, in view of their costs at the existing price. If demand remains unchanged, any producer can sell more by increasing output and shading his price a relatively small amount.

When an increase in demand occurs, price will be marked up because no additional output is available at the existing price. Price will have to rise until demand and supply are once again in balance—either through contraction of sales as a result of the price increase, or because the higher price induces firms to increase output by working overtime, or using obsolete plant.

When demand declines, prices will move downward; but initially, most firms will find that they are selling less than they are willing to supply. Further shading of prices has to continue until supply and demand are once more balanced by increases in sales or reduction in output.

When there are many small firms, there is no reason for anyone to refrain from price cutting as long as there is excess supply, since competitors may do so anyway. The firm cutting the price would take a little business from each of a number of firms without influencing the action of any of them.

In such industries, prices will move upward and downward with short run changes in demand. The range of movement will be sufficient to keep supply and demand in balance.

Over longer periods, of course, supply can be increased or decreased by the construction of additional plant, or the abandonment of old plants. The adjustment of capacity places a limit on the extent to which price can deviate from average cost in efficiently operated new plants, except for short periods.

Prices of the products of highly concentrated industries are much less responsive to short run movements in demand than prices in highly competitive industries.

When demand declines, managements tend to avoid open price cutting, because each firm expects that others would retaliate if it cut prices.

On the other side, when demand increases, large firms often refrain from raising prices, even though they could sell more than they can produce at the existing price.

It is easy to see why large firms tend not to cut prices when sales are low. Unless sales are very responsive to price, it will be unprofitable for any firm to seek more volume by cutting prices when its rivals are fairly sure to retaliate.

In order to insure price stability when sales are declining, it is necessary to refrain from raising them when sales are rising.

In addition, large firms are usually sensitive about their share of the market and are, therefore, unwilling to risk the loss of customer good will by frequent price changes.

At least some large firms are sensitive to customer relations and political considerations.

Finally, if prices are raised during periods of high demand, unions may attempt to capture some of the increased profits in the form of a wage increase which cannot be reversed if prices should fall.

When there are only a few large firms in an industry, the relation between prices and direct operating costs tends to be very unresponsive to changes in the relation between demand and capacity.

However, when an industry is fairly heavily concentrated, but contains a certain number of small firms which together account for an appreciable proportion of output, the picture may be somewhat different.

When demand declines, the smaller firms may lead the way in cutting prices—either openly or, more commonly, through various types of unannounced discounts and other concessions to buyers. They tend to do so partly because each small firm can gain a substantial percentage increase in volume by taking a small percentage of sales from the larger ones if they can cut prices for a time without retaliation.

The small firms may lead prices down, eventually forcing the large ones to follow them. To the extent that prices decline when demand declines in the industry, they will also tend to rise when demand increases.

In general, then, it can be said that as the proportion of an industry's output produced by small firms increases, the tendency for prices to vary with demand will also increase. That proposition is, of course, only a broad and loose generalization.

Price movements are influenced by many other aspects of industrial structure besides the size distribution of the firms in the industry.

If demand moves upward and downward, relative to capacity, prices—in relation to direct costs—will tend to move upward and downward as well. The variation in both directions will tend to be larger in industries in which a large share of output is produced by small firms than in those which most of the output is produced by a few large ones.

If demand fluctuates, the prices in industries with a low degree of concentration will fluctuate more widely than those in highly concentrated industries; but over the cycle, difference in the amplitude of price fluctuations need not affect the average level of prices.

It cannot, therefore, be said that the small business sector intensifies the secular upward trend of prices in any way.

However, the fluctuations in prices may have an indirect influence on the long term trend of prices. Price increases during boom periods raise the cost of living. Increases in living costs intensify demands for higher wages.

An increase in wages granted during a boom is not likely to be reversed even when demand declines. Wage increases tend to be built into the cost level and to prevent prices from falling as far during slack periods as they rise during booms. Hence, price fluctuations may not cancel out over the cycle.

The temporary price increase in each boom has a permanent effect on the wages and costs that contribute to the upward drift of prices.

The competitive structure of an industry also influences the industry's response to trade-union wage pressures. There is some reason to believe that managements in highly concentrated industries can grant wage increases with less fear of loss than those in less concentrated industries.

Profit margins in highly concentrated industries seem to be limited by the possibility that customers will supply themselves, that firms in related industries will enter the field, or that small firms will expand by giving price concessions.

In those circumstances, an increase in wage costs can be reflected in prices since it affects potential competitors in the same way as it affects existing firms.

Moreover, trade-unions in these industries try to obtain similar concessions from all firms whether there is industry-wide bargaining or not.

Finally, there seems to be a general belief that sales are not very sensitive to industry-wide price changes. Under these conditions, managements may feel that they can grant wage increases and raise prices without losing business.

In less concentrated industries the situation is different. If wage increases are granted, they cannot be reflected in prices by the decisions of a few managements. Wage increases will lead to price increases only because the increase in costs induces some firms to contract output so that demand exceeds supply at the old price.

The amount of price increase which results depends on the sensitivity of output to prices and the sensitivity of sales to prices in the industry as a whole.

Individual managements cannot judge those factors very well.

As a consequence, it is more risky for managements in highly com-

petitive industries to grant wage increases than for those in highly concentrated ones. That risk is increased by the fact that there may be more
unorganized firms in an industry containing many small firms than in an
industry with a few large ones.

Those considerations suggest that the cost-push element making for
inflation may be somewhat less powerful in highly competitive industries
than in highly concentrated ones.

However, there appear to be a number of industries in which trade-
union pressures on wages are very effective in spite of the large number
of small firms in the industry.

Construction is the most impressive example.

Thus, small firms may provide some resistance to cost-push inflation, but they do not always do so.

Moreover, comparisons between wage and price movements in
competitive and highly concentrated industries have to be made with
care, because other factors besides the degree of concentration are important.

To sum up, then, prices fluctuate most in some manufacturing fields
in which small business predominates, and these price fluctuations may
contribute indirectly to the long term upward drift of prices.

On the other hand, these same highly competitive sectors may
resist the cost-push component of inflation somewhat more strongly than
industries dominated by a few large firms.

Neither of these considerations relates to a dominant force causing
inflation, and it is important to take account of numerous other factors
when judging comparisons of wage and price movements in industries
with different competitive structures.

Competition plays an important role in connection with incentives
for investment and innovation. We have argued that there are strong incentives for cost-reducing investment and innovation even in very highly
concentrated industries. But the continued operation of these incentives
would not be guaranteed if the whole manufacturing sector consisted of a
few hundred very large firms.

If the management of every large firm could feel that its resources
permitted it to be a follower rather than a leader, the incentive to innovate would be greatly reduced.

It is not necessary to have very large numbers of firms competing in
order to provide adequate incentives for investment and innovation, but
the adequacy of investment incentives is not guaranteed in industries
dominated by a very small number of firms.

We have argued that large firms have a distinct advantage in conducting industrial research, but that small firms can make significant con-
tributions to technical development. In this connection, new firms play a
particularly important role.

When we attempt to take all those considerations into account at once, it is apparent that an optimal industrial structure is not one in which all firms, even in a single industry, are cast in the same mold. Too many diverse considerations have to be reconciled for that.

There is a place in an efficient, progressive economy for the very large industrial firm capable of supporting large scale research activities and able to venture millions of dollars on the success of a new product or process.

But we would be unwise to entrust our fortunes wholly to three or four such large firms in each industrial sector.

For all their large resources, and even when they have adequate incentives, large firms may and actually have neglected to develop important processes and products which smaller firms have exploited.

Moreover, while there is no doubt that large firms have adequate resources for research and for the investment required to put their results into practice, their incentive to take the necessary risks is not so securely based.

It is true that rivalry among a few large firms provides more incentive for a progressive investment policy than is sometimes thought to be the case, but the rivalry among very large firms might very well atrophy —or be reduced in intensity by various types of market sharing—without the constant threat of aggressive behavior on the part of small and medium sized rivals hungry for a larger market share.

I might add that my colleague, Professor Galbraith, has made some comparison of wage and price movements between industries, and given particular attention to a comparison of wages and prices in textiles and apparel as against steel. It strikes me that the particular comparisons which he makes are a good example of the many other factors that I have mentioned, because it is clear that the textile and apparel industry are relatively slow-growing demand industries in which there are special conditions in labor supply, owing to one migrating to the south and the other having the benefit of a lot of migration. Textiles have tended to have excess capacity because of the regional shifts toward the south. Steel, on the other hand, is an industry with increasing capital costs in addition to having a market structure and union situation different from those of textiles and apparel.

One cannot get reliable results by comparing industries for particular practices and not taking into account their other features. In many cases it will happen that particular comparisons will produce mistaken results.

I wish to emphasize two points: There is some reason to think that industries with more price competition and more price flexibility contribute—in an indirect way and in some periods—to inflation when the demand for their products is increasing very fast. Their price increases raise the cost of living generally and the cost of production in other industries.

On the other hand, the more highly concentrated industries contribute to inflation through a different route, that is, not so much through raising their profit margins but through being in a position where it is fairly easy for them to give wage increases and pass them on into prices. So one cannot draw any simple conclusion to the effect that strong market power in itself gives us a great deal more inflation than we would have with a different structure.

In closing, I would like to make this point about long run price policies: Industries in which there is a strong competitive element from what I have called fringe competitors may be industries that give us the best of both worlds. It is very important that conditions be as favorable as possible for the relatively small firms in industries that otherwise are heavily concentrated.

8. THE PROCESS OF CREATIVE DESTRUCTION*

Joseph A. Schumpeter

SYNOPSIS

1. Competition and economic growth are the result of continual improvements in product quality and of cost reductions—or of the process of creative destruction, which replaces old forms of consumption and production with new.

2. The process is a part of the evolutionary development of capitalism, and the development is affected by external changes, like war and revolution; semi-automatic changes, like population growth and capital accumulation; and most importantly, by an inherent tendency toward new products, new production methods, and new forms of business organization.

3. Large, imperfectly competitive firms are more often responsible for creative destruction than small, competitive firms.

4. Effective, as distinct from formal, competition consists in firms seeking a decisive quality or cost advantage.

5. Creative destruction will be overlooked if one views capitalism as a static system and appraises it by the efficiency of resource use at any time. Short period inefficiency may be necessary for long term growth.

The theories of monopolistic and oligopolistic competition and their popular variants may in two ways be made to serve the view that capitalist reality is unfavorable to maximum performance in production. One may hold that it always has been so and that all along output has been expanding in spite of the secular sabotage perpetrated by the managing bourgeoisie. Advocates of this proposition would have to produce evidence to the effect that the observed rate of increase can be accounted for by a sequence of favorable circumstances unconnected with the mechanism of private enterprise and strong enough to overcome the latter's resistance. However, those who espouse this variant at least avoid the trouble about historical fact that the advocates of the alternative proposition have to face. This avers that capitalist reality once tended to favor maximum productive performance, or at all events productive per-

* Reprinted by permission and shortened from *Capitalism, Socialism, and Democracy* (3d ed.; New York: Harper, 1950), pp. 81–87.

formance so considerable as to constitute a major element in any serious appraisal of the system; but that the later spread of monopolist structures, killing competition, has by now reversed that tendency.

First, this involves the creation of an entirely imaginary golden age of perfect competition that at some time somehow metamorphosed itself into the monopolistic age, whereas it is quite clear that perfect competition has at no time been more of a reality than it is at present. Secondly, it is necessary to point out that the rate of increase in output did not decrease from the nineties from which, I suppose, the prevalence of the largest size concerns, at least in manufacturing industry, would have to be dated; that there is nothing in the behavior of the time series of total output to suggest a "break in trend"; and, most important of all, that the modern standard of life of the masses evolved during the period of relatively unfettered "big business." If we list the items that enter the modern workman's budget and from 1899 on observe the course of their prices not in terms of money but in terms of the hours of labor that will buy them—i.e., each year's money prices divided by each year's hourly wage rates—we cannot fail to be struck by the rate of the advance which, considering the spectacular improvement in qualities, seems to have been greater and not smaller than it ever was before. If we economists were given less to wishful thinking and more to the observation of facts, doubts would immediately arise as to the realistic virtues of a theory that would have led us to expect a very different result. Nor is this all. As soon as we go into details and inquire into the individual items in which progress was most conspicuous, the trail leads not to the doors of those firms that work under conditions of comparatively free competition but precisely to the doors of the large concerns—which, as in the case of agricultural machinery, also account for much of the progress in the competitive sector[1]—and a shocking suspicion dawns upon us that big business may have had more to do with creating that standard of life than with keeping it down.

The essential point to grasp is that in dealing with capitalism, we are dealing with an evolutionary process. It may seem strange that anyone can fail to see so obvious a fact. Let us restate the point and see how it bears upon our problem. Capitalism, then, is by nature a form or method of economic change and not only never is but never can be stationary. And this evolutionary character of the capitalist process is not merely due to the fact that economic life goes on in a social and natural environment which changes and by its change alters the data of economic action; this fact is important, and these changes (wars, revolutions and so on) often condition industrial change, but they are not its prime movers. Nor is this evolutionary character due to a quasi-automatic increase in

---

[1] [That is, imperfectly competitive big business (of which agricultural machinery is an example) may so improve the quality of its products as to promote progress in competitive industries (like agriculture).]

population and capital or to the vagaries of monetary systems of which exactly the same thing holds true. The fundamental impulse that sets and keeps the capitalist engine in motion comes from the new consumers' goods, the new methods of production or transportation, the new markets, the new forms of industrial organization that capitalist enterprise creates.

The Process of Creative Destruction

As we have seen in the preceding chapter, the contents of the laborer's budget, say from 1760 to 1940, did not simply grow on unchanging lines, but they underwent a process of qualitative change. Similarly, the history of the productive apparatus of a typical farm, from the beginnings of the rationalization of crop rotation, plowing, and fattening to the mechanized thing of today—linking up with elevators and railroads —is a history of revolutions. So is the history of the productive apparatus of the iron and steel industry from the charcoal furnace to our own type of furnace, or the history of the apparatus of power production from the overshot water wheel to the modern power plant, or the history of transportation from the mailcoach to the airplane. The opening-up of new markets, foreign or domestic, and the organizational development from the craft shop and factory to such concerns as U.S. Steel illustrate the same process of industrial mutation—if I may use that biological term—that incessantly revolutionizes[2] the economic structure *from within*, incessantly destroying the old one, incessantly creating a new one. This process of Creative Destruction is the essential fact about capitalism. It is what capitalism consists in and what every capitalist concern has got to live in. This fact bears upon our problem in two ways.

First, since we are dealing with a process whose every element takes considerable time in revealing its true features and ultimate effects, there is no point in appraising the performance of that process *ex visu* of a given point of time; we must judge its performance over time, as it unfolds through decades or centuries. A system—any system, economic or other—that at *every* given point of time fully utilizes its possibilities to the best advantage may yet in the long run be inferior to a system that does so at *no* given point of time, because the latter's failure to do so may be a condition for the level or speed of long run performance.

Second, since we are dealing with an organic process, analysis of what happens in any particular part of it—say, in an individual concern or industry—may indeed clarify details of mechanism but is inconclusive beyond that. Every piece of business strategy acquires its true significance only against the background of that process and within the situ-

---

[2] Those revolutions are not strictly incessant; they occur in discrete rushes which are separated from each other by spans of comparative quiet. The process as a whole works incessantly, however, in the sense that there always is either revolution or absorption of the results of revolution, both together forming what are known as business cycles.

ation created by it. It must be seen in its role in the perennial gale of creative destruction; it cannot be understood irrespective of it or, in fact, on the hypothesis that there is a perennial lull.

But economists who, *ex visu* of a point of time, look for example at the behavior of an oligopolist industry—an industry which consists of a few big firms—and observe the well-known moves and countermoves within it that seem to aim at nothing but high prices and restrictions of output are making precisely that hypothesis. They accept the data of the momentary situation as if there were no past or future to it and think that they have understood what there is to understand if they interpret the behavior of those firms by means of the principle of maximizing profits with reference to those data. The usual theorist's paper and the usual government commission's report practically never try to see that behavior, on the one hand, as a result of a piece of past history and, on the other hand, as an attempt to deal with a situation that is sure to change presently—as an attempt by those firms to keep on their feet, on ground that is slipping away from under them. In other words, the problem that is usually being visualized is how capitalism administers existing structures, whereas the relevant problem is how it creates and destroys them. As long as this is not recognized, the investigator does a meaningless job. As soon as it is recognized, his outlook on capitalist practice and its social results changes considerably.[3]

The Meaning of Competition

The first thing to go is the traditional conception of the *modus operandi* of competition. Economists are at long last emerging from the stage in which price competition was all they saw. As soon as quality competition and sales effort are admitted into the sacred precincts of theory, the price variable is ousted from its dominant position. However, it is still competition within a rigid pattern of invariant conditions, methods of production, and forms of industrial organization in particular, that practically monopolizes attention. But in capitalist reality as distinguished from its textbook picture, it is not that kind of competition which counts but the competition from the new commodity, the new technology, the new source of supply, the new type of organization (the largest scale unit of control, for instance)—competition which commands a decisive cost or quality advantage and which strikes not at the margins of the profits and the outputs of the existing firms but at their foundations and their very lives. This kind of competition is as much more effective than the other as a bombardment is in comparison with forcing a door, and so much more important that it becomes a matter of

---

[3] It should be understood that it is only our appraisal of economic performance and not our moral judgment that can be so changed. Owing to its autonomy, moral approval or disapproval is entirely independent of our appraisal of social (or any other) results, unless we happen to adopt a moral system such as utilitarianism which makes moral approval and disapproval turn on them *ex definitione*.

comparative indifference whether competition in the ordinary sense functions more or less promptly; the powerful lever that in the long run expands output and brings down prices is in any case made of other stuff.

It is hardly necessary to point out that competition of the kind we now have in mind acts not only when in being but also when it is merely an ever-present threat. It disciplines before it attacks. The businessman feels himself to be in a competitive situation even if he is alone in his field or if, though not alone, he holds a position such that investigating government experts fail to see any effective competition between him and any other firms in the same or a neighboring field and in consequence conclude that his talk, under examination, about his competitive sorrows is all make-believe. In many cases, though not in all, this will in the long run enforce behavior very similar to the perfectly competitive pattern.

Impermanence of Collusion

Many theorists take the opposite view which is best conveyed by an example. Let us assume that there is a certain number of retailers in a neighborhood who try to improve their relative position by service and "atmosphere" but avoid price competition and stick as to methods to the local tradition—a picture of stagnating routine. As others drift into the trade, that quasi equilibrium is indeed upset, but in a manner that does not benefit their customers. The economic space around each of the shops having been narrowed, their owners will no longer be able to make a living, and they will try to mend the case by raising prices in tacit agreement. This will further reduce their sales, and so, by successive pyramiding, a situation will evolve in which increasing potential supply will be attended by increasing instead of decreasing prices and by decreasing instead of increasing sales.

Such cases do occur, and it is right and proper to work them out. But as the practical instances usually given show, they are fringe-end cases to be found mainly in the sectors furthest removed from all that is most characteristic of capitalist activity. Moreover, they are transient by nature. In the case of retail trade the competition that matters arises not from additional shops of the same type, but from the department store, the chain store, the mail-order house, and the super-market, which are bound to destroy those pyramids sooner or later.[4] Now, a theoretical construction which neglects this essential element of the case neglects all that is most typically capitalist about it; even if correct in logic as well as in fact, it is like *Hamlet* without the Danish prince.

---

[4] The mere threat of their attack cannot, in the particular conditions, environmental and personal, of small scale retail trade, have its usual disciplining influence, for the small man is too much hampered by his cost structure and, however well he may manage within his inescapable limitations, he can never adapt himself to the methods of competitors who can afford to sell at the price which he buys.

9. PUBLIC POLICY AND MARKET POWER*

Harold M. Levinson and Otto Eckstein

SYNOPSIS

1. Market power contributes to inflation, retards growth, and restricts consumer choice. It should be dealt with directly, and a policy that does will indirectly assist policies for stability and growth.

2. Efficiency and competition are not as inconsistent as supposed. Firms need not be large in all industries to be efficient; and where they must be, a competitive environment still is possible.

3. The government can deal with market power by enforcing competition, or by persuading firms and unions to use their power in the public interest, or by intervening in the fixing of prices and wages.

4. The basic method should be the enforcing of competition by enlarging the Antitrust Division, empowering it to subpoena records and to require pre-notification of mergers, by reviewing the work of agencies that regulate exempt industries, and by developing ways to prevent parallel action.

5. Continuing reciprocal tariff reductions are a necessary part of such a policy.

6. The market power of unions should be controlled by means other than the anti-trust laws which, however, in themselves can indirectly reduce union power.

7. It is not desirable or effective to persuade those with market power to use it for the benefit of others. Nevertheless, bringing them together in an annual conference to examine the state of the economy could lead to more informed price and wage decisions in key industries.

8. When serious inflation threatens, the government may intervene by the President's appointing a group to study the facts about key price and wage changes and to make recommendations.

The analysis in chapter V has indicated that at least some of the inflationary pressure of the past several years can be attributed to the exercise of market power by large industrial and labor groups. In addition, market power may well have contributed in some degree to the

* Reprinted from *Staff Report on Employment, Growth, and Price Levels,* Joint Economic Committee, U.S. Congress (Washington, D.C.: U.S. Government Printing Office, 1960), pp. 431–40. Mr. Levinson had main responsibility for this chapter of the report, while Mr. Eckstein, technical director of the staff, was responsible for the report in its entirety.

downward rigidity of both prices and wages during post-war recessions.

If this is so, an adequate public policy for inflation must try to reduce the impact of such power. This is necessary because monetary and fiscal devices, the major alternatives, approach the problem primarily from the *demand* side of the market, whether in an aggregative or in a selective way. What evidence we have, however, indicates that these alternatives probably would be effective only at a quite high cost of unemployment of labor and capital. Public policy, therefore, must also deal *directly* with the problem of market power.

Market power is not only undesirable because of its impact on inflation; it can also have important adverse effects on the rate of economic growth. Competitive markets permit consumers through their choices to determine the composition of output of consumer goods. Furthermore, competitive industry provides the environment in which new ideas are most likely to flourish and in which the firms with the greatest skill in responding to the wishes of consumers, in improving products and in reducing costs, will prosper and grow.

In order to have a more competitive environment in industry, it is not necessary that all business be small. In many fields, technology requires that the size of plants be large, and economies of mass production can be reaped through large scale production. Large firms also are capable of supporting sizable research efforts, and of making the long run commitments of capital that are sometimes necessary in the development of new products and new techniques.

However, the objectives of large scale production and competitive markets are not, as has often been supposed, inconsistent. Most of the giant corporations in industry enjoy no greater economies of production and provide no greater improvements through research than do firms one quarter or one eighth their size. But the presence of these giant firms does encourage the development of monopolistic pricing and other restrictive practices. By the same token, the merger of already large firms into even greater ones typically provides little or no gains to society, but does provide more favorable conditions for limiting competition.

THREE ALTERNATIVE APPROACHES

Essentially, there are three alternative lines of approach to this problem. First, we can attempt to reduce or eliminate, directly or indirectly, the source of the market power itself by policies designed to increase competition. Second, we can accept the situation as it is, but attempt to induce those industries and unions which have considerable power to exercise it in a socially desirable—in this case, in a noninflationary—way. Or, third, we can have government participate in or control the price- and wage-setting process. The proposals of this latter group cover a wide range, the most important being discussed briefly below. It should also be noted before proceeding that these alternatives are not necessarily mutually exclusive. It is quite possible to consider them as shorter versus longer run approaches, or as being applied variously to different types of industries and at different times. Their basic features, however, are quite easily delineated.

POLICIES TO REDUCE MARKET POWER AND INCREASE COMPETITION

Anti-trust Action

The most fundamental policy approach to excessive market power has been the anti-trust laws. This approach has the immense advantage of not only reducing this source of inflationary pressure, but also increasing the effectiveness of the economy for growth, for reducing undesirable concentrations of power in private hands, and accomplishing all this without increasing the amount of government intervention in the private economy.

The basic legislation of anti-trust is the Sherman Act of 1890, and the Clayton and Federal Trade Commission acts of 1914. In essence, the Sherman Act prohibits (1) every contract, combination, or conspiracy in restraint of trade, and (2) every attempt to monopolize any part of trade or commerce. In the 1914 legislation, Congress attempted to deal with the problem by proscribing certain activities which might *develop* into monopoly, particularly by prohibiting certain types of mergers if their effects were substantially to lessen competition.

Undoubtedly, both the Sherman and the Clayton acts have had a profound and beneficial effect on the character of the American economy, insofar as they have prevented open cartelization and have limited the extent to which producers have utilized their potential market power. Nevertheless, the enforcement of the anti-trust laws on the whole has been disappointing. The courts have often interpreted the Sherman and Clayton acts in ways which make it virtually impossible to show that market power is being exercised in violation of the laws. The delays of legal processes have been long; and the remedies that the courts have imposed have often been either ineffective, or made long obsolete by changing conditions in the industries. Finally, the resources of the Anti-trust Division of the Department of Justice, and of the other responsible agencies in this field, have been hopelessly inadequate to cope with the very important tasks they are attempting to perform.

Within the past few years, however, there has been some indication that the courts are becoming more aware of the wider economic implications of size as a factor in market power and have also broadened the frame of reference by which to judge the potentially adverse effects of mergers upon competition in an industry or area. Thus, in the Bethlehem-Youngstown merger case of 1958, the courts ruled against the planned merger on the grounds that it threatened substantially to reduce the degree of competition in the sale of certain steel products. Since this decision, the Antitrust Division has placed considerable emphasis on early action to prevent the completion of mergers before the assets of the companies involved have become so intermingled as to make subsequent dissolution much more difficult to achieve.

Recommendations for Strengthening Anti-trust. In general, *we recommend that the basic approach toward the problem of market power should be through a considerably expanded anti-trust program.* Some of the most important specific recommendations in this area are:

1. The budget of the Antitrust Division should be very considerably expanded from its present meager level, even after recent increases, of less than $4.5 million. The Antitrust Division should be able to enlarge its professional staff considerably, and to establish a salary level which will prevent the present continual drain of experienced man power into private industry.

2. Notification of proposed merger action to the Antitrust Division should be provided within some reasonable time prior to the date when the merger is to be effectuated. In this way, prior judgment can be made and effective action taken if it is believed that the proposed merger will substantially lessen competition.

3. Serious re-evaluation should be given by the Congress to the existing policies of regulatory agencies in industries which are specifically granted major exemption from the anti-trust laws. The activities and decisions of the Federal Power Commission, the Federal Communications Commission, the Civil Aeronautics Board, and the Interstate Commerce Commission should be reviewed for their effect on competition. A similar evaluation of the Federal Reserve Board's policies toward bank mergers would be desirable.

4. The Antitrust Division should be given greater power to subpoena records in civil cases. The existing limitations on this power circumscribe severely the ability of the division to carry out its investigations effectively.

5. A more effective method should be developed for dealing with industries "in which a high degree of monopoly power over price and competitive opportunity is possessed and exercised through coordinated and interdependent economic actions by the companies involved, *without overt agreement,* but each acting with full awareness of what the others are doing or will do in response to the actions of any one of the group. Such coordinated parallel action may take the form of price leadership, common adherence to a delivered price system, common distribution practices, common buying practices, and the like."[1] [Italics provided.]

The problems of establishing appropriate criteria in this area are most difficult. Nevertheless, it is here that much market power is concentrated. It may be desirable for Congress to make clear its intent that a record of consistent parallel policy, even without evidence of collusion, combined with some degree of concentration of *group* market

---

[1] Quoted from a statement by E. V. Rostow, in *Report of the Attorney General's Committee to Study the Antitrust Laws,* March 31, 1955, p. 40.

share, is a presumptive violation of the Sherman Act. It is probably in this area, more than any other, that the courts have failed to deal effectively with industrial developments of the past few decades.

Reduction of Tariffs

A tariff is essentially a protective device to minimize competition—in this case, competition from foreign-made goods. An increase in such competition from abroad can be and often has been a stimulus to American producers to modernize their technology, increase their efficiency and productivity, and hold their costs and prices down; in recent years, it has probably been the most effective constraint on the exercise of market power in several key industries. A continuation or increase in tariff levels, on the other hand, would invite the charging of higher prices and the negotiation of higher wages. *It is therefore recommended that, as part of our over-all policy measures to limit and if possible reduce the role of market power in our economy, we should continue to reduce tariffs.*

The Anti-trust Laws and Labor Unions

Should the provisions of the anti-trust laws be applied to labor union activities as well? This has been very widely proposed in recent years. Yet the fundamental characteristics of the labor market are such that we do not feel that this approach would be desirable. This is not to say that the exercise of market power by strong unions has not been a factor in the inflation; it very probably has been. But an appropriate solution is not to be found in the anti-trust laws.

Perhaps the most basic difficulty lies in the fact that, strictly speaking, the application of the anti-trust laws to the labor market would strike at the very existence of unionism and collective bargaining. The very reason for unions is to limit competition, and the philosophy underlying our entire public policy toward collective bargaining has been that unions per se are desirable, because the unrestrained forces of a "free" competitive labor market place the individual worker at a grave disadvantage before the employer. We must presume, therefore, that the phrase "application of the anti-trust laws to labor unions" is not to be construed literally to mean that *any* restraint on competition will be unlawful, since this is tantamount to stating that unions per se will be unlawful.

But if this is not what is meant, then it is necessary to specify in some detail those particular aspects of union policy which *will* be considered violations of the anti-trust laws. To begin with, it should be noted that in at least a few areas, the present anti-trust laws already apply. Where a union attempts to affect the price at which a product is sold *on the product market by direct collusion with the producer*, there is no doubt that such collusion is unlawful and proscribed by our present anti-trust policy. Furthermore, there has been some tendency in recent years to expand the scope of applicability of anti-trust to other areas. In general, however, the activities of unions which are subject to anti-trust restrictions are quite limited at the present time. In addition, several other union activities have been prohibited or severely restricted by the Taft-Hartley and Landrum-Griffin acts. Among the most important of these have been the restrictions placed on the closed shop, secondary boycotts, jurisdictional disputes, and several others. The activities of labor unions today, therefore, are not as free of government restraints as is sometimes suggested.

The fact remains, however, that these existing restrictions do not deal in a direct way with the great majority of situations where union market power may be excessive. Consequently, two additional recommendations have been widely suggested, viz., to make industry-wide bargaining unlawful, and to make national union participation in bargaining unlawful. Both, it will be noted, are directly related to *wage setting*, as contrasted to other areas of concern to unions such as seniority provisions, grievance procedure, etc.

Industry-wide bargaining is that in which negotiations are carried on at one time for all or most of the firms and employees within an industry. Actually, there are very few industries in the United States where this type of bargaining occurs—railroads, steel, and coal are the major ones. In most industries, bargaining is between one company and representatives of the local and the national union in that company. There is no evidence to suggest that this latter type of bargaining results in any lower settlements than where industry-wide bargaining occurs; in fact, most industry-wide bargaining has developed as a device to strengthen the bargaining position of the *employer* rather than the union. The elimination of industry-wide bargaining, therefore, would have little or no effect on the problem at hand.

The alternative approach—to greatly restrict or eliminate the role of the national union in bargaining—is much more far-reaching. This approach is based on the premise that it is the power of the national union which creates the upward pressure on wages, so that local union bargaining would result in less inflationary pressure.

This is again a doubtful premise; it may well be that in many instances, precisely the opposite is the case. Some of the strongest unions in the United States, where wages have risen at least as rapidly as elsewhere, place primary responsibility for bargaining on the local union, with the international union having virtually no role—the building trades unions are a clear case in point. Of greater importance, however, is the fact that there is much evidence to suggest that local bargaining units may well be more aggressive in fighting for wage increases than are national union representatives. In general, national officers are insulated from the internal political pressures of the membership and are more able to understand the broader economic problems of the industry. Local union bargaining, therefore, could create an atmosphere of inter-local rivalry which would accentuate rather than reduce the pressure for wage increases.[2]

We believe, therefore, that the anti-trust approach to the problem of power in the labor market is neither feasible nor desirable, and would create many more problems than it would solve. It may well be, nevertheless, that stricter anti-trust enforcement in the *product* market, as well as a gradual lowering of tariff barriers, would have favorable *indirect* effects on wage pressures. The analysis of the wage-setting process in chapter V indicated that wage adjustments in "key" industries were greatly affected by the level of profits and by the severity of competition in the industry. Thus, both profits and degree of competition are important variables in the wage-setting process. If stronger competitive conditions and lowered profit margins could be achieved by a stronger anti-trust approach and more foreign competition, it is likely that wage increases would also be dampened. In any case, however, additional legislation in this area should be considered with an understanding of the unique characteristics of collective bargaining rather than in the framework of anti-trust.

Policies to Encourage Businessmen and Labor to Restrain Their Use of Market Power

This approach attempts to deal with market power by inducing businessmen and labor unions to adopt a policy of self-restraint in reaching decisions on price-wage matters. Certainly, it can be said that public admonitions and appeals by the President and other national leaders can do no harm and perhaps some good. But the experience of the United States in the past several years, as well as that in most other countries, casts serious doubts on the effectiveness of such a policy. Furthermore, reliance upon the "social consciousness" of large private power groups represents a highly questionable method of solving such a critical economic problem. A democratic society cannot place this degree of responsibility or power in the hands of private individuals.

Aside from such philosophical considerations is the fact that such an approach is most unlikely to succeed in the economic and social environment existing in the U.S. Businessmen are expected to earn profits; in fact, the effectiveness of the economic system itself requires that they should if competitive conditions permit. An appropriate movement of prices and wages to reflect changing demand and cost conditions is an important mechanism by which resources are shifted from declining to expanding industries, or from declining to expanding occupations.

[2] For a discussion of this issue, see the testimony by John Dunlop in the hearings of the Joint Economic Committee, Part 7.

The structure of the labor movement in the U.S. also makes it virtually impossible to expect that a self-imposed policy of "wage restraint" will be successful.[3] The greatest barrier to such a possibility is the very high degree of decentralization of power in American unions. Any policy of restraint, if it is to be effective, must be accepted by a very large proportion of, if not all, unions; the more decentralized the power to affect wages, the less likely is it that such a broad acceptance will be obtained. And if, as in the U.S., there are strong internal rivalries between important union leaders, this likelihood becomes extremely small.

In recent months a more specific proposal has been put forth suggesting an annual conference of business, labor, and government leaders. Such a conference, if it were held in the spring, could discuss the President's Economic Report, the hearings of the Joint Economic Committee, and the over-all economic outlook. Advocates of such a conference suggest that as a result, price and wage decisions in important industries could be reached with a greater understanding of their possible impact on the economy as a whole. Such a conference approach would have to be managed most skillfully, however, if it were not to become a mere public forum for presenting the viewpoints of special interests. *Nevertheless, we believe such an annual conference could yield beneficial results, particularly over the longer run, if care is taken to avoid this danger.*

At least for the immediate future, however, we conclude, with Professor Redford, that it is *"too much to expect that management and labor will be able consistently to view specific questions of wages and prices in terms of public interests rather than of the interests of the groups which they are under compulsion to represent."*[4]

Greater Government Participation in the Price-Wage-Setting Process

We turn, finally, to the whole spectrum of potential courses of action which involve a greater or lesser degree of government participation in the price-wage-setting process. Before proceeding with this, however, the point must be emphasized that, as a general rule, there should be a strong presumption *against* any type of government interference or control unless the circumstances are such as to make it essential. There is always the danger that government participation in the determination of wages and prices will interfere with the proper allocation of resources, will reduce the incentives of labor and capital, and will,

---

[3] According to a study by Mark Leiserson, the success of such policies has been quite limited in several European countries where the underlying economic and social environment was relatively much more favorable than in the U.S. See his paper, "A Brief Interpretive Survey of Wage-Price Problems in Europe," Study Paper 11.

[4] Emmette S. Redford, "Potential Public Policies to Deal with Inflation Caused by Market Power," Study Paper No. 10.

particularly in the long run, create more serious problems than it solves. Nevertheless, society also has the right to impose limits on market power, if it feels that market power is detrimental to its basic interests. Our studies suggest that market power has, in fact, contributed to the inflation of recent years. The problem of balancing these divergent considerations is, of course, a judgment only society can make.

If an approach of this kind were to be used, there are several kinds of government participation.[5] The mildest would be to establish a study group to advise the President on key price and wage changes which might threaten economic stability. Such a group could recommend occasional intervention through fact-finding procedures only when there was a threat of serious inflation. The ultimate decision to initiate fact finding, however, should be left to the President.

A somewhat more drastic step would require that certain clearly defined key industries notify the government at the time prices and/or wages are raised. Hearings of the type already noted could then be initiated at the discretion of the President.

A further and much stronger form of government intervention would be to give the President, or some designated agency, the power to suspend price and/or wage increases while hearings were held.

Assuming some approach of this type were adopted, there is a question of the action which would follow the investigation of the board. The weight of experience suggests that the board should be given the power to make definite recommendations, though they should not be binding upon the parties (at least until we have considerably greater experience as to the desirability and effectiveness of the entire procedure). Unless recommendations are made, it is virtually impossible to bring to bear the pressure of public opinion. For the facts themselves are often difficult to interpret, let alone to understand; and statistical data, no matter how impartially set forth, cannot be expected to convey any impression to the public as to the merits of the issues at hand. Furthermore, many of the most serious implications of a given price increase or wage settlement are not matters of fact, but of judgment—of the potential indirect effects on other prices or wages, for example.

All these elements strongly suggest that any fact-finding procedures, if initiated, should culminate in a series of specific recommendations in order to make the procedure effective.

There is finally the extreme possibility of compulsory arbitration of labor-management disputes combined with compulsory regulation of prices similar to that now used in public utilities. It must surely be presumed that such an approach would entail a far greater degree of public control than is either desirable or necessary at this time.

In sum, it would seem far better at this state of our knowledge and

[5] The discussion in this section draws heavily upon the study paper by Redford, *op. cit.*

experience to confine our efforts in this area to the introduction of a fact-finding procedure to be invoked at the discretion of the President and to result in the issuance of a report and recommendations regarding the justification and desirability of proposed increases in wages and prices.

In the coming years, if the exercise of market power continues to constitute a serious problem, further steps may be deemed desirable.

SUMMARY

1. A vigorous anti-trust program is fundamental to any attempt to reduce market power; in the long run, it is on this approach that we must rely. By making the economy more competitive, anti-trust activities serve not only to reduce inflation; they also help encourage a more rapid rate of growth.

2. If the anti-trust approach is to be relied on, it must be considerably strengthened. The professional staff of the Antitrust Division should be expanded, with a salary scale sufficient to attract and retain able personnel.

In addition, Congress should give serious consideration to several other aspects of our present anti-trust enforcement procedures. Prenotification of proposed mergers would be desirable; greater power to subpoena records in civil cases should be provided; and a more effective method for dealing with market power which is not based on overt collusion should be developed.

Finally, the present policies of our regulatory agencies should be re-evaluated with particular regard to the effect of these policies on competitive practices within their respective jurisdictions.

3. We also recommend, as part of an over-all program to limit and possibly reduce market power, that tariffs be steadily reduced in exchange for concessions from other countries.

4. The anti-trust approach to the problem of union market power is neither feasible nor desirable, except in instances where there is collusion between unions and firms to fix product prices. Making industry-wide bargaining unlawful would be unwise; nor would it be sound policy to prevent national unions from participating in collective bargaining. This is not to say that union market power has not contributed to the inflation problem; it has. But increased competition in product markets, as the result of tariff reductions and a vigorous anti-trust program, can do much to check the exercise of this power.

5. We do not believe that moral suasion can be relied upon to check the exercise of market power. We do believe, however, that an annual conference for business and labor leaders, at which they can be apprised of the economic outlook and the implications of their actions

for this outlook, would yield some benefits and should therefore be instituted.

6. We believe there should be a presumption against government intervention in wage and price determination, unless the circumstances involved make it necessary. If this approach were to be utilized, several alternatives are available, reflecting increasing degrees of intervention. These would include establishment of a study group to advise the President on important price and wage changes; the use of fact-finding procedures, with or without the issuance of a report and recommendations; the requirements of prior notification to the government of proposed price or wage increases in certain key industries; the power to suspend such increases; and, finally, direct price and wage controls.

At this stage of our knowledge and experience, we believe that if such an approach were to be utilized, it should be limited to the establishment of fact-finding procedures to be invoked at the discretion of the President and to result in the issuance of a report and recommendations regarding the justification and desirability of price or wage increases. In the coming year, historical developments will determine the extent to which such measures prove unavoidable.

10. SOME REFLECTIONS ON SYNDICALISM*

Henry C. Simons

SYNOPSIS

1. The interests of labor unions conflict with those of the working class and of others in society whose real income is reduced in proportion to the unions' success in raising money wages by restricting the supply of labor. Eventually, the unions themselves are injured.

2. Democracy is based upon the dispersion of power and cannot tolerate the concentration of power by unions or other monopolies. If it does not eliminate them, democracy will give way to an authoritarian government which will substitute political force for the discipline of competition.

3. Monopoly power is inherently pernicious and never voluntarily moderated. When exercised by unions, it is more damaging than when used by business firms. A rationally conducted union could force an industry out of existence by continuously increasing wage rates and prohibiting entry into the labor market.

4. By enforcing standard wage rates for workers of varying efficiency, unions (*a*) retard the industrialization of unproductive areas like the south; (*b*) deny low-paid workers access to better employments; (*c*) force inferior workers into unemployment; and (*d*) by imposing high labor costs on new firms, give monopoly power to old firms.

5. The ideal wage pays workers the amount they could obtain in an alternative employment and so permits the maximum mobility of labor. Such a wage requires free entry into labor markets, and any obstruction to free entry makes high wages higher and low wages lower.

6. The ideal wage has no necessary relation to a particular industry's profits which, when high, do not justify a permanent wage increase but instead denote the necessity of increasing employment and output. If higher wages invariably absorb higher earnings, expansion is prevented.

7. Investment is restricted by the expectation that unions will appropriate profits or otherwise raise costs, and the ultimate burden of less investment is not borne by enterprises but by the economy in the form of a lower real income.

8. The proper remedy for inequality is the progressive taxation of income and inheritance. It is not syndicalism, which is an irresponsible assertion of power by organized minorities.

9. Syndicalism cannot be justified by the democratic right to form

* Reprinted by permission and shortened from *Journal of Political Economy*, March 1944, pp. 1–25.

voluntary associations. Nor can labor monopolies be justified because they do not always exercise their full power. Monopoly power, whether active or potential, threatens the basis of economic and political order.

10. Continuous inflation via massive fiscal and monetary measures can postpone the unemployment and declining investment which unions lead to, but real income will be much less than it could be.

Let me indicate from the outset that my central interest, and the criterion in terms of which I wish to argue, is a maximizing of aggregate labor income and a minimizing of inequality. If unionism were good for all labor, that would be the end of the issue for me, since the community whose welfare concerns us is composed overwhelmingly of laborers.

Our problem here, at bottom, is one of broad political philosophy. Advocates of trade-unionism are, I think, obligated to present a clear picture of the total political-economic system toward which they would have us move. For my part, I simply cannot conceive of any tolerable or enduring order in which there exists widespread organization of workers along occupational, industrial, functional lines. Sentimentalists view such developments merely as a contest between workers who earn too little and enterprises which earn too much. What we generally fail to see is the identity of interest between the whole community and enterprises seeking to keep down costs. Where enterprise is competitive—and substantial, enduring restraint of competition in product markets is rare—enterprisers represent the community interest effectively; indeed, they are merely intermediaries between consumers of goods and sellers of services. Thus, we commonly overlook the conflict of interest between every large organized group of laborers and the community as a whole. What I want to ask is how this conflict can be reconciled, how the power of strongly organized sellers can be limited out of regard for the general welfare. No insuperable problem arises so long as organization is partial and precarious, so long as most unions face substantial non-union competition, or so long as they must exercise monopoly powers sparingly because of organizational insecurity. Weak unions have no large monopoly powers. But how does a democratic community limit the demands and exactions of strong, secure organizations? Looking at the typographers, the railway brotherhoods, and metropolitan building trades, among others, one answers simply: "It doesn't!"

In an economy of intricate division of labor, every large organized group is in a position at any time to disrupt or to stop the whole flow of social income; and the system must soon break down if groups persist in exercising that power or if they must continuously be bribed to forgo its disastrous exercise. There is no means, save internal competition, to protect the whole community against organized labor minorities and, indeed, no other means to protect the common interests of organized groups themselves. The dilemma here is not peculiar to our present economic order; it must appear in any kind of system.

All the grosser mistakes in economic policy, if not most manifestations of democratic corruption, arise from focusing upon the interests of people as producers rather than upon their interests as consumers. One gets the right answers usually by regarding simply the interests of consumers, since we are all consumers; and the answers reached by this approach are presumably the correct ones for labor as a whole. It is only in terms of general rules or principles that democracy, which is government by free, intelligent discussion, can function tolerably or endure. Its nemesis is racketeering—tariffs, other subsidies, and patronage dispensations generally and, outside of government, monopoly, which in its basic aspect is impairment of the state's monopoly of coercive power.

Trade-unionism may be attacked as a threat to order under any kind of system. The case against it is crystal clear if one thinks of purer types of systems like democratic collectivism. A socialist government, faced with numerous functional minorities each organized to disrupt the whole production process unless its demands are met, would be exactly in the position of recent Chinese governments faced with great bandit armies continuously collecting ransom from the nominal sovereign. It would either deprive such minorities of their power or be displaced by a non-democratic authority which could and would restore monopoly of violence. There is no place for collective bargaining, or for the right to strike, or for effective occupational organization in the socialist state, save in the sense that revolution against established authority is an undeniable privilege and violent chaos always an imminent possibility.

Power in a Mixed Economy

I am arguing, however, not as a socialist, but as an advocate of the elaborate mixed system of traditional economic liberalism. The essence of this practical political philosophy is a distrust of all concentrations of power. No individual may be trusted with much power, no organization, and no institution save the state itself. The state or sovereign must, of course, possess great reserves of power, if only to prevent other organizations from threatening its monopoly of violence. But the exercise of power inherent in government must be rigidly economized. Decentralization of government is essential. Indeed, the proper purpose of all large scale organization is that of dispersing power.

Governments can be trusted to exercise large power, broad functions, and extensive control only at levels of small units like American states and under the limitations imposed by freedom of external trade. Especially in the higher levels or larger units of government, action must follow broad principles. Only by adherence to "constitutional" principles of policy can the common interest be protected against minorities, patronage, and log-rolling; and only in terms of broad principles can government by free, intelligent discussion (democracy) prevail. Most important here are the presumptions in favor of free trade and against dispensations to producer minorities. Constitutional principles or accepted norms are also peculiarly important, and lacking, in fiscal (monetary, budgetary) policy.

Other implications of this older liberalism may be mentioned briefly. The government must not tolerate erection of great private corporate empires or cartel organizations which suppress competition and rival in power great governmental units themselves. It must guard its powers jealously both against the combination of numerous pressure groups and against powerful lobbies. Finally, and most important for the future, it must guard its powers against great trade-unions, both as pressure groups in government and as monopolists outside.

The danger here is now most ominous, in the very nature of such agencies and also because the danger is least well recognized and commonly denied entirely. In other areas we are at least on our guard; nothing is likely to happen that cannot be undone if we will; but labor monopolies and labor "states" may readily become a problem which democracy simply cannot solve at all. There must be effective limitations upon their powers; but I do not see how they can be disciplined democratically save by internal competition or how that discipline can be effected without breaking down organization itself. Here, possibly, is an awful dilemma: Democracy cannot live with tight occupational monopolies; and it cannot destroy them, once they attain great power, without destroying itself in the process. If democratic governments cannot suppress organized extortion and preserve their monopoly of violence, they will be superseded by other kinds of government. Organized economic warfare, if allowed to spread, must lead to total revolution, which will, on very hard terms, restore some order and enable us to maintain some real income instead of fighting interminably over its division among minorities.

The Control of Economic Power

A community which fails to preserve the discipline of competition exposes itself to the discipline of absolute authority. Preserving the former discipline, we may govern ourselves and look forward to a peaceful world order; without it, we must submit to arbitrary authority and to hopeless disorder internationally. Observance of such [competitive] norms *does not* preclude wholesale redistribution of income afterward, if such redistribution proceeds even-handedly on the basis of definite, broad rules. There is room for much socialized consumption, made available without price restraints or at prices well below costs. The policy requires both deliberate supplementing of earnings at the bottom of the scale (relief, family allowances, old-age assistance, etc.) and, especially under free enterprise, progressive taxation of the most fortunate and their heirs and assigns. But the supplementing of public spending and the scaling-down by taxation must proceed even-handedly among functional groups, in terms of objective economic (income) circumstances and without arbitrary occupational differentiation. Thus, poor farmers may properly be subsidized, like others of similar income and needs, because they are poor, but *not* because they are farmers; and wealthy manufacturers may be taxed heavily, not because they are manufacturers of this or that, but because their incomes are large. Incidentally, it is one merit of our present (past) system that inequality is measured closely by income and can most easily be modified systematically through taxation and spending. Inequalities of political power, which alternative systems are likely to produce in extreme form, are likely to be more obscure and certainly are not amenable to quantitative measurement or to continuous, systematic correction

Every organized group of sellers is typically in a position to gain by raising price and restricting sales; the popular notion that they commonly are more exploitative than their own interests would dictate (that we need only more enlightened price and wage policies by organized groups) is simply mistaken, for inadequacy of monopoly power usually leaves them far short of ideal monopoly restriction. When organization becomes widespread, however, the common interest in increased production may greatly outweigh particular interests in restriction, even for those practicing restriction; but, I repeat, the common interest may be implemented only by competition or by authoritarian dictation. There is little hope that mass organizations with monopoly power will submit to competitive prices for their services while they retain their organization and power. No one and no group can be trusted with much power; and it is merely silly to complain because groups exercise power selfishly. The mistake lies simply in permitting them to have it.

Monopoly power must be abused. It has no use save abuse. Some people evidently have believed that labor organizations should have monopoly powers and be trusted not to use them. Collective bargaining, for the Webbs, was evidently a scheme whereby labor monopolies were to raise wages to competitive levels, merely counteracting monopsony among buyers, but eschewing further exercise of organizational powers. A trade-unionism, affecting wages and working rules only within such limits, and doing all the many other good things that unions can do, would be a blessing all around.[1] No one could seriously question its merits in

---

[1] It has seemed best in this essay simply to recognize that unions perform many functions besides those having to do with wage rates, labor costs, restrictive practices, and monopoly or bargaining power—without attempting to detail or to appraise the salutary aspects of activities. This deliberate omission implies no inclination to minimize the good things of unionism, but merely a disposition to emphasize considerations which are the special business of economists. To stress those things which are espe-

the abstract. But monopsony in the labor market is, I think, very unsubstantial or transitory; and it is unreasonable to expect organizations to exercise powers only for the common interest. All bargaining power is monopoly power. Such power, once attained, will be used as fully as its conservation permits and also used continuously for its own accretion and consolidation.

I do not assert that our only monopoly problems lie in the labor market. Save for the monopolies which government is promoting in agriculture, however, no others seem comparably important for the future. It is shameful to have permitted the growth of vast corporate empires, the collusive restraint of trade by trade associations, and the gross abuse of patent privilege for extortion, exclusion, and output restriction. But enterprise monopoly is a skin disease, easy to correct when and if we will, and usually moderate in its abuses, since its powers are necessarily small, and since the danger of political reckoning is never very remote. Enterprise monopoly, enjoying very limited access to violence and facing heavy penalties for unfair methods against rivals, is always plagued by competition, actual and potential, and must always operate against a deeply hostile, if lethargic, attitude of courts, legislatures, and the public. In exceptional cases it has acquired vast power and sustained power over long periods. In many cases it has transformed salutary price competition into perverse and wasteful "competition" in merchandising and advertising. But, to repeat, the proper remedies here are not very difficult.[2]

Labor monopolies are, now or potentially, a different kind of animal. If much violence has been used against them as they struggled into existence, this should not obscure the fact that, once established, they enjoy an access to violence which is unparalleled in other monopolies. If governments have tolerated flagrant violations of law by employers, they are nearly impotent to enforce laws against mass minorities even if majority opinion permitted it.

---

cially amenable to quantitative or abstract analysis is not to imply that others are unimportant.

The closed shop, like overt violence, is an invaluable device for acquiring power and yet, as an explicit privilege or contract provision, is of almost no importance for the exercise of power once acquired and strongly held. The notion that labor monopolies can be frustrated or mitigated merely by forbidding the closed shop is, I submit, almost wholly ingenuous and mistaken.

I wish I could honestly and tactfully propose that large unions be fostered in their good functions and deprived of their socially bad ones (monopoly power). Like others, I can *wish* for this solution, but, also like others, I cannot honestly propose it, for I have no notion *how* it could be done. However, it is perhaps not merely wishful to suggest that many of the good features of unionism *could* be preserved, and monopoly powers perhaps kept within reason, by limiting the size of unions and proscribing collusion among them.

[2] It is difficult to focus attention upon the potentially greater problem of labor monopoly without seeming to under-estimate the corresponding and complementary problem of enterprise monopoly. My best defense against this charge may be found elsewhere, e.g., in "Postwar Economic Policy: Some Traditional-Liberal Proposals," *The American Economic Review*, March 1943, pp. 431–45.

Patently restrictive practices are now commonly deplored and, perhaps because unnecessary, seem somewhat on the wane. But there have been many cases of severe limitations upon entry—high initiation fees, excessive periods of apprenticeship and restrictions upon numbers of apprentices, barriers to movement between related trades, and, of course, make-work restrictions, cost-increasing working rules, and prohibition of cost-reducing innovations, notably in the building trades—not to mention racial and sex discriminations against which effective competition in labor markets is probably a necessary, if not a sufficient, protection.

The Basis of Union Power

It is not commonly recognized, however, that control of wage rates *is* control of entry, especially where seniority rules are in force, and, even failing such rules, where qualitative selection is important and turnover itself very costly to firms. If able to enforce standard rates, experienced, established workers can insulate themselves from the competition of new workers merely by making their cost excessive, that is, by establishing labor costs and wage expectations which preclude expansion of production or employment in their field. New and displaced workers typically migrate, not to high wage occupations but to places where employment opportunities exist; high wages are less attractive if jobs cannot be had. Wage control, determining a major element in operating cost, also determines the rate at which a whole industry will expand or, more likely, with strong organization, the rate of contraction.

Frankly, I can see no reason why strongly organized workers, in an industry where huge investment is already sunk in highly durable assets, should ever permit a return on investment sufficient to attract new capital or even to induce full maintenance of existing capital. If I were running a union and were managing it faithfully in the interest of the majority of its members, I should consistently demand wage rates which offered to existing firms no real net earnings but only the chance of getting back part of their sunk investment at the cost of the replacement outlays necessary to provide employment for most of my constituents during their own lifetimes as workers. In other words, I should plan gradually to exterminate the industry by excessive labor costs, taking care only to prevent employment from contracting more rapidly than my original constituents disappeared by death and voluntary retirement.

If I were operating, as labor leader, without the valuable hostages of large sunk investment, I should be obliged to behave more moderately. But I should still seek, controlling prices via labor costs, to restrict production as rapidly as consistent with decline of my membership by death and retirement and, while permitting some return to investors, should try always to induce only as much employment and production as my original constituents could take care of without new members. If investors disliked my high wages, they would like the high prices which I could assure them by excluding lower wage competitors. In both cases I should, of course, not serve my constituents well toward the end unless I utilized the opportunity of permitting some newcomers, by payments of heavy tribute, to enter, to acquire skill and experience, and to become established with my older cronies; for the initiation fees would contribute handsomely to our retirement annuities.

The situation is more complicated, of course, where unions do permit and facilitate entry, that is, where work is shared equally between newcomers and others. Here the advantages of high wages are dissipated by the sharing of unemployment; and annual wages may even drop below a competitive level, if workers value leisure highly or are usually able to find other remunerative work during their periods of layoff. The outcome resembles that of the pure cartel among enterprises, where price is fixed by voluntary agreement, output divided by quotas, and newcomers admitted freely and granted quotas on the same basis as old firms. No one gains, and everybody as consumer loses. There is great social wastage of resources, of labor in one case, of investment in the other; and the two wastes are likely to occur together, as in coal mining.

But free entry and division of work are not likely to characterize unionism of the future and have rarely prevailed in the past. Employees increasingly seek seniority rights; employers prefer to exercise qualitative selection; and the demands from both sides are roughly consistent, especially in large established firms where workers are carefully selected in the first place and experience is important. Some conflict arises, fortunately, between the rank and file, who want the highest possible wage rates, and labor leaders, whose power and influence, in government and in labor circles, depend on the number of their constituents; but this conflict will usually be reconciled in favor of the interests of the rank and file or avoided via organizational imperialism (jurisdictional conquests).[3]

The Effect of Standard Wage Rates

Personnel experts tell us that qualitative dispersion in labor markets is enormous; that among workers regarded as belonging to the same class (i.e., apart from the upgrading that accompanies large increases of employment) the best workers are worth several times as much to a firm as are the poorer ones. In any case, it is instructive to consider an analogy in agricultural policy to the device of the standard rate in unionized industry.

It is a familiar axiom that the existence of poorer grades of land serves to keep down rents on the better grades. The poorer grades, adding to output, keep down product prices and thus diminish productivity

[3] [Higher wages mean fewer jobs, fewer union members, and less power for their leaders. They can seek them, however (to satisfy the rank and file), and still increase their power if they bring additional skilled groups into the union.]

and rents of other land. Suppose now that wheat producers, protected by prohibitive tariffs, should organize and prohibit, by night-riding or by securing appropriate legislation, the use for wheat raising of any land whose net annual rental value is less than $10 per acre. (Thus, renters could not use land for wheat unless they paid at least $10 per acre; and owners could so use their own land only if annual net returns averaged above $10 per acre.) The effects of such a measure would be fairly complex, since some land excluded at the start would become eligible for use after output fell and price rose; but its virtues for owners of the best land, and its grave diseconomies for the community, are obvious enough. No one (outside the Department of Agriculture) would purport to defend such a policy or suggest that it would be less objectionable if extended to cover all forms of agriculture. In principle, however, there is little to distinguish it from the standard wage in industry.

The argument need not be extended to support extensive differentiation among employees within establishments. It is the proper business of personnel officers to classify employees by tasks and to standardize rates within categories, with perhaps some regard for length of service. Differentiation among individuals is to be avoided, in the interest of both workers and management.[4] A less strong case can be made for considerable standardization of rates within cities or localities. The issue becomes critical when standardization is enforced over wide areas, between small and large cities, and among regions in a vast economy.

Even with such differentiation, however, the argument for standardization of wage rates between communities comes near to denying all advantages of inter-regional trade and is fundamentally on a level with the preposterous Republican (and Democratic!) principles of tariff policy. If standard wage rates are desirable, then tariffs should everywhere be adjusted to offset all differences in labor cost between domestic and foreign producers. This differs slightly from the Republican principle of equalizing all costs, but not enough to merit separate attention. If fully applied in tariff policy, it would practically prohibit all trade and all territorial specialization. One difference here may, however, be noted. If a domestic industry and its workers are protected by duties which compensate for wage differences, say, in Argentina, Argentinean workers are excluded from an American product market. If American workers can enforce their wage rates on Argentinean and other producers, they get both the American and the Argentinean markets—if they are superior workers and/or if they have access here to better and more abundant capital and management. If northern enterprises and workers can enforce

---

[4] One finds here a source of both economies and diseconomies in large as against small firms. The former can afford more elaborate methods of selecting and grading, while the latter can tolerate wider quality dispersion and more differentiation in remuneration. Smallness has much to commend it socially, since it promises better utilization of exceptionally good workers and employment rather than unemployment for substandard workers.

northern wages in particular southern industries, they can largely exclude southern enterprises and workers from both northern and southern markets.

Southern workers may be intrigued by the wage expectations held out by organizers from northern unions and by the Fair Labor Standards Act. They may in a few cases get such wages; but, if they get much employment at such wages, it will be only in spite of the intentions of the northern unions and the Massachusetts senators. Again, it is simply contrary to the interests of northern workers to permit competitive expansion of southern industry in their respective fields.

The great American problem of poverty and under-privilege concerns southern labor. Climate, culture, poverty, and scarcity of complementary resources (especially capital) account for chronically low productivity. A bad situation has been profoundly worsened by world changes which have narrowed the market for our great export staple. This, in turn, gave rise to governmental intervention on behalf of land owners—to a modern counterpart of the inclosure movement, which further diminished agricultural output and accelerated displacement of labor where alternative employment opportunities were inadequate even for slower adjustment.

Two growing southern industries—textiles and coal—offered escape from the hills in many areas; but both developments were alarming to northern workers and employers, who, using the slogans of sentimentalist reformers, obtained legislation which protected them against the south as tariff subsidies had earlier protected them against foreigners. The Fair Labor Standards Act was designed, and will serve primarily, to retard migration of textile production and textile capital into southern states. The Guffey-Vinson Act was intended to sustain a cartelized and unionized northern industry, which the competition of southern coal would have disrupted considerably.

I am here arguing merely the classical case for free trade, free markets, and free occupational migration. The argument is equally sound whether invoked against external or internal barriers, against governmental restrictions on trade, or against those imposed by private monopolies. If its application is more obvious when one considers problems of our south, the same argument may be invoked as regards our whole economy or as regards the special interests of the north itself. The public interest demands free exchange and free movement of workers among occupations. Above all, it demands the easiest possible access by workers in low wage occupations to highly productive and remunerative employment. Unionism implies ability of established workers in high wage areas and occupations to insulate themselves from competition, excluding inexperienced new workers and qualitatively inferior labor from their markets. It enables an aristocracy of labor to build fences around its occupations, restricting entry, raising arbitrarily the costs and prices of its products, and lowering the wages and incomes of those outside, and of the poor especially.

In passing, let me propose, as something better than half-truth, the generalization that, by and large, employers get the kind of labor they pay for.[5] Highest enterprise earnings usually go with highest wage rates; and so-called marginal firms commonly pay both their workers and their owners rather poorly. As between firms and even between industries, large differences in wage rates may persist without corresponding differences in cost. A single firm, offering higher wages than its competitors, may get better morale and cooperation which are well worth the cost; and surely it will be able to enlist and maintain a qualitatively superior labor force. A whole industry may accomplish the same thing, competing for labor with other industries. Depending upon prevailing rates of pay, one industry may get high quality labor in all firms; another, very mediocre workers. Thus, wage concessions to organized groups may at the outset cost nothing at all, to a firm as against other firms or to an industry as against other industries. All that happens is that quality standards are raised and inferior workers more rigidly excluded. But downgrading cannot go on forever; the trick works only if it is confined to a few cases; we should guard here against fallacies of composition. The automobile industry may employ only the best human material, leaving other industries to absorb lower grades. But beyond narrow limits, wage increases will not permit corresponding improvement in quality, even for a single firm. When all industry or many industries try the trick, poorer labor is simply frozen out and driven into unemployment or into much less remunerative and less socially productive employment where standards are less severe. In the old days the steel industry, the garment industry, and coal mining, with all their abuses, did absorb and train a great mass of low grade immigrant labor. What industries will do this job for us in the future? Where, to repeat, is our surplus agricultural labor going to be absorbed? Surely not in steel, which has now little place for anything but the best.

Consider also the untoward effects of standard rates on new and venturesome enterprise. The most vital competition commonly arises from firms content to experiment with new locations and relatively untrained labor. Such enterprises must offer workers better terms than they have received in alternative previous employment but cannot offer the wages paid to highly specialized, selected workers in established centers. If compelled to offer such terms, they will not arise. Yet it is obviously one of the finest services of new and venturesome enterprise to find bet-

[5] This persuasion will explain my diffidence about problems of labor monopsony, i.e., about the one or only argument from pure economic theory which condones labor monopolies. There are, I believe, no important cases in fact where employers face, and act in terms of, wide discrepancy between average cost (wage) and marginal cost of labor. In any event, such phenomena are short-lived; and the remedies proposed (save those suggested below, n. 7) are worse than the affliction.

ter uses for existing labor and to employ more productively than theretofore labor resources which need not be confined to activities of low value. Indeed, every new firm must do this in large measure. Old established firms have skimmed off the cream of the labor supply and have trained their workers to a substantial superiority over the inexperienced. If potential competitors must pay the same wages as old firms, the established enterprises will be nearly immune to new competition, just as high grade workers are immune to the competition of poorer grades. Here again, one sees an alarming identity of interest between organized workers and employers and a rising barrier to entry of new firms, as well as to entry of new workers.

An Ideal Wage Policy

Let me now propose some generalizations about wages and ideal wage policy. The proper wage in any area or occupational category is the lowest wage which will bring forth an adequate supply of labor in competition with other employment opportunities. "Adequate supply" is ambiguous as it stands but will usually be interpreted correctly if not defined. It may, of course, be defined as the supply necessary to equate the productivity of transferable labor as between the industry or occupation in question and alternative employments. In other words, it is the wage which will permit the maximum transfer of workers from less attractive, less remunerative, less productive employments. Broadly, for factory employment in general, it is the wage or wage level which will condemn the minimum number of workers to casual labor and to subsistence agriculture. We imply that any wage is excessive if more qualified workers are obtainable at that wage than are employed—provided only that the industry is reasonably competitive as among firms.[6] This amounts to saying that any relative wage may be presumed to be too high if it requires the support of force (organization) or law.

The basic principle here is freedom of entry—freedom of migration, between localities, between industries, between occupational categories. If such freedom is to exist—and it is limited inevitably by costs and by defects of training and experience—wages must fall to accommodate new workers in any area to which many qualified persons wish to move. Freedom of migration implies freedom of qualified workers, not merely to seek jobs but to get them; free entry implies full employment for all qualified persons who wish to enter. Other things equal, the wage is too high if higher than the wage in actually alternative employments. Ethically, one cannot go beyond the opinion of qualified workers seeking to transfer. If in large numbers they prefer employment here to the alternatives and cannot get it, the wage is exces-

---

[6] [It is possible for a monopolistic industry to pay higher than alternative wages, for which the remedy would not be lower wages but the elimination of the enterprise monopoly.]

sive. A case may be made for supplementing, by governmental expenditure, the family incomes of workers of low productivity, but not for keeping them idle or for confining them to less productive as against more productive employment.[7]

Now, freedom of entry is peculiarly essential in the case of unusually remunerative employments, if one believes in greater equality of opportunity. Only by permitting the freest movement upward through wage categories can we minimize economic inequality and maximize incomes at the bottom of the scale. But it is exactly the high wage industries which invite and facilitate organization; and it is the favorably situated who have most to gain by exclusion, restriction, and monopolistic practices.

Organization is a device by which privilege may be intrenched and consolidated. It is a device by which the strong may raise themselves higher by pressing down the weak. Unionism, barring entry into the most attractive employments, makes high wages higher and low wages lower. Universally applied, it gets nowhere save to create disorder. Surely we cannot all get rich by restricting production. Monopoly works when everyone does not try it or when few have effective power.

The Relation of Wages to Profits

Unionism is only incidentally a means for raising labor incomes at the expense of profits or property income. Profits are usually a small moiety, sometimes positive and often negative; and all property income is a margin whose reduction by particular wage increases reacts promptly and markedly upon employment, production, and product price. Labor demands may be rationalized and popularized as demands for a larger share of earnings—as part of a contest over the shares of labor and capital in particular outputs. But enterprises remain essentially intermediaries between sellers of services and buyers of product. The semblance of struggle between labor and capital conceals the substantial conflict between a labor monopoly and the community; between organized workers and consumers; and especially between established workers in more remunerative occupations and workers elsewhere. The masses of the unorganized and unorganizable lose as consumers; they lose by being denied access to higher wage area; and they lose by an artificial abundance of labor in the markets where they must sell, that is, by being forced to compete with workers who should have been drawn off into the higher wage occupations. And let no one infer that their problem would be solved if they too were organized. The monopoly

[7] Perhaps the best investment by government in better labor standards is improvement of public employment agencies, facilitation of labor mobility and migration, and systematic informing of enterprisers about areas of labor redundancy, actual and prospective. Labor markets should be made more competitive as among firms, industries, and localities and more flexible, as well as less monopolistic, on the supply side. All this is proper and urgent public business.

racket, like that of tariffs and subsidies, works only so long as it is exceptional—works only to advantage minorities relatively, with over-all diseconomy and loss.[8]

Let me now explain an earlier dictum that proper wages are a matter of alternative employment opportunities and not of enterprise earnings or profits. In wage negotiations the level of business earnings is usually given much stress. This plausible notion, however, does not bear much examination.

In a world of continuous innovation, change in relative costs, and change in consumer tastes, new industries appear and old ones vanish; and among enduring industries, some are always rising and others declining in the economy. When one industry enjoys an unexpected or inadequately anticipated improvement of demand conditions or production methods, earnings will rise markedly; and, with strong labor organization, this will mean larger wage demands. But should the industry meet such demands and share its earnings more largely with its existing employees?

Such adjustment, at least temporarily, is to be commended so far as it would occur in a free market. Employers would naturally seek to expand their outputs by drawing workers from competitors and by drawing them from other industries. However, the relative increase here would be temporary, serving to attract young workers and to induce transfer where costs and sacrifices were moderate; and the long term effect would be, not an increase in relative wages but in the quantity and proportion of various kinds of labor in this as against other industries using similar kinds.

Where labor resources are not much specialized, the proper correction for inordinate rates of return on investment is not higher wages, but larger investment, larger employment, larger output, and lower relative product prices. If the large earnings reflect monopoly restraint upon output by enterprises, as they occasionally will, measures should be taken to extirpate such restraint; monopoly in the labor market will only aggravate and consolidate restriction. Temporary increases in relative wages are justified if necessary to attract additional supplies of labor from other industries. If attained by collusive, collective action of workers where supply is adequate or redundant, increases will serve, not to facilitate expansion of output, but to prevent it.

[8] One may recognize the possibility that, with wide or universal organization of workers, federations of unions might enforce some moderation of wage demands and of exclusive, restrictive practices among the labor aristocracies. Such internal discipline among and between unions is a real contingency in small, homogeneous nations like Sweden (especially if complemented by a strong free-trade tradition). In a vast, culturally heterogeneous population, the possibility may be dismissed as utterly unsubstantial. Moreover, the development of such effective "regulation" would involve radical constitutional change in the political system, i.e., reduction of the Congress to a status not unlike that of the British crown.

With strong organization, increased earnings will always be accompanied by demands for higher wages. If the earnings increase in general, and if there is little unemployment, the wage increases will be economically necessary and desirable. Gradual secular increase is to be expected in a progressive economy. But note the awful effects of adjusting *relative* wages continuously to relative earnings. Even in a vigorous and healthy system, some industries and employments will always be contracting, relatively and absolutely. Given free markets, the slack will readily be taken up by industries where demand conditions are improving. Expanding industries will absorb the labor released by those which contract—but only if the opportunities for expansion are not blocked by arbitrary increases of costs, that is, if the stimulus of relatively high business earnings reacts mainly upon employment rather than upon wage rates.

With strong organization, established workers in expansible employments are in a position to prevent expansion and must do so to capture for themselves the full advantage of favorable changes affecting their industry or product market. Ethically, they should share their gains with the community as consumers and with outside workers for whom expansion of output would permit transfer from less remunerative employment. But no group will practice such sharing if it has power to prevent it.

Union Power and Investment Decisions

The situation here is especially alarming when one considers it from the viewpoint of enterprises or investors. In a free-market world, every commitment of capital is made in the face of enormous uncertainties. One may lose heavily or gain vastly, depending on unpredictable contingencies. For reasonably intelligent investors, however, the gamble, with free markets, is a fairly even one, with chances of gain balancing roughly the risks of loss—relative to a conservative commitment, say, in government bonds. The willingness to take chances, to venture with one's property, especially in new and novel enterprises, of course, is the very basis of our whole economic and political system. It is now gravely jeopardized by developments which tend ominously to diminish the chances of gain relative to the chances of loss.

Investors now face nearly all the disagreeable uncertainties of investors in a free-market world plus the prospect that labor organizations will appropriate most or all of the earnings which would otherwise accrue if favorable contingencies materialized. Indeed, every new, long term commitment of capital is now a matter of giving hostages to organized sellers of complementary services. Enterprisers must face all the old risks of investing in the wrong places—risks of demand changes, of technical obsolescence in plant facilities, and of guessing badly only because too many others guessed the same way. Besides, they must risk being unable to recover the productivity which their assets would have if there were free-market access to complementary factors. The prospect for losses is as good as ever; the prospect of profits, is, in the main, profoundly impaired.

If we are to preserve modern industrial production without totalitarian control, we must solve the problem of private investment. There is now much profoundly foolish talk of economic maturity and of technically deficient outlets for new investment. I believe that investment opportunities were never so large; that our highest thrift would not for generations permit enough investment to lower interest rates substantially, if owners of new capital assets could be assured of free-market access to labor and other complementary factors (mainly indirect labor).[9] But the prospect of such access has diminished everywhere. Every new enterprise and new investment must now pay heavy tribute to labor (and other monopolies) in acquiring its plant and equipment; and it faces the prospect of increasing extortion in its efforts to utilize facilities after they are constructed.

In the name of equalizing bargaining power, we have sanctioned and promoted the proliferation of militant labor monopolies whose proper, natural function is exploitation of consumers. The ultimate burden of their exactions will not fall mainly upon industrial investors or enterprises; but enterprises, as intermediaries, will bear the impact of new exactions and may expect to see earnings continuously pressed down to such extent that average expectations are utterly discouraging.

The Remedy for Inequality

We face a real problem in economic inequality. This problem can be handled easily and without serious diseconomies, if one is not hysterically in a hurry, by progressive taxation of income and inheritance. Merely by repairing a few structural flaws in our income tax, we could assure steady reduction of inequality in property incomes and continuous correction of wide disparities in non-property incomes. But radicals and power seekers have little interest in such dull, peaceful, orderly, efficient, gradualist methods. So they have simply ignored critical issues in tax reform and plumped for labor organization. They have promoted the organization of innumerable industrial armies, with implicit sanction to employ force, coercion, and violence, at least to prevent competing sales of services at rates below their own offers. We are told that violence is essential only in the organizing phase; that it will disappear after organization is achieved and recognized—which, of course, is true. Organizations which have attained power need use little overt violence to maintain it. However, it is only the middle phase of unionism or syndicalism which is non-violent. There is much violence at the

[9] [Complementary factors, like raw materials, may be produced by union labor and hence be prohibitively priced.]

start inevitably; but there is more and worse violence at the end, involving total reconstitution of the political system. Somehow, sometime, the conflict between the special interests of labor monopolies and the common interest must be reconciled. Beyond some point their exactions become insufferable and insupportable; and their power must be broken to protect the general welfare.

Progressive taxation is a workable, democratic method for dealing with inequality. The alternative of unionists is to send workers out in packs to exploit and expropriate by devices which resemble those of bandit armies. The one device is inherently orderly, peaceful, gradualist, and efficient. It is the device of law. The other is inherently violent, disruptive, and wasteful in the extreme. One calls for debate, discussion, and political action; the other, for fighting and promiscuous expropriation.

Few Americans will straightforwardly espouse syndicalism or look with approval on Il Duce's corporative state.[10] Few likewise will face the patent fact that we are rushing pell-mell toward and into that political order in the United States. Our formal political structure, of course, retains its traditional character. Our legislators, state and federal, still represent geographic sections of the nation. But alongside this formal political structure arises now a structure of powerful organizations of labor, immune to prosecution as monopolies and largely immune to the proscriptions or penalties of other laws. An essentially syndicalist order (or disorder) may, of course, evolve or arise without formal participation of industrial or occupational organizations in the legislative process. Indeed, such organizations may exercise greater power as extra-constitutional political agencies than they could if they had direct representation in Congress, in state assemblies, and in county and local government.

The intricate pluralism of modern democracies is, of course, a commonplace among students of sociology and politics. Equally commonplace, however, is the fact that organized minorities are a continuing threat to democratic order and internal peace. The danger may arise dramatically in the case of churches, secret societies, vigilante movements, a Ku Klux Klan, or less dramatically in the case of political machines, tariff lobbies, silver senators, veterans' organizations, and farm blocs. In the main, however, we have rarely or briefly endured political usurpation by minorities practicing violence and intimidation.

But, to repeat, we have never faced the kind of minority problem which widespread, aggressive national and regional unions and their federations present. They are essentially occupational armies, born and reared amidst violence, led by fighters, and capable of becoming peaceful only as their power becomes irresistible. Other groups practice violence, of course; but few others practice it with general public approbation or employ it at all without grave risks of punishment or loss of power.

---

[10] [Mussolini's plan for a corporative state was ostensibly based on syndicalist doctrine.]

Unions and the Right of Association

Some conservatives will defend labor organization in terms of the right of voluntary association as a basic privilege in a democratic system, while deploring the use of violence and intimidation. But there are no absolute rights; and the right of voluntary association must always be qualified, *inter alia*, by prohibitions against monopolizing. Failing ability to use violence, particular organizations could not practice heavy extortion indefinitely; but they could often tax the community for a time and subject it to substantial, if minor, disturbances. Protection of the public interest demands limitation of the right of association where the association is of people as suppliers of particular commodities or services.

The point, in any case, is rather academic, for labor organization without large powers of coercion and intimidation is an unreal abstraction. Unions now have such powers; they always have had and always will have, so long as they persist in their present form. Where the power is small or insecurely possessed, it must be exercised overtly and extensively; large and unchallenged, it becomes like the power of strong government, confidently held, respectfully regarded, and rarely displayed conspicuously. But, to repeat, this apparent peacefulness of a maturing syndicalism is unsubstantial and deceptive. It marks a fundamental disintegration of the very bases of political order—a disappearance of free exchange and of the state's monopoly of coercion. Individual groups, securely organized and secure in their monopoly positions, may levy their exactions without overt violence and merely through peaceful political maneuvering (via the arbitration device especially). However, they necessarily restrict drastically the normal flows of trade, destroying general prosperity in their struggle for relative advantage, and reducing enterprisers and investors to a defensive, defeatist task of withdrawing their property.

A maturing syndicalism is the mature economy of our monetary and fiscal extremists. It is inherently unstable and unmanageable. It may be kept going, at income levels far short of our potentialities, by sufficiently large fiscal and monetary stimulation; and no one may wisely condemn policies which postpone revolutionary upheaval if postponement alone is possible. But we should face the fact that nothing else is ahead along this route. Especially, we should be skeptical of economic analysis and prescription which rests on the political premise that mass monopolies (and increasing enterprise monopoly) are assured for the future beyond any recourse of democratic discussion and orderly political process.

The Problem: Labor Monopolies versus Free Markets

Our great minority and monopoly problem of the present and of the discernible future is the problem of labor organization. One may stress the right of voluntary association or, rather, the right of free entry into occupations.[11] One may stress the right to bargain collectively on a national or regional scale or, rather, the right of free occupational migration. In neither case can one sensibly defend both categorically. If one is accorded and exercised, the other is curtailed or destroyed. The issue is simply whether wage rates should be determined competitively or monopolistically.

The obvious struggle within particular industries over division of earnings tends largely to obscure the more substantial identity of interest and functional complementarity of labor and employer organizations. Popularly regarded and defended as counterpoises to industrial concentration or enterprise monopoly, unions in fact serve mainly to buttress effective monopoly in product markets where it already obtains and to call it into existence when it does not.

While extremely ill-informed, I know of no instance where a powerful union has proposed reduction of a monopolistic product price or given real support, singly or in federations, to anti-trust policy. On the other hand, N.I.R.A., like extreme tariff protection, was strongly supported by organized labor.[12] The enforced cartelization of the coal industry may be credited largely to the U.M.W. And if some proposals of C.I.O. leaders for labor participation in management are not pure cartel schemes, I cannot identify the beast when I see it. If labor remains and becomes increasingly cartelized along industry lines, enterprises must be similarly organized for bargaining purposes—not only to present a united front and to recoup wage increases from consumers but because labor itself will prefer and, in any case, compel such employer organization.

We must alter our labor policy or abandon our anti-trust policy. If one big union is a *fait accompli* in, say, the automobile industry, that industry is all through as a competitive sector of our economy—and damned to full cartelization, if not to General Motors. Thanks largely to Thurman Arnold and, now, to an unprecedented sprinkling of intelligent business leaders, the prospects for sound anti-trust policy are perhaps better than they have ever been, here or anywhere. Even if these prospects materialize abundantly after the war, however, the achievements must be frustrated and then sharply reversed unless accompanied or followed closely by reversal of recent trends in labor organization. If labor is tightly cartelized or syndicalized, enterprises must adjust themselves to the political realities.

Business leaders, even when qualified in terms of tolerance and wisdom, are hopelessly disqualified, by their fiduciary responsibilities if not

[11] [The "right of voluntary association" as used here does not mean the right to form monopolies but to enter an occupation.]

[12] [The N.I.R.A. (the National Industrial Recovery Act, 1933–34) was an effort to direct the economy by granting each industry the power to determine output, prices, employment, wages, etc.]

merely by what they symbolize, for leadership in the hard part of this task. They can and may put their own house in better democratic order. That is no small job; but it is all that they can do toward reversing the syndicalist trend. And it is not enough—not more than a beginning. Labor baiters of dubious repute will volunteer in hordes for the real task, and thereby aggravate enormously the sufficient difficulties. Much the same must be said of the conservatives who now dominate our two great political parties—men whose negligible capacity for frankness and whose stupid smartness in devious maneuver are perhaps a greater obstacle to solution than are the prospective harangues of demagogues on either side.

It is easy to argue that the whole problem is so hard and ominous politically that no effort should be made to solve or even to see it —that the real choice lies between a certain, gradual death of economic democracy and an operation or treatment which would cure if successful but is almost certain to kill. I am no forecaster and am not in direct communication with the Almighty. Consequently, I can only maintain that it is immoral to take such absolute dilemmas seriously. Democracy would have been dead a thousand times if it paid much attention to historical extrapolations; and it is perhaps unnecessary to discuss now the shortcomings of temporizing expedients or appeasement.

11. LABOR MONOPOLY AND ALL THAT*

Edward S. Mason

SYNOPSIS

1. Unions are necessarily monopolies, and the important questions are what determines their power and what are the proper limits to it.

2. Their power depends on their control of the demand and supply of labor including the technical conditions that fix the number of jobs, on the elasticity of product demand, and on how well-informed they are about these things.

3. They cannot operate in labor markets as a pure monopoly can operate in a product market, and their nearest business analogue is a cartel that does not engage in profit pooling.

4. There is no striking evidence that union wages are higher than non-union, and hence their wage performance is not a test of their market power. A better test is to compare what a union actually does with what it would have to do in order to control a market completely.

5. Collective bargaining presupposes market power, and hence union practices necessarily limit competition; but the limitations are not always serious, and those which are do not always strengthen unionism.

6. It has been contended that government should not restrain unions so long as they peaceably pursue their own interest. But restraint per se does not impair collective bargaining. Union power is not inevitably checked by countervailing business power, and may produce socially unacceptable results.

7. Equality of bargaining power is not helpful in distinguishing between reasonable and unreasonable union power. It is not operational, does not have the same meaning in all markets, and is not necessarily consistent with efficiency.

8. In pursuing its own interest, a union cannot stay out of the product market, because its power is affected by the number of firms, by prices and output, by who is eligible for membership, and by managerial decisions. Hence, it is impossible to distinguish between reasonable and unreasonable power according to whether a union acts only in the labor market or in the product market also.

9. To determine the proper limits of union power requires a political reconciliation of conflicting values. It may be that the conflicts are more serious than the supporters of unionism acknowledge but less serious than the opponents contend.

* Reprinted by permission from *Proceedings,* Industrial Relations Association, December 1955.

Whether labor unions are monopolies is a question hardly worth asking and, if asked, hardly worth discussion. Whatever else a union is, it is certainly an agreement among workers not to compete for jobs. If unions are not monopolies, working men have been deliberately sold a "bill of goods" for many long years by slick operators who have repeatedly promised to "take labor out of competition." The interesting questions would appear to be: Of what are unions monopolists; how much market power do they have, and how do they use it; are there degrees of power and types of use that call for public intervention; and if so, are "unreasonable" manifestations of labor monopoly appropriately handled by policies primarily designed to deal with monopoly problems in product markets, or is another type of policy required? It is obviously impossible adequately to discuss so many questions in the time available. What I propose to do is to consider some of the determinants of the degree of market power and its use by "labor monopolies" and to do a little prospecting around and about the concept of "unreasonable" power.

Unions in the Market

Monopoly power is obviously a question of degree. In commodity markets a pure seller's monopoly, if it means anything at all, can only mean that buyers confronting this seller have no alternative except to purchase from him. But since, in some sense, all commodities and services compete with each other for consumer dollars, it follows that to be "pure," the monopolist would have to control the sales of all goods and services. Even then he might encounter competition from the "do it yourself" contingent. Certainly, if his control falls short of all goods and services offered for sale, his market power will be limited by the alternative open to buyers to spend more or less on the products of other sellers. Similarly, a pure labor monopoly can only mean the total control of the supply of labor by a single seller or, if you prefer, a single negotiator for the sale of labor services. Anything short of that would confront the seller, or negotiator, with competitive limitations to his market power.

Unions are, of course, organized for purposes other than bargaining advantage. Consequently, it is possible—though barely possible—to imagine a union with no market power. Unless, however, its members think there are advantages in wages, hours, and working conditions greater than could be obtained by individual negotiation, the union is not apt to be long-lived. If we accept the degree of market power essential to the continued existence of a union as the lower limit, and a monopoly of all labor as the upper limit, the market power of present unions is somewhere between. They are all monopolists to a degree, and the degree will be largely determined by their success in controlling the alternatives open to employers.

Each employer must be denied access to alternative sources of labor. The number of employers to be controlled will depend on competitive relations in product markets. If product transport costs are high, it may be sufficient to organize employees in a regional market only. If there exists a national market for the product, the market power of the union will depend either on organizing employees on a nation-wide basis or on devising means of keeping competing products out of organized local markets. Nor may it be enough to deny all employers in a relevant product market access to alternative sources of labor. Under certain circumstances, the power of the union can be increased by denying the employer access to labor-saving techniques. Market power is dependent not only on control of the supply of labor but also on control of the supply of jobs. Finally, assuming adequate control of the supply and demand for labor, the power of the union may be increased if advantage can be taken of elasticities of the demand for the employers' product. This may, on the one hand, involve control of the entry of new firms and, on the other, control of the product price.[1]

The power of a union may be roughly measured by its ability to raise the price of labor above the level attainable in the absence of the union. What for reasons of simplicity is here called price is better considered as a utility index of acceptable combinations of wage rates, hours worked, and other "working conditions." What is here called labor is some group of working men in whose interest the union negotiates. For the present we are concerned with the determinants of market power, leaving for later consideration the characteristics of the unit that exploits it. Even if a union has complete control of the supply of labor, wields substantial influence over the number of job opportunities, and is in a position to determine the conditions of entry of new firms and the way existing firms take advantage of the elasticity of demand for the products they market, the power of the union is still limited. There may be close substitutes produced by firms whose employees are outside the control of the union. Furthermore, there may be a wide discrepancy between the union's judgment of its market power and the fact. This happens all the time in product markets, and there is no reason to believe that unions are immune from such mistakes. A union, for example, that hopes to strengthen its position by denying employers access to superior technology may wake up to find that demand has shifted away from the products in which it has interest to others. No union is likely to have sufficient market power to be able to ignore competitive influences from areas outside its control.

It is obvious that in the process of acquiring and using market

---

[1] The demand for labor is, of course, a derived demand; and for particular types of labor services which are complementary to others, the derived demand may be highly inelastic. Hence, an organization—say, a craft union—capable of taking advantage of this inelasticity may, at least in the short run, command a high degree of market power.

power, union activities may impinge either on the labor market or on the product market. But it is not at all clear where the labor market leaves off and the product market begins. Nor, assuming we know where the product market begins, is it at all easy to determine what types of labor intervention lessen competition in the product market and what do not. If union rules deny the use of spray guns to painting contractors, is competition among these contractors thereby lessened? Presumably, if there is a large number of contractors in the market and they continue to act independently of each other, competition, as the term is explained in the textbooks, remains intact.

If the labor market embraces those economic activities which a union may seek to influence in order to improve wages, hours, and working conditions, there is really no tenable distinction between labor markets and product markets. There is literally no entrepreneurial activity in the production and sale of goods that cannot conceivably be influenced by union activities to the advantage of union members. Certainly the attempt of the Antitrust Division, preceding the decision in the Hutcheson case, to draw a distinction between "legitimate" union concern for improving wages, hours, and working conditions and "illegitimate" activities that interfered with business competition, was ludicrously ineffective.[2] Any attempt to set out the limits of the market power of unions will have to consider union activities on both sides of

---

[2] It is interesting in this connection to compare the Antitrust Division's statement (Thurman Arnold) of "illegitimate" union practices with the A.F.L. replies (T.N.E.C. Hearings, Part 31 A, pp. 18, 175–79).
1. "The strike of one union against another union certified by the N.L.R.B. to be the only legitimate collective bargaining agency with whom the employer can deal."
Reply: "A union certified by the N.L.R.B. may certainly be guilty of negotiating an unfavorable wage contract or imposing arbitrary dues or arbitrary leadership."
2. "A strike to erect a tariff wall around a locality."
Reply: "His illustrations prove that he considers it to be unlawful for unions to seek as much work as possible for their members. Surely it cannot be denied that efforts on the part of a labor union to increase the amount of work for its own members have a direct connection with wages."
3. "The exclusion of efficient methods or prefabricated materials from building construction."
Reply: "Surely unions may, in the language of Mr. Justice Brandeis, 'join in refusing to expend their labor upon articles whose very production constitutes an attack upon the standard of living.'"
4. "The refusal of unions to allow small independent firms to remain in business."
Reply: "The so-called independent contractors or vendors are in truth employees, and certainly the competitors of employees."
5. "The activities of unions in imposing and maintaining artificially fixed prices to consumers."
Reply: "The crux of the problem is, when are prices artificially fixed? Would it, for example, be an unreasonable restraint of trade for unions to enforce a price so as to maintain a living wage by cutting out sweatshop competition?"
6. "The make-work system."
Reply: "Employers will always claim that a few extra hours of work by a smaller number of employees renders useless and unnecessary a greater number of employees."

the market—its success in controlling not only the supply of labor but the demand for labor. And any exploration of union activities on the demand side of the labor market will inevitably penetrate deeply into the functioning of product markets.

What Kind of Monopoly?

Having set out some of the factors that influence the degree of monopoly power that a union may possess, let us turn now to the nature of the organization that presumably exploits this power. An examination of business monopoly makes it clear that a given degree of market power can be variously used, depending, in part, on relationships among those who hold it. Market power may be held by a single seller, a small group of sellers each of whom acts with regard to the reaction of others, a cartel, a trade association, and, no doubt, by other combinations. The market conditions external to the group may be similar, but differences in relationships within the group can produce a wide variety of responses to these external conditions. Insofar as the theory of the firm has attempted to explain business behavior where power is held by a group the members of which act independently or in collusion, it has done so by asking how firms attempting to maximize profits would act subject to various restraints imposed either by the probable reactions of other firms or by the regulations of a collusive agreement. But it has proved very difficult to specify restraints that have any generality, and the meaning of profit maximization under such circumstances itself becomes ambiguous. Consequently, examination of business behavior tends at this point to abandon theoretical models and to retreat into the institutional atmosphere of industry studies. The rock on which the more general analysis founders is the complexity of relations within a group possessing market power.

If we attempt to relate this experience to the study of labor monopoly, the first thing we need to recognize is that whatever else it may be, a trade-union is not a seller of labor services. If a union controlling the supply of labor were to act as a monopolistic seller, it would presumably, on the analogy of a monopolistic seller in a product market, attempt to take advantage of differences in demand elasticities in different segments of the market via a policy of wage discrimination and, in other ways, so act as to maximize total receipts for services rendered.[3] How to distribute these receipts among union members would rationally be de-

---

[3] Although it is probably correct to say that, in general, unions do not act like systematic discriminators, my colleague Martin Segal has called my attention to a number of interesting examples of discriminatory action: The rubber workers not only discriminate among tire-making firms but also negotiate different rates (for the same job) within one firm, depending on the nature of the product and the elasticity of demand for the product. The teamsters, at least in certain geographical markets, appear to consider the elasticity of the demand for the service in setting rates for virtually identical trucking jobs.

termined by some calculation of incentives required to bring forth the necessary services. Obviously, unions not only do not but cannot act as rational monopolistic sellers of labor services.

In the first place, even though the union is the sole negotiator in a given market, there is considerable ambiguity in determining the numbers for whom it negotiates. Not all may be union members; and within the union, certain members may have preferred positions that, at the least, may influence acceptable gradations among wage rates. In other words, the union view of the quantity axis in the familiar diagram that depicts the results of quantity-times-price calculations is not quite the same as the perspective, say, of a seller of cement.

In the second place, there is a still greater ambiguity about the nature of the unit of sale, i.e., of labor services. The union presumably negotiates with respect to a bundle of benefits called wages, hours, and working conditions. But "working conditions" in particular have a way of appearing on both sides of the bargain. The terms affecting "working conditions" offered by the buyer of labor services as a part of the "price" for these services may affect the size of the unit of services he in turn receives. In other words, the supply and demand functions for labor services may not be completely independent of each other.

In the third place, the union is clearly not in the same position to package, ship, and otherwise dispose of its product as, say, a seller of cotton grey goods. In fact, if the union does not handle its material very carefully, it is not likely to have any product at all. The necessity to persuade, discipline, cajole, and take the other steps required to maintain morale and cohesiveness in the organization clearly sets important limits to what the union can and cannot do in negotiating. For all these and other reasons the union is not a seller of labor services but a negotiator for the sale of a not very clearly defined product, representing a not very easily determinable number of men, and operating in an environment that pretty seriously limits the application of any maximizing principle.

To say, however, that a union is not a monopolistic seller of labor services is not to say that it is not a monopoly organization. If we are permitted again to draw analogies from the commodity market, the form of business monopoly that most closely resembles the union is a price cartel with sufficient control over entry and output to make its price policy effective, but lacking the device of profit pooling. Such a cartel can obviously not pursue the price and output policies that would be followed by a single seller operating in the same market. The prices that would maximize the profit of the various firms constituting the cartel will normally be different, and consequently the cartel price has to be some sort of compromise. Since profits are not pooled, each firm has an interest in its continued existence as a firm, and consequently the cartel cannot do what a single seller would supposedly do—shut down inefficient facilities and attempt to minimize costs for the total output. The union is normally faced with somewhat the same problem of reconciling divergent interests and taking care of employees in high cost locations even though it might be better for the union as a whole if jobs could be concentrated in high profit concerns.

Although a cartel is not a single-firm monopoly, no one has any hesitation in describing it as a monopolistic organization. Nor should there be any hesitation in so characterizing a trade-union. The exploitation of its market power by a cartel—or similar loose business arrangements—has been characterized by Fellner as "limited joint profit maximization."[4] Any attempt so to characterize a union's exploitation of its market position would probably have to stress the "joint" and the "limited" and play down the element of "maximization."

Structural and Performance Tests of Market Power

We have now said something about the character of the market confronted by unions and the varying degrees of "occupancy" of the market—if I may be permitted this term—that a union may possibly achieve. We have also considered briefly some of the relations between the union and its membership that might be expected to influence the way in which a market position is exploited. Given the market position and the internal organization of a union, would it be possible to say anything useful about the wages, hours, and working conditions that collective bargaining is likely to produce in that market? Or conversely, given the performance of a union as revealed in the terms and administration of its collective agreements, would it be possible to say anything about the market power possessed by the union?

There has been a good deal of examination in recent years of at least one aspect of union "performance"—the effect of labor organization on hourly wage rates—with fairly inconclusive results. Paul Douglas, writing in 1930, found that while in the 1890's and early years of this century "unionists were able to secure for themselves appreciably higher wages and shorter hours than the mass of the workers," since 1914 "the wages in the non-union manufacturing industries have risen at least as rapidly as have those in non-manufacturing trades."[5] Arthur Ross, on the other hand, after a study of B.L.S. wage data for 1933–45, concludes that: "Real hourly earnings have advanced more sharply in highly organized industries than in less unionized industries, in periods of stable or declining membership as well as periods of reorganization."[6] Studies by

---

[4] William Fellner, *Competition among the Few: Oligopoly and Similar Market Structures* (New York, 1949). Cf. in particular chap. vii.

[5] Paul Douglas, *Real Wages in the United States* (1930).

[6] Arthur M. Ross, "The Influence of Unionism upon Earnings," *Quarterly Journal of Economics*, February 1948, p. 284.

Dunlop[7] and Garbarino[8] cast doubt on any very strong influence of unionization on inter-industry wage structures. Clark Kerr, summing up the results of these and other investigations, concludes: "One consequence of contemporary institutional controls in the labor market is evident. They conduce to the single rate within the craft or industrial field which they cover. The best, although not thoroughly convincing, evidence now indicates they have surprisingly little effect, however, on inter-industry differentials, confirming the conclusions of Paul Douglas of a quarter of a century ago."[9]

If we turn to the writings of those who have most strongly emphasized the dangers of labor monopoly, we find many ominous statements about distortions of the wage structure and sabotage of the price system, but almost no factual information to support such statements.[10] Are we to conclude that because the factual investigators of union performance have found no striking evidence of wage differentials and the theorists of labor monopoly have failed to demonstrate their case empirically, the market power possessed by unions is small? Some writers appear to think so, but the conclusion seems to me premature.

Similar difficulties confront judgments, based on evidence regarding business performances, of market power in product markets. Repeatedly, in the administration of the anti-trust laws, the courts have wisely refused to answer the question whether the prices—or some other aspects of performance—of a combination are "unreasonable," by some test of what would be reasonable under competitive conditions, and have found violation in the mere existence of the combination. And insofar as the courts have tended to move away from "abuse of power" and to the existence of "power itself" as evidence of monopolizing or its attempt in cases involving large firms, the tests of market power have emphasized structure rather than performance. If the firm's degree of monopoly is to be estimated by comparing its prices, output, investment, and profits with what they would be if the firm were subject to competitive restraints, two major difficulties arise. First, there is the question of standards: Are the restraints to be those associated with pure competition or

[7] John T. Dunlop, "Productivity and the Wage Structure," in Lloyd A. Metzler *et al., Income, Employment and Public Policy: Essays in Honor of Alvin H. Hansen* (New York, 1948).

[8] J. W. Garbarino, *A Theory of Inter-industry Wage Structure Variations* (Institute of Industrial Relations, University of California, 1950).

[9] "Labor Markets: Their Character and Consequences," I.R.R.A. *Proceedings*, 1949, p. 78.

[10] E.g., various writings of Charles E. Lindblom, Fritz Machlup, and Henry Simons. Cf. Lindblom, *Unions and Capitalism*, p. 5: "Unionism will destroy the price system by what it wins rather than by the struggle to win it. It sabotages the competitive order, not because the economy cannot weather the disturbance of work stoppages but because it cannot produce high output and employment at union wage rates. Nor can the economy survive the union's systematic disorganization of markets and its persistent undercutting of managerial authority."

with some sort of "workable" competition, and, if the latter, what sort? Second, there is the problem of isolating the effect of market power on the prices, output, investment, and profits from other influences. The study of business performance has its uses in estimates of market power in conjunction with structural evidence, but only in rather special situations can performance tests alone yield unambiguous findings.

So far as I can see, the same difficulties plague attempts to estimate the market power of unions by observing union performance. Again, there is the question of standards. Are we comparing the behavior of union wage rates with their assumed behavior in a purely competitive market, which is apparently what Machlup has in mind?[11] Or is the standard the assumed behavior of wage rates in the absence of unionization, which is apparently what Reynolds and various other people consider appropriate?[12] Secondly, assuming we have chosen our standard, will we find it possible to isolate statistically the influence on wage rates, or other dimensions of performance, of union power from all the other influences at work in a changing economy? A failure to establish empirically a clear connection between unionization and the terms of the wage bargain does not, to my mind, dispose of the question of labor monopoly.

In product markets, it is much easier to assemble information relevant to the market power of a firm by considering the limitations imposed by the firm's position in the market than by observing the firm's performance, and I suspect this is true of the market power of unions. Needless to say, it is not at all easy in either case to evaluate this information. If we are to consider the area of freedom open to the union in wage negotiations as well as the limitations imposed by the external market environment, we must presumably start with the product market which defines the employers with whom, and the number of jobs with respect to which, the union will desire to negotiate. Unless all the employers in a well-defined product market are included, the union's area of freedom is bound to be severely circumscribed by the product substitution of non-union for union output. Given complete control of the jobs in a well-defined product market, the union may be able to increase its market power by setting limits to the introduction of labor-saving technological changes or by increasing the number of jobs by "feather-

[11] Fritz Machlup, "Monopolistic Wage Determination as a part of the General Problem of Monopoly," in *Wage Determination and the Economics of Liberalism* (Economic Institute of the U.S. Chamber of Commerce, 1947), pp. 69, 70.

[12] Lloyd Reynolds, *Structure of Labor Markets: Wages and Labor Mobility in Theory and Practice* (New York, 1951), p. 259. Kerr, "Labor Markets: Their Character and Consequences," distinguishes between "perfect" labor markets in which "physical movement of workers and the wage setting process" are intermingled with the emergence of "one wage for labor" and "natural markets." He reports of the latter that all the evidence indicates a wide range of wage rates for equal qualifications—due to limited knowledge on the part of the worker and a "restricted conception of himself."

bedding" operations. There may also be opportunities of taking advantage of demand elasticities in the sale of the product by controlling or influencing output and price. The union might be said to occupy its market fully when all opportunities of improving wages, hours, and working conditions within the unavoidable limits imposed by the elasticity of product demands and unalterable production functions lie within its control.

The union, in the course of acquiring its market position, may find it necessary to engage in organizing strikes and secondary boycotts; to press for closed shops; to absorb "independent businessmen-workers" into the union or drive them out of business; to insist on the employment of non-working stand-by crews, and do many other things designed ultimately to improve wages, hours, and working conditions. All or most of these are "well-established practices" of trade-unions, and Lester admonishes us, "Merely to condemn as 'monopoly' almost every well-established practice of trade-unions serves, therefore, to confuse rather than to shed light on, the significant issues."[13] I agree that to *condemn* these practices as monopolistic is wrong since condemnation implies a judgment based on some public interest standard. But to *analyze* these practices in relation to the market power or degree of monopoly achieved or achievable by unions seems to me not only desirable but necessary. Needless to say, the conclusions of such analysis have no necessary relevance to a public interest finding of "unreasonable" power or "abuse of power."

I take it for granted that all these and other union practices contribute—or are thought to contribute—to improvement of wages, hours, and working conditions. Consequently, I agree with Lester that there is no reason for selecting out certain of these practices, such as the closed shop or industry-wide bargaining, as monopolistic to the exclusion of others. Certainly, these particular practices may in various circumstances increase the degree of union power, but so does any kind of labor organizing. The union is a monopolistic arrangement by definition, and it may be reasonably assumed that a union will take such steps as it can to increase the degree of its monopoly control in order the better to perform the functions for which it was organized.

At the same time, it has been emphasized that the union is a very special kind of monopoly organization, negotiating on behalf of its members rather than selling their services, and constrained by various internal and external political considerations in its conduct of negotiations. There is no reason to expect, then, that the market power possessed by a union will be translated into a certain predictable pattern of economic performance via some sort of wage-maximizing motivations and procedures. If we turn to commodity markets, the closest resemblance is a

[13] Richard A. Lester, "Reflections on the Labor Monopoly Issue," *Journal of Political Economy*, December 1947, p. 526.

particular kind of cartel which, though it does not behave as a single monopoly seller would behave, is a monopoly organization for all that. And so is a labor union.

Unreasonable Union Power

It needs to be recognized at the outset of any discussion of "appropriate" limits to union power or its use that this is a political question. There is no possibility, by means of an application of the principles of economics, the philosophy of the common law, or any other technique of analysis or body of doctrine, of arriving at an "optimum" solution to this problem. The determination of wages and working conditions by collective bargaining is highly valued by important elements of the community not only because of "bargaining" considerations but because it permits the participation of labor in a process of industrial self-government. Under the Wagner Act, collective bargaining was the preferred method of wage determination; and even under Taft-Hartley, it is an approved method. But collective bargaining inevitably requires the existence of unions with a substantial degree of market power. In general, the more power unions have, the more rapidly unorganized sectors of the economy can be brought within the framework of collective bargaining, and the more deeply union representatives can penetrate into the process of joint labor-management decision making. Those who set a high value on this process are apt to take the position that since collective bargaining is a "good thing," public policy should favor whatever measures are necessary to expand it.[14]

It is equally clear, on the other hand, that a substantial degree of union power can adversely affect the functioning of competition in both labor and product markets. I say *can* rather than *will* both because the evidence is unclear and because there is a difference between the possession and the exercise of market power. There is a substantial body of opinion favoring the maintenance of competition and, *ipso facto*, whatever measures are necessary to attain it. Furthermore, some attach value to continued opportunities for self-employment even in areas where so-called "businessmen-workers" are in competition with union members.[15] And others point out that individual workers can be "oppressed"

---

[14] Cf., for example, the statement of Nathan Feinsinger in *Hearings on the Taft-Hartley Law before the Senate Committee on Labor and Public Welfare*, 81st Cong., 1st sess., Parts 4–6, p. 2569: "If our national policy is to be effectuated through collective bargaining, we cannot simultaneously encourage a competing system of individual bargaining. If collective bargaining is to be free and voluntary, we cannot have governmental intervention, except to insure the conditions under which free bargaining can take place."

[15] Cf. the opinion of Frankfurter, J., in the case of *International Brotherhood of Teamsters, Local 309*, v. *Hanke*, 339 U.S. 470 (1950), at p. 475: "Here we have a glaring instance of the interplay of competing social-economic interests and viewpoints. Unions obviously are concerned not to have union standards undermined by non-union shops. This interest penetrates into self-employer shops. On the other hand, some of our profoundest thinkers from Jefferson to Brandeis have stressed the importance to a democratic society of encouraging self-employer economic units as

by union as well as business power. Thus, there appears to be a set of respectable values held by a considerable number of people that is unlikely to be realized without some check to union power, and I suppose it would have to be said that for those who esteem highly the benefits—supposed or real—of a competitive price system, the check would need to be sharp and severe.

A conflict of *some* magnitude between the values of collective bargaining and the values of competition seems to me inescapable.[16] Under these circumstances, how much of the one, as against how much of the other, a democratic society will permit itself to have will, in the last analysis, be determined at the polls. All that an "independent" and "objective" student can hope to contribute is a somewhat clearer understanding of the question of how much must be sacrificed in order to secure some part of the other. This seems to me a fruitful field of inquiry for those interested in public policy. Even if we set a high value on collective bargaining, we can recognize that there are some union practices that seriously damage the competitive process without adding very much to the union's ability to attain its ends. And, no doubt, similar conclusions could be reached by asking the question whether the competitive process would really be damaged very much by certain union practices that are essential to effective collective bargaining. But this type of inquiry is detailed and difficult, and I propose here to avoid it in favor of the much easier task of commenting on certain proposed solutions to this question of the appropriate limits to union power and its use.

Let us consider first the implications of the so-called self-interest doctrine: that so long as a union acts in its own interest and eschews violence and coercion, no limits should be placed on it by government. So far as federal legislation is concerned, this doctrine was, of course, in effect between 1941 and 1947, after the Hutcheson decision[17] and before the enactment of Taft-Hartley.

---

a counter-movement to what are deemed to be the dangers inherent in excessive concentration of economic power."

[16] This conflict is stated in somewhat exaggerated form by Neil Chamberlain, commenting on a statement of Joseph Spengler's on unions' monopolistic control of the wage rate: "Here is a problem couched in terms which are familiar to generations of economists bred on liberal economic traditions. But its very statement in these terms robs it of its real significance—that the developments in industrial relations represent not just a threat to the workability of the price system but a challenge to its philosophical and ethical foundations. . . . Satisfaction in the process of production, enjoyment of the job and the worker society which it represents, are important parts of living." (Joseph J. Spengler, "Power Blocs and the Formation and Content of Economic Decisions," I.R.R.A. *Proceedings*, 1949, p. 174. Chamberlain's statement is at p. 200.)

[17] *U.S.* v. *Hutcheson*, 312 U.S. 219 (1941). In Justice Frankfurter's famous phrase, "So long as a union acts in its self-interest and does not combine with nonlabor groups, the licit and the illicit under Section 20 are not to be distinguished by any judgment regarding the wisdom or unwisdom, the rightness or wrongness, the selfishness or unselfishness of the end of which the particular union activities are the means."

I should like to state with respect to this doctrine three not very startling or novel propositions. There is really not much basis in either logic or experience for believing that an unimpeded economic struggle among large interest groups will lead to socially acceptable results. Government can, in fact, go rather far in limiting the acts of unions in pursuit of their interest without substantially damaging the collective bargaining process. The view that a free enterprise economy implies no constraint of the self-interest pursuits of economic units has as little validity for labor as it has for business.

There are some, of course, to whom the struggle of large groups means competition. "I have seen the suggestion made," said Justice Holmes sixty years ago, "that the conflict between employers and employed is not competition. But I venture to assume that none of my brethren would rely on that suggestion. . . . it is plain from the slightest consideration of practical affairs, or the most superficial reading of industrial history, that free competition means combination, and that the organization of the world, now going on so fast, means an ever increasing might and scope of combination. . . . Whether beneficial on the whole, as I think it, or detrimental, it is inevitable. . . ."[18]

Justice Holmes was a very great man, but his ideas on the nature of competition, I confess, have always struck me as being rather peculiar. The stricture that unions should act only in their own interest is really not very much of a stricture, as experience since the Hutcheson case has shown; and despite the writings of my colleague Galbraith, I do not really believe that there is an historic law to the effect that the appearance and use of power will be inevitably checked by the appearance of a countervailing power.[19] The historic forces may have to be nudged and assisted by the state to moderate, in their own interests, the action of economic groups. This has been found desirable, in this country at least, with respect to business enterprises, and there is no reason to believe that the self-interest of labor groups is any more closely identified with the public interest than that of General Motors.[20]

Nor do I think that government intervention to limit unions in the pursuit of their interest means the end of collective bargaining. One does not have to be a supporter of Taft-Hartley to hold that after eight years' experience under that law, American workers are not yet slaves. After

[18] O. W. Holmes, J., in *Vegelahn* v. *Gunter*, 167 Mass. 92 (1896). My colleague Archibald Cox calls to my attention, however, that a review of Holmes's labor decision reveals his position as falling substantially short of full acceptance of the self-interest doctrine.

[19] Cf. J. K. Galbraith, *American Capitalism: The Concept of Countervailing Power* (Boston, 1952).

[20] On the relation of the labor interest to the public interest, see an interesting paper by E. H. Chamberlin, "The Monopoly Power of Labor," in *Impact of the Union: Eight Economic Theorists Evaluate the Labor Union Movement*, edited by David McCord Wright (New York, 1951).

all, as McCabe has pointed out, "The Wagner Act took unions out of the category of private clubs in which the Supreme Court found them in Adair v. United States and Coppage v. Kansas."[21] And they have never returned to that category. There is a view, vigorously expressed by various labor leaders in the hearings on Taft-Hartley,[22] that any public interference with the self-interest pursuits of a union is incompatible with the operation of a free enterprise economy. But, in the words of Justice Holmes, "I venture to assume that none of my brethren would rely on that suggestion."

We must, of course, recognize that in the United Kingdom and the Scandinavian countries, public policy in effect sets little or no limit to the self-interested action of trade-unions. It we had time, and the competence, it might be useful to speculate on the lessons of this experience for the United States. Certainly, on one definition of "good labor relations," it might be said that in these countries labor relations are better than they have been over the last two decades in the U.S. But this definition appears to exclude from the meaning of "good labor relations" certain adverse effects on consumer interests; and, in England at least, some considerable part of the good relationship between labor and management seems to have been purchased by effective collusion against the consumer.[23] In certain of the Scandinavian countries, notably Norway, the management of labor relations appears to have required a large step toward the application of a public wage-price policy as an essential element in the administration of a planned economy. I am very far from contending that even this cost of attaining good labor relations is necessarily excessive. But if these are the costs, they should be recognized; and in the political

[21] Testimony of D. A. McCabe, *Hearings*, Senate Committee on Labor and Public Welfare, 81st Cong., 1st sess., Parts 1–3, p. 1564.

[22] Cf., for example, the testimony of John L. Lewis, *Hearings*, Senate Committee on Labor and Public Welfare, 80th Cong., 1st sess. (1947), p. 1984. The statement of William Green (*Hearings*, pp. 992–94) is equally illuminating regarding labor attitudes toward any limitation of self-interest pursuit by unions. When Senator Ives pointed out that there was probably going to be legislation regulating secondary boycotts and jurisdictional strikes and that it was important that this legislation be as sensible as possible, Mr. Green replied in effect: (1) The present proposals are impossible. (2) It is all a very difficult question, and a commission ought to be set up to study it. (3) What can Congress do about it, anyway? Are you going to put people in jail for refusing to work? (4) The whole question should be left to the "House of Labor" to determine.

Philip Murray's contribution was that if there are any abuses in the labor movement, the Committee should persuade "Willie" Green to sit down with "Phil" Murray to see how they can be ironed out (p. 1089).

[23] See, e.g., the comment of W. Arthur Lewis on the decision in *Crofter Handwoven Harris Tweed Co., Ltd.* v. *Veitch and Another*, 1 All. E. R. 142 (1942) in *Overhead Costs* (London, 1949), chap. vi: "Businessmen seeking to advance their private trade interest may not only combine with each other, but also bring their workers into the scheme, and promise them part of the swag; even this was hardly in doubt after the decision in Reynolds v. Shipping Federation, Ltd. (1923, Ch. 28). Now we know that they may use not only their own workers, but workers in any other industry who happen to belong to the same union."

process through which public policy gets determined, they should be compared with the supposed advantages that might accompany an unimpeded pursuit of self-interest by organized labor.

There is, furthermore, the question whether institutions and policies that work in another country would function in the U.S. In this connection, I am impressed by the words of Judge Amidon in *Great Northern Railway* v. *Brosseau*.[24] After pointing out that Section 20 of the Clayton Act was pretty much copied from Section 2 of the British Trades Dispute Act of 1906, he emphasizes the enormous differences in the application of these two sections in the two countries and concludes, "The contrast between the situations in England and the United States presents an impressive example of how differently the same statute works in countries whose habits of life are different."

The facts cited here refer, of course, to the early 1920's when labor relations in this country were vastly different from now. But the observations of Judge Amidon are still relevant to the question of whether in this country an unlimited pursuit by trade-unions of their interest would produce the same kind of labor-management relations as in England, with or without the presence of a Sherman Law.[25]

I do not know what the answer to this question is. Here, I wish merely to emphasize that the self-interest doctrine will inevitably lead to action that impinges on various values that may, somewhat loosely, be said to be bound up with the maintenance of competition. The self-interest doctrine then can be pushed to an extreme only by those who are willing to assign zero magnitudes to these values. If it is not to be pushed that far, what kinds of limits have been or may be suggested?

The Doctrine of Equal Bargaining Power

One of the oldest defenses of union organization depends on the supposed desirability of equalizing bargaining power between employees and employers. This argument appears in every textbook in economics and as a statement of policy is written into paragraph 2 of the Wagner Act.[26] One clear implication of this defense is that there are appropriate

---

[24] 286 F. 414 (1923): "In Great Britain strikers and the new employees are a part of the common life of the community. They mingle freely with one another. The opportunities for peaceful persuasion are a part of the daily intercourse. There the private armed detective is unknown. . . . The writ of injunction in strike cases has been unknown in England during the period when it has attained such universal use with us."

[25] It should be noted, furthermore, that trade-unions in the United Kingdom are substantially limited in their pursuit of self-interest by extensive foreign competition, and the balance of payments considerations involved in a heavy dependence on foreign trade, and by their association with a political party that has been and at any time may be asked to assume the responsibilities of government.

[26] National Labor Relations Act of 1935, par. 2: "The inequality of bargaining power between employees who do not possess full freedom of association or actual liberty of contract, and employers who are organized in the corporate or other forms of ownership association substantially burdens and affects the flow of commerce, and

limits to union power. If equality of bargaining is desirable, a growth of union power beyond the extent necessary to secure equality would appear to be undesirable. Do we have here a useful suggestion concerning the proper distinction between reasonable and unreasonable union power?

I think not. Although there is some minimum of market power without which a union cannot bargain effectively or even exist, to attempt by public action to equalize power on different sides of the labor market is neither possible nor desirable. In the first place, the standard suggested by the doctrine of equal bargaining power is clearly non-operational. Does the U.A.W. have greater or less bargaining power than General Motors? I don't know. Not only do I not know, but neither I nor anybody else has a very good idea what information, if diligently collected, would permit an answer to that question. It is difficult enough—some would say impossible—to form an objective judgment on whether the market power of a business firm exceeds or falls short of some permissible standard. But to estimate whether a labor union and a business firm confronting each other in wage negotiations have or do not have approximately equal bargaining power seems to me, by at least another order of magnitude, more difficult.

In the second place, equality of bargaining power, if attained, has a very different significance in different market contexts. If the negotiating parties are surrounded, on either side of the market, by effective competitors, the results are likely to be quite different than if both are entitled to be called monopolists. The theory of bilateral monopoly tells us that stalemate is a distinct possibility; and the more equal the negotiators, the more likely is this possibility.

In the third place, the doctrine implicitly assumes that the attainment of equality is compatible with the efficient operation of organizations on both sides of the market. Why should this be necessarily so? If workers are unorganized, we would not recommend, I presume, that firms be reduced to that size necessary to the attainment of equality of bargaining power with individual workers. Nor should we, I think, suppose that there is any virtue in the proposition that the size of the union, or of a union bargaining unit, be adapted to the scale considerations that influence the size of firms. Both firms and unions have scale problems of their own, and there is no reason for believing that what is optimum on one side of the market will produce an equality of bargaining power with the optimum size on the other side of the bargaining table.

For all these reasons, I suggest that the doctrine of equal bargaining power, having done its duty in the early history of trade-unionism, be decently interred and quietly forgotten.

---

tends to aggravate recurrent business depressions, by depressing wage rates and the purchasing power of wage earners in industry and by preventing the stabilization of competitive wage rates and working conditions within and between industries."

Union Interference with Business Competition

Finally, let us consider briefly the suggestion that at least one guide line to the proper limitation of union powers may be provided by considering the effect of union action on business competition. Since the Hutcheson decision there has been much discussion of this possibility, and many bills designed to accomplish it have been presented to Congress. Unfortunately, the line separating trade-union action limiting competition in labor markets from trade-union action limiting business competition in product markets is not self-evident. As we have seen, union efforts to improve wages, hours, and working conditions can spread rather indiscriminately among labor and product markets, and business competition may be adversely affected at a number of points. Let us consider briefly some of the possibilities.

First, there is the question of the effect of union action on the number of firms in the market. Should unions be permitted to drive independent businessmen-workers out of the market? It is clear that their continuing competition may adversely affect union wage scales. On the other hand, to eliminate them may adversely affect competition in the product market. Should unions control the entrance of new firms through what is essentially a licensing process, as allegedly has been done in the Pacific northwest under conditions locally and familiarly known as "Dave Beck's N.R.A."? Should unions exclude from a local market the competition of firms located outside the market by refusing to work on their products? This appears to have been a fairly common practice in recent years, and by no means all boycotts of this sort have been attempts to organize the unorganized employees of outside competitors.

Second, there is the question of union action interfering with the independence of price and output decisions by firms within the market. Should unions there be allowed to do what would be condemned as a per se violation of the anti-trust laws if undertaken by business firms? My colleague Professor Cox, in what is by far the most penetrating discussion of labor and the anti-trust laws that I have seen, favors an amendment of these laws condemning "agreements with employers, fixing prices, limiting production or cutting off access to a market."[27] It is not altogether clear, however, how far this condemnation is meant to go. Cox admits that union action limiting output presents a difficult problem. Were John L. Lewis' famous memorial days merely an attempt to spread the available work among union members, or did they represent an attempt to maintain the price of coal by limiting output? Cox apparently also does not want to include in this condemnation union action designed to exclude the introduction of labor-saving techniques and equipment and to "make work" by requiring the employment of non-workers,

[27] Archibald Cox, "Labor and the Anti-trust Laws: A Preliminary Analysis," *University of Pennsylvania Law Review*, November 1955.

though this type of action would almost certainly be struck down by the anti-trust laws if attempted by a combination of employers.

Third, there is the bothersome question of who is a worker and who is a businessman. However far one goes in supporting the self-interest activity of unions, it is assumed that certain limitations to union power are provided by the arms'-length and independent bargaining of businessmen on the other side of the market. But what if the wages of labor are essentially a share of the proceeds and dependent on the quantity and price of the workers' output as in the case of various east and west coast fishermen's associations? In this situation the only limitation to be found is the elasticity of the demand for the product. And what may become of arms'-length bargaining if managerial employees up to and including the president of the company are brought within the ranks of union membership? The United Mine Workers, at least before Taft-Hartley, frequently proclaimed their aims to include organizing everyone up to and including the mine superintendent. The Wagner Act defined employee as "any employee" and, as Justice Douglas pointed out in his dissenting opinion in the Packard case, if foremen are employees, so are "vice presidents, managers, assistant managers, superintendents, assistant superintendents—indeed all who are on the payroll of the company, including the president."[28] He goes on to say that if the majority view of the Court prevails, "The struggle for control or power between management and labor becomes secondary to a growing unity in their common demands on ownership" or, one might add, on the consumer.

Finally, there is the most bothersome question of all, the question of so-called "management prerogatives." We expect from our system of enforced competition, I take it, not only a limitation to business power but an environment in which business rivalry will produce a continuous flow of better products and better ways of producing existing products. One important presumption underlying this policy is that business has a substantial area of freedom to innovate and to explore ways of achieving cost reduction and product improvement. Union action *could* diminish this area of freedom rather drastically, and this diminution *could* at all points be closely related to a legitimate union concern with wages, hours, and working conditions. E. Wight Bakke, in a perceptive paper on collective bargaining, points out that a business enterprise is a risk-taking organization in which management wants to preserve as much freedom of action as possible. The union, on the other hand, is a security-seeking organization, one of whose objectives is a reduction in the area of employer discretion.[29] At the Labor-Management Conference in 1945, management representatives wanted an assurance that collective bargaining

---

[28] *Packard Motor Co.* v. *N.L.R.B.*, 330 U.S. 483.

[29] E. Wight Bakke, "Organizational Problems in Collective Bargaining," in *Wage Determination and the Economics of Liberalism* (Economic Institute of the U.S. Chamber of Commerce, 1947).

would not be allowed to encroach on a specific set of "management prerogatives." The labor representatives, while recognizing that "the responsibilities of management must be preserved," took the position that collective bargaining is an "expanding process" which must necessarily encompass new subjects.[30] One can agree with Richard Lester that unions do not normally desire to "take over" the functions of management but at the same time be impressed by the potential limitations to the effectiveness of business competition that inhere in a gradual curtailment of management's area of freedom through the process of collective bargaining.[31]

These seem to me the principal ways in which union power may impinge upon business competition. There may be others.[32] I do not propose to attempt here an evaluation of the effects on competition of various lines of union action, but wish merely to emphasize that those who consider that the appropriate limits to union power should be established at the point where union action adversely affects the process of business competition may be embracing a lot of territory.

In conclusion, let me re-emphasize the view that the determination of the "proper" limits to union power is not completely amenable to logic and experience. We are concerned here with values that are to some degree conflicting, and how these values are to be reconciled is a part of the political process. At the same time, I feel that the gulf between those on the one hand who believe that there is no problem of labor monopoly worth mentioning and those on the other hand who believe that it is the problem of our generation is unnecessarily wide. Is it not possible for those who set great store by collective bargaining to recognize that there are areas in which union action may encroach rather seriously on other values and where limitations may be imposed without significant injury to the process of collective bargaining itself? And is it not also possible for those who set great store by the maintenance of a competitive society to recognize that the spread of unionism does not necessarily mean that all is lost?

[30] Cf. George W. Taylor, *Government Regulation of Industrial Relations* (New York, 1948), pp. 237–38.

[31] Richard A. Lester, *Labor and Industrial Relations; A General Analysis* (New York, 1951), p. 209.

[32] I have not discussed at all the so-called wage-price problem, though this is probably the area in which there is the greatest latent concern for the effects of trade-union action on the functioning of the economy. Insofar as there is a wage-price problem, it certainly involves the relationships of large groups, unions and firms, but it is not very amenable to analysis in terms of particular markets. Industry-wide wage increases, whether or not negotiated by industry-wide bargaining, provide an excellent rationalization for simultaneous price increases and probably facilitate price leadership. Furthermore, business will be less reluctant to increase prices if "key" wage bargains bring about similar wage increases in economically adjacent industries. And such reluctance as union leaders have to pressing for a continuous succession of wage-rate increase or that business may have in granting such increases will be considerably mitigated if both groups can count on a fiscal policy that in effect guarantees full employment regardless of what happens to the price level.

THE CONTROL OF MARKET POWER

Market power is the ability to make prices and quantities different from what they would be under competitive conditions. The presence of such power necessarily means a departure from competition, and is therefore a problem in an economy which values competition. Market power also may impair other values, although in a less evident way, and so present other problems for policy to manage. A firm has market power if by its own action it can change the prices of what it sells or buys or prevent them from changing, and a union has market power if it can raise wages or prevent them from falling.

Most firms have some power over the market in which they operate. No actual market conforms to the idea of perfect competition in economic theory, because that idea is an analytical device and not a descriptive statement. No firm has absolute power over price, because no product has a completely inelastic demand at all prices. About the power of unions there is less agreement. Some economists believe their power in labor markets is greater than that of firms in product markets, while others believe it is not. The disagreement may in time be removed by the empirical studies of union behavior, especially of its effect on wages.

Market power at the present time presents more problems than it did in the past, and the control of it is a more complex endeavor. At one time (and not very long ago) the standard case against market power —or monopoly—consisted of two arguments. It was contended that monopoly reduces the efficiency with which resources are used by preventing them from moving from competitive industries where their productivity is low to monopolistic industries where it is higher. Hence, the total income of the economy is less than it could be. It also was contended that monopoly increases the inequality of the distribution of income: by charging higher than competitive prices, thereby increasing the income of the owners of the monopolistic industries relative to that of others, and by increasing the size of firms relative to the size of the industry, thereby making the distribution of wealth more unequal.

The arguments are as valid as they ever were, but they no longer comprise the total case. Today, economists want to know what is the effect of market power on the entire price level, not just on individual prices, and what is its effect on growth, that is, on changes in income from year to year and not just on the income of any one year. The problem of market power now has four aspects; and policy, if it were perfect, would serve four purposes. It would be conducive to an equitable distribution of wealth and income, would make aggregate income as large as possible, would help to increase it at an appropriate rate each year, and would aid in stabilizing the price level. At the risk of being obvious, we wish to say that no perfect policy has yet come forward. The imperfections do not come from the fairly simple fact that there is no suitable means of securing any one of the separate purposes. There is the more troublesome problem that the purposes may not be entirely consistent with each other, and we may have either to decide which shall be sacrificed for which or (what is more difficult) to decide how much of one should be sacrificed for how much of another.

The Meaning and Limits of Competition

Before these decisions can be made, we must be clear about what market power means. To say that it means a departure from competition is, in the United States, more than a factual statement. It implies a problem for policy, because competition here is a value or a means to values. Yet, as J. M. Clark explains, it is a value we are not as willing to practice as to praise. American economists want competition between firms in such areas as large scale manufacturing, and between industries in such areas as transportation. But they do not want it in agriculture, and about merchandising they are ambiguous. They do not believe that workers should compete as strenuously for jobs as firms should for sales, but that nevertheless there should be more competition in labor markets than there now is.

There are reasons why opinion about competition is complex. One is that the theory of competition is not an entirely certain guide to understanding actual competition and to formulating a policy to foster it. Another is that competition does not produce all the results we want for an economy. Theory states that what a competitive firm does is determined entirely by the market and can have no effect on it. The implication is that a firm is not competitive if what it does has an effect on other firms. The ability of a firm to affect others is market power. If a policy for controlling market power were derived from the theory of competition, that policy would outlaw all behavior by a firm that affected other firms. Such a policy would be mistaken, in Clark's view, because market power may be temporary and it may produce desirable results. It is more helpful, he states, to think of competition as rivalry among firms, with each trying to secure an advantage over others or reacting to avoid disadvantage. As one firm offers its buyers a lower price or improved quality or some other inducement, the other firms must respond with inducements of their own; and as they do, the advantage of the first is neutralized. Actual competition is therefore neutralizing behavior. There usually is a lag between the initial inducement and the responses, giving the initiator temporary market power. Yet it does not imperil competition but is a part of it.

Competition is desirable, according to Clark, because it promotes efficiency, lowers prices, and fosters growth. It also enlarges opportunity, mobility, and freedom. A competitive economy permits an expression of the competitive impulses that, he believes, are common to most people. But they have other values and impulses as well, and a competitive economy is not consistent with them. People want security and want to identify themselves with others. Clark believes that a policy for market power should try "to superimpose competitive incentives and fluidities on an underlying structure of group solidarity and security."

Market Power, Growth, and Price Stability

The incentives are more likely to be present in an industry with a large number of firms. But they may be present also in one with only a few, according to James S. Duesenberry. Each of the few firms may be able to increase its profits by doing things that increase the efficiency of the economy—such as cutting costs—but it also is able to increase profits by doing things that reduce efficiency—such as engaging in collusion. While the incentives for efficiency can operate in a concentrated industry, they do not operate as surely or as forcefully. Yet there are advantages to the economy in having large firms. They can better afford efficient research, are more likely to make it pay, and can make better use of its results. In this way, they foster growth.

The implication seems to be that we must choose between competition with static efficiency and concentration with growth. But actually, we need not. There is a third market structure, which Duesenberry calls concentration with fringe competition. It is an industry with a few large firms surrounded by a number of small but tough and aggressive firms. They can initiate changes that increase efficiency, and the large firms must do the same in order to survive.

Market power is also important for its effect on the price level, especially when inflationary forces are operating. What that effect is depends on where the forces originate. If they come from an increase in aggregate spending, firms with market power are not likely to raise their prices as much as competitive prices rise. That is because large firms prefer stable prices, do not want to incur the ill will of customers and the government, and do not want to give unions a reason to ask for higher wages. Competitive firms, on the other hand, do not have these choices. If inflation comes from rising costs, such as higher wages, firms with market power are more likely than those without it to raise prices. Competitive firms, in order to survive, must resist higher costs. In a concentrated industry with a competitive fringe, the large firms are likely to resist inflation that comes from rising aggregate demand, and the small firms will have to also; while inflation that comes from rising costs will be resisted by the smaller firms, and the larger will have to also. So again, this particular structure seems to yield the best of both concentration and competition.

Monopoly, Innovation, and Competition

It is usual to ask whether different market structures cause different rates of growth and to define structure by the characteristics of a market at a particular time. Neither is done by Joseph A. Schumpeter, and some novel results emerge. Structure is what a market is like over a long period, he states, and it then is usually more competitive than in the short run. A firm may have power over the market; but in time, it will be challenged by another, its power being taken from it, or reduced, or retained, depending on how it responds by challenges on its own. They consist of improvements in the product, of more efficient methods of production, or of organization; or the challenges can arise outside the economy in changes of population, tastes, and technology, or of social and political institutions. The successive challenges and responses—and the consequent changes in market structure—are what Schumpeter calls the process of creative destruction. It is creative in replacing old forms of consumption and production with new and better forms. It is destructive in removing positions of power and in making them transitory.

Creative destruction is a part of growth, because growth consists not only of increasing the quantity of output and capital of familiar kinds but also of improving it. Growth alters the structure of markets and makes them more competitive. Over the long period a firm is likely to have less power than at the moment of its zenith, and the entire market is likely to perform better. The idea has still another bearing on competition. The rivalry among a few large firms, each seeking to take power from the others, can yield product improvements that reduce the costs of firms in other industries and make them more competitive. Schumpeter's idea of creative destruction resembles Clark's idea of competition as neutralizing behavior, but applies to a longer period of time. The ideas of both imply that policy which seeks to enforce competition must be inclusive enough to allow numerous forms of rivalry and must judge performance over the long rather than the short period.

Alternative Policies for Market Power

How best to control market power is the question to which the analysis of it leads. There are, in principle, three answers. The government can put firms and unions under the control of the market by enforcing competition, or it can regulate them itself, or it can make them a part of the state. According to Harold M. Levinson and Otto Eckstein, in product markets it should rely most on enforcing competition. (In labor markets, power should be controlled in other ways.) That requires increasing the size of the Antitrust Division, empowering it to require firms to notify it of an intention to merge, and to subpoena records in civil cases. Congress should review the work of federal agencies that regulate industries exempt from anti-trust laws, and the Federal Reserve System should do the same in banking, so that regulation is made as consistent as possible with an otherwise competitive system. Congress should also try to prevent parallel action. That consists of firms independently acting in a way that produces the same result that would be produced by explicit collusion. The remedy may be to declare parallel action a presumptive violation of the Sherman Act if the firms have more than a specified share of the market.

Levinson and Eckstein do not believe it desirable or effective for the government to urge those with market power to use it in the public interest. Nor do they believe the government should regulate that power. They do believe there is a value in an annual conference of business, labor, and government leaders to consider the state of the economy and so be able to make informed decisions about prices and wages. When serious inflation threatens, the government might go further, the authors state, and intervene by the President's appointing a board to study the facts of wage and price decisions and to make specific recommendations.

Controlling the market power of unions is more difficult than controlling that of firms. Although nearly everyone believes in some control, there is much disagreement about which union practices are to be controlled, how it is to be done, and who is to do it. There are two issues here: Do unions have market power; and if so, what is its effect? If they do have power, should they be controlled in the same way as firms?

The Monopoly Power of Unions

The principle of comparing alternative returns is used by Henry C. Simons to ascertain the market power of unions. He states that a wage is monopolistic if it is greater than the worker could receive in an alternative employment. A union is a monopoly if, by restricting the number of workers who can enter a labor market or by other artificial means, it prevents wages from falling. Simons contends that employers have little power over wages and that in the absence of unions, wages would be competitively determined. By forcing wages up, unions cause a misallocation of resources, including unnecessarily low investment, the loss being borne by unionists as well as others, although in smaller amount. Less productive workers are forced out of employment or into low-paying jobs, the effect being to increase inequality. Unemployment, however, can be averted by continuous inflation.

Unions also have political consequences. As organized producer groups—syndicates—they recognize no limits to their power except those imposed by other organized groups. The contests for power among them create political disorder which can have only two issues: the imposition of a power greater than all of them in the form of a giant state or the elimi-

nation of the contesting groups by the enforcement of competition. Simons proposes that unions be treated like other monopolies and subjected
to the anti-trust laws.

The Nature and Limits of Union Power

Edward S. Mason presents a much different view of unionism. They
are monopolies, he states; but the more important questions are where
their power comes from, how much they have, and what limits should
be put on it. It depends on how well they control the supply and demand for labor and the technical conditions that set the number of jobs,
on the elasticity of demand for the product made by organized workers,
and on how well-informed unions are about such matters and how effectively they use their information. Mason does not believe it is useful to
think of unions as being analogous to pure monopolies in product markets. Unions cannot control and sell the supply of labor in the way a firm
can market its output. If they resemble anything in product markets, it is
a loosely organized cartel with limited objectives.

The amount of power unions have is usually judged by the difference between union and non-union wages. But, as Mason states, there is
no conclusive evidence that union wages are higher. He suggests that
their power be estimated by comparing what they actually do with what
they would have to do in order to control a market completely. Their
power is, by definition, a limit on competition in labor markets. But the
limit is not always a serious one; and when it is, it does not always work
to the advantage of the union. Hence, the market power of unions is
less important than their opponents—and they themselves—usually believe it to be.

It is not always unimportant, however, and a policy for controlling
it is necessary. Mason finds the customary standards for labor policy un-
satisfactory. One cannot, he states, allow unions to do what they choose,
subject only to the condition that they do it peacefully. That can lead to
a dangerous contest between big unions and big business. Nor can they
be allowed whatever power is necessary in order to give them bargaining
equality with employers, because that rule is impractical. Nor can unions
be allowed to do whatever they choose so long as they do not interfere
in the product market, because their action necessarily affects that market. What, then, should the standard be? The values held by union members may conflict with those held by others; and the reconciliation, Mason
states, must be done by political process. What is hopeful is that it may
possibly be done without jeopardizing either competition or unionism in
any serious way.

The Control of Market Power: A Summary Statement

Market power is the ability to influence prices or wages. It is power
over the market rather than control *by* it, and hence is the opposite of

competition. It is a problem because it affects total income and growth, the stability of prices, and the distribution of income and wealth. But the effect is not always an undesirable one. In the short period a firm with market power can provoke its rivals to increase efficiency, and total income then will rise. In longer periods, market power can be favorable to innovation and so will promote growth. Its effect on price stability is determined by where destabilizing forces originate. Just what the effects are of power in product markets depends on their structure, particularly on the size distribution of firms. The effects in labor markets depend both on the power of the union and on the characteristics of the market for the product made by the organized workers. The problem usually is quite different in the long than in the short run and usually is less serious.

It does not, however, carry its own remedy. That must be the work of policy, and policy can take three forms. The government can force firms and workers to act competitively or it can regulate them or it can make them a part of the state. The competitive solution is the favored one in this country, but its application is limited. It is not favored in all markets or in any one at all times. It must not conflict with institutions that provide security and group solidarity. Where the competitive solution is used, it must be based on standards that are more operational than those now available in economics and in law. In labor markets, the appropriate policy is much less clear. There is less agreement about the extent of power, about the standards for controlling it, and whether or not the competitive solution should be applied in the same way as in product markets.

PART 3

Inequality

Editorial Introduction

THE PROBLEM OF INEQUALITY

Equality as a social goal has its origins in the belief in the dignity of man. If men are created equal, why should some of them enjoy superior opportunities and larger incomes? Yet there is another common belief: It is that people should be rewarded according to their contribution—that a man's labor is his own and all that it yields belongs to him. Out of this conflict has come a series of policy compromises, with each generation balancing the gains from individualism and from equality to arrive at a set of policies which serve both the goal of "to each according to his need" and the goal of "to each according to his contribution."

The mixed economies of the west are constantly experimenting with means of re-distributing income, hoping to keep the advantages of individualism while ameliorating their effect on the distribution of income. The social security systems, particularly those of the Scandinavian countries, take money from one group and give it to another. In the United States, the public support of education is a massive effort to reduce inequality. Progressive taxation, combined with government expenditures on social products, represents another attack on inequality. The unanswered question in all of these efforts is how far they can go without compromising both the effectiveness of the price mechanism as a means of allocating resources and individual initiative as a source of economic growth.

Inequality is a deceptively simple problem. The facts seem clear. So do the causes and the remedies. Actually, none are. This section, therefore, begins with a statement of the facts by Emanuel T. Weiler, and the reader will note that they are not unambiguous and that each of them must be examined in relation to the others. The facts do clearly show the existence of poverty in the U.S. Robert J. Lampman explains the kinds of poverty, how they probably are affected by economic growth, and what can be done to hasten their disappearance.

What it is that determines the distribution of income and indeed the meaning of income itself are neither of them as simple and straightforward as they are usually made out to be. What they are and how they relate to individual power are explained by Frank H. Knight, and the reader will find the essay worth all of the effort it requires. The alternative methods of reducing inequality are explained by Allan G. B. Fisher:

175

those that go to the root of the problem (the radical methods) and those that modify its effect (the direct methods). Of the radical methods, the most important is education. It is investment in human beings, it can reduce inequality and foster growth, and it is explained by Theodore W. Schultz.

12. THE DISTRIBUTION OF INCOME IN THE UNITED STATES, 1959*

Emanuel T. Weiler

SYNOPSIS

1. The poorest 20 per cent of all families had about 5 per cent and the richest 20 per cent about 45 per cent of all personal income in 1959.

2. However, the figures exaggerate inequality because: (*a*) Over a period of time, there is less inequality than in one year. (*b*) The distribution of income per person is less unequal than the distribution by families. (*c*) When account is taken of the occupational costs of high income families, their net income is less above other incomes than their gross income is. (*d*) Low incomes are received more often than not by persons living in areas where the cost of living is low, while high incomes more often are earned and spent in high living cost areas. (*e*) The figures ignore the effect of government payments and tax collections which together raise the lower incomes and reduce the higher.

3. Although these corrections reduce the amount of inequality, they do not eliminate it. There is a significant number of persons who are poor throughout their life because of race, deficient education, personal misfortune, disability, and kind of occupation.

4. The richest groups receive income mainly from working, although property income is a larger proportion of their total income than it is of others.

5. The distribution of property income is more unequal than that of labor income, although at least one fourth of all units have a net worth of $5,000 or more. However, the distribution of property is less important than the distribution of labor skills, talents, and earning power, because about four fifths of the national income is wages and salaries.

6. Between 1913 and 1948 the income of the richest 1 per cent increased less than the income of the lower 99 per cent, and the difference between the per capita income of the two groups was reduced by one half.

The United States, it is sometimes charged, is characterized by "poverty in the midst of plenty," with the "rich getting richer and the poor getting poorer." To prove their point, those who make these alle-

* Adapted by permission from *The Economic System: An Analysis of the Flow of Economic Life*, (New York: Macmillan, 1952), from pp. 791–99.

gations frequently cite income distribution figures such as are reproduced in Table 1.

Using the figures in this table, they might argue that about one out of seven families in 1959 had annual income of less than $2,000 and about one third of the families had income of less than $4,000. Or they might argue that while the seventh of the families with incomes of less than $2,000 received only 2 per cent of the nation's personal income, the seventh receiving income of $10,000 and over received about 37 per cent

TABLE 1

PERCENTAGE DISTRIBUTION OF CONSUMER UNITS AND THEIR INCOME BY FAMILY INCOME
LEVEL, 1947, 1955, AND 1959.

	Consumer Units			Aggregate Family Personal Income		
	1959	1955	1947	1959	1955	1947
Under $ 2,000..........	14	16	25	2	3	7
$ 2,000–$ 3,999..........	21	25	38	10	14	28
4,000– 5,999..........	23	26	20	18	23	24
6,000– 7,999..........	18	16	9	19	20	14
8,000– 9,999..........	10	7	3	14	11	7
10,000– 14,999..........	9	6	3	16	12	8
15,000 and over..........	5	4	2	21	17	12
Total...............	100	100	100	100	100	100

SOURCE: Selma Goldsmith, "Size Distribution of Personal Income, 1956–1959," *Survey of Current Business*, April 1960. These figures are based on annual surveys of family income made by the Census Bureau, Federal Reserve Board, and Survey Research Center of the University of Michigan. Consumer units are defined as combined groups of families and unattached individuals. Later, we shall use census figures on "families" which are defined as units of two or more persons related by blood, marriage, or adoption and residing together. "Unattached individuals" are persons other than institutional inmates who are not living with any relative.

of the total. They might also argue that while the percentage receiving less than $2,000 has been reduced by about a third in the twelve years from 1947 to 1959, there still is a large number of families living in poverty, despite a 60 per cent increase in average family income during this period.

Are these figures correct? The answer is that to the best of our knowledge, they are correct. Each year a new study is made, and each year the results fit into the same pattern. What is more, different groups have made the same studies for the same years, and their findings have been consistent.

Does it follow, then, that the U.S. is in fact a country in which there are a few rich families getting large incomes and many poor families struggling for subsistence? The answer is that these figures have to be interpreted with care before they can be used to throw light on the distribution of income in the U.S. It has been said of astronomy that it consists largely of making corrections (for atmospheric conditions, etc.) to the original observations because uncorrected data would lead to misleading conclusions. And so it is in the use of income distribution figures. Unless used with care, they can be misleading. In the paragraphs that follow, we shall use data from the 1959 survey of consumer income conducted by the Bureau of the Census to shed light on the figures cited above.

Correction: Shifting between Income Classes

Suppose we were to think of the distribution of income as being like a great apartment house with as many different floors as there are income classes. We could then think of all the families and unrelated individuals (in place of spending units) having an annual income of $0 to $999 as living on the first floor, of those having an income of $1,000 to $1,999 as living on the second floor, and so on to the top floor, which would be occupied by those having an annual income of $10,000 or more.

Now, if each family stayed on the same floor throughout its life, we could say that an annual distribution (of the type we have been considering) would represent accurately the distribution of lifetime incomes. Those in the lower income groups would continue to be poor, and those in the upper income groups would continue to be rich. Indeed, we could go further: We could then talk about *the* lower third or *the* upper third of the income recipients as if they consisted of the same people.

But if families moved from year to year to different floors, an annual income distribution would not necessarily reflect the way lifetime incomes were distributed. Suppose that people have small incomes when they are young, large incomes in middle age, and small incomes when they are old. Or suppose that some people were employed in establishments where they were paid high wages when they were working but where the work was unsteady. They would then be paid high incomes in some years and low incomes in others. Even though lifetime incomes were equal, the annual distribution of income would indicate inequalities. It would show that some people were getting low incomes (the young, the old, and the unemployed) and others were getting high incomes. Annual figures, unless supplemented by other data, can be misleading.

How much shifting between income classes occurs? We cannot answer this with a precise figure. We do know that about four out of every ten spending units reported that their 1958 incomes were higher than their 1957 incomes, about two out of every ten reported that their 1958 incomes were lower than their 1957 incomes, and the remaining four out of ten reported that their incomes did not change significantly.[1] We also know that in 1954 about a half of those in the lowest income class were in a higher income class the year before and that about a fifth of

---

[1] *Federal Reserve Bulletin*, July 1959, p. 702.

those in the highest income class had been in a lower income class the year before.[2] This suggests that there is considerable shifting between income classes. Consider the reasons.

Shifting Due to Age and Family Formation or Dissolution

The first and probably the most important is that people are paid less when they are young, more in middle age, and less again when they retire. Your attention is directed to Table 2, showing the median incomes

TABLE 2

AGE OF HEAD AND MEDIAN INCOMES OF FAMILIES AND UNRELATED
INDIVIDUALS IN 1959

Age of Head	Median Income	
	Families	Unrelated Individuals
14–24..........................	$3,865	$1,481
25–34..........................	5,524	3,284
35–44..........................	6,141	2,828
45–54..........................	6,137	2,621
55–64..........................	5,439	1,861
65 and over.....................	2,831	1,006
All ages....................	5,417	1,556

SOURCE: *Current Population Reports: Consumer Income Series*, P–60, No. 35, Bureau of the Census, January 5, 1961, p. 6.

of families and unrelated individuals classified by age groups. (The median is the middle item in an array of items arranged by size.) You will note that the median income of families whose head was between 14 and 24 years old was 3,865, while the median income of families whose head was between 45 and 54 years old was about $2,200 more. The *age-income* relationship was about the same for unrelated individuals, except that the peak was in the 25–34-year group. Unrelated individuals, you will note, received much less income than families in all age brackets.

Shifting between income classes also occurs because of family formation and dissolution and changes in the number of earners in a family. Initially, let us suppose that two young people, John and Mary, are earning $1,500 each but are living at home. Their incomes will be added to the incomes of their parents, thus putting their families in the middle or upper income classes. Then suppose that both John and Mary leave home. The incomes of their families will shrink and will appear in the lower part of the income distribution. If John and Mary are then married and Mary continues to work, a new family will be formed; their combined income may put them in the middle part of the income distribution. When Mary quits her job to raise a family, their income will fall, although

[2] *Ibid.*, March 1955, p. 231.

by this time John may be earning more. In time, their children may go to work and augment the family's income. Finally, when the children have left home and John is too old to work, their income is likely again to be small.

Also Due to Multiple Workers per Family

We know that family income is closely related to the number of earners in a family. Table 3 shows the median incomes of families and

TABLE 3

MEDIAN INCOMES OF UNRELATED INDIVIDUALS AND FAMILIES
WITH SPECIFIED NUMBER OF PERSONS

Number of Persons	Median Income
Unrelated individual	$1,801
2	4,701
3	5,963
4	6,355
5	6,439
6	6,036
7 or more	5,945

SOURCE: See Table 2.

unrelated individuals with specified numbers of earners. You will see that the larger the number of earners, the higher the median income.

And to Fluctuating Incomes

Some incomes show more year-to-year variations than others. Salaried workers' incomes are fairly steady. Workers employed in the construction trades are likely to have high incomes in some years and low incomes in others. Farmers, too, have fluctuating incomes. Heads of small businesses, real estate brokers, salesmen dependent on commissions, and lawyers are likely in one year to be in the upper part of the income distribution and in the next in a lower part. Even if the average money incomes of all families over, say, a ten-year period were the same, the year-to-year distribution of income would show considerable inequality because of fluctuations in annual income.

And to Part-Year Incomes

The movement of workers in and out of the labor force also introduces a bias. People who work only part of a year, like college graduates who get jobs in July, are likely to show up in the lower part of the income distribution, even though their annual rate of pay is quite high. Deaths during the year also account for the reporting of part-year incomes (and part-year incomes are likely to be near the bottom of the distribution). The labor force is constantly changing, with people entering and people leaving it. It has been estimated that during 1958 an average of 3 million persons entered the labor force each month and nearly as many left it, showing that there would be included in the distribution of incomes a considerable number of part-year incomes.

Shifting between income classes makes it difficult to interpret the annual distribution of income. To what extent do they reflect year-to-year changes in income due to such factors as (1) the age-income cycle, (2) family formation and dissolution and changes in the number of earners per family, (3) fluctuating incomes, and (4) the entry into and exodus of workers from the labor force? The answer is that we do not know. We do know that the factors are important. We know that even if lifetime incomes were equal, the annual distributions would show considerable inequality.

Correction: Per Capita Distribution of Income Not Shown

Another correction is that the larger families, until the family exceeds five persons, tend to have larger incomes. Table 4 shows the me-

TABLE 4

MEDIAN INCOMES OF FAMILIES AND UNRELATED INDIVIDUALS
WITH SPECIFIED NUMBER OF EARNERS—1959

	Median Incomes	
Number of Earners	Families	Unrelated Individuals
None	$1,682	$ 784
1	4,976	2,654
2	6,269	
3 or more	7,814	
All	5,417	1,556

SOURCE: See Table 2.

dian incomes of unrelated individuals and families with specified numbers of persons. You will note that the median income of unrelated individuals was about $1,800 in 1959 and the median incomes of five-person families was about $6,400. The generalization does not hold for the very large families: Families of six or more had smaller median incomes than five-person families. This tendency for income to increase with the size of the family reflects a number of factors. We have already seen in Table 2 that income tends to rise with age for those 55 and under. Then, too, as is apparent from Table 4, the families with multiple workers tend to have larger incomes.

Correction: Occupational and Educational Costs Not Shown

The higher incomes go to the persons who must spend more time and money acquiring skills. Table 5 shows the median incomes of families classified by the occupation of the head of the family. You will note that the median incomes in Group A are markedly higher than those in

TABLE 5

MEDIAN INCOMES OF FAMILIES, CLASSIFIED BY OCCUPATION OF HEAD, 1959

Group A:
Professional workers	$8,132
Managers, officials, and proprietors (except farm)	7,517
Sales workers	6,655
Craftsmen, foremen, and kindred workers	6,324
Clerical and kindred workers	5,978

Group B:
Service workers, except private households	4,594
Laborers, except farm and mine	4,259
Farmers and farm managers	2,423
Farm laborers and foremen	2,035
Private household workers	1,625

SOURCE: See Table 2.

Group B. You will also note that Group A occupations typically require more years of preparation than do Group B occupations. To make Group A incomes strictly comparable to Group B occupations, we should deduct an allowance for what might be called the "cost of investment in skills." Were both groups to get the same annual incomes, those in Group A—the occupations requiring more preparation—would be at a disadvantage: They or their families would get no return for financing their education and apprenticeship.

Also interesting in this connection is the relation between investment in education and family income. Table 6 shows the median incomes

TABLE 6

MEDIAN INCOMES OF ONE-EARNER FAMILIES, BY EDUCATION OF HEAD, IN 1956

Educational Attainment	*Median Income*
Less than 8 years	$2,310
8 years	3,366
High school—4 years	5,457
College—1–3 years	5,299
College—4 years or more	7,059

SOURCE: *Consumer Population Reports: Consumer Income Series*, P–60, No. 27, April 1959.

for one-earner families with heads classified by educational attainment. You will note that in 1956 the high school graduate was making about $150 a month more than the person who had quit school after completing the eighth grade. You will also note that the college graduate was making about $150 a month more than the person who had finished high school, but who had not gone on to college. Other factors also influence these incomes. Presumably, the persons who had the diligence and other personal qualifications to complete a block of schooling also had other qualifications sought by employers. But the return to the investment in education is also involved.

Correction: Income Distribution Figures Ignore Differences in Costs of Living

Were we to use income distribution figures for welfare purposes, we should also have to consider the differences in the costs of living of the various income classes. We could take account of certain obvious differences. The cost of living in cities is larger than in the country, and median incomes of urban families are larger than those of rural families. In 1959, as is clear from Table 7, the median income of urban families was about $5,800, while the median incomes of rural non-farm and rural farm families was about $5,400 and $3,000, respectively. Corrected for differences in the costs of living, the difference between urban and rural

TABLE 7

MEDIAN INCOMES OF FAMILIES AND UNRELATED INDIVIDUALS, CLASSIFIED BY SIZE OF COMMUNITY

Size of Community	Median Income
Urbanized areas:	
1,000,000 and over	$6,366
250,000 to 1,000,000	5,732
Under 250,000	5,350
Towns not urbanized:	
25,000 and over	5,348
All urban	5,755
Rural—non-farm	5,361
Rural—farm	2,800

SOURCE: See Table 2.

incomes would be much less marked, although urban incomes would probably still be higher than rural incomes. Then, too, the upper income classes tend to have certain expenses or financial obligations associated with their jobs not borne by the lower income classes: They must do more entertaining, belong to more clubs, contribute more to charitable organizations, and so on. Were account taken of these differences in financial obligations associated with differences in income, the inequalities of income would be less marked.

Correction: Redistribution via Government Taxes and Benefits Not Shown

Another correction is necessitated by taxes and governmental benefits. The income distribution figures we have been considering do contain transfer payments, such as unemployment benefits, old-age pensions, and the like. They do not, however, show effects of taxes on the distribution of income. Nor do they show the effects of governmental benefits other than transfer payments. The income distribution figures we have been considering exaggerate the inequalities of income. Measured after taxes and benefits, we would find the income of the nation to be more equally distributed than before taxes and benefits.

To appraise the way federal, state, and local governments affect the distribution of income, we would have to consider the effect of both taxes and benefits on the various income classes. This is not easy to do. We would have to make estimates of the percentage of each tax—and there are many taxes—paid by each income class. Then we would have to consider the distribution of benefits—and there are many of them also— between income classes. Once we had allocated taxes and benefits, we could make a new estimate of the real income going to each of the income classes. The available evidence suggests that the tax structure of the U.S. is progressive and that the benefit structure is regressive—so that, on balance, government appears to take from the rich and give to the poor. You are referred to Table 8, prepared by Dr. John H. Adler, for

TABLE 8

REDISTRIBUTION OF INCOME THROUGH FEDERAL, STATE, AND LOCAL TAXES AND BENEFITS, 1946–47*

Income Class	Total Income, Including Government Transfer Payments in Millions	Taxes as a Percentage of Income	Benefits as a Percentage of Income	Redistributed Income as a Percentage of Original Income
$0– $ 999	$ 5,632	19.6%	93.0%	173.4%
1,000– 1,999	20,940	15.1	37.5	122.4
2,000– 2,999	33,073	17.3	28.4	111.1
3,000– 3,999	34,320	17.7	24.3	106.6
4,000– 4,999	23,038	22.9	21.4	98.5
5,000– 7,499	31,431	24.2	16.9	92.6
7,500 and over	56,635	36.3	14.9	78.6
Total	$205,069	24.2%	24.2%	100.0%

* SOURCE: John H. Adler, "The Fiscal System, the Distribution of Income, and Public Welfare." Reprinted by permission of Prentice-Hall, Inc., from *Fiscal Policies and the American Economy*, ed. Kenyon E. Poole (New York: Prentice-Hall, Inc., 1951), pp. 412 and 418.

the fiscal year 1946–47. While the estimates in this table are no doubt tentative, and while they apply to the immediate post-war period, they do indicate a considerable amount of redistribution via taxes and benefits. The rise in prices and hence in money incomes has more than offset adjustments in tax rates since 1947, probably leaving the pattern of redistribution about the same as indicated in this table. You will see that after taxes and benefits the lowest income class would have about 75 per cent more income and the highest income class about 20 per cent less.

Corrections Summarized

The corrections come, then, from (1) the year-to-year shifts between income classes as a result of the age-income cycle, family formation and dissolution, multiple workers, part-year workers, and so forth; (2) family size; (3) occupational costs; (4) costs of living; and (5) governmental taxes and benefits. They make it difficult to interpret the usual income distribution statistics.

Who Are the American Poor?

Granted that the uncorrected figures are misleading and that the distribution of lifetime incomes after taxes would show much less inequality, is it not true that there is still "poverty in the midst of plenty"? The answer is, probably, yes: There are many families (although we are not in a position to say how many) and single individuals whose average lifetime incomes are below $2,000 a year (to pick an arbitrary dividing line). Who are they? Are their low incomes due to the malfunctioning of the economy, or are their low incomes due to other causes? Consider the groups whose average incomes are low.

1. Non-Whites. The median income of non-white families, largely Negro families, is much lower than the median income of white families. In 1959, white families and individuals received a median income of $5,643, while non-white families and individuals received a median income of $2,917. While about 11 per cent of the white families (including unrelated individuals) received less than $2,000 per year, 36 per cent of the non-white families were below this figure.

2. Broken Families. The incomes of broken families are lower than the incomes of normal families. In 1959 the median income of normal families was about $5,600, while the median income of families headed by a woman, with the husband dead, disabled, or missing, was half this figure. This means that three eighths of the 4.5 million broken families, whether due to death, divorce, desertion, or disability, had annual incomes of less than $2,000.

3. Disabled. It has been estimated that about 4.5 million persons, exclusive of the very young and the aged, are disabled at one time. Many are only temporarily out of the labor force, but between a third and a half are permanently unemployed. There are few data available to indicate their median incomes, but fragmentary information indicates that their incomes tend to be below $2,000.

4. Unmarried Women. The incomes of women workers are much lower than those of men. When the husband and wife both work, the lower wage rate typically paid women does not lead to poverty. But in 1959, there were about 6.5 million women workers living alone. The median income of urban women workers was about $1,300 in 1959, compared to the median income of male workers of about $4,000.

5. Subsistence Farmers. There are large differences in the incomes of farm families. Those farmers using modern methods to till fertile soils have incomes well above the poverty level. But many families live on subsistence farms and earn only a meager living. In 1959, a fairly prosperous year, 1.1 million farm families, many of them large, had incomes of less than $2,000. Many were Negroes living on share-crop land in the south.

6. Educational Deficiencies. About two thirds of the families with incomes of less than $2,000 were headed, in 1957, by persons with no education past the eighth grade. In the population as a whole, 45 per cent of the families were headed by persons with this little education—indicating that the educational deficiencies of the head greatly increased the probability that the family will have low lifetime average income.

7. Old Age. Finally, we have already seen that unrelated individual families headed by persons over 65 years of age tend to have low incomes. The median income of these groups tends to be about half as large as the median income for the nation as a whole. Some of this poverty does not represent low lifetime average incomes. Indeed, many of the older persons have paid for their homes and other consumer durable goods and have savings they can use to offset their low incomes; and in a sense, their apparent poverty is illusory. But at the same time, a substantial number of the older persons have, through low lifetime earnings, misfortune, or lack of providence, failed to prepare for old age, and their poverty is real.

In answer to the question, "Who are the American poor?" we can say that in 1959 they consisted of (1) minority groups to whom many of the better-paying jobs are closed by reason of social prejudice, (2) broken families in which the wife has had to become the breadwinner, (3) the families struck by chronic illnesses and permanent disabilities, (4) women who never marry, (5) subsistence farmers, (6) families headed by persons who have gone no further than grammar school, and (7) older persons who for one reason or another have not accumulated the means to finance their declining years. In many cases, poor families fit into a number of these categories, as a Negro share-cropper in the south would.

Where Do Those in the Upper Income Groups Get Their Income?

Those in the upper income groups, it is sometimes argued, are primarily "coupon clippers" depending on income from investments to maintain their preferred position. It is true that incomes from property are less equally distributed than are incomes from wages and salaries. But the bulk of those in the upper income groups depend on wages and salaries and self-employment income, and not on income from investments, for the major part of their income. In 1950, about 56 per cent of the spending units receiving $7,500 or more (and hence in the upper 6 per cent of the income distribution) received no income from interest, dividends, trust funds, and royalties. About 84 per cent received less than $1,000 from these sources. In the same year, 73 per cent of those in the $7,500 or more income class received no income from rent, and 90 per cent received less than $1,000 from this source. While it is true that the rich typically receive more interest, dividends, and rent than the poor, it is also true that the poor receive more pensions and allowances than the rich. In large part, then, the inequalities in the distribution of incomes are due to inequalities in the distribution of wages, salaries, and self-employment income. And this is what we should expect, since about four fifths of the personal income consists of wages, salaries, and self-employment income.

Such information as we have on the distribution of individual wealth also supports these findings.[3] In early 1950, about 40 per cent of all spending units had a net worth—assets owned less debts owed—of $5,000 or more. About a quarter of those receiving less than $1,000 per year reported a net worth of $5,000 or more, thus indicating that they had once been in a higher income group. At the same time, about a fifth of those receiving $5,000 or more per year had a net worth of less than $5,000, thus indicating that they were either disinclined to save or had not been in the upper income classes long enough to accumulate substantial holdings of assets. Even though some of those in the lower income classes had sizable holdings of assets and some of those in the upper income classes had very limited holdings of assets, the distribution of assets was more unequal than the distribution of incomes, thus reinforcing the finding that income from the sale of personal services is a much more important source of income than income from the sale of property services.

Are the Poor Getting Poorer and the Rich Richer?

Is there any evidence that the poor are getting poorer and the rich richer, as is so often alleged? The answer, based on the work of Professor Simon Kuznets, is that the reverse is true. The poor and the middle income groups, taken together, are getting richer, and the rich are getting poorer, measured in annual income.[4] The top 1 per cent of the income recipients received 16 per cent of the total income before taxes in 1913, 14 per cent in 1920, 17 per cent in 1929, 13 per cent in 1939, and 9 per cent in 1948.[5]

Professor Geoffrey Moore, in commenting on the Kuznets findings, writes:

Taking the period as a whole, the average per capita income for the upper groups rose from $5,700 in 1913 to $12,500 in 1948, a gain of $6,800; the average for the lower 99 per cent rose from about $300 to $1,300, a gain of only $1,000. Nevertheless, relatively the gain was much larger for the lower group; that is, the mass of the population. Their per capita income in 1948 was more than four times what it was in 1913, whereas the income of the upper group had little more than doubled. Moreover, a doubling of dollar income

[3] *Federal Reserve Bulletin*, December 1950, p. 1588.

[4] Simon Kuznets, *Shares of Upper Income Groups in Income and Saving*, Occasional Paper 35 (National Bureau of Economic Research, Inc., 1950). See also Geoffrey H. Moore, "Secular Changes in the Distribution of Income," *The American Economic Review*, May 1952, pp. 527–34.

[5] Moore, *op. cit.*, p. 531.

in this period does not appear to have been enough even to maintain real income; the BLS consumers' price in 1948 was two and a half times its 1913 level. In real terms, if this index is representative, the "poor" grew richer and the "rich" poorer. Certainly there was a shift towards a smaller relative difference: the individuals in the upper 1 per cent had an average per capita income nearly twenty times as large as the average in the lower 99 per cent in 1913 and only ten times as large in 1948.[6]

The increase in income taxes, which take more out of the incomes of the rich than the poor, also has contributed to the shift toward greater equality. From 1929 to 1948 "the advance in taxes paid by the upper 1 per cent was sufficient to convert a rise of 21 per cent in per capita income before taxes to a decline of 9 per cent after taxes."[7] Drastic though the

TABLE 9

PERCENTAGE OF AGGREGATE WAGE OR SALARY INCOME (BEFORE
TAXES) RECEIVED BY EACH FIFTH OF WAGE AND SALARY RECIPIENTS,
RANKED BY INCOME, FOR THE UNITED STATES:
1939 TO 1952

Year	Highest Fifth	Fourth Fifth	Middle Fifth	Second Fifth	Lowest Fifth
1939......	49.3	23.9	15.0	8.4	3.4
1945......	43.9	25.7	17.4	10.1	2.9
1947......	44.3	24.7	17.8	10.3	2.9
1948......	42.8	25.5	18.6	10.2	2.9
1949......	42.4	26.2	18.7	10.1	2.6
1950......	44.0	25.7	18.3	9.7	2.3
1951......	41.6	25.9	18.9	10.6	3.0
1952......	42.9	25.7	18.5	10.2	2.7

SOURCE: "Income of Persons in the United States: 1952," *Current Population Reports*, Series P–60, No. 14, Bureau of the Census, 1953, p. 22.

changes were, the rise in income taxes accounted for no more than a fourth of the decline in inequality of income after taxes. Most of the decline was due to changes in factor prices and from one type of occupation to another. The wage rates of the lower paid urban workers and farm workers rose more than the wage rates of the higher paid workers and professional people from 1920 to 1948. Meanwhile, interest rates and rents declined. The major part of the shift toward greater equality seems to have been due to the functioning of the price mechanism.

The post-war figures showing the distribution of wage and salary income also support these conclusions. (See Table 9.) During the thirteen-year period 1939–52 the share of the aggregate wage and salary income received by the upper fifth of the recipients declined from about 49 per cent to about 43 per cent. During the same period the middle three fifths of the recipients received a larger share of the total. The share re-

[6] *Ibid.*, pp. 529–31.
[7] *Ibid.*, p. 541.

ceived by the lowest fifth declined, indicating that the gain in equality during this period was due to a redistribution of income between the upper and middle income groups. And this is what we would expect, since we have already seen that poverty is largely due to the lack of earning power.

Conclusion

We must conclude, then, that the uncorrected figures are grossly misleading. The nation's income is not as unequally distributed as the figures at first indicate. Moreover, recent studies have shown that the functioning of the economy over the last quarter of a century has tended to reduce inequalities in income. While there is still "poverty in the midst of plenty" in the U.S., it tends to be due to specific causes, such as race prejudice, broken homes, disabled workers, educational deficiencies, unequal opportunities for female workers, and the immobility of farm workers, rather than to the alleged tendency in a capitalistic economy for the rich to become richer and the poor poorer.

13. THE FUTURE OF THE LOW INCOME PROBLEM*

Robert J. Lampman

SYNOPSIS

1. If trends continue, within a generation only 10 per cent of consumer units will have incomes under $2,000, compared to 20 per cent now.

2. J. K. Galbraith has argued that poverty today is different from that of the past, there being more island and case poverty (caused by immobility and personal handicaps, respectively) and less generalized poverty. Unlike the last, the first two are not likely to be reduced by economic growth.

3. It would appear that the facts are not consistent with Galbraith's conclusions. Migration from the farms has substantially reduced the island poverty in agriculture, and the case poverty associated with insufficient education has been alleviated.

4. Nonetheless, some groups do not benefit by economic growth, namely, families headed by women or by older people, and the disabled.

5. However, other groups, mainly Negro and large families, do benefit, and they comprise about two thirds of the groups with incomes under $2,000.

6. The percentage of total income going to the lowest fifth of families has not increased. We have been overcoming poverty more by raising the general level of income than by redistributing it.

7. There is evidence that the distribution of income and wealth is less unequal now than earlier, but the changes have occurred in the top half of the distribution.

8. A program to hasten the reduction of poverty would include a high rate of growth, greater opportunity for labor to move into higher income areas and for capital to move where greater productivity is needed, enlarged private assistance to eliminate the causes of poverty, more opportunity for retraining and education of the poor, together with greater social security, elimination of racial discrimination, and better education of children of the poor.

Projections for the Future of Numbers in Low Income Status

One way to estimate what will happen in the future is to project the experience of the past. The percentage of all persons in low income

* Reprinted from *The Low Income Population and Economic Growth* (No. 12), prepared for the Joint Economic Committee (Washington, D.C.: U.S. Government Printing Office, 1960), pp. 24–32.

status fell from 26 per cent in 1947 to 19 per cent in 1957. A similar fall in the succeeding ten-year period could result in a 14 per cent figure in 1967 and 11.5 per cent in 1977.

A different way to project past experience is to refer to changing levels of average income. The group of consumer units with income under $2,000 in 1957 was roughly the lowest one fifth of consumer units. The median income of this group was $1,465.[1] Projecting past rates of growth in that median puts it at $2,000 within thirty years from 1957. This would mean 10 per cent would have incomes under $2,000. A still different way to refer to experience is to call upon differences within the U.S. New York, one of our wealthiest states, had a per capita income 23 per cent higher than that of the U.S. in 1956—16 per cent of consumer units in New York had incomes under $2,000, while 23 per cent of the nation's consumer units had incomes that low. This would suggest that when the national per capita income rises 23 per cent, the national consumer units with under $2,000 of income would fall to 16 per cent. This might be expected within fifteen years from 1957.

These several methods of projection all yield approximately the same answer. By 1977–87, we would expect about 10 per cent of the population to be in low income status as compared to about 20 per cent now. These methods all assume that the process of growth and development of the economy will be as effective in reducing poverty in the future as it has been in the past.

Will Reduction of Poverty Be Slower in the Future?

It is argued by some that the future rate of change will be slower because present-day poverty is qualitatively different from the poverty found in earlier days. Whereas old-time poverty was general, the new poverty, it is alleged, is specific and associated with a limited number of groups. These groups are in turn said to be those which are not likely to be improved by a generalized type of national economic growth because they are "immune" to such progress. This immunity arises out of personal characteristics or an environment which insulates them from opportunities for earning higher income.

Professor John Kenneth Galbraith, in his book, *The Affluent Society*, writes of three kinds of poverty—namely, generalized poverty, island poverty, and case poverty. The first is the kind which yields to the process of economic growth in which the average productivity of labor is increased. The latter two, he asserts, are the principal kinds of poverty remaining in the U.S. today, and these are caused respectively by (1) inability or unwillingness to move out of low income areas or regions, and (2) ". . . some quality peculiar to the individual or family involved—mental deficiency, bad health, inability to adapt to the discipline of mod-

---

[1] It is interesting that increasing the average wage by $1,000 for 12 million units would only amount to $12 billion, or less than 5 per cent of the national income.

ern economic life, excessive procreation, alcohol, insufficient education, or perhaps a combination of several of these handicaps. . . ."[2]

Galbraith states that in the early 1950's, "The hard core of the very poor was declining, but not with great rapidity."[3] Further, he argues:

> The most certain thing about modern poverty is that it is not efficiently remedied by a general and tolerably well-distributed advance in income. Case poverty is not remedied because the specific individual inadequacy precludes employment and participation in the general advance. Insular poverty is not directly alleviated because the advance does not necessarily remove the specific frustrations of environment to which the people of these islands are subject. This is not to say it has no effect. Secure job opportunities elsewhere, a concomitant of industrial advance, work against the homing instinct. And so, even more directly, does the spread of industrialization. The appearance of industry in parts of the Tennessee Valley area has had a strong remedial effect on the insular poverty of those areas. But it remains that advance cannot improve the position of those who, by virtue of self or environment, cannot participate or are not reached.[4]

Evaluation of the Galbraith Thesis

We submit that Professor Galbraith has misinterpreted the low income problem in several ways. In the first place, our finding that the percentage of the total population in low income status fell from 26 to 19 per cent in ten years would seem to contradict, or at least not to confirm, his statement that "the hard core of the very poor was declining but not with great rapidity." In the second place, with regard to island poverty, the record suggests that movement was a leading factor working for the reduction of numbers in low income status. For instance, the number of rural farm families with under $2,000 income (1947 dollars) actually fell during the 1947–57 period from 3.3 to 2.4 million because of movement off the farm. Similarly, there were great shifts among occupations and industries which contributed to the reduction of low income units. Third, with respect to "case poverty," it should be pointed out that some of these characteristics of persons are moderated over time. For example, average educational attainment levels will rise in future years simply because younger people presently have better education than older people. Hence, as the current generation of old people passes from the scene, the percentage of persons with low educational attainment will fall.[5]

[2] *The Affluent Society*, p. 325.

[3] *Ibid.*, p. 324.

[4] *Ibid.*, p. 327.

[5] Between 1950 and 1957 the median educational level increased one full year. "Most of the improvement was due to the fact that persons reaching adult ages . . . had been better educated than their parents and grandparents, many of whom were leaving the population through death" (*Current Population Reports*, No. 77, p. 20). ". . . The educational level of young persons considerably exceeds that of older workers. In March, 1957, 18 to 34 year old labor force members had completed over 12 years of school (on the average) as compared with only 9½ among middle-aged workers and 8½ years among those over 65" (No. 73, p. 50).

Whether the reduction of low incomes due to such improved levels of educational attainment should be attributed to economic growth or to social policy is a semantic problem. It is part of the adaptation to new and higher skill occupations and hard to separate from the whole process of growth. This process, in turn, pulls people into areas where educational opportunities are greater. This is not to deny that increased educational opportunity will not in itself contribute to the rate of growth.

Fourth, we would take exception to Professor Galbraith's list of causal variables since he excludes the important ones of age, color, and sex of head.

Suppose now we take up the question as Galbraith implicitly, if quite awkwardly, puts it. Which groups among the contemporary low income population are likely to diminish in the future, assuming a rising average level of income; and which ones are not likely to diminish? Do the answers to these questions suggest a slowing-down of the rate at which we have been reducing the share of the population in low income status?

What Groups Do Not Benefit by Economic Growth?

It is true, of course, that some groups will not benefit from the process of growth in the same ways that others do. Those who are outside of the labor force tend to have an immunity to growth. (Here we are ignoring property income. Those who hold equity claims will tend to share in the growth of the economy thereby, even though they may be out of the labor force.) Those who cannot or will not move or change occupation, or who cannot otherwise adapt to changes in the economic environment, will run a greater risk of low income status at some time in their lives than will others. In general, consumer unit heads who are least mobile and adaptable are seen to have a handicapping characteristic such as old age, non-white color, female sex, or low education. Old age is a handicap in the sense that older people typically have greater difficulty in getting re-employed than do younger people and in getting into new and rapidly growing occupations and industries. (In one sense, the aged group may be said to participate in growth if average old-age insurance and assistance payments rise with average income of the community. To the extent that the formula for computing old-age, survivors', and disability insurance benefits accounts for rising average monthly wages, those benefits will rise over time.) Non-white color is a handicap to the extent that color is a bar to higher income occupations. Female sex also operates to limit occupational choice and even, to some extent, geographic mobility. Low education limits mobility and adaptability by barring entry to and perhaps limiting knowledge of and motivation toward new occupational possibilities.

It is significant that the contemporary low income population is disproportionately made up of persons having one or more of these characteristics. In the discussion of "Who are the low income people?" above, it was concluded that while about 50 per cent of the total population have one or more of the four handicapping characteristics, 70 per cent of the low income population of 32.2 million persons had one or more of these characteristics.

There is plausibility in the idea that each one of these characteristics has causal significance in determining the numbers in low income status. As we have already mentioned, one can confidently predict that the numbers having low educational attainment will fall and from that deduce that the percentage of persons having low income will fall.

While low educational attainment will diminish in importance over time, the other three "handicapping" characteristics of old age, non-white status, and female headship will not. It was estimated that while only 20 per cent of the total population have one or more of these three characteristics, 50 per cent of the low income population have one or more of them. Old-aged persons, who now make up 8.5 per cent of the population, will be 9.5 per cent of the population within twenty years. The importance of families with female heads changed very little, and that of non-whites increased slightly between 1947 and 1957. Since none of these groups will diminish in importance in the future, the question then is: Will economic growth reduce the incidence of low income within the old-aged group, the non-white group, and the female head group?

With regard to the old-aged group, it is striking that the 1947–57 period saw virtually no reduction in the incidence of low income. Therefore, on the basis of past experience, we may identify this group as one that is "immune" to economic growth.

The female head group shows little change in incidence of low income over the recent ten-year period. In 1947, 46 per cent of the families headed by women had incomes under $2,000; in 1957, 38 per cent had incomes that low. (This compares with percentages of 25 and 15 for all families.) The failure of this rate to fall very much is doubtless due in part to the lower labor force participation of women heads. The latter in turn is associated with the higher proportion of aged among women and also with the fact that many of the younger women family heads have children to care for in the home. Hence, units with aged or female heads would seem to be identifiable as having "immunity" to economic growth.

With respect to the third "handicapping" characteristic of non-white color the picture is different. Non-white persons have shared and no doubt will continue to share in the processes of growth, i.e., higher earnings on present jobs, shifts into higher paying employments, and increasing numbers of earners per family. Between 1947 and 1957 the percentage of non-white families with income under $2,000 fell from 62 to 36. The comparable percentages for white families were 24 and 12. Hence, non-whites are not immune to economic growth.

There are two other causal variables which should be accounted for in an appraisal of the "hard-core" nature of contemporary poverty. Some persons are disqualified from full participation in economic life because of physical or mental or emotional difficulties. Data are inadequate in this area, but some evidence is provided by a study of the prevalence of long term disability. On the average day in 1954, it is estimated, there were 5.3 million persons with a disability lasting more than six months.[6] Of these persons, 2.2 million were 65 years of age and over, and 2.9 million were aged 14 through 64 years. Of the latter group, perhaps over half would have been in the labor force if they were not disabled. How many of these disabled persons were in fact low income persons is not known. Nor is there any good way of estimating the importance of other related "personal" causes of low income, such as anti-social habits and attitudes or what Galbraith refers to as "inability to adapt to the discipline of modern economic life." But we can say that disability does result in an important degree of immunity to economic growth.

Then there is the cause Galbraith refers to as "excessive procreation." While only one fourth of the total population is found in families of six or over, one third of low income persons are in such large families. Looking to the future, it does not seem that very large families will increase as a proportion of all families, so this will not in itself cause an increasing share of all persons to be found in poverty. Further, large families are not immune to economic growth. In 1947–57 the incidence of low income fell just about as much for large families as it did for all families.

By way of summary of this discussion, Table 1 is presented. It serves to underline the idea that several factors are working against reduction, via economic growth, of the size of the low income population. These are old age, disability, and female headship. As persons having one or more of these three characteristics come to be a larger part of the remaining low income population, it would seem probable, unless offsetting factors work in the other direction, that subsequent general growth would do proportionally less to reduce the number of low incomes. However, the composition of the low income population changes very gradually, and it does not appear that the characteristics of old age, disability, and female head, which now account for about one third of the group, will account for as much as one half of the low income population for many decades. Further, it should be recalled that these same factors had to be overcome in the 1947–57 period and, in fact, were overcome by economic growth and social policy.

[6] *Social Security Bulletin*, June 1955, pp. 20–21.

TABLE 1

IMPORTANCE OF SELECTED CHARACTERISTICS IN FUTURE DETERMINATION OF LOW INCOME

Characteristic	Percentage of Low Income Population Having This Characteristic, 1957	Will Numbers with Characteristic Increase or Decrease with Time?	Degree to Which Persons Having This Characteristic Are Immune to Economic Growth
Low education	67	Decrease	High
Old age	25	Increase	High
Non-white color	20	Increase	Low
Female headship	25	No change	High
Disability	*	No change	High
Large family size	33	No change	Low

* Not available.

From this investigation of Galbraith's claim that "modern poverty" will not yield to general economic growth, we conclude, for reasons quite different from his, that there is limited validity to his claim and that the future rate of reduction in the percentage of the population in low income status will tend to be slightly slower than in the recent past.

Low Income Group's Share of Income

All of this thinking about extending past experience assumes that the lowest income groups will not increase their share of total income. The only way for their income to rise faster than the income of the rest of the population is, of course, for them to get a larger share of the total. To make faster progress in eliminating poverty than the above calculations suggest would require such an increasing share of income.

The lowest fifth of income receivers now get 5 per cent of all income. It received 5 per cent of income in 1947. It apparently received about 5 per cent of income in the 1930's. In general, we have been overcoming poverty more by raising the general level of income than by increasing the share of the bottom fifth at the expense of upper income groups.

Changes in Economic Inequality

There is evidence for the belief that the distribution of income and wealth are less unequal now than in earlier days. But the greatest part of the change seems to have occurred within the top half of the distribution. That is, the top group's share has been lowered at the expense of a gain in share by the upper middle group. Two leading studies into changes of the size distribution of income have established that a noteworthy fall in the income share of the top 5 per cent of income receivers took place between 1939 and 1945. Professor Simon Kuznets found that the top 5 per cent of persons' share of disposable income fell from 27 to 18 per cent, or well over three tenths.[7] Dr. Selma Goldsmith and colleagues found a similar fall in the share of the top 5 per cent of families in personal income.[8]

A study by the present author into the share of wealth held by top wealth holders offers the finding of a gradual loss of share of wealth by top-ranking persons and families.[9] Between 1922 and 1953 the top 2 per cent of families' (ranked by size of wealth holdings) share of wealth fell from 33 per cent to 29 per cent. However, it is found that the concentration of wealth is increasing in the years since 1949. The lesser fall in inequality of wealth than in inequality of personal income calls attention to the fact that disposable personal income has changed more in its distribution that has national income.[10] Apparently, the top income group has been able to offset its losses on income account to some extent by gaining on capital account. This has occurred in large part through corporate saving.

Government Policy toward Inequality

These changes toward less inequality of wealth and income are apparently in some part due to the workings of "the market" and private responses to economic changes. They are also in some part due to government policies and programs. Principal among these government activities are education, health, and welfare service programs which improve the ability and motivation of poorer persons to compete in the market place. Also important are tax and money transfer programs. Several studies have been made which confirm the fact that over-all taxing and spending policies of federal, state, and local governments operate to diminish the inequality which arises in the market.[11] Comparison of the over-all tax systems of pre-war and post-war years suggests that the historical trend is, while very moderate indeed, toward a more equalizing tax system. In both the depression period and the post-war period the combined tax burden of the lowest fifth of consumer units has been heavy, about 19 per cent of their income going to taxes of all kinds in 1938–39 and about 25 per cent in 1948–54. The tax burden on the top fifth in the

---

[7] *Shares of Upper Income Groups in Income and Savings* (National Bureau of Economic Research, Inc., 1953), p. xxxvi.

[8] Selma F. Goldsmith, George Jassi, Hyman Kaitz, and Maurice Liebenberg, "Size Distribution of Income since the Mid-thirties," *The Review of Economics and Statistics*, February 1954.

[9] *The Review of Economics and Statistics*, November 1959.

[10] Selma F. Goldsmith, "Change in the Size Distribution of Income," *The American Economic Review*, May 1957, p. 506.

[11] See Richard A. Musgrave, "The Incidence of the Tax Structure and Its Effects on Consumption," *Federal Tax Policy for Economic Growth and Stability*, Joint Economic Committee, November 9, 1955, pp. 96–117. Also John H. Adler, chap. viii in *Fiscal Policies and the American Economy*, ed. Kenyon Poole (New York, 1951).

same period moved from 22 per cent to 34 per cent. The relative tax burden on the lowest fifth of consumer units is perhaps over-stated in the more recent period because of the structural changes in the composition of that group. In short, the lower fifth of units has come to contain a smaller part of the total population with less of the nation's total of consumer needs than it once did.

In the same period, government transfer payments have become a more important part of the income of the lowest fifth of consumer units. According to the Survey of Consumer Finances, about half the spending units in the lowest fifth received some transfer payments, and transfer payments were 40 per cent of the total money income of the group.[12] It seems clear that both the composition of this group and its share of income would be very different were it not for the tremendous growth of social insurance and related programs in recent years. In the last thirty years, government transfer payments have increased from 1 per cent to 5 per cent of national income.

Possibilities for the Future

It is concluded, then, that progress in the elimination of poverty has been made with only a minor change in the share of income and wealth in the hands of the lowest fifth of consumer units. Continuation of past policies and past experience for another generation (thirty years) or so may be expected to result in the virtual elimination of what may reasonably (by present standards) be thought of as low income status. On the other hand, a relaxation in the rate of economic growth or a drop in the rate of increase of government transfer programs could make the goal of eliminating poverty recede into the far distant future. A higher rate of growth in average incomes, or a more aggressive government policy aimed at increasing the post-tax, post-transfer share of total income received by the lowest fifth of consumer units (or a combination of both growth and wide sharing) could lead to this result in less than a generation.

A Program to Hasten the Reduction of Poverty

The primary motive power in reducing the share of the total population in low income status has been and should continue to be a vital, progressive private economy yielding increasing average product per worker. Therefore, the basic part of any program directed against poverty must be that of insuring high levels of employment and production. As part of this program, efforts should be made to preserve and expand freedom and opportunities for individuals to move from low income areas and occupations to high income areas and occupations and, conversely, for capital to flow toward the lower income regions of the country. In a

[12] *Federal Reserve Bulletin*, September 1958, p. 1030.

national market free from barriers to such movement, it may be expected that economic self-interest will work as a powerful engine to propel many people out of low income status.

In the discussion above, it was urged, however, that the groups within the low income population vary in susceptibility to or immunity against this process of economic growth. In general, those groups with low labor force participation are quite immune. The groups referred to under this heading are the aged and the family units headed by women. The long run private approaches to reducing the incidence of poverty within these groups are many, including more saving, more private insurance, improved family responsibility, and adaptation of employment opportunities to the needs and limitations of aged persons and women with family responsibilities. Public approaches, on the other hand, include the provision of more education and retraining opportunities and social insurance programs (particularly old-age, survivors', and disability insurance) and public assistance programs (particularly old-age assistance and aid to dependent children). These programs in turn can be associated with guidance and counseling and rehabilitation work aimed at increasing participation in the economic life of the community.

Similarly, increasing public effort should be made to encourage more efficient participation in economic progress by the non-whites in the low income population. Negroes, Indians, and other non-white minorities are often barred or alienated from such participation. Elimination of occupational barriers and especially improved educational opportunities for these groups would seem to be minimum steps in the direction of reducing their disproportionate representation in the low income population.

It has been noted that low income status is particularly marked on farms and more particularly on farms in certain regions of the country. Any program to overcome poverty must make special provision for this group, offering better opportunities to earn a satisfactory living. Such better opportunities may be brought about (1) by encouraging these low income farmers to move elsewhere, (2) by encouraging non-agricultural employers to move their operations into these areas, and (3) by technical and financial aid to improve their farming productivity. Ability and motivation of the next generation of adults in the depressed agricultural communities to achieve greater economic well-being would be improved by a sharply expanded program of education for those currently of school age.

Probably no public program has made and can continue to make so important and fundamental a contribution to the elimination of poverty as free public education. Education offers children a way to rise in occupational status above their parents and hence is a way to break the vicious circle of poverty breeding poverty. About a fifth of the nation's children are being reared in low income status, and it is of critical importance that these children have educational opportunities that are not inferior to the national average. It is, of course, true that there is a tendency for children of low income families to have below average educational opportunity. We would agree with Galbraith that:

> . . . poverty is self-perpetuating because the poorest communities are poorest in the services which would eliminate it. To eliminate poverty efficiently we should invest more than proportionately in the children of the poor community. It is there that high quality schools, strong health services, special provision for nutrition and recreation are most needed to compensate for the very low investment which families are able to make in their own offspring. The effect of educational and related investment in individuals is to enable them to contend more effectively with their environment, to escape it and take up life elsewhere on more or less equal terms with others.[13]

In 1956 the Joint Economic Committee set forth a program for the low income population at substandard levels of living.[14]

In that statement, which is still applicable to the situation today, they concluded that:

> To meet the problems effectively will require the concerted efforts of all segments of our national life—all levels of government working with labor and management and private community groups and organizations. With such coordinated, positive action, we are confident that, in overall terms, the total cost will be low when measured by the positive economic gains which will be generated throughout the total economy and also when measured by the resultant strengthening of the forces which produce an alert, productive, and democratic society.[15]

[13] *The Affluent Society*, pp. 330–31.
[14] 84th Cong., 2d sess., Senate Report 1311.
[15] *Ibid.*, pp. 2, 3.

14. THE DETERMINATION OF JUST WAGES*

Frank H. Knight

SYNOPSIS

1. In deciding what is a just distribution of income, one must separate (*a*) the *facts* of how income is determined from (*b*) the *wishes*, or
non-discussible personal preferences, about how it ought to be distributed,
and from (*c*) the discussible ethical *values* which ought to determine distribution.

2. In its factual aspect, income measures the marginal productivity
of a resource. One can compare the income from different uses of a given
resource and so determine that in which it is most productive. The factual
meaning would be the same in a simple as in a complex economy.

3. In the latter, resources are provided by four specialized groups:
entrepreneurs, workers, lessors, and owners, who may share the uncertainty of economic decisions in seven distinct ways, the most common
being the corporation. In it, entrepreneurs buy, lease, or manage labor
and property resources from workers, lessors, and owners, paying the
latter three groups relatively certain incomes and accepting the responsibility of using resources productively and the consequent relatively uncertain returns.

4. Wages, rent, and interest measure the productivity of labor and
property. If the productivity of a given resource differs among alternative
uses, the difference is profit or loss. However, the efficiency of the economy is greatest only when the productivity is the same in all uses. Therefore, profit or loss denotes a mistaken allocation which, however, is inevitable because of the impossibility of knowing perfectly the present and
future productivities of resources in all uses. All resource owners accept
uncertainty when they choose between employments.

5. The entrepreneurial economy is a device which divides unequally the sharing of uncertainty. Those who want to accept as little as
possible can provide resources as workers and lessors and receive a relatively certain income. Those who are willing to accept uncertainty can
act as entrepreneurs, receive a variable income, and maximize the possibility of profit and loss. The way uncertainty is shared is determined by
the free choice of individuals, and hence the consequent distribution of
income is freely determined.

6. There is an element of profit and loss in all income, including
wages, if resource productivity differs among alternative uses. Wages then

* Reprinted by permission and shortened from *Twentieth Century Economic
Thought*, ed. Glenn Hoover (New York: Philosophical Library, 1950), pp. 470–510.

cannot be distinguished from rent and interest, all three of which can contain profit or loss. Wages are similar to property income also in being produced at a cost and in being the return to a resource which depreciates. The difference between labor and property income is non-economic: Labor cannot be bought and sold (as slaves were) but only hired for a specified period; hence, its earning power cannot be capitalized in order to guarantee its owner a permanent income.

7. The income of an individual depends on the value of the resources he owns, which consist of his labor as well as property. This value is determined by two kinds of decisions freely made: by a decision made at some past time of how much to invest in the resources, and by a current decision of how best to use them.

8. In determining how income ought to be distributed—its *value* aspect—the primary considerations are the preservation of free choice, the determination of which deficiencies of distribution are remediable, the cost of the remedies, and the comparison of the present distribution of income with that of an alternative economic system.

9. Neither an ethical nor a factual distinction can be made between wages and property income, both being the result of free choice affected by knowledge, error, and luck.

10. To distribute income according to need or to merit is impracticable, and to distribute it equally even more so.

11. A market economy creates a much less unequal distribution than is popularly believed, and it provides what alternative economic systems do not, which is the power of free choice.

12. The principal ethical deficiencies of a market economy originate either outside the economy or in two economic conditions which change only slowly: the concentration of power which freedom produces, and the inability of an individual or a generation to alter the conditions which determine power and hence income.

A candid discussion of the problem of just wages should make clear in general terms the ultimate values that are accepted as premises. The present essay accepts and is based upon the world view of modern liberal civilization, specifically the ethics of individual liberty and progress based upon the growth of knowledge and its application to human problems. But these concepts require much interpretation and qualification, some of it involving real or apparent limitations. The central value is freedom—in social life, free association by mutual assent and on terms accepted voluntarily by all parties concerned. But this formula is by no means as simple in application as it sounds in statement. Individual freedom is clearly inseparable from individual responsibility, and any possible social life sets both physical and moral limits to individual independence, for it entails many obligations, both mutual and one-sided. The concept of knowledge, or particularly of science, raises thorny questions with respect to application to problems of human association.

As an introductory word it must suffice to point out that our topic of just wages involves both economic and moral issues. Now, economics deals with wants and their satisfaction, and these things cannot be observed, compared and measured in anything like the way in which the objects of nature are treated by the natural sciences. Even more strikingly, ethics deals with things as they ought to be, in contrast with what they are, with norms rather than even mental facts. Natural science has a clear general objective—to increase the power of man over nature. Nature itself has no interests, to say nothing of rights. But social problems arise out of conflicts of interests and of rights, and differences of opinion about rights. Power of man over man is objectionable; the objective in human relations is accord, not "prediction and control." Such issues must be settled, if they are to be settled and harmony established, by a procedure very different from the testing and verification of theories in science.

This means that we accept the *spirit* of science, the objective and impartial quest of truth; but the scientific *technique* is applicable to human and social data only up to the point of ascertaining facts which are the same for all, and ceases to apply when conflicting interests or ideals come into the picture. There is limited room for science, in any strict meaning, in finding out what the interests are, and little or none in the crucial step of establishing the knowledge of norms by which the merits of opposed desires are weighed and decision reached as how they "ought" to be reconciled, favored or frustrated.

INCOME FORMS IN AN INDIVIDUAL ECONOMY

We now embark on the more "scientific" or quasi-scientific part of our study, the task of explaining what wages are, apart from any question as to what they ought to be. The quotation marks are a reminder that even with "justice" (and moral issues in the broadest sense) left out, wages is an "economic category"; i.e., it is relative to ends, motives, purposes, and to economy of means, and these notions find no place in an objective description of scientifically observable and verifiable facts. Motives are similar to physical forces, or analogous, up to a point, since the latter also are not directly observable. But motives are far less objective still, since forces can be unambiguously inferred from the phenomena to which they give rise, and measured by these, but motives cannot; for we know that purposive action differs from cause-and-effect sequences in being subject in all degrees and many ways to *error*.

Fact, Wish, and Value

We have referred to the "hornet's nest" of problems stirred up by any attempt to give a concrete meaning for the word "justice." The case of "wages" is in fact not very different. This is largely because in the field of human relations men generally are unable or unwilling to make a clear separation between the three kinds of propositions: (*a*) a statement of fact; (*b*) an expression of liking or disliking; and (*c*) a judgment of approval or disapproval, or of "real value." Our inheritance from "primitive" modes of thinking, along with the inherent difficulty of the task, makes this double separation very hard. For example, words like "murder" and "theft" are regularly used in a factual meaning, though they obviously contain a moral judgment; only "wrongful" killing of a human being is murder, and appropriation of goods is not stealing unless they "rightfully"—or at least legally!—"belong" to someone else.

The weather of a crop season may be "good" or "bad," in the sense of favorable or unfavorable to human interests (and we should include the esthetic interest as well as those usually referred to as "crassly" utilitarian), but it is surely not good or bad in a moral sense. The preceding sentences have deliberately brought in categories outside the three (fact, wish and value) formally enumerated—legal as well as moral right and wrong and esthetic values alongside the moral—because these also have to be considered in any complete account of our topic, and its full complexity will still not be covered. The items that make up a "decent" or "necessary" standard of living, or one a human being may claim a "right" to have, derive their value in very large measure from esthetic considerations; and laws have to exist and be enforced, even in cases where they do not seem to do justice, or even (until they can be improved) to be the best general rules that could be drawn.

Still more to the point, "justice," though a very ambiguous term, yet can hardly be stretched to cover the whole field of human rights and duties. The question of just wages raises that of the rightness of the wage or employee-employer relationship itself, and of the economic order of which this relationship is a feature. But this question, and all questions of action, must be considered in explicit comparison with possible alternatives and the pro's and con's of methods for bringing about changes. The further course of the argument will suggest that when both wages and justice are clearly and correctly defined, the expression combining the two words is largely self-contradictory or redundant—that "a wage is a wage," is a fact merely; hence that while "justice" in some ideal sense may call for more or less *income*, just or unjust *wages* has little more meaning than a just or unjust weather.[1]

Finally, it must be kept in mind that judgments about justice and injustice in the abstract, or ideal right, carry no necessary implications for action. There are many "wrongs" that cannot be righted, and more that an attempt to right would lead to greater wrong. It is always a question, how much and at what cost, and whose cost, any condition can be

---

[1] [Wages are a fact, while justice is a value. So long as fact and value are kept separate, the words "just wage" are meaningless because they imply facts can be just or unjust. On the other hand, if fact and value are united, it can only be done by supposing that whatever is, is right. Wages then always would be ideal because they were whatever they were. Then the phrase "just wages" becomes redundant.

The word "income" is here used to describe a return which can be appraised by such ethical standards as justice and not to describe a fact.]

changed by men, or especially by laws and policemen, even if there is general agreement that it ought to be changed if possible.

Crusoe's Economic Problem

A study of social-economic organization needs to proceed step by step. The first essential step is a clear picture of individual economic life, for a free economy is in essentials individualistic—especially in the moral essential that in our liberal culture value is considered to reside in the individual. He is the end, and social order the means, not conversely; and the individual is considered to be in general the best judge of his own good and the means of achieving it. It is in fact advisable to begin with the economic life of an *isolated* individual, the famous hypothetical Robinson Crusoe.

We shall think of a Crusoe who acts rationally to use a given stock of resources to produce the highest standard of living, made up of the "goods and services" he desires, that is to be had from them. The term "resources" is to be taken in the inclusive meaning, to cover all his personal powers (knowledge, skill, technique) as well as external means, whether classed as natural or artificial. It will be convenient to consider all ends to be distinct from action using means, hence to ignore both the play and work aspects of conduct. That is, "consumption" is separated from "production," in contrast with activities which themselves have interest or value. Our economic man Crusoe will look to the future, planning and acting to maintain his standard of living, hence to repair and replace equipment used up or worn out; and we shall assume that he also, like a typical man in our civilization, adds to his productive capacities, including always his own knowledge and skills.

Crusoe's economic problem (the *economic* problem of anyone in any circumstances) is to allocate his resources among different lines of production—forms of goods and services for consumption and forms of additional productive capacity—in such a way as to secure the most satisfactory result. Underlying and conditioning this task are two famous "economic laws." The first is the psychological principle of diminishing utility (or satisfaction); it states the familiar fact that wants for particular goods are satiable, or, in precise quantitiative terms, that as more and more of any one good is consumed, each successive equal increment adds less and less to total satisfaction (until at some point it would add nothing, and then would begin to yield negative satisfaction). In consequence of this principle, an individual gets more satisfaction by spreading a given income among a variety of goods than by spending it all on one. It is a self-evident inference that he gets the *maximum* satisfaction from that apportionment which makes every equal increment of expenditure yield an equal addition to total satisfaction in all uses. If the satisfaction increments are unequal, the total can obviously be increased by shifting some expenditure from any use which yields less to one that yields more.

The second economic law is a technological one, parallel in form: the law of "diminishing returns." It relates to the fact that different kinds of resources are used in combination to produce a single final product. As more of any one resource is applied in any combination, an additional increment adds less to the total (physical) product. A corollary holds: Each *kind* of resource is most economically used if so apportioned among productive organizations that its product increments have *equal value* in all uses.

These principles apply also to the allocation of resources between present consumption and future requirements; and the whole "rigama-role" is merely a definition of "economic behavior." Actual behavior conforms more or less perfectly to this pattern because (*a*) of error, and (*b*) of action from motives which are not realistically described as achieving the greatest quantity of an end with a given quantity of means. E.g., in addition to play, but related to it, we often act from curiosity, to see what the result will be, not to secure a given result or even expecting any result of value.[2]

Income Forms in a Crusoe Economy

From this fact, that means used to achieve ends may be combined in variable proportions, it follows that one may be substituted for another in a definite ratio without changing the total result, and thus their relative effectiveness in production be compared; or, the total product may be divided up, "imputed" to the various resources on the basis of the amount by which a small unit of each alone *increases* the total, if the other "factors" are held constant. The two procedures are equivalent. The important point is that even a Crusoe, to manage his affairs intelligently, must make this division of the product between his personal activities or labor and each and every other resource which he employs. Only in this way can he effect the right apportionment (and combination) of these resources.

Thus arise the two most familiar "shares" into which produced income is divided. In this case, obviously, no moral issue whatever is involved, but only intelligent management, since both personal and property earnings go to the same person. It will also be evident that intelligent management, even on the part of a Crusoe, calls for what amounts to a price system. The solitary producer-consumer would have to know the relative significance to him of every consumption good or service and the relative significance of every productive agent or service in increasing the output of each of the former, and increasing the total in-

---

[2] [Actual behavior is not perfectly efficient, because (*a*) people can be mistaken about what economic returns they want and how best to get them, and (*b*) they sometimes act out of curiosity or for the sake of rivalry itself, as when they buy a product just to see what it is like or look for a better job just for the distinction it brings.]

come.[3] The shares so determined will be called *wages* and *rent*, as they are the earnings respectively of a human being and of a piece of "property." The distinction is based on tradition or "human" interest, not on economic principles, for these are the same in the two cases. Both incomes are the product of a productive agent, separated out of a joint product in the only way in which an effect is ever assigned to a particular cause.

We now have to consider the other two income forms or shares of the familiar classification, i.e., interest and profit. Both arise in connection with the economic subject's provision for the future. The essential fact is the twofold one that *productive instruments wear out*, and are *replaced*, implying the possibility of net increase.

Because productive agents are used up and replaced, and the supply regularly increased, every productive instrument must be viewed as the embodiment of a certain cost or "investment." Under the conditions of a continuing economy, in which the consequences of action are foreseen, this investment cost would be equal both to the total quantity of consumption value sacrificed in the past to create any instrument and to the amount that could be recovered—for consumption or transfer to another form of investment—by failing to provide for its maintenance and replacement.

The ratio between the annual net rental (after providing for perpetuity) and the investment cost is the primary meaning of a *rate of yield of capital*. Its meaning is exactly the same for a Crusoe economy as for any other. Under the "ideal" conditions to which theoretical generalizations must relate, the rent on an agent and the "interest" on the investment in the agent will be identical—merely different ways of looking at the same thing.

The fourth form of income, "profit," arises out of the fact that the economic subject does not have complete foresight of the consequences of his acts. The difference between rent and interest under real conditions is due to the same cause, and is in fact merely a profit (positive or negative).[4] Neither rent nor interest in the ordinary meaning of a pay-

---

[3] [Why Crusoe would have to compute income shares can be illustrated by supposing that in the production of wheat the marginal productivity of his labor (i.e., his wages) is 25 bushels and in oats is 35 bushels, while the marginal productivity of land (i.e., rent) is 15 in wheat and 10 in oats. If wheat and oats were of equal value to him, Crusoe would devote more labor to oats and more land to wheat. The transfer of a unit of labor from wheat to oats would add 10 bushels of grain to his total income, and the opposite transfer of land would add five bushels. Units would be transferred until wages were equal and rents were equal in the production of both products. If Crusoe did not compute wages and rents, he would be unable to use labor and land efficiently.]

[4] [The following illustrates the meaning of *investment cost, annual net rental, rate of yield on capital, interest,* and *profit*. Suppose that Crusoe devotes a certain amount of labor and materials to building a house and that the resources, if they had been used to prepare land for cultivation, would have yielded 20 bushels of

ment by one party to another would, of course, exist in a Crusoe economy, but a Crusoe who managed his affairs scientifically would have to "impute" them and take them into account in his managerial decisions. Crusoe would have to estimate the yield of concrete agents in their actual use, and compare this with what they "would" yield in any other employment; and he would further have to estimate the difference between the actual rate of yield of the investment in each agent and what might be had by converting this into some other form.

If there is a difference in favor of any particular agent, it means, of course, that other agents should be allowed to disappear and be replaced by that form until the return is equalized. Any such difference, either way, between what is actually secured by any operation and what might have been (and presumptively may be) secured through some alternative use of the same ultimate resources (capital) is the meaning of profit. It arises out of *error*, and if the errors are unbiased, the profit differential will be exactly as likely to be negative as to be positive; on the average and in the long run, gains and losses will be equal and aggregate profit zero. The question of bias in errors is one to be investigated; there is reason to believe a bias exists toward more "risky" activities, hence a negative profit on the whole.

ENTREPRENEURIAL ECONOMY AND INCOME DIFFERENTIATION

In turning to consider economic life in organized society, we continue to take an analytical-descriptive point of view, ignoring moral is-

---

wheat annually, or if they had been used directly to acquire consumer goods (as by hunting), would have yielded a value equivalent to 400 bushels of wheat. Suppose, finally, that when the house is completed, Crusoe finds it yields him a satisfaction equivalent to that provided by 25 bushels of wheat annually.

The annual net rental value of the house is 25; the investment cost of the house is 400; the rate of yield is 25/400, or 6.25 per cent, which is also the *actual* rate of interest. However, if the resources had been invested in developing wheat land (which would have cost 400), the rent would have been 20 annually; the rate of yield of capital, or the alternative rate of interest, would have been 20/400, or 5 per cent. The profit on investment in the house is the difference between 6.25 per cent and 5 per cent, or 1.25 per cent.

In these circumstances, Crusoe would devote more of his resources to providing shelter and less to wheat, causing the satisfaction derived from shelter to decline relative to that from wheat until the two yields were equal.

It will be noted that Crusoe's profit from investment in shelter is possible only because shelter yields a greater return than wheat and that the difference would not have occurred if he had invested less in wheat (making it more valuable) and more in shelter (making it less valuable) *before* the present investment was made. The fact that he did not indicates a mistaken allocation of resources. Because of ignorance or error, he invested too much in wheat and too little in shelter.

It will be noted also that Crusoe's profit from investment in shelter is in part attributable to the use of his labor as well as of other resources, that his wages are higher than they would have been as a wheat farmer, and therefore that there is an element of profit in his wages.]

sues. The fundamental principle of the organization is *freedom* in the relations between its responsible individual members.

Our primary concern here is with *economic* association, or *cooperation*, or acting in some sort of unity for the sake of increased efficiency, i.e., in order that each party may secure a larger product from the use of his various resources. The ends and the means are not (we assume) affected by the association, but the procedure is different, in that activity is *specialized*. Economic cooperation rests on the principle of common or mutual advantage, hence of *voluntary exchange* which leads at once to the institution of the *market*.

Certain requisites for theoretical analysis need to be set forth explicitly. Our analysis must envisage only the market, and the "ideal" or "perfect" market—in a theoretical, not a moral, sense. A market is simply a provision for each person to exchange with whoever offers or accepts the terms most favorable to himself. Since this applies to all, the result is maximum advantage to all.

The main warning that is called for is that analysis of the market organization takes individual wants for the things finally received and consumed as ultimate. It is not concerned with *why* the things are wanted, beyond the abstract reason of yielding some quantity of "satisfaction." All this has nothing to do with the mechanics of organization, and is ignored in its study. In particular, "competition," in the psychological meaning of rivalry, has nothing to do with the market, and is largely absent from ordinary buying and selling. There is little "higgling and bargaining"; conduct is controlled by matter-of-fact comparison of advantage among alternatives open.

In short, exchange is viewed simply as a method of production; it is a fallacy to think of it in terms of "surpluses," since these exist because they are produced for the purpose of exchange. If party A exchanges good *a* with party B for good *b*, this is merely an indirect method by which A and B use their resources to produce goods *b* and *a*. It will be done only because of increased efficiency, to the individuals concerned; each gets either a larger amount of the same good by exchange (because specialization increases efficiency) or, in the extreme case, obtains a good that he could not produce at all by direct use of his own resources.

Distinctive Features of an Entrepreneurial Economy

At some points, the fact that an individual lives in society affects his economic problem in ways that cannot finally be ignored without making the argument too unrealistic. The fact of specialization makes the mechanical difference that, insofar as it is complete, the individual does not apportion his own resources among the various modes of use (products, goods, and services) but devotes them all to a single one, that in which they yield the largest return. It is only on the social scale that apportionment is effected. But the social order makes available a far greater variety of final products among which consumption is apportioned. This suggests another mechanical detail, which is of very great importance in reality: Large-scale markets have to be carried on not through literal "exchange" but through purchase and sale for money. Important disturbances arise due to the use of money, because of speculation as to changes in its value. But these must be considered separately; our more general analysis will assume that money is used but that it is exclusively in practice what it is in theory, a mere intermediary, facilitating the exchange of goods and services (never hoarded).

The intervention of money divides the individual's economic problem into two steps or stages. The first is to secure the largest possible "income" in money (by putting one's resources to the most profitable use); the second is to buy the maximum "total satisfaction" with this income, by apportioning it in the best way among the goods and services available in the economy as a whole. But we must not forget that the individual is interested in the future and apportions some part of his income to the purchase of production goods, causing the economy to apportion a corresponding fraction of its resources to making net additions to its productive equipment.

We now have to make a sweeping qualification in our characterization of the theoretical model of the free-market organization as implied in referring to it as an "exchange" system. The individual typically gets his income by selling some *service* or services to one or more *business enterprises*. It is these units which do the producing and which alone own and sell products. This further subdivision of functions makes it practically inevitable that the individual laborer, or owner-supplier of any resource-service, shall receive his share of the product in the form of money.

But the form of employer-employee relation that is actually familiar results from a different specialization than this technical one. The organized productive unit "might" be a producers' cooperative, a pure or a representative democracy, in which all the participants, including any who performed managerial functions along with other "workers" and property owners, would "work together," and distribute the product, in any manner on which they might agree. They could even divide up the physical product and sell it individually. The relation of the member to the group might or might not take the form of employee and employer. It is well to think of these possibilities, even though they seem fanciful. For, in fact, practically every conceivable form of production unit has been tried, and that which has become typical must be regarded as resulting from a rough sort of natural selection of the fittest in a struggle for existence; those who do not like the individual businessman in small concerns, and the business corporation in large ones, are and have been free to try anything else and find out from experience why other forms are not generally capable of holding their own in a social milieu where the parties concerned are free to choose.

That which has in general survived to become typical is a large unit in the "corporate" form, with a fairly distinct—but far from complete— separation of the same four functions, with their corresponding forms of income, that we recognized in the Crusoe economy. There is (1) a group of controlling proprietors [or] entrepreneurs (but they also generally supply more or less of both personal and property services to the undertaking); (2) a group supplying primarily personal services (but owning varying blocks in the proprietorship, i.e., voting "stock"); (3) a group of lessors of property; but this has become relatively unimportant in comparison with (4) owners who lend "capital" (money) on various contractual terms. It is imperative to get behind the vagueness and confusion which surrounds these concepts and distinctions, to their real meaning. Perhaps the first offers the greatest difficulty, since the real, "responsible" managers of a business unit are *not* the salaried foremen, superintendents, production managers, who directly give orders, but those who hire these and for whom they act as agents. The real manager group is the owners of the voting common stock. Theirs is the real initiative, and they take the risk of being right or wrong.

One of the worst of the fallacies is the confusion of the entrepreneur and the property owner or "capitalist," which is directly suggested [by] the "capitalist system."[5] The term was popularized by the Marxists to stand for the false idea that the "capitalist" employs and controls the "laborer"; in reality, property owner and laborer are in the same position in the organization; both are hired and in the immediate sense controlled by the entrepreneur. Ultimately, he is himself controlled by market forces called "competition," meaning the sovereignty of consumers and those who supply the productive services, both labor and property; the business must produce what is most in demand and employ the most efficient methods or soon go into bankruptcy. Profit comes only to those most successful in this endeavour, while others incur a loss.

It must be made unmistakably clear that the basic functional specialization in a free economy is that arising between the entrepreneur as ultimate manager (though not in ultimate control) and all other roles in production, and that this specialization is the result of free choice by all parties. The whole arrangement is essentially a mode of cooperation, a form of partnership. To bring out its true character, we may consider a few simplified illustrations, beginning with one in which no property is

[5] [The entrepreneurial function is the making of decisions about what resources the firm should buy, how it should combine them, and what products it should produce and offer for sale. The function is not performed or delegated by any individual whose income is fixed and certain (as labor income usually is) but by those whose income depends on the success of the decision making (that is, the owners of common stock and those to whom they delegate authority).]

involved. If, say, two people are to work together, they must somehow reach agreement as to what is to be done and how, and for dividing between them whatever gain or loss is achieved. But such planning nearly always involves more or less uncertainty;[6] the result may be highly dependent on various details that have to be decided in some particular way, and it may be zero or negative if some decision turns out to be wrong.

Forms of Association among Income Receivers

We must keep in mind that in free society the parties may make any arrangement they please. Where a high degree of uncertainty exists, it is typical for people to disagree—the more so when a large number are involved. One simple way out is for one of the parties to take the responsibility. Either may offer terms to the other: "Do it my way, let me direct operations, and I will give you so and so much, however it turns out, and I will take what is left; and if there isn't enough to give you the amount specified, I will make it up to you." When such a proposition has been accepted, the result is the ordinary wage bargain. And this is just what happens, on a large scale, under market control, in the entrepreneurial economy. In the case of two persons, the active partner (entrepreneur) would presumably work at the task along with the passive one (wage earner); but in a larger and more elaborate unit, he would do nothing but direct and supervise; and in a still more complex situation, he would go farther, delegate the more routine activities of supervision itself to hired agents and use all his own energies in study of the market, of possibilities for improving technique and organization, and in making the major decisions of policy.

The same relationship in the case of entrepreneurship and property may be illustrated by an owner of a one-man farm and a "farmer" without capital means. Their problem is to arrange for the farmer to cultivate the owner's land. Several arrangements are possible. The one that may come first to mind is a lease "on shares"—the simple partnership. But this would call for agreement on operations, and it may be simpler for the farmer to pay a stipulated rent and be free to manage the enterprise as he sees fit—subject to protecting the owner against loss through "mining out" the value of his property. But it would be just as logical to adopt a third arrangement, the inverse of the second; the farm owner may hire the farmer and pay him wages. Or, it may happen (fourthly) that a third party—as entrepreneur—both leases the farm for a rental and hires the farmer for a wage. The important fact is that under "ideal conditions," meaning in substance the absence of uncertainty (hence of difference of opinion), all these arrangements would lead to exactly the same result,

[6] [Uncertainty and "risk" are used by the author to mean the possibility of a future event whose chances of occurrence cannot be predicted and which consequently cannot be insured against, such as the possibility of a change in the value of money.]

both as to the technique of operations and as to the division of the product, and the choice would be a matter of indifference to the parties. (With the exception, that under the condition of universal perfect knowledge and foresight the outside [third] party of the fourth arrangement would have no function to perform, and this scheme becomes meaningless.)

However, under realistic conditions (uncertainty present, and difference in expectations and in operational views and preferences), there is still another possible form of organization, one that is very familiar in practice. The farmer, lacking means to pay for the farm, instead of leasing it for a rental may buy it, borrowing the "money" from the owner, on a note (usually secured by a mortgage). In this case, the one will pay and the other receive "interest," instead of rent. But under ideal conditions, as before, the substance will be the same in all respects and the distinction between the two types of agreement a pure form and a matter of indifference.

The possibilities are still not exhausted. The farmer may borrow the money from a third party to buy the farm (instead of the former owner); or, finally, it is quite possible that a *fourth* party may borrow the money (from the former [third party]) and buy the farm and hire the farmer, for wages, to operate it. This is not very common in connection with farms, but is the most typical procedure in industrial enterprise. The entrepreneur, especially the large corporation, hires the use of (rents) comparatively little property; for the most part the "members" of the company (voting common stockholders) own (have title to) the property used; but it may to any extent be really theirs because it is to any extent pledged or over-pledged to "bondholders" (or other creditors) on all sorts of terms. (The distinction between the owner and creditor position is not sharp, and conditions vary widely from case to case.)

Income and Uncertainty-Bearing

The important fact is that the real differences among all the forms of association, in a free-market economy, center in the distribution of responsibility, i.e., control and uncertainty-bearing. The possibility of "talking sense" about the distribution of income in a free-market economy, in the way either of explaining what happens or of criticizing the result, depends first of all on understanding this division, between those who control operations (directly or through agents) and take the risk, and those who passively furnish productive capacity, in one form or another.

The problem is both more difficult and more important because of three facts. First, the separation is never complete, and the overlapping of functions of the same person varies all the way from nearly pure entrepreneurship to its nearly complete absence. Second, the working of "market competition" constantly *tends* to eliminate entrepreneurship (and the corresponding income, profit—always meaning profit or loss), since men tend to learn the conditions under which they are working. But this process is never carried through because of the *innovations* that are constantly being made, and other changes which cannot be foreseen and allowed for in advance by those affected by them. Third, differences in the role of contingency and in the contingent element in income enter into the forms of contract and into the classification of income forms, producing much confusion, all along the line. We cannot say anything true and relevant about wages, for instance, without understanding the actual relations of the wage receiver to the wage payer, and of both to receivers of other incomes, or income called by other names.[7] But the "profit receiver" (or sufferer of loss) is the payer both of wages and of the income received from "property" under different forms.

Finally, we must note a "methodological" point, a fourth source of difficulty. In consequence of the three facts explained, theoretical analysis must be concerned at its first stage with a hypothetical state of economic society in which the tendency toward complete foresight would be carried to perfection and the function of entrepreneurship, along with its peculiar income, profit, would be eliminated. In particular, economic theory must first discuss the *other* forms of income for the most part *as they would be* in the economy in which entrepreneurship and profit would be absent. (If everyone had complete and accurate foresight of the consequences of action, there would be no occasion for anyone to be directed by anyone else, or have the use of his property directed.) Thus the "theory" of profit and of wages and property incomes is expounded with reference to opposed sets of conditions.

Characteristics of Property Income

We must next give brief attention to the forms of property income, especially to different meanings of the concept of "rent," in relation to "interest" and to "profit," and take note of the difference in the position of a human being and his services. We have previously used the term "rent" to designate the income earned (per unit of time) by any piece of property, and for the payment made to the owner for the service of a piece of property when it is used by a person other than the owner. The identification rests on the assumption of "ideal conditions" just mentioned, in which profit would be absent. In real life, there is a tendency toward equality of rent and actual earnings, the approximation varying from case to case. We have presumably made it clear enough how it comes about that men borrow money and buy property instead of renting it (and lend money instead of buying property and renting it out). The

---

[7] [The income received by an employee is a literal wage only if it is completely independent of the profits of the firm. If he shares in the profits (as a hired manager might), his income is not a literal wage because it contains a contingent return for assuming uncertainty.]

all-important matter is the "risk"—who benefits or suffers from any unforeseen change in the value of the property that is in question; in case of a sale it is the owner-user—"owner" subject to the encumbrance (the lender of the "capital" being somehow made secure). In the case of a farm, in our previous illustration, both forms are familiar, and it is no strain on the imagination to think of them as equivalent alternatives.

It is easy to think of the farm as simply "there," since it has physical features that are nearly unchanging and even as a productive entity it is comparatively stable. But if we turn from a farm to, say, a manufacturing plant, the case is notably different. The stability, the "there-ness" is much less; it does not "come natural" to think of the rent on the property and the interest on its value as different terms for the same reality. An apparent reason for this attitude is the fact that manufacturing plants are not commonly leased for a rental, as we have noted before. But it is of course their "mutability" that underlies this fact, that those who operate them usually "own" them through the medium of borrowed money, if they do not possess the requisite wealth. It is an unreal sort of ownership, since the money lenders can take title if obligations to them are not met. It is essentially more like a lease, and the operator's position, analytically viewed, is more that of an entrepreneur than an owner. He is an entrepreneur in two senses of the word, and receives two forms of profit. Two "responsible decisions" have been made. One covers the commitment of a certain amount of wealth or capital to this particular form; the other is the group of decisions involved in managing the concrete capital instrument so as to create a net income.

The difference in degree between such property as farms and that of which industrial plant is the type has led in the history of economics to a classificatory distinction which is very misleading. The term "rent" has been restricted to income from "natural agents." This might not be serious, if economists had introduced some other term to refer to the rent of other things when they are leased, as they often are. And this term is universally employed in everyday discourse, whether the object in question is a farm, a dwelling, an auto, or a dress suit. What is utterly destructive of clear thinking is the idea that "interest" is subject to any corresponding restriction, that it consists of the earnings of a different class of productive agent—presumably "capital goods." The palpable fact is that the income from any productive agent (with some reservations as to the free laborer—see below) can be viewed at will under either of these forms, whether it is used by the owner or leased to another. It is a "rent" on the agent as a concrete thing, or it is "interest" on the "investment" which the thing represents. Under "ideal conditions," again, the investment would be identical with the historical cost, and also at all times with the amount that could be recovered by "real disinvestment," and further equal to the monetary sale value. All differentiation between these several amounts is due to uncertainty, error, and differences of opinion.

It especially calls for emphasis that "natural agents," typified by agricultural "land," are no special case, except for a difference in degree. They have also all had their historical cost in one form or another (except that any valuable object may be quite accidentally found). In some cases the cost has been less than the present value, but in others it has been vastly more; and there is no reason for believing that on the average, or on the whole, natural agents are at any time worth more than they have cost; indeed, they are almost certainly worth less, if we go back to the "beginning" and include all costs and sacrifices of exploration, pioneering, development, and waiting (quite certainly if we include taxes paid).

In sum, the economic difference between natural agents and capital goods is a relatively great prominence of *profit*—gain or loss—in connection with their *production*. But this is really not at all peculiar to them. If we think of the most highly *artificial* of all capital goods, those of *new kinds*, representing some *innovation*, either the launching of a new product or a new and original process of making one more or less familiar, we find an equal degree of uncertainty, and an equal prominence of profit or loss as a difference between yield or rental value and interest on cost.

Characteristics of Labor Income

We come to the question, more directly germane to our topic, of where the laborer and his income stand in relation to these complex and rather subtle distinctions. The question may be answered briefly by starting from the rather trite, but not therefore trivial, observation that the difference between laborers and "property" is that the laborer is not "property." The essential difference is that "ownership" of the laborer is limited to the natural person himself; it is "inalienable"; this productive agent cannot be bought and sold. As regards other agents, their services are to be had in either of two ways, rental from the owner or outright purchase. But transfer of ownership is excluded in the case of the laborer; his services (labor) are to be had only through lease—and this virtually cancelable at will, by him, since a labor contract can rarely be enforced, and a "long" contract would be quite illegal.

The principle of the sanctity of personal liberty has many implications disadvantageous to the individual whose productive capacity is embodied (his capital invested) chiefly in his own person. It is difficult for him to pledge his future earnings, even with the protection of any practicable insurance. This is a serious handicap in connection with assuming the role of entrepreneur. And (apart from public relief) the accumulation of some assets is virtually the only reliable assurance against distress through loss of earning power during life.

But in the more fundamental relations, "labor power" and "property" are alike. The laborer is a productive agent with the essential attributes of other such agents, i.e., the attributes common to either class are common to both. In particular, both have the essential qualities by which "capital goods" are defined. They are produced at a cost, require constant maintenance at a cost, and they wear out and have to be replaced out of their earnings during service life, if production in the economy is to continue. (And of course, the supply may also be increased, at a cost.) The mere fact that the agent is a human being has little economic significance, as will be apparent from the consideration that in a slave economy it would make no substantial difference.

The important question for the purpose of our discussion is that of freedom of choice of role, and it is especially in connection with this issue that prejudice and sentiment lead public opinion astray. The least reflection on facts known to everyone will make it clear that the way in which an individual comes into possession of the respective forms of productive capacity (property and personal qualities enabling one to render salable services) represent very much the same mixture of sources. The main items in both cases are on the one hand inheritance and luck, and on the other the efforts of the individual himself—in both cases more or less conscientious and intelligently directed. The great difference popularly assumed, from a social-ethical point of view, and made the basis of the familiar opposition of "human rights" to "property rights," cannot be rationally explained. It is of course absurdly obvious that the second expression is a figure of speech, that the rights of "property" (whatever they may be, and its duties also) inhere in its owners as human beings. Search for a more substantial basis for the contrast commonly drawn will probably point to disapproval of inheritance.

But critical reflection will raise doubt as to whether on the whole inheritance, biological and social-cultural, plays a larger role in inequalities (supposedly unearned or undeserved) in income-earning power or opportunity in the form of property owned than in that personal endowment. It is true that the majority of the largest incomes are now derived largely from property; but certainly no "abolition" of private property by political-legal process would give any assurance of a more equal distribution of real income. Such a step would more probably result in a much greater concentration of economic power. Besides investment in education, in the inclusive sense, there are many ways by which persons in a privileged situation will be in a position to secure a similar status for their children (or other heirs). Vast economic differences certainly exist; and they arise only to a limited extent from the free choice of those affected, or from any source likely to be judged to correspond with "merit"; but that fact and its bearing on the subject of just wages must be considered later, when we come to deal with appraisal and policy.

The Role of Choice in Setting Incomes

With respect to what is specifically in question at this point—the *freedom* of choice of roles—it should be clear without more explanation that *taking individuals as they stand*, with whatever means and capacities they actually have, selection among modes of use of *these capacities* is a matter of free agreement between the parties directly concerned, to the extent that the market is free and its organization effective. Entry into the role of wage earner versus that of property owner ("supplier" of one or the other class of productive service) is not at the moment a matter of choice, since one can only sell what one has to sell. The question is the validity of the sharp distinction in the longer view between these classes of productive agents and their services.

We have already shown that if we go back of the conditions at the moment, both labor power and property are the embodiment of pre-existing productive capacity; and the parties in possession of this capacity, at the time, could have chosen to invest it in either the one form or the other. Chance and error may cause nearly any divergence from the normal, but these factors presumably cancel out, and on the average, in a free economy, the individual gets the general rate of return, distorted by the good or bad results of risk *voluntarily assumed*.

Finally, the role of entrepreneur also is a matter of free agreement between all parties to any cooperative production arrangement. Anyone is "free" to hire labor and property service and produce goods, if he can offer terms a bit more attractive than others making similar offers, including under terms the security they are able to give that they will fulfill the agreements they make. Thus, profit, the theoretical antithesis or counterpart to other incomes, is, after all, the payment for a service—that of responsible management; true, it is not measurable with reference to any definite base, but accrues to the enterprise as a whole and falls to those persons who are responsible for its existence and its conduct.

But this means that the income of the entrepreneur is, in the most real and accurate sense of all, a payment corresponding to the actual value of the service he performs. Any positive profit he gets is due to his making productive services yield a result of greater value than do his competitors, whose bids fix the prices he pays; and any negative profit (loss) shows his failure to equal them. The difference in either case measures actual results of his performance. (What relation it bears to the "deserts" of the entrepreneur or of those who supply him with productive services is a question that would call for long discussion.) The explanation of profit, it will be kept in mind, disposes of the difference between rent and interest, and also, in the same connection, takes care of the gains and losses from changes in the capital value of relatively stable forms of property, such as "land" (and its "permanent improvements"). Finally, the theory of profit obviously covers all receipts from invention and successful innovation of every form, and losses arising out of such activities.

Summary of the Factual Aspect

We have now reached the point for a summing up of the main "scientific" part of our study. (1) Every productive resource (laborer or piece of property—ultimately every unit of "capital") will be directed into the use in which it will create the product of greatest value, determined by the choices of willing and able consumers, or saver-investors, as purchasers. (2) Every personal income (consumption plus investment) will exactly measure the value product contributed (added to the social total) by whatever resources that person actually furnishes to production. This implies that every product sells at a price exactly equal to its cost, leaving no profit (as defined by economists, including loss). With perfect foresight in possession of everyone, no "management" in the real sense of deciding and acting in the face of contingencies (of miscalculation or wholly unforeseen events) would be called for. Managers would perform only a routine function and would be paid "wages" only, plus rent (interest) for whatever property services they might also supply (to the same or another productive unit). In this situation, every individual member of the economy will receive the consequences of his own activity.

The first great step by way of bringing this abstract model into closer correspondence with reality is to consider the general effects of "uncertainty"—still under the conditions of a mechanically perfect market. For two reasons—because uncertainty implies differences of opinion, and because men have different emotional-volitional attitudes toward adventure versus security—the presence of uncertainty brings about specialization of the entrepreneur function—assumption of risk and of final direction—as already sufficiently described. "Final" direction here means "immediately final"—it is rather closely controlled even momentarily by the general conditions of the market and is constantly subject to over-ruling; the entrepreneur is forced to give up his role if he does not or cannot adapt his plans to bring what he can get for his product into line with what he must pay for productive services, to meet the competition of other producers. He takes the risks which he is willing to take on terms a little better than those offered by anyone else.

Finally, it must be kept in mind that in a free economy the parties to economic relations are not under any compulsion to accept the terms set by markets. Anyone may seek council of another, or give advice, and may give and receive gifts, or enter into arrangements for cooperation in production on any terms satisfactory to all concerned. In particular, the political machinery of the state may always be used for any economic function; economic freedom in the most rigorous interpretation is not violated if this is done by general agreement.

WAGES AND JUSTICE: EVALUATION AND ACTION

After so much theoretical analysis in the way of "scientific" economics (treating desires and their free expression in action as "facts"), what is further to be said in terms of ethics—of what ought to be—can (and anyhow must) be put briefly. A starting point may be the statement so often heard, that free competition is all right in theory, but it doesn't work in practice. This is true, "up to a point," but with fundamental limitations. The system works far more closely in accord with its theory than people generally suppose, and our economic ills (those that are remediable, not part of the nature of things) arise more out of inherent limitations of the underlying social philosophy than out of defects in the market mechanism. And yet they point not at all toward replacement of the latter with a radically different type of social order.

The market economy is based on the principle of freedom; this is imperfectly implemented, as well as inadequately limited by other values. But the one economic system that confers freedom on individuals in production and consumption and admits of political and social freedom must be preserved and perfected. Reforming policy must be directed to supplementing it by other types of social control—and not too far, for these involve the sacrifice of freedom. On this point, indeed, there is no disagreement in principle; it is a question only of the kind and amount of recourse to other forms. Collectivists of various schools propose to (and in power do) keep the framework of markets and prices; and our contemporary "capitalism" interferes and regulates and adopts "socialistic" measures on a vast scale.

Profit as an Element of All Income

Our topic requires us to think of wages in comparison with other forms of income, and of all forms in relation to the grounds on which they are received, and to accepted ethical ideals; and—"of course," but far too much neglected—in relation to possible alternatives of social action; and these must be realistically viewed, especially recourse to the state, meaning to politics. Wages include all income received for or through personal service, insofar as this can be currently evaluated. The other two income forms are (1) property return (ambiguous use of the words "rent," "interest," and "profit," leaves no accurate short designation) and (2) profit. Profit must be analytically defined, as already explained. It enters into all income, insofar as this differs from what it would be under universal perfect competition; but we may confine attention to the difference between the receipts of the formal entrepreneur and the competitive value of the services he supplies (a positive or negative quantity).

Profit is focal to the failure of market competition to work in close accord with pure economic theory;[8] in fact, its analytically important

---

[8] It is also the prime butt of moralistic sneering. The "profit motive" is really just the wish to be effective in action—either in achieving some concrete end actually pursued, or in rivalry with others. The latter interest is the mainspring of most play, affects work and all aspects of economic life, is still more characteristic of politics than of business, and figures prominently in cultural pursuits and in moral and religious zeal.

feature is the "tendency" of the competitive forces to eliminate it. And, to repeat, these forces work far more effectively than romantic critics and the general public imagine, and the main real affront to our moral sentiments lies elsewhere. In any case, analysis must begin with the fact that "perfect competition" would place every individual member of the economy in essentially the position of a Crusoe, *except* that he would reap all the gain in efficiency that is possible through specialization *on terms of mutual assent.* He would receive the product of his own resources, in the only meaning this can have for joint action; and "the consequence of one's own acts," received through exchange of equal values, represents a kind of natural justice.

The actual market economy diverges from this theoretical result, in consequence of uncertainty or ignorance (including ignorance of present and future facts that no one could possibly know) and because of such coercion and fraud as men's consciences, public reprobation, and the law and its officers fail to prevent; also in some cases from indivisibility of productive agents (especially men) and discontinuity of markets. The entrepreneurial organization has grown up as apparently the way most satisfactory to all concerned for combining competent direction with individual freedom. There has never been any question of the right of any aggregation of persons organizing themselves in any way they like for any economic purpose (not outlawed as anti-social). The facts making other forms less satisfactory lie at hand and need not be specified here. All that is in question is use of force to compel adoption of some other form, and its actual relative merit.

As to profit and wages: First, entrepreneurs as a *class* receive little income or none, or (probably) less than none, and have nothing out of which to pay higher wages. Second, there is no presumption that the profits made by some, when really unearned, are made at the expense of their particular employees, rather than of consumers, or owners of "capital." If they "justly" belong to anyone else, it is presumably those who "innocently" incur the corresponding losses. Anyhow, they cannot to any large extent be taxed away by the state or any monopolistic pressure group for any purpose, without making enterprise unattractive and bringing about forcibly a controlled economy, or chaos.

The Problem of Monopoly

The two main "mechanical" shortcomings of the market economy are monopoly and the business cycle. The latter is a purely scientific problem, not one of conflict of interest and hence not "ethical" in nature; for no considerable group gains from depression, and nearly all lose. The problem of monopoly is important, but is misconceived, and its evils grossly exaggerated. Prevention, as in the case of the business cycle, would be a matter of finding and applying effective measures that would not destroy essential freedom of economic action and place excessive power in the hands of political functionaries. The only case in which monopolists can be said to exploit wage earners rather than consumers and society at large is that of "monopsonistic" employers. Most of these are unimportant, except in a temporary and local sense. In any case, arbitrary price fixing is no cure for monopoly, and wage fixing is no exception. Imperfect competition, instead of justifying such measures, as commonly argued, makes it more certain that forcing up the prices (wages) will reduce the amount demanded. In free society, laws and pressures can only prevent; they cannot force people into economic arrangements they do not think to their advantage.

Discussion of the division of the social income between labor and property is fraught with many difficulties. Policy must be concerned with facts and possibilities as well as rights, but the latter are our main concern here. As is the case of profit, the most important fact is the foolish ideas people hold and act upon. The contrast between "human rights" and "property rights" is nonsensical, unless as a mere dogmatic denial that owners have any rights. And laws ordaining that labor, sold and bought, is not a commodity are on a par with laws fixing an arbitrary value of "pi," the ratio between circumference and diameter of a circle. The hoary dictum that "labor produces all wealth" is patently contrary to fact, whether it is used to argue current labor's right to the whole product (Marx and predecessors and followers) or to justify property ownership (Locke the most famous example).[9] Everyone knows that property cooperates in the production of replacements and new items (as well as current consumption), and this has been the case as far back as economic life can be traced.

What needs explanation is the virulent prejudice against "wealth"— along with veneration of far greater power and luxury in political and religious potentates, all so conspicuous in our western religious tradition. Human workers, with the qualities that enter into their labor power are, like all other productive agents, produced (out of natural materials and forces) in the same age-long cumulative social-cooperative process; if we accept the principle of free association, there is no general and significant difference in their economic nature or the rights of their "owners" to have and to use the two forms of economic capacity.

Income as a Reward for Effort

If we extend our notion of justice, or right, to cover the feeling that there ought to be some proportionality of reward to sacrifice in the sense of pain or effort, the existing state of things is of course monstrously unjust. But there is little correspondence between this contrast and that between property and personal earnings; rather, practically the whole

---

[9] One task of education is to cure workers of the notion that they are working for a "capitalist"; they work for themselves or, in a sense, for the consumers of their products.

range of relationship between burden and benefit can be found in both categories. Some work is pleasant but highly paid, other work onerous and the pay miserable; the cares and labors of investors and managers are even harder to gauge, but are naturally under-estimated by those who view them from afar; and the rewards are subject to more vicissitudes. If one thinks of justice as a rough equality, or at least of extreme inequality as the great injustice, it is again certain that the causal role of property is usually much exaggerated. Property return tends to predominate at the top of the scale, but many of the very large incomes are "earned." At the bottom, poverty of course reflects a lack of income, hence of salable productive capacity, in either form. An owner of much wealth will often have a small or even a negative income, but this does not cause immediate privation.

As noted earlier, the institutions protecting personal freedom make it hard for one who has only personal earning power to draw upon the future (in comparison with a property owner, or a slave). If income available for consumption is correctly determined and averaged out over the years, the difference in dispersion between incomes from the two sources will not loom so large. Equality as an ideal needs much qualification, apart from the need for incentive. Our moral tradition greatly, if not hypocritically, exaggerates the claims of weakness. Account must be taken of differences in need, which cannot be measured; and neither the individual nor the family can defensibly be taken as a unit for equalization of money income.

To repeat what was said before, the main affronts to tenderhearted sensibilities arise outside the mechanics of the market, ruthless as its workings often are. Modern psychology has revealed much about the personal and emotional relations of life as sources of unhappiness—surely much more important than economic injustice. In fact, these relations carry over into economic life itself; it is only in theory that buying and selling are purely impersonal. Many of the common attitudes are quite irrational; people personify institutions such as "the company," "Wall Street," or "capitalism," and feel animosity toward them—where in earlier history the attitude was veneration of the established [order], though it conformed much less than now to a liberal conception of justice. The great historical anomaly is the coincidence, in the nineteenth century, of unexampled progress in the well-being of the masses, and specifically of social and individual humanitarianism, with destructionist revolutionary propaganda based on the most violent denunciation of the existing social order.

The Ethical Limits of a Free Economy

In the field of economic organization, two related facts are overwhelmingly important. The more obvious is the tendency to progressive concentration of power that is inherent in free and progressive society;

for power can be used to get more power, making inequality cumulative. To him that hath shall be given. This is not at all a matter of the form of power; it applies to intellectual, social, and psychological as well as to economic power, whether property or salable working capacity or merely "position," and also to "taste"—fully as important and seriously neglected. Through the family and inheritance, this tendency operates beyond the individual life, through the generations. Again, it is negligibly if at all a question of the form of power (the forms are largely interconvertible); the abolition of "property," in favor of any political substitute, would almost certainly increase, not reduce, the ability of persons in a privileged position to secure special advantages for their heirs. And the form of the family, or "primary group"—some form is inevitable—is also relatively immaterial. Only profound intellectual and moral changes in "human nature" could do much about it—beyond what is already done by such familiar expedients as progressive taxation with use of the proceeds for public services to low income groups; these seem to have about reached their limit if they are not seriously to hamper production. The kind of human change really desirable calls for terribly serious thought, as do methods of effecting such changes.

Our second fact, which underlines the first, is that from a sociological or culture-historical standpoint, the individual is not the basic reality, but is rather insignificant. He is the ephemeral carrier of a "culture," a complex of institutions, beliefs, feelings, and usages—something like the proverbial waterdrop in a flowing river. Certainly the family is the real unit in what is called individualistic society, and many communities fill in between the family and the state and world order. The family is the economic unit in consumption, and for the most part in production. And a productivity system of distribution, even if defensible for the individuals who are "producers," does not seem very ethical in relation to non-producing "dependents," a majority of the population. These facts do not invalidate the principle of individual liberty; but this needs to be considered in the light of the limitations which they set.

We cannot pursue the problem of social justice or ideals into these philosophical deeps, though it is here that the issues really lie. Values *are* passions and if not "prejudices" it is only because this term is defined as "bad" values! And who is to discriminate, and how? We must end with the rather harsh reminder that "necessity knows no law," or rather (epigrams rarely say what they mean), the laws it knows do not conform closely to the moral ideals current in our society. The first necessity is to keep civilization going, and try to make a little progress, not to be destructive or do more harm than good. Too much of what passes for economic reform, enacted and proposed, fails to pass this primary test. Men need to be "educated," first of all to see what is obvious, then to know and understand things that call for more than bare willingness to see.

Radical versus Direct Redistribution

15. ALTERNATIVE TECHNIQUES FOR PROMOTING EQUALITY IN A CAPITALIST SOCIETY*

Allan G. B. Fisher

SYNOPSIS

1. Inequality can be reduced either by the superficially "direct" method of redistributing income after its distribution has been determined by market forces, or by the "radical" method of altering market forces.
2. The direct method is taxation and public expenditure, and its value is limited because (*a*) it must be repeated endlessly since it has little effect on the causes of inequality, and (*b*) the high taxes it requires can limit the productivity of the economy.
3. The radical method seeks to reduce inequality of labor income by extending educational opportunities and so making entry into higher paid occupations easier, and to reduce inequality of property income by limiting inheritance.
4. The fact that the wages of skilled relative to the wages of unskilled labor are lower in countries of extensive educational opportunity indicates the power of education to reduce inequality. It requires, however, at least a generation to show its effects, one of which paradoxically is to increase the income of the uneducated.
5. A more drastic limit to inheritance than now exists is necessary in order to alter this cause of inequality.
6. Both the direct and the radical methods may coincide in practice, but emphasis on the latter has the advantage of making an effective use of the price mechanism.

This paper takes as its starting point the postulate that in most countries a diminution of the current inequality of income distribution should be welcomed. There are important differences about the reasons for regarding inequality as excessive when it gets beyond a certain point, about the speed at which inequality should diminish, and about the earnestness with which one should insist upon the significance of the obvious distinction between diminishing inequality and establishing equality. An examination of these differences is, however, for the most part not necessary

*Reprinted by permission and shortened from *The American Economic Review*, May 1950, pp. 356–68.

for the purposes of the present discussion, which is designed primarily to bring out the contrast between the two main approaches for the diminution of inequality. For purposes of practical action, indeed, it will be suggested, the two approaches need not be mutually exclusive. There is much to be said for working along both lines simultaneously; and if we seriously wish to diminish inequality, this is what we shall most likely decide to do. Nevertheless, the decision to place the greater emphasis on one or the other of these approaches is a matter of considerable practical importance and is likely, moreover, to reflect still more profound differences in economic and social philosophy.

The causes which have produced the current pattern of income distribution are complex. Their general character is fairly well known to economists, and it is not necessary to recapitulate them in detail here.[1] They may be grouped in two broad classes: those which explain the differences in earnings arising from different kinds of work and those which explain the differences in the amount of property owned by individuals. The pattern of inequality has never been rigid and unalterable. Inequality has been greater at certain times than at others and in certain countries than in others. There has, especially in this century, been a powerful movement to establish a greater degree of equality. Even without any deliberate action, it is only to be expected that in time the relative strength of the influences which tend to produce inequality should alter; and economic policy decisions, even when they are motivated by considerations in which hostility to inequality plays little or no part, often have as a by-product some important effects upon income distribution.

"Radical" versus "Direct" Techniques

The decision to support any particular measure for diminishing inequality cannot, of course, be made exclusively on one's judgment of its probable efficacy for that purpose alone. Other effects it is certain to have, for example, upon the efficiency of production, and these may be of overwhelming importance. In the first instance, however, we may ignore these effects, and concentrate our attention upon the distinction between the two divergent points of view which have in fact determined the character of most recent efforts to diminish inequality.

If our preference favors what I shall later call the "radical" approach, we should begin by examining the causes of inequality, and, having determined which of them can be most easily removed or weakened, we should look about for instruments for this purpose. [Their] application might then be expected in time to facilitate the emergence from the "normal" processes of income distribution of a less unequal pattern of distribution.

[1] Cf. Edwin Cannan, *Wealth* (1928), chaps. xi–xii; and *A Review of Economic Theory* (1929), chaps. xii–xiii.

The effects produced in the pattern of income distribution by changes which weaken some of the causes of inequality are not likely to be seen at once. Those who are impatient for quick results have therefore often naturally enough preferred a more direct attack upon the income structure as it exists at the time; observing the inequalities which appear as the current "normal" process of distribution allocate their shares to each unit in the economy, they then attempt to remedy inequality by compulsory direct transfers from those to whom the "normal" processes allocate more than the average to those who are receiving less.

Direct transfers, by way of private charity, have long been practiced in economies at every stage of development and of every conceivable kind of structure and have found respectable support in appeals to both religious and ethical sentiment. There is no reason to suppose that they will ever cease. Their economic significance has, however, usually been slight and is likely to remain so. If uninstructed benevolence encourages, as it may easily do, a quasi-commercial attitude toward the receipt of alms, some people may be induced to make a business of the cultivation of potential donors while at the same time much privation is left unrelieved.

In recent years the redistribution of income through taxation and public expenditure has been much more important than private charity. Sometimes the redistribution has been fairly direct; money has been collected from one set of people and paid out to another, e.g., old-age pensioners. Sometimes it has been more indirect, the obligation to pay and the right to benefits financed by the state being formally shared by everybody, but both being so arranged that, in proportion to their means, the rich pay more than the poor, while at the same time they are also likely to make less use of the facilities and enjoyments which are financed by the states out of taxation.

Redistribution by such methods accepts, at least tacitly, the existing pattern of gross income distribution as a datum not to be questioned. The "normal" economic processes, from which emerges the real national income, are permitted to allocate a certain fraction of the whole to each individual. This original distribution is then corrected after the event by lopping off part of the gross income allocated to certain individuals and handing it over to others. This direct redistribution will have some effects upon production, which in turn will produce some incidental effects upon the pattern of gross distribution. By its very nature, however, redistribution along these lines must be endlessly repeated.

The Limits of Direct Techniques

This method of redistribution now has a lengthy and respectable history, and we are unlikely ever entirely to dispense with it. Redistribution by means of taxation and social services has become a commonplace, to which in principle few will seriously object. The controversies which still rage in this field are usually on questions of degree. There are still many countries where there is a strong case for pressing for more intensive use of this technique. Experience has shown that most economies can stand a great deal more of it than many supposed when the first modest experiments were made. There is always some risk that it may be pushed too far, and in some countries the view has recently been expressed—and not only by those who are lukewarm [to] measures of this kind—that the limits of redistribution by taxation have already been reached. The discouraging effects of high taxation upon production and in particular its effects upon willingness to undertake the risks associated with the more novel types of investment and work may be so serious as to justify restraint. The hard-boiled businessman who for the greater part of his life has been accustomed to paying income tax at a low rate, say x per cent of his income, may be indignant and resentful when with little notice the rate is doubled. His son, who has never known anything better, is likely to be less disturbed by the $2x$ per cent, and his record of initiative may be just as good as that of his father. Nevertheless, even for his son there is likely to be a limit which it would be imprudent to ignore.

Moderation in all things is usually a sound working principle. As the average level of taxation rises everywhere, the problem of maintaining incentives for economic activity may become acute, and the risk is increased that the limit may be passed beyond which it is unsafe to raise the level further. The limit is probably flexible, but it is not indefinitely extensible. The view that the limit has already been reached beyond which further income redistribution by way of taxation can safely be pressed without incurring losses in other directions may now possibly be justified in a significant number of countries; and if this is so, the case for considering alternative methods of dealing with inequality is greatly strengthened.

Objectives of the "Radical" Approach

It is in any event a little odd that so many people should have a marked preference for the continuous large scale transfer of income from the relatively wealthy to the relatively poor—motions which can never produce permanent results—and should show little interest in other techniques the results of which would be much more permanent. The alternative approach to the problem which was briefly indicated above is genuinely "radical" in the true sense of that word: It seeks to go to the root of the matter. The preference for the superficially more direct methods appears still more odd in face of the fact that the "radical" approach is also likely to have beneficial effects upon production. An anti-inequality policy based upon this approach would work simultaneously along two lines. It would seek to alter permanently the relative scarcities of different types of skill and service, which are the basis of many of the more striking inequalities in income derived from work, and it would also remodel inheritance—one of the most potent causes of inequality of incomes derived from the ownership of property.

If we seek to explain specific cases of inequality between the remunerations paid for different kinds of work, we usually find it necessary to say a good deal about certain influences which appear to be peculiar to the case in hand: trade-union organization, for example, or the influence of traditions of wage movements. None of these influences can safely be ignored in any realistic study of income distribution. It is, however, easy to exaggerate their importance. As a rule, they are factors of the second order of importance whose influence is superimposed upon a pattern of income distribution which, broadly speaking, reflects the current conditions of supply and demand for labor. When one kind of work is paid for at higher rates than another, it may usually be assumed that those who are competent to perform the better paid work are, relatively to the demand for their services, scarcer than those who are competent to perform work which is less remunerative.

So far from justifying the conclusion that the pattern of distribution is inexorably fixed, reflection upon the implications of this doctrine should direct our attention to the possibility of remolding the pattern by changing the basic structure of supply and demand upon which it rests. Social pressures and prejudices are in every society important—and sometimes overwhelmingly important—in limiting the range of choice of occupation open to certain sections of the community. These are, however, always subject to change, and some changes are always going on. Particularly on the side of supply, the institutional factors which greatly influence the allocation of labor are capable of much more modification than in most countries they have received. There can be little doubt that the most important influences determining, for example, the disparities between the normal earnings of men and women are the various obstacles, social and otherwise, which impede the entry of women into certain occupations. The institutional factors of which this is an obvious illustration are usually closely connected with educational practices, and the most obvious modifications on the supply side—which do not, however, necessarily exhaust all the possibilities—are in the field of educational policy.

Education and Relative Wages

There are no doubt many factors which may be grouped under the heading of "natural forces" which limit the number of people with the intrinsic qualities needed for the more highly paid types of work, and thus create "natural" scarcities, from which in the ordinary course definite and important inequalities would emerge. But upon the effects of these "natural" scarcities there are superimposed the effects of other scarcities, which are not at all natural, arising from the expense and other difficulties involved in the acquisition of many types of skill. The removal of these difficulties might be expected to have far-reaching and permanent effects upon income distribution.

The wide extension of educational opportunity during recent decades was for the most part not due to any respect for those considerations. For the most part, the consequences which have in fact followed in this field were not deliberately intended. To many people the fairly close connection which can be traced between variations in the "normal" wage differentials between skilled and unskilled labor and variations in current average standards of education in different countries comes as a surprise, and, what is more important for purposes of practical policy, when the consequences in this field of further extensions of educational opportunity become evident, they often provoke vigorous resistance from people who are unwilling to face the adjustments in their own mode of life which such consequences demand.

There are, of course, numerous individual exceptions; but the general rule is that the ranks of unskilled labor are recruited from the less educated members of the community, and some educational foundations are usually necessary to acquire even an ordinary artisan's standard of skill, and much more any of the skills demanded in still more highly paid occupations. If a change in educational policy makes it easier to gain the qualifications which command higher pay and thus to avoid entry into the ranks of unskilled labor, we may expect the wages of unskilled labor relative to the remunerations paid for other types of work to rise, just as the wages of carpenters or the incomes of medical men would tend to rise if it were made more difficult to become a carpenter or to enter the medical profession. The benefits to be derived from educational policy would often accrue to those whose level of education remained unchanged, for they would enjoy the advantages to be derived from increasing scarcity. The rest of the community would, however, have no legitimate ground for complaint, for in a reasonably well-ordered economy their real income standards would also be rising, though not so rapidly as the standards of those who were left in the lower income strata.

Short and Long Run Effects of Education

The immediate effects upon income inequality of even drastic changes in educational practice will seldom be very substantial. For the most part, they can affect only new entrants into the labor market; and the number of new entrants into any one occupation at any given time will usually be small in relation to the total supply. Changes in educational policy will increase or diminish their number only slowly, so that the effects of the consequential changes in degrees of scarcity will be comparable with the effects upon the price of houses or upon the value of gold of any influence which tended to alter the volume of new house building or the output of newly mined gold. At least a generation must elapse before the full effects of any radical educational reform can be felt. And it is of course necessary that the changes in relative values which a more liberal educational policy should produce shall not be impeded by the efforts of those already at work in the more highly remunerated occupations to maintain artificial scarcities by setting up barriers to the employment of others.

The whole of this analysis is extremely elementary. It is now more than sixty years since Marshall pointed out that "the normal earnings of a carpenter and a surveyor might be brought much nearer together than they are, by even so slight and easy improvement on our present social arrangements as the extending to all persons of adequate natural ability the opportunity of receiving the training required for the higher ranks of industry."[2] To this, indeed, Marshall added, "but we have to take things as they are." On the whole, however, we have been increasingly reluctant just to take things as they are; and though there are still few countries where it can yet seriously be claimed that "all persons of adequate ability" have been given "the opportunity of receiving the training required for the higher ranks of industry," social responsibility for the widespread extension of education has in nearly every part of the world been admitted now for a period sufficiently long to make possible a test of the hypothesis that this "slight and easy improvement on our social arrangements" would influence the distribution of income.

It was possible before the war to show that the ratio of skilled to unskilled wages tended to fall, as our hypothesis would lead us to expect, as one moved from countries where education was but little developed to countries with comparatively advanced educational systems.[3] The correlation is far from exact, and the examination of particular countries where the ratio is either higher or lower than our hypothesis would suggest throws some useful light on other factors which affect income distribution. By and large, however, the correspondence between hypothesis and facts is sufficiently striking to justify us in regarding this as a striking illustration of the way in which, while adhering to liberal economic principles in the strictest sense, changes in the basic institutions of society might be used to reshape income distribution.

It would be very useful at the present time to have a statistical analysis of the effects of alternative educational policies upon income distribution more detailed than the rough calculations mentioned above. When for most people education had to start from very low levels and those who were eager to extend it had little knowledge of its effects upon income distribution, it developed in a somewhat undiscriminating way with little regard to its effects upon the relative scarcities of specific types of labor. There can be little doubt that in the Middle Ages the

---

[2] *Memorials of Alfred Marshall* (1925), p. 214.

[3] "Education and Relative Wage Rates," *International Labor Review*, 1932; *Bulletin of International News*, June 27, 1942, pp. 563–64.

mere ability to read and write conferred upon the "clerk" economic advantages which have now practically disappeared everywhere where elementary education has reduced illiteracy to negligible proportions. It was argued in England before the war that while "the charitable endowments of universities and upper-class schools have had an important influence in reducing the remuneration and cheapening the products of the better paid employments," the systematic provision of primary education has "rather resulted in diminishing the remuneration and cheapening the products of the class of labor which requires a smattering of letters, but is scarcely above, if it is at all above, the average,"[4] and superficial observation seems to confirm the view that routine clerical work is now often economically no more advantageous for those who perform it than any kind of work which would traditionally be described as unskilled. These are no doubt considerations. For those who are concerned with income distribution in the future, they mean that we have a long way to go before exhausting the possible effects of basic reforms in the economy's institutions.

Even if we had no concern at all with inequality, and were interested exclusively in expanding the volume of production, the same reforms would necessarily occupy an important place in our program. In particular, they would make available adequate supplies of key types of labor the scarcity of which often slows down economic progress, and this should be a point of special interest to those for whom employment policy is the dominating concern. The risk that a high general level of effective demand may produce inflationary pressures should be diminished by an educational policy which widens some of the bottlenecks in the customary labor supply. If our efforts to correct income inequality start from this point, it is unlikely, therefore, that at any time we shall feel it necessary to restrain them less they should impair the progress of production. It is likely rather that the educational reforms most effective for expanding the volume of production will also be the most satisfactory from the standpoint of distribution.

The Treatment of Inheritance

The inequalities of income which result from inequalities in the distribution of property are, however, often much more important. Here the institution of inheritance stands out most clearly as something immediately susceptible to treatment. By means of inheritance, old inequalities are perpetuated and new inequalities injected into the situation. The institution of inheritance has itself varied widely, and another field of investigation is the effect of these variations upon income distribution. Even when the most careful precautions are taken, it is indeed usually difficult to maintain intact all the advantages associated with inheritance in individual cases; but even after taking account of fluctua-

[4] Cannan, *Wealth*, pp. 209–10.

tions in individual fortunes, the effects of inheritance upon income distribution over a long period of time might be expected to be cumulative. In general, and neglecting individual cases, there is no tendency for inequalities based on these foundations to disintegrate with the passage of time, and the inheritance taxes which were imposed in many countries before the war seem to have done little more than limit to some slight extent the cumulative general effects of inheritance.

This is not a convenient place in which to examine in detail the complicated and difficult practical problems which arise in any attempt to reform the institution of inheritance. The maintenance of an unlimited right of inheritance is indeed a comparatively modern phenomenon, and it has been subjected to much criticism upon a wide variety of grounds. If equality is to be promoted within a capitalist society, more drastic changes in inheritance rights will certainly have to be made.

In principle, the contrast between the two methods of [correcting] excessive inequality is obvious enough. In practice, the dividing line is less clear. A "radical" approach to inheritance will rely heavily upon taxation, and education is one of the most important of the social services to be financed by taxation. Nevertheless, the distinction between measures which modify the basic structure of income distribution and measures which attempt merely to modify its consequences remains valid. In recent years the emphasis has tended to fall on policies of the latter type, and the process of collecting taxes and redistributing their proceeds has become more complex. Increasing resort has also been made to subsidies, limitations of prices, and other "direct" devices, until the simple picture of redistribution by means of taxes and social services may seem to be quite inadequate. These complexities do not, however, fundamentally affect the contrast—a contrast which has not unfairly been compared to that between poulticing a sore and treating the disease from which it springs.

The Price Mechanism and "Radical" Techniques

Greater emphasis upon the "radical" approach means that greater trust will be placed in the price mechanism in the labor market. It requires that we should first take vigorous steps to modify the conditions which determine the supply and demand for different kinds of labor; as a result of these modifications, we may then confidently expect to see a less unequal income distribution pattern emerge. The defects of the price mechanism are well known, and there is probably no field in which its results have been more imperfect than in determining the price of labor. These imperfections are unlikely to disappear if the current institutional practices which to a large extent determine the allocation of the labor supply are left untouched. Contempt for the price mechanism here may, therefore, have the unexpected consequence of preserving, with some superficial modifications, a traditional order of magnitude for labor incomes for many parts of which there may even now be little rational justification.

The doctrine that the techniques of redistribution which conform most closely to the principles of a competitive economy are also the most likely to produce far-reaching and permanent results should not occasion any surprise. For so far in this field these principles have been applied only in the most hesitating manner and with all kinds of inhibitions and restraints imposed by extraneous institutional factors. Their courageous and systematic application would in the course of time result in something not far short of a complete transformation of most modern economies.

16. INVESTMENT IN HUMAN CAPITAL*

Theodore W. Schultz

SYNOPSIS

1. Economists usually have not treated the development of human ability as investment, but it may be one of the most important forms.

2. The evidence is indisputable that those with more education and better health have higher incomes.

3. Human capital that results from investment in education, training, and medical care has increased more rapidly than non-human capital.

4. The increases in human capital may account for the fact that the output of the nation has been increasing more rapidly than the apparent input of resources. Increases in labor productivity may in large part be a return to investment in human beings.

5. The more important types of human investment include health facilities and services, on-the-job training, formal education, adult study programs not organized by firms, and migration of individuals and families to better jobs.

6. Educational expenditures rose about three and a half times as much as gross investment in non-human capital between 1900 and 1956—indicating that the prospective returns to education were greater than those to non-human capital.

7. Rough estimates indicate that the stock of education in the labor force rose about eight and a half times from 1900 to 1956, whereas the stock of reproducible non-human capital rose about four and a half times.

8. Despite the increased number of high school and college graduates, the return to investment in education is still higher than the return to non-human capital.

9. Among the obstacles to investment in human capital are discriminatory tax laws, the deterioration of human capital when it is unemployed, barriers to entry in some professions, imperfections in the market for capital funds for human investment, the difficulty of internal migration, and racial discrimination.

10. In undeveloped countries the under-investment in human beings has limited investment in non-human capital.

Although it is obvious that people acquire useful skills and knowledge, it is not obvious that these skills and knowledge are a form of capital, that this capital is in substantial part a product of deliberate

* Reprinted with permission from *The American Economic Review*, March 1961, pp. 1–17.

investment, that it has grown in western societies at a much faster rate than conventional (non-human) capital, and that its growth may well be the most distinctive feature of the economic system. It has been widely observed that increases in national output have been large compared with the increases of land, man-hours, and physical reproducible capital. Investment in human capital is probably the major explanation for this difference.

Much of what we call consumption constitutes investment in human capital. Direct expenditures on education, health, and internal migration to take advantage of better job opportunities are clear examples. Earnings forgone by mature students attending school and by workers acquiring on-the-job training are equally clear examples. Yet nowhere do these enter into our national accounts. The use of leisure time to improve skills and knowledge is widespread, and it too is unrecorded. In these and similar ways the *quality* of human effort can be greatly improved and its productivity enhanced. I shall contend that such investment in human capital accounts for most of the impressive rise in the real earnings per worker.

I shall comment, first, on the reasons why economists have shied away from the explicit analysis of investment in human capital, and then, on the capacity of such investment to explain many a puzzle about economic growth. Mainly, however, I shall concentrate on the scope and substance of human capital and its formation. In closing, I shall consider some social and policy implications.

Shying Away from Investment in Man

Economists have long known that people are an important part of the wealth of nations. Measured by what labor contributes to output, the productive capacity of human beings is now vastly larger than all other forms of wealth taken together. What economists have not stressed is the simple truth that people invest in themselves and that these investments are very large. Although economists are seldom timid in entering on abstract analysis and are often proud of being impractical, they have not been bold in coming to grips with this form of investment. Whenever they come even close, they proceed gingerly as if they were stepping into deep water. No doubt there are reasons for being wary. Deep-seated moral and philosophical issues are ever present. Free men are first and foremost the end to be served by economic endeavor; they are not property or marketable assets. And not least, it has been all too convenient in marginal productivity analysis to treat labor as if it were a unique bundle of innate abilities that are wholly free of capital.

The mere thought of investment in human beings is offensive to some among us.[1] Our values and beliefs inhibit us from looking upon

---

[1] This paragraph draws on the introduction to my Teller Lecture [16].
[Numbers in brackets relate to references at the end of this paper.]

human beings as capital goods, except in slavery, and this we abhor. We are not unaffected by the long struggle to rid society of indentured service and to evolve political and legal institutions to keep men free from bondage. These are achievements that we prize highly. Hence, to treat human beings as wealth that can be augmented by investment runs counter to deeply held values. It seems to reduce man once again to a mere material component, to something akin to property. And for man to look upon himself as a capital good, even if it did not impair his freedom, may seem to debase him. No less a person than J. S. Mill at one time insisted that the people of a country should not be looked upon as wealth because wealth existed only for the sake of people [15]. But surely Mill was wrong; there is nothing in the concept of human wealth contrary to his idea that it exists only for the advantage of people. By investing in themselves, people can enlarge the range of choice available to them. It is one way free men can enhance their welfare.

Among the few who have looked upon human beings as capital, there are three distinguished names. The philosopher-economist Adam Smith boldly included all of the acquired and useful abilities of all of the inhabitants of a country as a part of capital. So did H. von Thünen, who then went on to argue that the concept of capital applied to man did not degrade him or impair his freedom and dignity, but on the contrary that the failure to apply the concept was especially pernicious in wars; ". . . for here . . . one will sacrifice in a battle a hundred human beings in the prime of their lives without a thought in order to save one gun." The reason is that ". . . the purchase of a cannon causes an outlay of public funds, whereas human beings are to be had for nothing by means of a mere conscription decree" [20]. Irving Fisher also clearly and cogently presented an all-inclusive concept of capital [6]. Yet the main stream of thought has held that it is neither appropriate nor practical to apply the concept of capital to human beings. Marshall [11], whose great prestige goes far to explain why this view was accepted, held that while human beings are incontestably capital from an abstract and mathematical point of view, it would be out of touch with the market place to treat them as capital in practical analyses. Investment in human beings has accordingly seldom been incorporated in the formal core of economics, even though many economists, including Marshall, have seen its relevance at one point or another in what they have written.

The failure to treat human resources explicitly as a form of capital, as a produced means of production, as the product of investment, has fostered the retention of the classical notion of labor as a capacity to do manual work requiring little knowledge and skill, a capacity with which, according to this notion, laborers are endowed about equally. This notion of labor was wrong in the classical period, and it is patently wrong now. Counting individuals who can and want to work and treating such a count as a measure of the quantity of an economic factor is no more meaningful than it would be to count the number of all manner of machines to determine their economic importance either as a stock of capital or as a flow of productive services.

Laborers have become capitalists not from a diffusion of the ownership of corporation stocks, as folklore would have it, but from the acquisition of knowledge and skill that have economic value [9]. This knowledge and skill are in great part the product of investment and, combined with other human investment, predominantly account for the productive superiority of the technically advanced countries. To omit them in studying economic growth is like trying to explain Soviet ideology without Marx.

Economic Growth from Human Capital

Many paradoxes and puzzles about our dynamic, growing economy can be resolved once human investment is taken into account. Let me begin by sketching some that are minor though not trivial.

When farm people take non-farm jobs, they earn substantially less than industrial workers of the same race, age, and sex. Similarly, nonwhite urban males earn much less than white males even after allowance is made for the effects of differences in unemployment, age, city size, and region [21]. Because these differentials in earnings correspond closely to corresponding differentials in education, they strongly suggest that the one is a consequence of the other. Negroes who operate farms, whether as tenants or as owners, earn much less than whites on comparable farms.[2] Fortunately, crops and livestock are not vulnerable to the blight of discrimination. The large differences in earnings seem rather to reflect mainly the differences in health and education. Workers in the south on the average earn appreciably less than in the north or west, and they also have on the average less education. Most migratory farm workers earn very little indeed by comparison with other workers. Many of them have virtually no schooling, are in poor health, are unskilled, and have little ability to do useful work. To urge that the differences in the amount of human investment may explain these differences in earnings seems elementary. Of more recent vintage are observations showing younger workers at a competitive advantage; for example, young men entering the labor force are said to have an advantage over unemployed older workers in obtaining satisfactory jobs. Most of these young people possess twelve years of school, most of the older workers six years or less. The observed advantage of these younger workers may therefore result not from inflexibilities in social security or in retirement programs, or from sociological preference of employers, but from real differences in productivity connected with one form of human investment, i.e., education. And yet another example: The curve relating in-

[2] Based on unpublished preliminary results obtained by Joseph Willett in his Ph.D. research at the University of Chicago.

come to age tends to be steeper for skilled than for unskilled persons. Investment in on-the-job training seems a likely explanation, as I shall note later.

Economic growth requires much internal migration of workers to adjust to changing job opportunities [10]. Young men and women move more readily than older workers. Surely this makes economic sense when one recognizes that the costs of such migration are a form of human investment. Young people have more years ahead of them than older workers during which they can realize on such an investment. Hence, it takes less of a wage differential to make it economically advantageous for them to move; or, to put it differently, young people can expect a higher return on their investment in migration than older people. This differential may explain selective migration without requiring an appeal to sociological differences between young and old people.

The examples so far given are for investment in human beings that yields a return over a long period. This is true equally of investment in education, training, and migration of young people. Not all investments in human beings are of this kind; some are more nearly akin to current inputs as for example expenditures on food and shelter in some countries where work is mainly the application of brute human force, calling for energy and stamina, and where the intake of food is far from enough to do a full day's work. On the "hungry" steppes and in the teeming valleys of Asia, millions of adult males have so meager a diet that they cannot do more than a few hours of hard work. To call them under-employed does not seem pertinent. Under such circumstances, it is certainly meaningful to treat food partly as consumption and partly as a current "producer good," as some Indian economists have done [3]. Let us not forget that western economists during the early decades of industrialization and even in the time of Marshall and Pigou often connected additional food for workers with increases in labor productivity.

Let me now pass on to three major perplexing questions closely connected with the riddle of economic growth. First, consider the long period behavior of the capital-income ratio. We were taught that a country which amassed more reproducible capital relative to its land and labor would employ such capital in greater "depth" because of its growing abundance and cheapness. But apparently, this is not what happens. On the contrary, the estimates now available show that less of such capital tends to be employed relative to income as economic growth proceeds. Are we to infer that the ratio of capital to income has no relevance in explaining either poverty or opulence? Or that a rise of this ratio is not a prerequisite to economic growth? These questions raise fundamental issues bearing on motives and preferences for holding wealth as well as on the motives for particular investments and the stock of capital thereby accumulated. For my purpose, all that needs to be said is that these estimates of capital-income ratios refer to only a part of all capital. They exclude in particular, and most unfortunately, any human capital. Yet human capital has surely been increasing at a rate substantially greater than reproducible (non-human) capital. We cannot, therefore, infer from these estimates that the stock of *all* capital has been decreasing relative to income. On the contrary, if we accept the not implausible assumption that the motives and preferences of people, the technical opportunities open to them, and the uncertainty associated with economic growth during particular periods were leading people to maintain roughly a constant ratio between *all* capital and income, the decline in the estimated capital-income ratio[3] is simply a signal that human capital has been increasing relatively not only to conventional capital but also to income.

The bumper crop of estimates that show national income increasing faster than national resources raises a second and not unrelated puzzle. The income of the United States has been increasing at a much higher rate than the combined amount of land, man-hours worked, and the stock of reproducible capital used to produce the income. Moreover, the discrepancy between the two rates has become larger from one business cycle to the next during recent decades [5]. To call this discrepancy a measure of "resource productivity" gives a name to our ignorance but does not dispel it. If we accept these estimates, the connections between national resources and national income have become loose and tenuous over time. Unless this discrepancy can be resolved, received theory of production applied to inputs and outputs as currently measured is a toy and not a tool for studying economic growth.

Two sets of forces probably account for the discrepancy, if we neglect entirely the index number and aggregation problems that bedevil all estimates of such global aggregates as total output and total input. One is returns to scale; the second, the large improvements in the quality of inputs that have occurred but have been omitted from the input estimates. Our economy has undoubtedly been experiencing increasing returns to scale at some points offset by decreasing returns at others. If we can succeed in identifying and measuring the net gains, they may turn out to have been substantial. The improvements in the quality of inputs that have not been adequately allowed for are no doubt partly in material (non-human) capital. My own conception, however, is that both this defect and the omission of economies of scale are minor sources of discrepancy between the rates of growth of inputs and outputs compared to the improvements in human capacity that have been omitted.

A small step takes us from these two puzzles raised by existing

[3] I leave aside here the difficulties inherent in identifying and measuring both the non-human capital and the income entering into estimates of this ratio. There are index number and aggregation problems aplenty, and not all improvements in the quality of this capital have been accounted for, as I shall note later.

estimates to a third which brings us to the heart of the matter, namely, the essentially unexplained large increase in real earnings of workers. Can this be a windfall? Or a quasi rent pending the adjustment in the supply of labor? Or a pure rent reflecting the fixed amount of labor? It seems far more reasonable that it represents rather a return to the investment that has been made in human beings. The observed growth in productivity per unit of labor is simply a consequence of holding the unit of labor constant over time although in fact this unit of labor has been increasing as a result of a steadily growing amount of human capital per worker. As I read our record, the human capital component has become very large as a consequence of human investment.

Another aspect of the same basic question, which admits of the same resolution, is the rapid post-war recovery of countries that had suffered severe destruction of plant and equipment during the war. The toll from bombing was all too visible in the factories laid flat, the railroad yards, bridges, and harbors wrecked, and the cities in ruin. Structures, equipment, and inventories were all heaps of rubble. Not so visible, yet large, was the toll from the wartime depletion of the physical plant that escaped destruction by bombs. Economists were called upon to assess the implications of these wartime losses for recovery. In retrospect, it is clear that they over-estimated the prospective retarding effects of these losses. Having had a small hand in this effort, I have had a special reason for looking back and wondering why the judgments that we formed soon after the war proved to be so far from the mark. The explanation that now is clear is that we gave altogether too much weight to nonhuman capital in making these assessments. We fell into this error, I am convinced, because we did not have a concept of *all* capital and, therefore, failed to take account of human capital and the important part that it plays in production in a modern economy.

Let me close this section with a comment on poor countries, for which there are virtually no solid estimates. I have been impressed by repeatedly expressed judgments, especially by those who have a responsibility in making capital available to poor countries, about the low rate at which these countries can absorb additional capital. New capital from outside can be put to good use, it is said, only when it is added "slowly and gradually." But this experience is at variance with the widely held impression that countries are poor fundamentally because they are starved for capital and that additional capital is truly the key to their more rapid economic growth. The reconciliation is again, I believe, to be found in emphasis on particular forms of capital. The new capital available to these countries from outside as a rule goes into the formation of structures, equipment, and sometimes also into inventories. But it is generally not available for additional investment in man. Consequently, human capabilities do not stay abreast of physical capital, and they do become limiting factors in economic growth. It should come as no surprise, therefore, that the absorption rate of capital to augment only particular non-human resources is necessarily low. The Horvat [8] formulation of the optimum rate of investment which treats knowledge and skill as a critical investment variable in determining the rate of economic growth is both relevant and important.

Scope and Substance of These Investments

What are human investments? Can they be distinguished from consumption? Is it at all feasible to identify and measure them? What do they contribute to income? Granted that they seem amorphous compared to brick and mortar, and hard to get at compared to the investment accounts of corporations, they assuredly are not a fragment; they are rather like the contents of Pandora's box, full of difficulties and hope.

Human resources obviously have both quantitative and qualitative dimensions. The number of people, the proportion who enter upon useful work, and hours worked are essentially quantitative characteristics. To make my task tolerably manageable, I shall neglect these and consider only such quality components as skill, knowledge, and similar attributes that affect particular human capabilities to do productive work. Insofar as expenditures to enhance such capabilities also increase the value productivity of human effort (labor), they will yield a positive rate of return.[4]

How can we estimate the magnitude of human investment? The practice followed in connection with physical capital goods is to estimate the magnitude of capital formation by expenditures made to produce the capital goods. This practice would suffice also for the formation of human capital. However, for human capital there is an additional problem that is less pressing for physical capital goods: how to distinguish between expenditures for consumption and for investment. This distinction bristles with both conceptual and practical difficulties. We can think of three classes of expenditures: expenditures that satisfy consumer preferences and in no way enhance the capabilities under discussion—these represent pure consumption; expenditures that enhance capabilities and do not satisfy any preferences underlying consumption—these represent pure investment; and expenditures that have both effects. Most relevant activities clearly are in the third class, partly consumption and partly investment, which is why the task of identifying each component is so formidable and why the measurement of capital formation by expenditures is less useful for human investment than for investment in physical goods. In principle, there is an alternative method for estimating human investment, namely, by its yield rather than by its cost. While any capability produced by human investment becomes a

---

[4] Even so, our *observed* return can be either negative, zero, or positive because our observations are drawn from a world where there is uncertainty and imperfect knowledge, and where there are windfall gains and losses and mistakes aplenty.

part of the human agent and hence cannot be sold, it is nevertheless "in touch with the market place" by affecting the wages and salaries the human agent can earn. The resulting increase in earnings is the yield on the investment.[5]

Despite the difficulty of exact measurement at this stage of our understanding of human investment, many insights can be gained by examining some of the more important activities that improve human capabilities. I shall concentrate on five major categories: (1) health facilities and services, broadly conceived to include all expenditures that affect the life expectancy, strength and stamina, and the vigor and vitality of a people; (2) on-the-job training, including old-style apprenticeship organized by firms; (3) formally organized education at the elementary, secondary, and higher levels; (4) study programs for adults that are not organized by firms, including extension programs, notably in agriculture; (5) migration of individuals and families to adjust to changing job opportunities. Except for education, not much is known about these activities that is germane here. I shall refrain from commenting on study programs for adults, although in agriculture the extension services of the several states play an important role in transmitting new knowledge and in developing skills of farmers [17]. Nor shall I elaborate further on internal migration related to economic growth.

Health activities have both quantity and quality implications. Such speculation as economists have engaged in about the effects of improvements in health,[6] has been predominantly in connection with population growth, which is to say with quantity. But surely health measures also enhance the quality of human resources. So also may additional food and better shelter, especially in under-developed countries.

The change in the role of food as people become richer sheds light on one of the conceptual problems already referred to. I have pointed out that extra food in some poor countries has the attribute of a "producer good." This attribute of food, however, diminishes as the consumption of food rises, and there comes a point at which any further increase in food becomes pure consumption.[7] Clothing, housing, and perhaps medical services may be similar.

---

[5] In principle, the value of the investment can be determined by discounting the additional future earnings it yields, just as the value of a physical capital good can be determined by discounting its income stream.

[6] Health economics is in its infancy; there are two medical journals with "economics" in their titles, two bureaus for economic research in private associations (one in the American Medical and the other in the American Dental Association), and not a few studies and papers by outside scholars. Selma Mushkin's survey is very useful, with its pertinent economic insights, though she may have underestimated somewhat the influence of the economic behavior of people in striving for health [14].

[7] For instance, the income elasticity of the demand for food continues to be positive even after the point is reached where additional food no longer has the attribute of a "producer good."

My comment about on-the-job training will consist of a conjecture on the amount of such training, a note on the decline of apprenticeship, and then a useful economic theorem on who bears the costs of such training. Surprisingly little is known about on-the-job training in modern industry. About all that can be said is that the expansion of education has not eliminated it. It seems likely, however, that some of the training formerly undertaken by firms has been discontinued and other training programs have been instituted to adjust both to the rise in the education of workers and to changes in the demands for new skills. The amount invested annually in such training can only be a guess. H. F. Clark places it near to equal to the amount spent on formal education.[8] Even if it were only one half as large, it would represent currently an annual gross investment of about $15 billion. Elsewhere, too, it is thought to be important. For example, some observers have been impressed by the amount of such training under way in plants in the Soviet Union.[9] Meanwhile, apprenticeship has all but disappeared, partly because it is now inefficient and partly because schools now perform many of its functions. Its disappearance has been hastened, no doubt, by the difficulty of enforcing apprenticeship agreements. Legally, they have come to smack of indentured service. The underlying economic factors and behavior are clear enough. The apprentice is prepared to serve during the initial period when his productivity is less than the cost of his keep and of his training. Later, however, unless he is legally restrained, he will seek other employment when his productivity begins to exceed the cost of keep and training, which is the period during which a master would expect to recoup on his earlier outlay.

To study on-the-job training, Gary Becker [1] advances the theorem that in competitive markets, employees pay all the costs of their training and none of these costs are ultimately borne by the firm. Becker points out several implications. The notion that expenditures on training by a firm generate external economies for other firms is not consistent with this theorem. The theorem also indicates one force favoring the transfer from on-the-job training to attending school. Since on-the-job training reduces the net earnings of workers at the beginning and raises them later on, this theorem also provides an explanation for the "steeper slope of the curve relating income to age," for skilled than unskilled workers, referred to earlier.[10] What all this adds up to is that the

[8] Based on comments made by Harold F. Clark at the Merrill Center for Economics, summer 1959; also, see [4].

[9] Based on observations made by a team of U.S. economists of which I was a member; see Saturday Review, January 21, 1961.

[10] Becker has also noted still another implication arising out of the fact that the income and capital investment aspects of on-the-job training are tied together, which gives rise to "permanent" and "transitory" income effects that may have substantial explanatory value.

stage is set to undertake meaningful economic studies of on-the-job training.

Happily, we reach firmer ground in regard to education. Investment in education has risen at a rapid rate and by itself may well account for a substantial part of the otherwise unexplained rise in earnings. I shall do no more than summarize some preliminary results about the total costs of education including income forgone by students, the apparent relation of these costs to consumer income and to alternative investments, the rise of the stock of education in the labor force, returns to education, and the contribution that the increase in the stock of education may have made to earnings and to national income.

It is not difficult to estimate the conventional costs of education consisting of the costs of the services of teachers, librarians, administrators, of maintaining and operating the educational plant, and interest on the capital embodied in the educational plant. It is far more difficult to estimate another component of total cost, the income forgone by students. Yet this component should be included, and it is far from negligible. In the U.S., for example, well over half of the costs of higher education consists of income forgone by students. As early as 1900, this income forgone accounted for about one fourth of the total costs of elementary, secondary, and higher education. By 1956, it represented over two fifths of all costs. The rising significance of forgone income has been a major factor in the marked upward trend in the total real costs of education which, measured in current prices, increased from $400 million in 1900 to $28.7 billion in 1956 [18]. The percentage rise in educational costs was about three and a half times as large as in consumer income, which would imply a high income elasticity of the demand for education, if education were regarded as pure consumption.[11] Educational costs also rose about three and a half times as rapidly as did the gross formation of physical capital in dollars. If we were to treat education as pure investment, this result would suggest that the returns to education were relatively more attractive than those to non-human capital.[12]

Much schooling is acquired by persons who are not treated as income earners in most economic analysis, particularly, of course, women. To analyze the effect of growth in schooling on earnings, it is therefore necessary to distinguish between the stock of education in the population and the amount in the labor force. Years of school completed are far from satisfactory as a measure because of the marked in-

[11] Had other things stayed constant, this suggests an income elasticity of 3.5. Among the things that did change, the prices of educational services rose relative to other consumer prices, perhaps offset in part by improvements in the quality of educational services.

[12] This of course assumes among other things that the relationships between gross and net have not changed or have changed in the same proportion. Estimates are from my essay, "Education and Economic Growth" [19].

creases that have taken place in the number of days of school attendance of enrolled students and because much more of the education of workers consists of high school and higher education than formerly. My preliminary estimates suggest that the stock of education in the labor force rose about eight and a half times between 1900 and 1956, whereas the stock of reproducible capital rose four and a half times, both in 1956 prices. These estimates are, of course, subject to many qualifications.[13] Nevertheless, both the magnitude and the rate of increase of this form of human capital have been such that they could be an important key to the riddle of economic growth.[14]

The exciting work under way is on the return to education. In spite of the flood of high school and college graduates, the return has not become trivial. Even the lower limits of the estimates show that the return to such education has been in the neighborhood of the return to non-human capital. This is what most of these estimates show when they treat as costs all of the public and private expenditures on education and also the income forgone while attending school, and when they treat all of these costs as investment, allocating none to consumption.[15] But surely

[13] From [19, Sec. 4]. These estimates of the stock of education are tentative and incomplete. They are incomplete in that they do not take into account fully the increases in the average life of this form of human capital arising out of the fact that relatively more of this education is held by younger people in the labor force than was true in earlier years; and, they are incomplete because no adjustment has been made for the improvements in education over time, increasing the quality of a year of school in ways other than those related to changes in the proportions represented by elementary, high school, and higher education. Even so, the stock of this form of human capital rose 8.5 times between 1900 and 1956, while the stock of reproducible non-human capital increased only 4.5 times, both in constant 1956 prices.

[14] In value terms, this stock of education was only 22 per cent as large as the stock of reproducible physical capital in 1900, whereas in 1956 it already had become 42 per cent as large.

[15] Several comments are called for here. (1) The return to high school education appears to have declined substantially between the late thirties and early fifties and since then has leveled off, perhaps even risen somewhat, indicating a rate of return toward the end of the fifties about as high as that to higher education. (2) The return to college education seems to have risen somewhat since the late thirties in spite of the rapid influx of college-trained individuals into the labor force. (3) Becker's estimates based on the difference in income between high school and college graduates based on urban males adjusted for ability, race, unemployment, and mortality show a return of 9 per cent to total college costs including both earnings forgone and conventional college costs, public and private, and with none of these costs allocated to consumption (see his paper given at the American Economic Association meeting, December 1959 [2]). (4) The returns to this education in the case of non-white urban males, of rural males, and of females in the labor force may have been somewhat lower (see Becker [2]). (5) My own estimates, admittedly less complete than those of Becker and thus subject to additional qualifications, based mainly on lifetime income estimates of Herman P. Miller [12], lead to a return of about 11 per cent to both high school and college education as of 1958. See [19, Sec. 5].

Whether the consumption component in education will ultimately dominate, in the sense that the investment component in education will diminish as these ex-a part of these costs are consumption in the sense that education creates a form of consumer capital[16] which has the attribute of improving the taste and the quality of consumption of students throughout the rest of their lives. If one were to allocate a substantial fraction of the total costs of this education to consumption, say one half, this would, of course, double the observed rate of return to what would then become the investment component in education that enhances the productivity of man.

Fortunately, the problem of allocating the costs of education in the labor force between consumption and investment does not arise to plague us when we turn to the contribution that education makes to earnings and to national income because a change in allocation only alters the rate of return, not the total return. I noted at the outset that the unexplained increases in U.S. national income have been especially large in recent decades. On one set of assumptions, the unexplained part amounts to nearly three fifths of the total increase between 1929 and 1956.[17] How much of this unexplained increase in income represents a return to education in the labor force? A lower limit suggests that about three tenths of it, and an upper limit does not rule out that more than one half of it came from this source.[18] These estimates also imply that between 36 and 70 per cent of the hitherto unexplained rise in the earnings of labor is explained by returns to the additional education of workers.

A Concluding Note on Policy

One proceeds at his own peril in discussing social implications and policy. The conventional hedge is to camouflage one's values and to wear the mantle of academic innocence. Let me proceed unprotected!

1. Our tax laws everywhere discriminate against human capital. Although the stock of such capital has become large, and even though it is obvious that human capital, like other forms of reproducible capital,

---

penditures increase and a point will be reached where additional expenditures for education will be pure consumption (a zero return on however small a part one might treat as an investment), is an interesting speculation. This may come to pass, as it has in the case of food and shelter, but that eventuality appears very remote presently in view of the prevailing investment value of education and the new demands for knowledge and skill inherent in the nature of our technical and economic progress.

[16] The returns on this consumer capital will not appear in the wages and salaries that people earn.

[17] Real income doubled, rising from $150 to $302 billion in 1956 prices. Eighty-nine billions of the increase in real income is taken to be unexplained, or about 59 per cent of the total increase. The stock of education in the labor force rose by $355 billion, of which $69 billion is here allocated to the growth in the labor force to keep the per worker stock of education constant, and $286 billion represents the increase in the level of this stock. See [19, Sec. 6] for an elaboration of the method and the relevant estimates.

[18] In per cent, the lower estimate came out to 29 per cent and the upper estimate to 56 per cent.

depreciates, becomes obsolete, and entails maintenance, our tax laws are all but blind on these matters.

2. Human capital deteriorates when it is idle because unemployment impairs the skills that workers have acquired. Losses in earnings can be cushioned by appropriate payments, but these do not keep idleness from taking its toll from human capital.

3. There are many hindrances to the free choice of professions. Racial discrimination and religious discrimination are still widespread. Professional associations and governmental bodies also hinder entry— for example, into medicine. Such purposeful interference keeps the investment in this form of human capital substantially below its optimum [7].

4. It is indeed elementary to stress the greater imperfections of the capital market in providing funds for investment in human beings than for investment in physical goods. Much could be done to reduce these imperfections by reforms in tax and banking laws and by changes in banking practices. Long term private and public loans to students are warranted.

5. Internal migration, notably the movement of farm people into industry, made necessary by the dynamics of our economic progress, requires substantial investments. In general, families in which the husbands and wives are already in the late thirties cannot afford to make these investments because the remaining pay-off period for them is too short. Yet society would gain if more of them would pull stakes and move because, in addition to the increase in productivity currently, the children of these families would be better located for employment when they were ready to enter the labor market. The case for making some of these investments on public account is by no means weak. Our farm programs have failed miserably these many years in not coming to grips with the costs and returns from off-farm migration.

6. The low earnings of particular people have long been a matter of public concern. Policy all too frequently concentrates only on the effects, ignoring the causes. No small part of the low earnings of many Negroes, Puerto Ricans, Mexican nationals, indigenous migratory farm workers, poor farm people, and some of our older workers reflects the failure to have invested in their health and education. Past mistakes are, of course, bygones, but for the sake of the next generation we can ill afford to continue making the same mistakes over again.

7. Is there a substantial under-investment in human beings other than in these depressed groups? [2] This is an important question for economists. The evidence at hand is fragmentary. Nor will the answer be easily won. There undoubtedly have been over-investments in some skills—for example, too many locomotive firemen and engineers, too many people trained to be farmers, and too many agricultural economists! Our schools are not free of loafers, and some students lack the necessary

talents. Nevertheless, under-investment in knowledge and skill, relative to the amounts invested in non-human capital, would appear to be the rule and not the exception for a number of reasons. The strong and increasing demands for this knowledge and skill in laborers are of fairly recent origin, and it takes time to respond to them. In responding to these demands, we are heavily dependent upon cultural and political processes, and these are slow and the lags are long compared to the behavior of markets serving the formation of non-human capital. Where the capital market does serve human investments, it is subject to more imperfections than in financing physical capital. I have already stressed the fact that our tax laws discriminate in favor of non-human capital. Then, too, many individuals face serious uncertainty in assessing their innate talents when it comes to investing in themselves, especially through higher education. Nor is it easy either for public decisions or private behavior to untangle and properly assess the consumption and the investment components. The fact that the return to high school and to higher education has been about as large as the return to conventional forms of capital when all of the costs of such education, including income forgone by students, are allocated to the investment component, creates a strong presumption that there has been under-investment since, surely, much education is cultural and in that sense it is consumption. It is no wonder, in view of these circumstances, that there should be substantial under-investment in human beings, even though we take pride, and properly so, in the support that we have given to education and to other activities that contribute to such investments.

8. Should the returns from public investment in human capital accrue to the individuals in whom it is made?[19] The policy issues implicit in this question run deep, and they are full of perplexities pertaining both to resource allocation and to welfare. Physical capital that is formed by public investment is not transferred as a rule to particular individuals as a gift. It would greatly simplify the allocative process if public investment in human capital were placed on the same footing. What, then, is the logical basis for treating public investment in human capital differently? Presumably it turns on ideas about welfare. A strong welfare goal of our community is to reduce the unequal distribution of personal income among individuals and families. Our community has relied heavily on progressive income and inheritance taxation. Given public revenue from these sources, it may well be true that public investment in human capital, notably that entering into general education, is an effective and efficient set of expenditures for attaining this goal. Let me stress, however, that the state of knowledge about these issues is woefully meager.

[19] I am indebted to Milton Friedman for bringing this issue to the fore in his comments on an early draft of this paper. See preface of [7] and also Jacob Mincer's pioneering paper [13].

9. My last policy comment is on assistance to under-developed countries to help them achieve economic growth. Here, even more than in domestic affairs, investment in human beings is likely to be under-rated and neglected. It is inherent in the intellectual climate in which leaders and spokesmen of many of these countries find themselves. Our export of growth doctrines has contributed. These typically assign the stellar role to the formation of non-human capital, and take as an obvious fact the super-abundance of human resources. Steel mills are the real symbol of industrialization. After all, the early industrialization of England did not depend on investments in the labor force. New funds and agencies are being authorized to transfer capital for physical goods to these countries. The World Bank and our Export-Import Bank have already had much experience. Then, too, measures have been taken to pave the way for the investment of more private (non-human) capital abroad. This one-sided effort is under way in spite of the fact that the knowledge and skills required to take on and use efficiently the superior techniques of production, the most valuable resource that we could make available to them, is in very short supply in these under-developed countries. Some growth, of course, can be had from the increase in more conventional capital even though the labor that is available is lacking both in skill and in knowledge. But the rate of growth will be seriously limited. It simply is not possible to have the fruits of a modern agriculture and the abundance of modern industry without making large investments in human beings.

Truly, the most distinctive feature of our economic system is the growth in human capital. Without it there would be only hard, manual work and poverty except for those who have income from property. There is an early morning scene in Faulkner's *Intruder in the Dust*, of a poor, solitary cultivator at work in a field. Let me paraphrase that line: "The man without skills and knowledge leaning terrifically against nothing."

REFERENCES

1. G. S. BECKER. Preliminary draft of study undertaken for National Bureau of Economic Research. New York, 1960.
2. ———. "Underinvestment in College Education?" *Proceedings, The American Economic Review*, May 1960, pp. 346–54.
3. P. R. BRAHMANAND and C. N. VAKIL. *Planning for an Expanding Economy.* Bombay, 1956.
4. H. F. CLARK. "Potentialities of Educational Establishments outside the Conventional Structure of Higher Education," *Financing Higher Education, 1960–70* (ed. D. M. KEEZER). New York, 1959.
5. SOLOMON FABRICANT. *Basic Facts on Productivity Change*, Table 5. Occasional Paper 63. New York: National Bureau of Economic Research, 1959.
6. IRVING FISHER. *The Nature of Capital and Income.* New York, 1906.

7. MILTON FRIEDMAN and SIMON KUZNETS. *Income from Independent Professional Practice.* New York: National Bureau of Economic Research, 1945.

8. B. HORVAT. "The Optimum Rate of Investment," *Economic Journal*, December 1958, pp. 747–67.

9. H. G. JOHNSON. "The Political Economy of Opulence," *Canadian Journal of Economics and Political Science*, November 1960, pp. 552–64.

10. SIMON KUZNETS. *Income and Wealth in the United States*, Sec. IV, "Distribution by Industrial Origin." Cambridge, Eng., 1952.

11. ALFRED MARSHALL. *Principles of Economics*, Appendix E, pp. 787–88. 8th ed. London, 1930.

12. H. P. MILLER. "Annual and Lifetime Income in Relation to Education: 1939–1959," *The American Economic Review*, December 1960, pp. 962–86.

13. JACOB MINCER. "Investment in Human Capital and Personal Income Distribution," *Journal of Political Economy*, August 1958, pp. 281–302.

14. S. J. MUSHKIN. "Toward a Definition of Health Economics," *Public Health Reports*, September 1958, pp. 785–93. Washington, D.C.: U.S. Department of Health, Education, and Welfare, 1958.

15. J. S. NICHOLSON. "The Living Capital of the United Kingdom," *Economic Journal*, March 1891, p. 95. See J. S. MILL, *Principles of Political Economy* (ed. W. J. ASHLEY), p. 8 (London, 1909).

16. T. W. SCHULTZ. "Investment in Man: An Economist's View," *Social Service Review*, June 1959, pp. 109–17.

17. ———. "Agriculture and the Application of Knowledge," *A Look to the Future*, pp. 54–78. Battle Creek: W. K. Kellogg Foundation, 1956.

18. ———. "Capital Formation by Education," *Journal of Political Economy*, December 1960, Tables 3–7.

19. ———. "Education and Economic Growth," *Social Forces Influencing American Education* (ed. H. G. RICHEY). Chicago, 1961.

20. H. VON THÜNEN. *Der isolierte Staat*, Vol. 2, Part 2, 3d ed., 1875, translated by B. F. HOSELITZ, pp. 140–52. Reproduced by the Comp. Education Center, University of Chicago.

21. MORTON ZEMAN. *A Quantitative Analysis of White-Nonwhite Income Differentials in the United States.* Unpublished doctoral dissertation. University of Chicago, 1955.

INEQUALITY AND ITS REMEDIES

A policy for the distribution of income presents the following issues: (1) What are the facts of distribution? (2) What are the ethical standards that should determine distribution, and what are the relations among them? (3) What methods of redistribution are consistent with the appropriate ethical standards?

The customary standards are that income should be distributed in order to secure (*a*) efficiency in the use of resources and (*b*) justice in the distribution of power among individuals. Efficiency is the more easily defined. It consists, in a static economy, of allocating each kind of resource among the alternative uses in order that its productivity be the same in all of them. In a changing economy, it consists of an optimum utilization of an expanding supply of resources in order that the economy at all times can realize the maximum income which it is capable of producing. Justice consists in giving each individual that amount of power to act and to resist to which he is entitled. What he is entitled to or what he is "worth" is hard to define, and to give it monetary value is even harder. But it can be done and indeed is done each time society intentionally redistributes income. Not everyone is satisfied with the definition. Yet the behavior of the western world indicates it believes all men are of about equal worth because it has long approved of policies meant to reduce inequality and it continually considers fresh policies having the same intention.

The Facts of Inequality

There is a deceptive simplicity about the problem of inequality and an elusiveness that begins with the very facts about the distribution of income. As they usually are reported, they are misleading. What they are and how they must be corrected are explained by Emanuel T. Weiler. The extent of inequality in any one year between 1947 and 1959 is less than the figures suggest. They conceal the movement of families from one income class to another and so fail to show that the average annual income of a family over the entire period it receives income is not as high, or as low, as its income in any one year. The figures exaggerate high incomes in three ways: They often go to professional and other workers whose preparation for their jobs is expensive and whose incomes after adjustment for occupational costs are less than their reported incomes; higher incomes are more common in areas where the cost of living is high; and high incomes are more heavily taxed, and their recipients obtain fewer of the benefits from government expenditure, than is true of low incomes and their recipients.

There remains, however, an important amount of inequality, and it is revealed by the fact that in 1959 about one out of seven families had an income of less than $2,000. Some were in this class temporarily, but some are there year after year. They consist mainly of six groups: Negroes, especially those in southern agriculture; broken families which were provided for by the mother; unmarried women; subsistence farm families, also mainly those in the south; those with educational deficiencies; and disabled workers. Within these groups, persons beyond the age of 60 usually had the lowest incomes.

Poverty and Growth

Robert J. Lampman deals with the problem of how much of this poverty will be eliminated as a result of economic growth and education. He finds that within a generation (about thirty years) the proportion of the population receiving less than $2,000—now 20 per cent—will be reduced one half. Thus, what J. K. Galbraith calls "generalized" and "island" poverty can largely be eliminated. Poverty associated with racial discrimination and with large families can be reduced through economic growth and internal migration. However, there still are groups— and they account for about one third of those with incomes under $2,000 —whose lot will not be improved by economic growth or the other measures explained in this section. Theirs is the poverty associated with old age, disability, and female headship.

These groups, it may be noted, are poor because they have fewer resources to sell. The "radical" measures proposed by Schultz and Fisher will not benefit them. Nor would the increases in wage rates and the internal migration associated with economic growth.

It follows (although Lampman does not say this) that "case" poverty, as it might be called, is a particularly difficult type for a market economy to eliminate. The question that must be answered is, then: How far should a nation go in making "direct" transfers, either through social security measures or relief payments, from those in the middle and higher income groups to those suffering from "case" poverty? Whenever transfers of this kind are made, they limit the freedom of people of those groups to use their income as they please. They may also diminish the incentives of the resource-owning portion of the society to use their resources productively. How far a society can go in using "direct" methods to eliminate poverty without impairing its efficiency is an unanswered question.

Power, Income, and Freedom

To understand distribution policy, we must separate three issues, according to Frank H. Knight: (*a*) the factual aspect, which is about the way forms of income are determined and what they represent; (*b*) the ethical appraisal of the forms of income and whether or not its distribution should be changed; and (*c*) the wishful aspect, which consists of subjective preferences and hence cannot be discussed because they cannot be demonstrably true or false.

The principal facts about distribution, according to Knight, are:

1. Production requires both labor and property, and neither is useful without the other; labor is not the sole source of value.

2. The importance of each resource is that part of the total product attributable to it, and can be determined by marginal productivity analysis.

3. In ideally perfect competition, individuals receive the value of marginal product of the resources they own. Wages equal the value of the marginal product of labor, and rent (or, synonymously, interest) equals the value of the marginal product of property. There is no profit.

4. The income which resources produce—their value productivity—is ethically distinct from the income which the owners of resources receive. The value productivity of resources is relevant to the standard of efficiency, while the connection between value productivity and income received is a question of justice.

5. In all forms of economic organization, it is necessary to know the value productivities of resources in order to allocate them efficiently.

6. A perfectly efficient use of resources is impossible because those who allocate them can never be certain of their productivity in alternative uses. The owner of land cannot be certain that its use in, say, wheat will yield as great a return as its use in corn; the owner of capital cannot be certain that investment in industry X will be as productive as investment in industry Y; a worker cannot be certain that occupation A will be as remunerative as occupation B.

7. Hence, resources will be more productive in some uses than others. The difference in productivity is profit or loss. If the value productivity in industry X is 6 per cent while in industry Y it is 5 per cent, there is a profit of 1 per cent in X and a loss of 1 per cent in Y. If labor in occupation A has a value productivity of $95 a week and the same kind of labor in occupation B has a value productivity of $90, there is a profit of $5.00 to workers in A and a loss of $5.00 to workers in B. Profit and loss accrue to workers as well as to property owners.

8. Profit and loss cannot be eliminated because uncertainty is unavoidable, and is greater the greater is economic change.

9. It is possible, however, to divide the burden of uncertainty unequally, and the corporation is the most common device for doing it. The entrepreneurial group assumes greater uncertainty, and it consists of those resource owners whose returns depend on the success of the corporation in using resources productively. Customarily, they are the owners of common stock, but they may be managerial or other workers, or creditors.

10. The unequal sharing of uncertainty creates an unequal division of profit and loss. As the sharing of uncertainty is an arrangement freely made

by resource owners, the unequal division of profit and loss is the result of a choice freely made.

11. The distinction between labor income and property income is not, therefore, a distinction between wages on the one hand and profit on the other, because there are elements of profit in both. Labor and property are also similar in that both have a cost of production and depreciate.

12. The income produced by labor and property depends on the amount which at some time was invested in them and the effectiveness of the investment.

Although the facts in themselves are ethically neutral, they indicate the limits within which ethical choices have to be made. They imply that to equalize income, we would have to equalize the value of the labor and capital individuals own, give them equal ability to use it effectively, and eliminate uncertainty, which apart from unequal ability is the cause of ineffectiveness. All of this would require drastic limits on freedom. Knight believes little good can come from further efforts to reduce inequality and that the principal problem is to acquaint men with the facts of how income is determined in order that they will see the limits to redistribution and not set themselves the impossible task of going beyond them.

Radical versus Direct Redistribution

Given the limits of redistribution, there are two practical questions to be answered: (1) Shall the policy be directed principally to removing inequalities in the ownership of property or inequalities in the earning power of labor? A single policy can be directed to both purposes, of course, but its emphasis should depend on which form of income is more unequally distributed. (2) Should inequality be attacked at its causes or controlled in its effects?

It is the view of Allan G. B. Fisher that a "radical" policy, which attacks the causes or roots of inequality, is more effective and more consistent with the functioning of the price mechanism than is a "direct" policy, which tries only to control the effects of inequality. A radical technique distributes power more equally and alters the individual's ability to earn an income. A direct policy leaves the distribution of power untouched, and redistributes income after it has been earned.

The radical techniques proposed by Fisher are education and inheritance taxation, the former serving to reduce inequality in the distribution of wages and salaries and the latter to reduce it in the distribution of property income. Education increases the supply of labor to high-paying occupations and diminishes it in low-paying occupations. The distribution of income is altered for two reasons. The occupations that once paid relatively high wages and salaries now pay less, but the workers who entered the occupations because preparation for them was made less expensive through greater educational opportunity will earn more than they otherwise would be able to. The occupations that once paid relatively low wages will now pay more because the supply or labor to them decreases as workers move to the better jobs.

The taxation of inheritance reduces inequality by lessening the unequal distribution of property, but it has a somewhat different effect from education. Education lessens the unequal distribution of labor skills and increases the earning power of some workers as it reduces that of others. Inheritance taxes reduce the income of large property owners and increase the income of the government.

Human Capital, Distribution, and Growth

It is possible that the limits to redistribution can be made less confining by a redistribution of the human capital of the nation. In place of thinking of each individual as selling human services in the form of labor, on the one hand, and of property services in the form of control over reproducible capital on the other, Theodore W. Schultz proposes that we should think of human beings as an amalgam of "labor" and "capital" and as selling a stream of services stemming from their natural and acquired abilities. The latter abilities are the result of decisions to invest in human skills, just as the stream of services from a piece of reproducible capital is the result of decisions to invest in property.

This view of human beings is not common among economists. To treat them as wealth that can be augmented runs counter to some of the deeply held values of the west. Yet, human beings do sell much more than their capacity to do manual work; they also sell abilities they have acquired as a result of investment in themselves.

There has been investment in human beings for a long time, in the form of job training, health services, and better living conditions. It may resolve some of the paradoxes of economic growth. The empirical evidence indicates that real income per person has increased more rapidly than reproducible (i.e., non-human) capital. Thus the question: Where does the additional output come from? The answer, Schultz states, may be substantial unrecorded investment in human beings, and the increases in productivity are largely explained as returns to the investment in human beings.

What form does investment in human beings take? The first and most obvious is education. A second consists of investment in internal migration—i.e., to moving from islands of poverty to areas in which there are complementary resources and employment opportunities. A third, important for the undeveloped areas, is additional food and shelter, which increases the capacity of individuals to work. A fourth is health activities, which increase both the vigor and life span of individuals. It is difficult to compute the marginal percentage returns on the various types of human investment. It appears that despite a large increase in investment in education, its returns are still higher than those from reproducible capital. The expected lifetime income of college graduates is still much higher than the expected lifetime income of high school graduates, even though there has been a great increase in the former.

There are many ways that public policy can encourage further investment in human beings. Our tax laws discriminate against it; so do our capital markets; and the difficulties of deciding whether government or families should pay the costs of education and internal migration have also militated against it. Once investment in human beings is accepted as much as investment in reproducible capital, the opportunities (although Schultz does not say this) to achieve greater equality without the sacrifice of freedom are immense. Nobody who has the capacity to learn need be poor. Nobody living in a poor area need be penalized by the difficulty of moving. Possibly, the redistribution of capital through public and private investment in human beings is the way out of Knight's dilemma.

Inequality and Its Remedies: A Summary Statement

Inequality of income is caused by an unequal distribution of wealth, including the earning power of labor, by differences in the ability to put labor and capital to work, and by uncertainty. Uncertainty can be removed only by preventing economic change, and differences in ability and the value of labor power can be removed only by limiting inheritance—according to Knight, who believes the remedies would drastically curtail and probably destroy freedom. One way out of the dilemma is to emphasize the radical measures of education and other human investment suggested by Fisher and Schultz. The data on the distribution of income, even in their unadjusted form, show that inequality is not as extreme as it is usually thought to be and that it is declining. The corrected data show still less inequality.

Nevertheless, there remains a substantial amount of poverty. Some will disappear as a result of economic growth and continued investment in human beings. Some, however, seems not to be alleviated by economic growth. As a result, each generation must face anew the question of how far it is proper to go in eliminating poverty through direct transfers. This is partly a factual question: What are the effects of transfers on efficiency and growth? And it is partly an ethical problem: How much should efficiency and growth be sacrificed in order to reduce inequality?

PART 4

Trade and Development

Editorial Introduction

THE PROBLEMS OF TRADE AND
DEVELOPMENT

The post-war period has been marked by the rebuilding of the economies of western Europe and by the competition between the communist nations and the west for the support of undeveloped countries. In the economic sphere, this competition is taking the form of assistance to the undeveloped areas. The post-war changes have posed serious economic problems for the United States as a major participant in world trade. On the one hand, the economic recovery of western Europe has meant that the U.S. faces formidable competition in the markets of the world. The U.S. can no longer act as if there were a permanent dollar shortage, at least in western Europe. The industrial plant of western Europe is newer and in many cases technologically superior to that of the U.S. This, combined with lower wage rates, has made it possible for the European countries to under-price American products in many parts of the world, and many European countries are gaining gold and monetary reserves at the expense of the U.S. On the other hand, the undeveloped countries are looking to the U.S. for assistance in breaking the vicious circle of poverty. To do this, they need assistance in the form of grants and long term loans as well as ready markets for their products in the U.S.

Thus the dilemma: If the U.S. resorts to protectionism as a means of facing the competition from western Europe, it will weaken itself in the competition for support of the undeveloped countries. If the U.S. continues to liberalize its trade policy, as it has been doing since the end of the second world war, it must be prepared to face the discipline of the international market. Essentially, this is a question of where, given the political as well as the economic factors, the long run interests of the U.S. lie.

The articles in this section are about these problems. William Diebold, Jr., examines the broad question of national interest in a world divided by the power struggle. International trade is, according to him, a means of transmitting political as well as economic developments. Robert Triffin explains the factors that have led to the loss of gold and the increase of short term claims against the U.S. He proposes the establish-

261

ment of an international reserve fund within the International Monetary Fund.

Because of the rapidly increasing population of the undeveloped areas, H. W. Singer asserts that the per capita income in the world declined during the first half of the twentieth century. He also describes the vicious circle of poverty and the alternatives available to the developed countries in helping to break this circle. Two widely varying points of view have been developed as a means of starting the process of economic growth in undeveloped areas. Ragnar Nurkse proposes that "balanced investment," presumably planned by the state, will be necessary to accomplish this goal. On the other hand, Jacob Viner argues that the principle of comparative advantage, particularly as it is expressed in relative prices, should guide undeveloped countries in formulating their investment programs.

17. STATEMENT*

William Diebold, Jr.

SYNOPSIS

1. The foreign economic policy of the United States is unavoidably determined by the political problems inherent in its competition with the Soviet Union, such as military power, influence in under-developed areas, and trade between American allies and communist countries. But the U.S. should not engage in a growth race with Russia.

2. The U.S. recognizes that it will be affected for a long time by the development of other countries. Its aid should be varied and flexible, but the main work must be done by the countries themselves.

3. They will continue to face the problems of maintaining exports, of technologically caused decreases in the demand for their raw materials, of protectionism in the U.S., and of instability in world markets for raw materials.

4. Meanwhile, the U.S. must contend with its exports being reduced by aid, with protectionism in under-developed countries, and eventual competition from their manufactured products.

5. Western Europe has overcome its major post-war problems, and is in a strong position to meet its new problems and to bear a larger share of the cost of free world defense and development aid.

6. While the Common Market has strengthened the economies of the "Six," it should try to improve free world trade by reducing external tariffs, and the U.S. can promote this by tariff bargaining in GATT (General Agreement on Trade and Tariffs).

7. Other regional groupings may be advantageous, but in the undeveloped areas the gains from coordinating investment would probably be greater than those from liberalizing trade and payments.

8. But regionalism can retard the participating countries if it tries to be self-contained, and is of no help to countries that are unable to participate in it. The proper policy is to incorporate the regions and the independent trading countries into a global economy.

9. The effectiveness of our foreign policy depends on the strength of our economy and on the development and operation of that of the free world. We cannot control the changes that occur in the latter, and the way they affect us will be better managed the more flexible our foreign economic policy is.

* Before the Joint Economic Committee Hearings on Employment, Growth, and Price Levels, Part 5: *International Influences on the American Economy* (Washington, D.C.: U.S. Government Printing Office, 1959), pp. 921–30.

Not so many decades ago, it seemed reasonable to review the relation of the American economy to the world economy almost entirely in terms of exports, imports, over-sea investment, and foreign debts. For some time now, we have felt that a broader framework is necessary. Important as they are, foreign trade and payments are largely transmission belts, and we need to look beyond them to the conditions at home and abroad that they connect. My statement calls attention to some broad lines of development in the world economy that seem bound to raise a series of questions for national policy during a number of years to come. They will, therefore, have an important influence on employment, growth, and prices in the United States, even though it is not possible to give precise indications of their effects in advance.

I

The primacy of politics is not something that economists are always willing to accept, nor should they in every instance. But this survey would be out of perspective if it did not start with the dominant influence on the American economy that comes from the need to deter Soviet aggression and to prepare to meet it.

One has only to look at the level of arms expenditure in the U.S., the Soviet Union, and other countries, and at the proportion of world resources going into military production, to see that major changes in the relation between the two great powers would have great economic consequences. But even if there is neither war nor disarmament, we cannot assume that the economic effect of maintaining a high level of military preparedness will be constant. Changing military technology can spell the rise of one industry and the fall of another. It can radically alter the demand for particular raw materials and so affect the domestic economy, trade with other countries, and sometimes the attractiveness of investment opportunities in different parts of the world.

While the increasing cost of new weapons is well known, one often encounters the opinion that because destructive power is now so concentrated, the total cost of maintaining military strength is likely to fall. I am in no position to pass judgment on this matter, but one need not be an expert to see another possibility in the offing. There is much discussion of whether the U.S. should have the means of fighting sizable wars without the use of large scale nuclear weapons and should be prepared to move quickly to fight relatively small actions in far places. To do this in addition to maintaining an adequate nuclear deterrent might well raise the cost of military preparedness. The Soviet threat and the choice of western strategies can undoubtedly have a greater effect on employment, prices, and stability in the American economy than changes in the more obvious elements of our foreign economic relations. After all, a 10 per cent change in the military budget equals more than our total annual expenditures for foreign aid and a 5 per cent change exceeds our whole non-military aid. The goods and services for which our annual military budget provides considerably exceed our total foreign trade, exports plus imports.

Concern with military potential is only one of the elements in the now familiar debate about the comparative rates of growth of the Soviet and the American economies. Your committee already has the matter under study, and I cannot at this point add anything to the detailed discussion of data. However, since we shall have this problem with us for some time to come, it would be well to clarify some of our thoughts about it. Sometimes, over-simplified and rather crude comparisons are set forth which do not help us to understand these important issues and may prove misleading to people in the rest of the world. We need to sharpen our concepts of growth and look more critically at the relation between economic size and military and political power. We should not leave out of account either the other countries of the free world or China and the European satellites. When it comes to drawing conclusions that may affect national policy, two rather obvious points need to be borne in mind: First, we can have a major influence on only one side of the comparison, yet that side includes not only the U.S. but also other countries in the free world that have great potential for growth; second, while there are important reasons to be concerned with the growth of the American economy, too much is at stake to permit our policies to be dominated by comparisons with the Soviet Union. The "growth race" is important, but there are dangers in letting it acquire excessive symbolic importance.

In the last five years the U.S.S.R. and China have added a new complication to our problems of foreign economic policy by offering military, economic, and technical aid to under-developed countries while expanding trade with them. In these matters the communist powers are late-comers. They have thereby gained some political and psychological advantages. Some elements of their aid and trade policies seem designed to exploit frictions that have developed during the many years that the U.S. and other industrialized countries of the free world have been engaged in this kind of activity. Concentration of aid has given the U.S.S.R. a strong position in a few countries; but taken as a whole, the Soviet program is still quite small compared to what the western countries are doing. However, the U.S.S.R. has the means of expanding its trade and aid program substantially if it judges the gains to be worth the effort. To be sure, Moscow may change its policies or make enough mistakes to throw away its advantages; Pieping may find its own economic difficulties too great to permit expanding its outside activities. But it would be unwise to build American policy on any such assumptions.

Instead, we had best expect increased Soviet and Chinese economic activity in international trade and finance to be a continuing factor in the world.

There will then be continuing problems of what policies the U.S. should follow toward this communist activity. How great a danger is there in it? Are there means by which the under-developed countries can extract the maximum benefits from this additional aid while safeguarding themselves from Soviet pressure and influence? When should the U.S. make counter-offers? When should we stand ready to replace Soviet aid if it is withdrawn or a country wishes to give it up? Do new problems arise in giving American aid to a country that also gets aid from the U.S.S.R.? Should the U.S. change some of its own aid practices to compete more effectively with the U.S.S.R.? Do we need new trading agencies to offset some of the advantages of Soviet and Chinese government trading? These questions are only a beginning. Many of them probably cannot be answered in general terms. But they indicate lines along which our thought will have to move. There is also a fundamental consideration to be kept in mind: The risks of damage from communist trade and aid activity can be reduced by measures that improve the operation of the economy of the non-Soviet world. By reducing vulnerabilities—whether they be inadequate growth, a lack of capital, persistent or sporadic surpluses, or whatever—we reduce the opportunities for the Soviet Union to expand its influence by economic means.

Along with this new set of problems, an old and familiar one that has given us headaches in the past will need to be looked at again. There is a growing interest in western Europe, Japan, and perhaps the U.S., in trade with the communist countries. Some of this is political on the part of people who believe that trade will reduce tensions. Some of it is clearly commercial. While the economic importance of this trade for the U.S. may not be very great, there may be some advantages; in any case, American producers and traders are likely to show some interest, particularly if they see foreign competitors establishing regular relations with communist countries. We shall probably need some fresh assessments of familiar economic and political arguments. For instance, in conjunction with our allies, we might well look at the bearing of this trade on Soviet growth, at its potential economic importance to certain countries of the free world, at the validity of our distinction between strategic and non-strategic goods, at possible ways of controlling or organizing trade, and at the political implications of fostering or discouraging it.

II

The desire for economic improvement in the tremendous part of the world that is usually called under-developed now has a high place in any agenda of economic problems facing the U.S. The salient features of the problem and the range of considerations that make it important to the U.S. are well known. Later this week, you will devote a day to a discussion of some of the problems of economic development, and perhaps that session will provide an occasion to raise some of the intricate problems that I shall have to pass over—such as the means of mobilizing local capital, the possibilities of increasing private investment, the relation of private and governmental action here and abroad, and the relation of population growth to economic development. Here I can only comment broadly on a few loosely connected issues and trends.

In the course of the last few years, the U.S. appears to have recognized that for a long time to come, this country is going to be involved, in one way or another, in the economic development of foreign countries. We had better be sure, therefore, that our policies and methods, some of which were introduced on other assumptions, or even improvised, are reasonably well suited to the long haul. This does not mean that the issues are not timely, urgent, and critical. They are, but we should be sadly disappointed if we thought that a massive effort by all concerned would solve the basic problem in a few years.

Economic development is not only a long process, but a complex one that contains a wide range of problems. As development proceeds, problems change. Not all the problems result from lack of development or from the failure of an economy to begin moving rapidly. Quite the contrary. Many of the most difficult problems come from the acceleration of development. The rapid pace of growth, not the absence of it, is one of the principal causes of inflation and balance of payments difficulties in some Latin American countries, for instance. Part of India's difficulty in paying for imports results from a boom in the private sector of that country's economy.

Several inferences for policy can be drawn from the fact that "economic development" is shorthand for a wide range of problems that will last a long time. One is that we are likely to be misled if we think of economic development in terms of formulas or patterns. There are many common problems, of course, but the best combination of measures will differ from country to country and from time to time. Sometimes the first emphasis should be on agricultural development, sometimes on industry. The main need may be to get outside capital into the country, or it may be to find ways of using effectively the capital that already exists. It follows that effective aid to economic development is apt to require a wide range of devices; concentration on one or another of the familiar forms of aid is likely to leave us ill equipped to meet important problems. It is also very desirable to have a broad base of resources, skills, experience, and interests. Industrialized countries, other under-developed countries, private capital, and international organizations all can play useful parts, and do. Though there cannot be much quarrel with this description of needs, it seems clear that we have not yet secured the widest base for aid to economic development, provided a full array of means, or fully explored the possible combinations of methods.

There are however, some recent favorable developments in these respects. The growing importance of the Development Loan Fund, the inauguration of the U.N. special fund under Paul Hoffman, the increased activity of the International Monetary Fund, and the International Bank for Reconstruction and Development all move in this direction. Discussion of the proposed International Development Authority seems to be focusing on the means of bringing western European countries more fully into the process of aiding economic development. Some of these countries are already providing aid in one form or another, but it looks as if many of them have the means to do more. Skills and experience are involved, as well as funds and goods. While multilateral aid is not always preferable to bilateral aid, the increased interest in international arrangements seems to have a fairly solid basis. A more economical disposition of resources may be achieved through broader participation. There are increased opportunities for developing countries to help one another, especially through the exchange of specialists and experience. In some circumstances, an international agency can help greatly in exercising some of the pressure that is necessary for hard decisions about development. The Fund and the Bank are playing a valuable part in this. It should not be a surprise, however, to discover—as some recent Latin American reactions remind us—that there are times when it is no easier to accept the political consequences of financial discipline under international pressure than under any other kind of pressure.

Though the growing complexity of the free world's aid-giving machinery has caused some people qualms, it also has its good aspects. Look, for example, at the way different kinds of aid were combined to help Turkey and India during 1958. Britain, Canada, Germany, Japan, the U.S., and the World Bank concerted their efforts to help India meet its balance of payments difficulties. American aid to India comprises DLF (Development Loan Fund) loans, Export-Import Bank loans, and Public Law 480 sales. Turkey was helped by the International Monetary Fund, the U.S., and several western European countries acting through the EPU (European Payments Union). The American share of that operation involved DLF loans, Public Law 480 sales, defense support grants, money from the contingency fund, and postponement of instalments of past debt. Assuming that it was wise to provide aid in these cases, it looks as if the multiplicity of forms made it possible to accomplish things that might otherwise have been very difficult or impossible.

Aid is, of course, only one part of the problem of economic development and only one of the ways it affects the American economy. Crucial as foreign assistance is, the main job of development must be done by the people of each country. One of the main assets a country has that will sustain its own economic development is its ability to produce goods for export. If the U.S. accepts the fact that it has an interest in the growth of the under-developed countries, then it must give at least as much attention to trade relations as to ways and means of aid. A strong under-pinning is provided by the fact that a high level of economic activity in western Europe and the U.S. automatically produces a strong demand for the principal products of the under-developed countries. If we assure the continued growth of the American and western European economies, we can be reasonably optimistic about the ability of the under-developed countries as a whole to increase their export earnings. But this does not mean that each and every one of them can count on that, or that the long run upward movement will be stable.

Some countries may have trouble maintaining exports while meet-ing rising domestic demand. Some commodities may be plentiful enough so that their producers may suffer some disadvantage in the terms of trade. Technological change has a great effect on raw materials markets and can change demand rather more rapidly than is convenient for sup-pliers. In 1937, rubber, silk, and tin accounted for nearly 50 per cent of the value of U.S. imports of crude materials (excluding food); last year, they were less than 15 per cent. Though our economy has expanded greatly, and the value of raw material imports has nearly tripled, we im-port substantially less of each of those basic products than we did twenty years ago. We cannot gear technological innovation to the interests of under-developed countries, but it is of some importance that we should try to anticipate the effect of significant changes, especially on countries that depend heavily on sales of a product that is due for slow or rapid decline.

There is also American raw material protectionism to be reckoned with. The U.S. is a major raw material producer. Over a wide range of products, domestic output can hold its own with potential imports. But domestic producers of some raw materials feel threatened by imports. Sometimes, only a portion of the producers in an industry are affected, and the level of imports determines the size of the domestic industry, not its existence. Sometimes, the impact is broader, and a large part of the domestic industry is clearly in decline. Sometimes, what is at issue is pri-marily a price structure. Our record of public policy has been mixed. Recently, partly under the impact of the recession, we have extended protection, notably for oil, lead, and zinc. (Ironically, but not surpris-ingly, the main effect of this protection is felt after the recession.) Our agricultural policies make tariffs or quotas necessary on a number of products. In other cases, domestic producers have failed to get the protection they sought. It would be out of place to enter into the details of particular commodities. The general problem is simply that when an issue of this sort is being considered in the U.S., it is important to realize that in addition to the usual arguments about the pro's and con's of protecting high cost producers, we ought to take into account the effect of contracting the market for the products of under-developed countries and so adding to their problems of economic development. The result is bound to be a series of indirect effects on other elements in the American economy.

Another set of factors concerning raw material trade bears on the notorious instability of world markets for these products and the trouble-some consequences for the producing countries, especially those which depend heavily on income from sales of a few products. The decline in raw material prices after Suez revived an old interest in possible stabilization measures. Moved in part by its concern for the course of events in Latin America, the U.S. has taken a more sympathetic view than it often expressed in the past and has gone along with an agreement among producing countries aimed at holding coffee off the market. Although raw material markets are now improving once more, we can reasonably expect to hear more of these matters in years to come. That the U.S. should be willing to examine these problems with producing countries is certainly desirable. It would be unfortunate, however, to fool either ourselves or them with the idea that the prospects of effective long run action are good. Emergency action may always be possible, but whether acceptable, long run stabilization measures can be devised is much more doubtful. This is not one of those cases in which the economists have a selection of good, workable arrangements to propose if only untoward political obstacles were removed. On the contrary, while there are scores of proposals, there is little agreement. This is one of the most troublesome areas of economic analysis, marked by great differences as to what is desirable and also as to what can be accomplished. There is no room here for a close analysis of these matters, but a few questions will suggest the range of difficulties.

What is to be stabilized? Prices, foreign exchange earnings, or the income of producers? The problems and the means of coping with them will differ substantially according to the answer.

Do raw material producing nations really want "stability," or do they want a floor put under the markets, without a ceiling? Both the kinds of machinery that could be used and the willingness of consuming nations to accept such measures might depend on the answer.

Can effective stabilization measures be devised that do not seriously interfere with long run changes of price and volume of trade of the sort that are necessary if markets are to serve their purpose of guiding production?

Buffer stocks have appealed to many as the best way of moderating raw material fluctuations, but there is a nagging doubt about the workability of the neatest schemes in the face of producer pressure to prevent the liquidation of stocks once they have been accumulated. Some have advocated special loans to producing countries when surpluses appear that would keep up their current income and enable them to hold supplies off the market. Because of the difficulties of getting international agreement, national action in both producing and consuming countries has appealed to others. Countries as different as Ghana and New Zealand have done reasonably well in stabilizing returns to domestic producers in spite of fluctuations in world prices. But continued success depends on reasonably good world markets. Some countries are prevented from taking effective short run stabilization measures because they lack storage facilities. Sometimes, a relatively small shift in world demand has greatly magnified effects on the economy of a small nation heavily dependent on one export.

The U.S. is also an important exporter of raw materials and food. The sale of agricultural surpluses for local currency has become a major form of American aid. We have been made aware of the difficulties of avoiding the displacement of commercial trade by these shipments. We may find a growing problem of the relation of aid shipments of such products as rice and cotton to the opportunities that under-developed countries have to sell their own expanding output of these products. Our calculus must somehow be large enough to relate the advantages of giving rice to India and Indonesia, for example, and the disadvantage of narrowing the market for rice exports from Burma or Thailand.

We need also to think about the expansion of exports of manufactured products from under-developed countries. This trade may first be important in nearby markets in other under-developed countries. However, it is only reasonable to expect that in time, sizable quantities of cheap goods will make their appearance in American and European markets. Some of this will be made possible by the low wages that will prevail for some time in most under-developed countries. We can look forward to problems comparable to those we have long faced with Japanese goods and that England now faces with textiles from India and Hong Kong. We are doing nothing more than temporizing with the Japanese problem by so-called voluntary quotas, and the same method has caught on in Europe. We do not seem rich in ideas about what to do next; but unless we can find some means of permitting developing countries to make the most of these assets, we shall be further complicating the problems of economic development.

Another trade problem concerns protectionism in the under-developed countries. The justification of some protection for an infant industry is widely accepted by economists and has deep roots in American tradition. But before the phalanx of factories from San Francisco to Magnitogorsk and from Stockholm to Milan, almost every industry in an under-developed country may look like an infant industry, and some kind of blanket protection is likely to be tempting. There is considerable risk that the governments of some under-developed countries, under familiar economic and political pressures, will indulge in protection on a scale that will damage their own interests, and in the process slow down, or at least distort, their own economic development, instead of fostering it. No one has ultimate wisdom in this matter; good fortune and economic expansion may serve to overcome some serious mistakes. GATT provides some help. The other international agencies are in a position to take account of commercial policies in their activities in the under-developed countries. The U.S. and western Europe have a part to play because of their intimate links with the under-developed countries through aid, trade, and private investment. Pursuit of good examples is not the most marked characteristic of nations, and it would be unrealistic to call on the advanced countries to conduct themselves as paragons; but their chances of success in this matter will be helped if their own protectionism is kept to a minimum.

III

If we turn away from the endless panorama of the problems of the under-developed countries and look toward Europe, we see not the end of a story, surely, but the end of a phase and the opening of a new age. The great European problems of the post-war decade are behind us: recovery, the dollar shortage, tight restrictions of trade and payments, the difficulties of removing wartime controls. New heights of production and consumption, coupled with a great improvement in balances of payments, have now led to a considerable measure of convertibility. Of course, Europe continues to have economic problems: some recent stagnation or recession, the coal surplus, uncertainty about the area's long run energy position, Algeria's continuing threat to French financial reforms, the under-developed areas of southern Europe, inflationary pressures. The big difference is that these problems arise now against a background of prosperity and growth. The picture is not only greatly changed from that of 1947, but it is a different Europe from that which existed fourteen years after the end of the first world war, in 1932.

One mark of the improvement of the European economy was the slight effect on it of the last (1957–58) American recession. That was partly, of course, because of the character of the recession, but already in 1953–54 the European economy had weathered an American slump with less damage than was expected. The fears that existed at the end of the war that Europe's economy would always be at the mercy of fluctuations in the U.S. and would be buffeted seriously whenever there was a drop in economic activity here should by now have disappeared. With them should have disappeared the arguments that Europe's prime need was for a series of controls capable of putting buffers between it and the U.S. Another set of measures, those based on assumptions of a permanent dollar shortage, are also due for scrapping. Since convertibility, several European countries have taken important steps to liberalize their trade with the U.S. There is some distance left to go, and the leader of the American delegation to the last session of GATT was quite right in calling for the removal of remaining discriminations against dollar goods, since these no longer have any justification on balance of payments grounds. This kind of progress will be a direct advantage that the U.S. can gain from the improvement in Europe's economy. In addition, we can hardly count it as anything but a gain for our broad national interest that western Europe can play a greater role in the world economy.

One of the effects of Europe's expansion has been the stronger competition that the American exporters are meeting in markets around the world. This is inevitable. We cannot have a healthy Europe without it. While some export markets may be lost for good, I have reasonable confidence in the ability of American producers to meet a good bit of competition once they face the challenge. European recovery has also played its part in the gold flow from the U.S. It is to western Europe that the gold has gone. This is probably an important long run gain because a Europe with good reserves will be more stable and better able to hold its own place in the world. It is through such developments, supplemented by measures like those which increase the reserves of the International Monetary Fund, that we create the conditions in which current and future difficulties can be met as more or less normal problems rather than as emergencies.

The improved position of western Europe also raises the question whether the countries of that area can be expected to play a greater part in meeting the costs of some of the common free world measures. I have already mentioned the possibility of mobilizing more European capital for economic development. Edward Bernstein's analysis of the gold flow from the U.S. points a finger at U.S. military payments in western Europe as one of the factors that may have to be adjusted to prevent the outflow of gold from becoming a source of weakness. This suggests a re-examination of what NATO used to call burden sharing, to see whether a pattern of payments established some years ago is still the most desirable. This is clearly a very delicate issue, involving strategy as well as economics. It suggests other questions about the relations of defense and trade that are likely to be with us for some time. The recent "Buy American" cases concerning heavy electrical equipment and past arguments about watches and other products are familiar examples. There is a cogent Canadian argument that a single land mass with much common air defense is not easily divisible into two economic units on defense grounds. The conferences about shipping a few weeks ago suggest some of the complexities of defense economics. European complaints seem to have been directed not only at American subsidies and cargo preferences, which have been defended largely on strategic grounds, but also at the increasing use of "flags of convenience," which are regarded as an economic threat to some of our allies. To know where we stand we shall have to keep reviewing the economic requirements of our defense needs as strategy and military technology change. With this must be coupled sensitivity to the political requirements of our alliance policy. Throughout we have to weigh the arguments for protecting or subsidizing domestic production of strategic products against the long run need to make the most economical use of resources and to maintain the highest possible level of economic health and activity throughout the free world.

Western Europe has not only gained new economic strength; it has taken on a new shape. At its core is the Common Market—the European Economic Community, comprising France, Germany, Italy, and the Benelux countries. Though the reduction of trade barriers among the six countries is scheduled to take more than a dozen years, the initial response of business has been so strong that we may find the process speeded up. In any case, even if the original schedule is kept, and though there are always possibilities of failure, we must base our policy on the assumption that a customs union will be formed with a common tariff— and perhaps eventually a common commercial policy—toward the outside world. This is an extraordinary change from the traditional Europe. While keeping a clear eye out for the inevitable difficulties and for the effectiveness of the forces that will resist change, one can hardly fail to be rather optimistic about the long run effects of this economic union.

There will, however, be some problems for American policy, and perhaps some difficulties for some parts of the American economy. Some American exports will be put at a disadvantage; how serious this will be is hard to judge in general. The Common Market countries have professed a willingness to lower barriers to trade with the rest of the world; but, as in most countries, there are conflicting internal forces. It is of some concern to the U.S. that internally the Common Market should function as freely as possible, and that its external trade barriers should be low. The principal means we have of pursuing this aim is by tariff bargaining in GATT. The Europeans say they are ready for this, but I get the distinct impression that the importance of the result will depend on the willingness of the U.S. to bargain seriously, which means to offer some real concessions in return for better access to the enlarged European market.

Later this week, when you discuss American relations with the Common Market, you will undoubtedly get into the intricacies of the various free-trade area proposals. Essentially, this is a matter of the impact of the Common Market on the neighboring countries. This is not just Britain; Switzerland, Austria, and Denmark have an even greater interest, so far as trade is concerned. It is certainly important to the U.S. that a serious economic and political split in Europe should not result from the creation of the Community. It is not so easy, however, to see along what lines an agreement can be reached. We have also to compare the effects on American foreign trade of further removal of trade barriers among the European countries with extending the area of discrimination against American products that this entails. The matter grows more complex as we explore the possibility of some kind of association of the British Commonwealth countries, and their system of imperial preference, with the new European arrangements. We may be faced with some hard choices if, instead of a true free-trade area with all internal barriers removed, a series of special arrangements should be proposed, in which different countries would be associated with the Community in differing degrees and special understandings would cover trade in certain products. This is already the case for agriculture. Such a development might begin to look like the kind of world-wide trade discrimination we have long sought to eliminate. Convertibility has removed one of the arguments for discrimination that was most often advanced in the past and at the same time has reduced some of the risks of trade distortion from the creation of regional or other selective groupings of countries. We shall have to look very hard to determine how seriously our interests are affected by these possible developments and what courses of action are open to us. The commitments that most free world countries have under GATT are gaining in relevance, and it is likely to seem increasingly important to the U.S. to maintain them and increase their effectiveness.

The creation of the European Common Market has repercussions beyond the potential free-trade area countries. Africa is a clear case. French and Belgian territories are linked with the Common Market, while British and independent countries are outside it. If matters are left this way, there are likely to be implications for relative rates of development, and there would be some danger to the growth of closer relations among the African territories. There is evidence of some concern with this problem among African leaders, who may take the initiative in working out relations among themselves. In Latin America, there is worry about the preferred position of some competing African producers inside the Common Market's tariff wall, and about the bargaining position that Latin America will have in facing a large European bloc. In Asia, there is also concern about these matters, perhaps especially in India and Japan. Here again, GATT is relevant because up to a point the Common Market countries are bound by GATT rules and because in that setting the outsiders have a chance to join forces in presenting their cases.

Partly because of what has been happening in Europe, there is a stirring of interest in other parts of the world in the possibility of forming new regional groupings. Several proposals are being studied in Latin America; a limited arrangement has been approved in Central America. The U.S. recently reversed a policy of long standing and lent support to the drafting of a charter for an Inter-American Development Bank of which this country would be a member. The President has indicated that we would aid a Middle Eastern bank of the same sort, but without becoming a member. Various kinds of African development organizations have been proposed. We may expect to hear more of this kind of thing. Quite a wide range of questions opens up for the U.S., as well as for countries that would be directly involved in these groupings. The applicability of western European models is probably quite limited. In most under-developed areas, for instance, while there would be gains from liberalization of trade and payments, an effective integration arrangement would have to be more closely geared to investment and development plans. Difficulties from divergences in monetary and fiscal policies might be much more serious than in Europe, where they have not been negligible. There are unresolved questions about whether a development bank or some other regional financial arrangements would promote broader measures of integration.

Only rarely is the case for regionalism based on a clear-cut demonstration that a certain grouping is the natural economic unit in which to carry on certain functions. Usually, the argument is linked to political considerations or is based on simple pragmatism: These countries can agree among themselves, a larger group could not. If, by getting together with a small group of others, countries can go farther along the path of liberalization and sensible allocation of resources than they can on a national or global basis, then there is a good case for seriously looking at regional possibilities. There are also some advantages in having each country's economic policies judged to some extent by its peers who are immediately associated with it in some common venture and not only by the more remote officials of distant countries or international agencies.

At the same time, regional economic relations have their price. I have indicated some of the issues that arise in my remarks about the European Common Market. It is not only the outside countries that are affected. The members of the regional arrangement may find themselves deprived of some of the benefits of wider economic relations if they are tied too closely to a grouping that is restrictive in important ways. This is not an issue that can be resolved by generalities; it depends very much on circumstances and on the terms of particular arrangements. We shall probably have to give much attention to such questions in the future.

The U.S. probably does not have to make a sharp choice between regionalism and globalism. It can look sympathetically on efforts of countries to work out problems for themselves by regional groupings, and may be able to encourage or help some of these efforts. But it is also important to insist that regional arrangements be looked at in a global— or at least free world—perspective and that they be subjected to rules of the sort laid down in the GATT agreement. More than rules are involved; the constant testing of the actual working of the arrangements by discussions and negotiations in international forums is also of great importance. We must be concerned, too, about the effect of regional developments on our own trading and investment interests, and on the position of other countries that are left outside. Some of these will be small countries, with limited bargaining power. Others will be countries that for one reason or another, sometimes political, cannot join particular groups but ought not to be deprived of opportunities to expand their economic links with the world. Among the great trading nations, Japan is perhaps the one beside the U.S. that is least apt to find a place in a regional trading arrangement. It is quite important, politically and economically, that the world economy should be able to accommodate single countries as well as regional groups, and without great disadvantages. Eventually, there may also be a question about American membership in some regional group—but to explore that hypothetical possibility now would require far more space than is available.

IV

This survey has had to be conducted at a level of generality that forbids the drawing of any sharp conclusions. It has been something of a catalogue of major problems and trends, each of which must be examined more fully than I have been able to, in order to judge just what its effects are likely to be on employment, growth, and prices in the U.S. Even so, this statement has omitted a number of important issues. For instance, I have said almost nothing about the relations of the U.S. with such important countries of Canada and Japan, which present a whole series of problems quite different from one another. Private investment needs to be examined, not only as to possible future amounts and direction, but in its relation to domestic needs, imports, and exports; when we talk about the American economy, we have increasingly to keep in mind that an important element in it is the economic activity of American firms abroad. Agricultural problems are global, not just national; the international trade in farm products is to a high degree controlled by governments. What will happen to this important segment of the world economy? What are the implications of widespread agricultural protectionism for the industrialized countries and the under-developed ones? The world's energy supply presents an interesting series of problems: How long will the oil surplus last? How much use can be made of nuclear energy how soon? The use of local currency sales and loans has eased a number of aid problems, but it is piling up questions for the future. It is easy to add to the list.

If there is one general observation that can be drawn from the wide range of diverse developments that this survey has mentioned, it is that the world economy is in the process of substantial change, as it has been so often in the past. Some of the mainsprings of change lie outside the U.S. Up to a point the U.S. can influence the course of economic events, but only rarely can it control them. In a broader sphere, the effectiveness of American foreign policy is linked both with our economic strength and with the growth and proper functioning of the free world economy. The economic welfare of the U.S. is, in turn, affected to a considerable extent by what happens in the rest of the world. In this situation, we are, and will continue to be, faced with a series of choices. They may look very different from one case to another; but by and large, most of them will have in common the fact that they are choices between flexibility and rigidity. Usually, the economic advantage for the U.S. and also the ability of this country to influence the course of events abroad will lie on the side of flexibility. This has been apparent for a long time in our domestic economy. We have not always applied the same principles to our foreign economic relations, but there is increasing reason to do so.

18. THE INTERNATIONAL MONETARY POSITION OF THE UNITED STATES*

Robert Triffin

SYNOPSIS

1. The balance of payments position of the United States raises two questions: Does the deficit on current account indicate the U.S. is pricing itself out of world markets? Does the outflow of gold endanger the convertibility of the dollar at its present value?

2. The U.S. should be able to secure a $4 billion current account surplus annually and spend it for investment and defense in undeveloped countries. The U.S. has been spending that amount, but its surplus on current account has been much less. The result is a deficit in the over-all balance of payments.

3. If in remedy the U.S. should reduce foreign aid, exports would drop because many are now paid for by aid. If it should restrict imports, other countries would do the same; and again, U.S. exports would fall.

4. Policy in the short run should be higher interest rates and some reduction in capital exports; and in the long run (*a*) a reduction of world tension, making possible smaller military outlays, (*b*) elimination of discrimination against American goods, (*c*) an increase in Europe's share of the cost of development programs, (*d*) a stop to creeping inflation in the U.S., and (*e*) investment in the U.S. to increase efficiency and growth.

5. There has been a substantial loss of U.S. gold and an increase in its short term debt to foreigners; but in themselves, they do not endanger the nation's solvency. That is determined by numerous and more complex factors, such as its long term credit position, which has risen much more than the sum of its short term debts and gold loss.

6. The basic reason for the U.S. balance of payments position is the increase in the world's output and trade, which has caused other countries to increase their reserves of money that can be used in foreign trade. The newly mined gold can supply only one third of the increase, and most of the remainder has been the currency of the U.S.

7. To supply it, the U.S. has had to buy more than it sells on current account; and if it were to reverse the practice, it might provoke an international financial crisis.

8. The use of national currencies for international reserves is ir-

* Reprinted from *Constructive Suggestions for Reconciling and Simultaneously Obtaining the Three Objectives of Maximum Employment, an Adequate Rate of Growth, and Substantial Stability of the Price Level*, Joint Economic Committee (Washington, D.C.: U.S. Government Printing Office, 1959), pp. 2905–14.

rational, and should be replaced by all countries depositing their reserves in the International Monetary Fund and using them to buy the currencies of other countries as needed.

9. The IMF would become an agency for lending the currency of one country to another and for making investments on its own, both operations to be limited to certain percentages of its total assets.

10. The U.S. would gain from the plan by being protected from volatile short term funds and by no longer having to be the only net lender to the IMF.

I

The evolution of the last ten years has now brought us to a point where we can no longer ignore the impact of our domestic policies upon our balance of payments and reserve position. I must admit that this way of looking at things is still very unfamiliar to most of my colleagues in the academic world, although it has recently begun to force itself upon the attention of economists in business and government.

For many years after the war, our only problem in this field was to reduce to more manageable proportions our enormous surpluses with the rest of the world, and to find adequate means to finance them. The so-called "dollar shortage" theory dominated economic thinking and inspired economic policy, both here and abroad. The authors of these theories, however, and policy makers themselves were extraordinarily slow in realizing the full extent of their own success in dealing with the problem. Only our large gold losses of 1958 finally woke us all to the fact that our balance of payments had shown persistent deficits on over-all account ever since 1949, and that our net international reserve position had been declining continuously at a rate of about $1.25 billion over the eight years, 1950–57. This latter figure rose abruptly to $3.3 billion in 1958, and is likely to exceed $4 billion this year. While our gold losses have been dammed up somewhat this year (1959) by sharp increases in interest rates, they have nevertheless continued, and been accompanied by a further upward spiraling of our short term indebtedness abroad. Finally, and for the first time in many years, this country—the richest in the world, by far—is now experiencing large and growing deficits even in its current account, i.e., its purchases of goods and services abroad far exceed its sales to foreign countries, even though a substantial portion of these sales are financed and supported by extraordinary aid programs, particularly in relation with the disposal of our agricultural surpluses. More and more is being heard about our producers "having priced themselves out of the world markets."

The situation clearly calls for an "agonizing reappraisal" of our foreign economic policies, but we are in great danger of misinterpreting the evidence and of taking refuge in the kind of policies which, although extremely plausible on the surface, are not likely to be as effective as one might think in redressing our own position and are most likely, on the other hand, to trigger off a disastrous reversal in the post-war trend toward freer and expanding world trade.

II

Two major questions emerge from any objective examination of our current balance of payments and reserve position. Does the evolution of our balance of payments on current account suggest that we may be in danger of pricing ourselves out of the world markets? Does the evolution of our international reserve position suggest that we might have difficulties in maintaining the free convertibility of the dollar at its present value in terms of gold and foreign exchange?

I do not pretend to be able to give you a definite answer to the first of these two questions, but I might point out some reasons for serious concern in this respect.

As the richest country in the world, with far-flung responsibilities, we should be able to finance a large and steady capital outflow to the under-developed countries to help sustain their economy and their defense. With far less resources than we have, the British estimate that they should aim, for such purposes, at a current account surplus averaging more than $1 billion a year. On a comparable basis, an average surplus of, let us say, $4 billion a year in our own balance of payments would not seem excessive. This is indeed just about the level around which our capital exports—public and private—have fluctuated, rather narrowly, over the last nine or ten years. Our current account surplus, however, has long been insufficient to cover such exports. It averaged slightly more than $2 billion over the years 1952–57, fell to $1.5 billion in 1958, and turned into an annual deficit rate of more than $1 billion in the first half of this year.

Even more disturbing as an indication of our competitive position in world trade is the evolution of our current account with western Europe. This area is most directly in competition with us in manufactures, while our balance with the rest of the world is more responsive to cyclical conditions and to the level of foreign aid and capital made available to it. Discounting some highly abnormal movements connected with the peak of the European boom and the Suez crisis in 1956–57, our current account with western Europe has shown a pronounced and markedly unfavorable trend ever since 1951. Our surpluses of the immediate post-war years had thinned out rapidly even before then, falling from $5 billion a year in 1947 to $1.8 billion in 1951. They averaged less than $100 million a year in 1952–57, and have now shifted to an annual deficit rate of $800 million in 1958 and more than $2 billion in the first half of this year.

The combination of a relatively stable level of capital exports— about $4 billion a year—with much smaller and fast-declining surpluses on current account, turning into an actual deficit in 1959, has left us with a persistent and growing deficit on over-all account, running today at the rate of about $5 billion a year. A small portion of this, however, is covered by long term foreign capital exports to the U.S. and by other untraceable transactions appearing as "errors and omissions" in our balance of payments estimates. The remainder has given rise to annual gold losses and increases in our short term indebtedness abroad totaling, on the average, more than $1 billion a year in 1952–57, $3.4 billion in 1958, and, at an annual rate, $3.7 billion in the first half of this year.

A continuation of this trend would clearly be untenable in the long run. Among the policy measures which suggest themselves, two are particularly plausible and yet likely to prove both ineffective and unwise. The first and most obvious one would be a sharp curtailment of our foreign aid programs. The trouble with this is that such curtailment would be offset, in very large part, by corresponding cuts in our exports. Of a total capital flow of $5.4 billion in 1958, less than $800 million went to western Europe, and more than $4.6 billion to the rest of the world, i.e., mostly to the under-developed countries. A comparison of our capital exports to this area with our current account surplus with it shows a high degree of correlation, as the ability of these countries to run deficits with us on current account depends primarily on the financing made available to them by our own capital exports and foreign aid. A lesser flow of capital to them is thus likely to be matched, in very large part, by declining purchases of U.S. exports by them, and to bring relatively little improvement in our over-all balance of payments.

We must also note that most of our aid programs and official capital exports are closely linked to political objectives which we would hardly abandon on mere balance of payments grounds.

This may yet leave some room for so-called tied loans, insuring that the recipients of aid use it to buy in this market rather than to add to their reserves or to spend the dollars in other areas. This would be a palliative at best, the practical results of which are likely to prove disappointing, as a great deal of our aid—such as the financing of our exports by agricultural surpluses—is already tied in this manner, or is, in any case, used in fact for purchases in the U.S.

A second and even more disastrous line of action would be to reverse the liberal trading policies pursued by us for more than twenty years, which have helped so spectacularly in the recovery and liberalization of world trade in general. This could hardly fail to trigger off similar reactions abroad, to arrest and reverse the current trend toward liberalization by foreign countries, and to stifle further our own export trade.

The remedies, I feel, should be sought in a different direction. First of all, the current relaxation of world tensions may possibly enable us to reduce the terrifying and disproportionate defense burdens—internal and external—which probably account, more than any other single factor, for the revolutionary shift in the international dollar balance from pre-war to post-war days. This is, however, only a hope yet, and one about which I feel totally incompetent to hazard any guess or suggestion.

We should, secondly, continue to press vigorously for the elimination of remaining discrimination on dollar goods and the further reduction of other obstacles to trade and payments by foreign countries, particularly in Europe. A more determined support for GATT (General Agreement on Trade and Tariffs) and its efforts to outlaw unjustified discrimination and liberalize other damaging restrictions on world trade should also serve as a basis for greater efforts on the part of our own producers to prospect foreign markets and expand the level of our exports.

We should, in the third place, do everything we can to encourage European countries to assume a larger share of the burden of development financing, and to allow the recipients to spend the proceeds of such financing in the U.S. as well as in Europe itself. (This is another reason, by the way, for us to be chary of "tying" our own lending operations any more than they already are.) Success along these lines should probably involve some redirection of our own programs away from bilateral assistance, and toward multilateral assistance, such as is implicit in the present IDA (International Development Association) project.

Fuller European participation in the financing of developmental needs seems to me particularly crucial at the present juncture, since I am not confident that the various measures mentioned above will be adequate to bring about a sufficiently rapid and drastic improvement in our over-all balance of payments position. Time will be needed to restore, in a politically desirable and feasible manner, full competitiveness in our external trading position. Creeping inflation here must be arrested, while our rates of growth and productivity are stepped up at the same time by appropriate investments in research and technology. We should also be aided by the inevitable adjustment of foreign wage and consumption levels to the steep increases in production and the large balance of payments surpluses achieved by foreign countries over recent years. In the meantime, we shall probably be forced to keep our interest rates high enough to retain and attract foreign funds to this market, and to slow down somewhat our own capital exports. While unavoidable in the short run, this policy would be difficult to reconcile with our longer run policy objectives, internally as well as externally. The last part of my statement will come back to this point and make concrete suggestions to help us out of this dilemma.

III

The second major question which I raised above related to the evolution of our international reserve position and the threat which it may raise for the future stability of the dollar.

I have already mentioned the fact that the largest portion of our persistent balance of payments deficits on over-all account has been financed, year after year, for nearly a decade, by a growing deterioration in our net reserve position. At the end of 1949, our gold stock exceeded the liquid dollar claims of foreign countries by more than $18 billion. This exceedingly comfortable cushion was down to less than $3 billion in June 1959. At the rate of loss experienced in 1958 and early 1959, these $3 billions would be wiped out within a year, and our short term indebtedness abroad would begin to outstrip our total gold stock.

The financial press, here and abroad, has sometimes exaggerated the significance of these figures. First of all, we are not in any danger of becoming insolvent as a nation. Our gold losses and the increase in our short term liabilities abroad are matched—and far more than matched—by the enormous growth of our foreign investments since the war. Most of these investments, however, are long term investments on private account and could not be mobilized quickly to meet any demand of foreigners for conversion of their liquid dollar holdings into gold.

Secondly, however, there is nothing unusual or necessarily alarming, for a country like ours, in this rough equivalence between our gold assets and the dollar balances held abroad. Sterling was made convertible in December 1958, and has shown considerable strength ever since—as reflected in its persistent premium over the dollar on the exchange market—in the face of a level of foreign sterling balances three to four times larger than the total gold and convertible currency reserves of the United Kingdom.

The strength, and the weaknesses, of our international position cannot be gauged from any simple formula or calculation of this sort. Account should also be taken of our short term, and even long term, assets abroad, and also of other assets held here by foreigners and which might, under certain circumstances, be liquidated by them for re-investment elsewhere or for repatriation to the owners' countries. Continued mismanagement of our own affairs might even prompt a flight from the dollar by our own citizens and find us unwilling or unprepared to take effective measures against it. The future of the dollar is far less dependent on transitory fluctuations in our balance of payments than on the maintenance of people's confidence in our determination to preserve its basic and still formidable strength, in our own interest as well as in the interest of the world at large. Our capital is very high in this respect, and there is no reason to think that it is in serious danger of being jeopardized by excessive complacency, or dissipated by sheer irresponsibility, on the part of the monetary and political authorities of this country.

IV

Even the most successful re-adjustment of our over-all balance of payments, however, will leave in its wake two major problems. The first is the impact which such a readjustment will entail for the maintenance of an adequate degree of international liquidity in an expanding world economy. The second is the need to protect our own economy and the freedom of our internal economic policies against the dangers inevitably associated with the existence of such a huge backlog of foreign short term funds in our financial and exchange markets. The concrete but somewhat revolutionary suggestions presented below aim at solving rationally both of these problems together. First, however, it is necessary to state them more precisely and to place them in their historical perspective.

The present international monetary system of the world can be sketchily described as follows. A number of countries—particularly the old industrial countries of western Europe—are both anxious and able to maintain relatively high levels of monetary reserves and to increase them more or less *pari passu* with increases in production, money supply, and international trade turnover. Other countries—particularly in the underdeveloped areas of the world—are content with much lower levels of reserves and a more continuous recourse to foreign aid and short term capital, currency devaluation, or trade and exchange restrictions as alternative techniques of balance of payments adjustment. Current increases in the world monetary gold stock meet only a fraction (about one third) of the combined demand for monetary reserves defined above. Most—although not all—countries, however, have shown themselves willing to accumulate a substantial portion of their monetary reserves in the form of foreign exchange rather than gold. In choosing a particular foreign currency for this purpose, they naturally tend to select the currency that appears safest, i.e., that of a major creditor country: primarily the United Kingdom in former days, and primarily the U.S. today. This accumulation of a key currency as international reserves by the rest of the world necessarily entails a large amount of "unrequited" capital imports by the key currency country. Coal is brought to Newcastle, from which it should be exported instead. The international liquidity shortage, moreover, is not thereby relieved, unless the key currency country allows its resulting short term indebtedness to grow continually and persistently at a faster pace than its own gold assets. (It may otherwise disguise the basic gold shortage into a scarcity of the key currency itself.)

This is an exact description of what has happened in fact since the war, and a major explanation of the growing threat to our own liquidity position. We have been lending long—and even given funds away—while borrowing short and losing gold. Foreign countries' gold reserves and dollar holdings have risen by $20 billion (from $15 billion to $35 billion) between the end of 1949 and the middle of this year, but only one fourth ($5 billion) of this increase has come from new gold production—including Russian gold sales in western markets. The remaining three fourths ($15 billion) were derived from our own gold losses and increasing short term liabilities to foreigners.

The restoration of over-all balance in the U.S. international transactions would put an end to this process and deprive the rest of the world of the major source, by far, from which the international liquidity requirements of an expanding world economy are being met currently in the face of a totally inadequate supply of monetary gold. This might trigger off tomorrow—as it did under very similar circumstances in the early 1930's—a new cycle of international deflation, currency devaluations, and trade exchange restrictions.

The other problem that would be left unsolved by the readjustment of our current balance of payments is that of the huge legacy of short term foreign indebtedness inherited from the past, and the huge handicap that might be placed thereby on sound policies for economic growth and stability of our own economy. Such funds are extremely volatile and may, at any time, move out of our market in response to interest rate differentials or to foreign conditions over which we have no control.

The experience of the United Kingdom, in the late 1920's and early 1930's, is particularly eloquent in this respect. The pound had been stabilized in 1925 at an over-valued level with the help of large amounts of speculative foreign funds and refugee capital, particularly from the continent, during the period of currency depreciation that followed the first world war. The dangers of this situation were well perceived and led to various exchanges of views between Montague Norman of the Bank of England and Benjamin Strong of the Federal Reserve Bank of New York. Both men agreed, in general terms, that interest rates should be kept higher in London than in New York, in order to prevent an outflow of short term funds from the first to the latter. This soon entered into conflict with domestic policy criteria in both countries. A rise of interest rates in the U.S. seemed highly desirable at times to slow down excessive lending here, particularly in connection with the boom in Wall Street. Even greater pressure arose in England to ease credit conditions in order to fight the economic stagnation and mass unemployment which plagued the British economy in the late twenties.

The enormous repatriation of French refugee capital after the Poincaré stabilization of the French franc heralded the beginning of the end. The pound still held out for a few years, but had to be bolstered in various ways, including urgent pleas to the Bank of France and other central banks to refrain from converting, at an unpropitious time, the huge amounts of sterling absorbed by them from private traders and speculators. Some reluctant cooperation was given to the British in answer to these pleas, and substantial exchange losses were incurred as a result by several central banks when the pound finally devalued in September 1931.

A disquieting parallel could be drawn between those events and our own situation today. The extent of foreign currency devaluation since the war may have given a competitive edge to those countries after their production potential had recovered from the early post-war low. Some foreign currencies may now be under-valued in relation to the dollar, as they were in relation to the pound in the late twenties. Refugee capital flew here in large amounts after the second world war, as it had flown to London after the first world war. Some of it may again return home, as currency conditions become definitely stabilized in Europe. Our huge gold losses of last year were due in part to such a movement. They have been slowed down this year by an extremely sharp rise in interest rates, prompted by our domestic concern with creeping inflation in this country. In this case, external and internal interest rate policy criteria happily coincided, but they may diverge tomorrow. When we feel reassured about our internal price and cost trends, we are likely to turn our attention increasingly to our laggard rates of economic growth as compared not only with Russia, but also with most countries in western Europe. We may wish to ease credit and lower interest rates to spur new investments and technological progress. At this point, however, interest rates abroad might again become more attractive to financial investors, and the gold dammed up this year by our high interest rates might flow out at a rate comparable to that of 1958, or even worse.

I cannot resist quoting here an incisive remark of Santayana, which the dynamic managing director of the International Monetary Fund, Per Jacobsson, has used most aptly in some of his recent speeches: "Those who do not remember the past will be condemned to repeat it." John Steinbeck wrote in the same vein: "The study of history, while it does not endow with prophecy, may indicate lines of probability."

V

My final remarks will attempt to sketch, in very succinct form, the most logical policy answer to the two problems which I have just discussed. Those of you whom this summary might leave both interested and unconvinced may find a somewhat more detailed presentation of these suggestions in my paper on "The Gold Shortage, the Dollar Glut and the Future of Convertibility" and a fuller and more technical treatment in another publication of mine on "Tomorrow's Convertibility: Aims and Means of International Monetary Policy."[1]

The keystone of my proposals lies in the true "internationalization" of the foreign exchange component of the world's monetary reserves. The use of national currencies as international reserves constitutes indeed a totally irrational "built-in destabilizer" in the present world monetary system. In time, it is bound to weaken dangerously the key currencies—primarily sterling and the dollar—used as reserves by other countries un-

[1] Published (in English) in the June 1959 issue of the *Banca Nazionale del Lavoro Quarterly Review* and in *Gold and the Dollar Crisis: The Future of Convertibility* (New Haven, 1960), pp. 77–147.

der this system. These difficulties are then bound, in turn, to endanger the stability of the whole international monetary superstructure erected upon these key currencies.

The logical solution of the problem is obvious enough, and would have been adopted long ago if it were not for the enormous difficulties involved in overcoming the forces of inertia and reaching agreement among several scores of countries on the multiple facets of a rational system of international money and credit creation. This is, of course, the only explanation for the survival of gold itself as the ultimate means of international monetary settlements. Nobody could ever have conceived of a more absurd waste of human resources than to dig gold in distant corners of the earth for the sole purpose of transporting it and reburying it immediately afterward in other deep holes, especially excavated to receive it and heavily guarded to protect it. The history of human institutions, however, has a logic of its own. Gold as a commodity enjoyed undoubted advantages over other commodities that could alternatively be used as money. The substitution of debt or paper money for commodity money within each country's national borders was a slow, gradual, and still recent phenomenon in world affairs. Its extension to the international sphere is even more recent and has also developed haphazardly under the pressure of circumstances rather than as a rational act of creation on the part of any national or international authority. This explains the present, and totally irrational, use of national currencies as international reserves. Yet the proliferation of regional, international, and supranational agencies since the war is slowly laying the groundwork for further and long overdue adaptations in the international monetary system, and particularly for the internationalization of the fiduciary portion—foreign exchange—of countries' monetary reserves. This portion should be made up of international deposits rather than of national currencies.

The United States and the United Kingdom should bar the use of sterling and dollars as monetary reserves by other countries. All countries should simultaneously renounce the use of these, or other, national currencies as international reserve holdings. They would be offered instead the opportunity of keeping in the form of deposits with the International Monetary Fund any portion of their reserves which they do not wish to hold in the form of gold. Deposits with the Fund would be constituted initially by transferring to the Fund the national currencies—primarily dollars and sterling now held as reserves by the central banks of member countries, plus any amount of gold which they might also wish to exchange for such deposits.

Reserve deposits at the Fund would be as fully usable as gold itself in all international settlements. They could be drawn upon by their holders to procure any currency needed in such settlements or for stabilization interventions of central banks in the exchange market. The amounts withdrawn would be merely debited from the withdrawer's deposit account and credited to the account of the country whose currency has been bought from the Fund.

Fund deposits would carry exchange rates and convertibility guarantees which would make them a far safer medium for reserve investment than any national currency holdings, always exposed to devaluation, inconvertibility, blocking, or even default by the debtor country. They would, moreover, earn interest at a rate to be determined, and varied from time to time, in the light of the Fund's earnings on its own loans and investments.

These various features, combining the earning incentive of foreign exchange holdings with the safety incentive of gold holdings, should insure in time a large and continuing demand for Fund deposits by central banks, once they become sufficiently familiar with the system and confident in its management. In order to take account of initial diffidence and inertia, however, and to guarantee the system against the vagaries of sudden and unpredictable shifts between gold holdings and Fund deposits, all members should undertake to hold in the form of Fund deposits a uniform and agreed proportion of their gross monetary reserves. They would be entitled, but not compelled, to convert into gold at the Fund any deposits accruing to their account in excess of this minimum requirement.

A minimum deposit ratio of 20 per cent would probably be ample to initiate the new system, and would substitute for the present exceedingly complex and rigid system of IMF quotas. This ratio might have to be increased in time, however, in order to provide adequate lending power to the Fund and to insure beyond any shadow of doubt the full liquidity and convertibility of Fund deposits, necessary to make them as unquestionably acceptable by all countries as gold itself in all international settlements. On the other hand, prudent management of the system would, in all likelihood, make it unnecessary to resort to compulsion for that purpose, as member countries' own interests would lead them to maintain with the Fund, rather than in gold, a much larger proportion of their total reserves than the minimum percentages imposed by the Fund.

The major objection to this proposed reform in the Fund's operations would be the same as that raised against the Keynes plan for an International Clearing Union. Such a system would endow the Fund with a lending capacity which, if improperly used, might impart a strong inflationary bias to the world economy. This is no reason, however, to fall back upon a system whose deflationary bias can only be combatted through an ever-increasing dependence upon the haphazard constitution of reserves in the form of national currencies, and an increasing vulnerability to unfavorable developments in one or a few key countries. The threat of inflationary abuses can be guarded against far more simply and directly by limiting the Fund's annual lending authority to the amount necessary to preserve an adequate level of international liquidity.

Various alternative criteria could be retained for this purpose. The simplest one might be to limit the Fund's net lending, over any twelve-month period, to a total amount which would, together with current increases in the world stock of monetary gold, increase total world reserves by, let us say, 3 to 5 per cent a year. The exact figure could not, of course, be determined scientifically and would, in any case, depend in practice upon the compromise between divergent national viewpoints which would emerge from the negotiation of the new Fund agreement.

The Fund's lending operations, moreover, should be no more automatic than they are at present, and this discretion should enable it to exercise a considerable influence upon members to restrain internal inflationary abuses. The experience acquired in the twelve years of operation of the Fund is extremely valuable in this respect. Fund advances should continue to require full agreement between the Fund and the member with relation not only to the maturity of the loan, but also to the broad economic and financial policies followed by the member to insure long run equilibrium in its international transactions without excessive recourse to trade and exchange controls.

A second broad category of Fund lending would take the form of investments in the financial markets of member countries. These operations would be decided at the initiative of the Fund itself but always, of course, in agreement with the monetary authorities of the countries concerned. Such agreement would be necessary in any case to attach to these investments the same guarantees against exchange and inconvertibility risks as those which protect the Fund's own deposit liabilities.

The first investments of this character would be imposed upon the Fund by its absorption of the outstanding national currency reserves transferred to it by members in exchange for Fund deposits. The bulk of these reserves would be in the form of bank deposits, acceptances, and treasury bills previously held by the central banks themselves in New York and London. The Fund would have no immediate need to modify the pattern of these investments, but should be empowered to do so, in a smooth and progressive manner, insofar as useful for the conduct of its own operations. This purpose would be served by giving the Fund an option—which it would not necessarily wish to use every year—of liquidating such investments at a maximum pace of, let us say, 5 per cent annually. The resources derived from such liquidation would normally be re-employed in other markets whose need for international capital is greater than in the United States and the United Kingdom. A portion of such investments might even be channeled into relatively long term investments for economic development through purchases of bonds of the International Bank for Reconstruction and Development or securities of a similar character.

The acceptance of the basic reforms proposed above should eliminate all existing balance of payments grounds for permissible discrimination under GATT. This should constitute a powerful incentive for U.S. support of these proposals, as the U.S. has long been the main target of such discrimination by other countries.

The gradual liberalization of remaining trade, exchange, and tariff restrictions could also be given a new impetus by these reforms if they were allied to a continuous and world-wide negotiation of *reciprocal* liberalization commitments, similar to that successfully undertaken regionally by the OEEC (Organization for European Economic Cooperation) on the basis of the EPU (European Payments Union) agreement.

Finally, some fundamental reforms in the cumbersome administrative machinery of the Fund have long been overdue. Greater efforts should be made to preserve effective contacts at all levels between the Fund and the national administrations of its members.

VI

May I close with a few words about the advantages and disadvantages which such a reform would entail for the U.S. itself.

Its major advantage emerges clearly, I hope, from our previous discussion. The U.S. would no longer have to bear the burden and court the danger, inseparable from the use of the dollar as a reserve currency by other countries. This would, it is true, deprive us of unrequited capital imports which have, in the past ten years, allowed us to carry a heavier burden of foreign lending and aid programs than we could have financed otherwise. We would now have to share these responsibilities—and the political influence that might accompany them—with other countries, through processes of multilateral decision making which would, at times, be irritating and frustrating. We would, on the other hand, have consolidated in the hands of the Fund a large portion of highly volatile foreign funds, whose sudden and unpredictable outflow might otherwise unleash, at any time, an unbearable drain on our gold reserves. Most of all, we would have shed thereby the strait jacket which the need to prevent such an outflow would impose upon monetary management and interest rates in this country, whenever the success of our price stabilization efforts allows us to give primary consideration once more to the furtherance of maximum feasible rates of employment and economic growth.

A second and closely related consideration is that these reforms would put an end to an absurd situation under which we have been in practice—with only minor exceptions—the sole net lender in the IMF, in spite of our persistent deficits and of the equally persistent and huge surpluses accumulated over the last ten years by other IMF members. We would, moreover, be able for the first time to obtain assistance from the IMF ourselves—through the more flexible procedure of IMF investments rather than loans—without triggering off the dangerous psychological reactions which would now accompany a U.S. request for such assistance. The IMF itself would need to look for safe investment outlets for its expanded resources, particularly during the initial years of the new system, and this would fit in particularly well with our own need to buy the time necessary for effecting, in as smooth a manner as possible—in the interest of other countries as well as in our own—the readjustment of our current over-all balance of payments deficits.

19. ECONOMIC PROGRESS IN
UNDER-DEVELOPED COUNTRIES*

H. W. Singer

SYNOPSIS

1. The median income of the world is probably less than in 1913, because in countries with an increasing majority of the world's population the standard of living has risen less than elsewhere. Moreover, there is greater inequality, and less stability of world income.

2. One cause of inequality is the fact that the undeveloped countries receive about 40 per cent less of manufactured goods for a given quantity of primary materials. A more favorable exchange ratio would enable undeveloped countries to buy many of the capital goods needed for industrialization.

3. Economic development is arrested if its results are imposed on a country instead of growing out of its industrialization.

4. Undeveloped countries are poor because they have no industry, and are without it because they are poor. They can break out of the impasse only by massive initial investment, which, however, is long in yielding results and beyond the resources of many. Meanwhile, the population increases faster than total income, and per capita real income falls.

5. It is difficult for such a country to employ domestic savings for its development because they cannot be secured by the government and, left to themselves, often go to unproductive uses.

6. Nor will inflation promote development, because it will not increase the output of primary products and will delay the transition to a monetary economy.

7. Development in such countries is undertaken by governments. They are unstable because of undevelopment which itself is partly caused by political instability.

The economist, surveying for the first time what is undoubtedly one of the world's key economic problems, namely, that of under-developed countries, cannot fail to be struck by the extraordinary neglect of this field by his own science. There is no doubt that economic research and the literature have been deeply conditioned by a purely national approach, generally the approach of a major industrialized country.

* Reprinted by permission from *Social Research*, March 1949, pp. 1–11.

This concentration on the problems of industrialized countries, and particularly their short term problems of economic stability, is perhaps most clearly epitomized in the often-quoted statement of Keynes, "In the long run we are all dead." But this statement has a peculiar poignancy if applied to under-developed countries and peoples. For them, it is a physiological fact rather than a logical preference.

As a result of the preoccupation of economists with national data and national problems—which has been only secondarily followed by analysis of foreign trade problems and foreign trade relations—there is a general tendency to assume that there has been a rise in per capita incomes the world over during the last two generations and also that there has been some progress toward a more equal distribution of income. This optimism cannot be seriously sustained if we abandon the national approach and think in terms of world income, of John Cosmos rather than John Citizen. While it is true that in some of the *individual* countries, incomes and even per capita incomes have been rising, though at very uneven rates, the average or median world income is almost certainly smaller now than it was in 1913. The reason for this is that in the determination of average international incomes the under-developed countries, with their expanding populations, acquire a constantly increasing weight. This situation is perhaps best described as follows: A shrinking proportion of the world population has been rapidly raising its standard of living, while the living standard of an increasing majority of the world population has been rising much more slowly or has remained stationary. The improvement within the first group and the very slow improvement in the second group are, however, swamped by the shift in relative numbers from the first group to the second. Marxist analysis, in which rising standards of living for given groups and sections are somehow held to be compatible with general deterioration and impoverishment, is much truer for the international scene than it is for the domestic.

In terms of world income, the situation has probably deteriorated during the last three generations in respect to all three Pigovian criteria: average size, equality of distribution, and stability over time. If we define the "average" world income as that of the median world citizen, the spectacular improvement which has occurred at one extreme and which has fascinated economists and other observers becomes irrelevant. Such considerations perhaps lean over backwards in the direction of gloom, but they may be a useful corrective of the prevailing view of the situation.

Nor is it even true to say that this way of looking at things in terms of world income is futile because the decisive motive force of economic development, or lack of it, is purely national or domestic. Later in this article, the self-perpetuating weaknesses of the domestic economies of under-developed countries will be discussed and fully taken into account as the formidable obstacles to economic development that they are. At this stage, however, it may be useful to point out that the growing inequality in the distribution of world income is at least partly attributable to a major structural change in international economic relations—that is, the change in price relations between primary materials and manufactured goods. From the published data, it would appear that over the two generations preceding World War II, the quantum of manufactured goods obtainable for a given quantum of primary commodities declined by more than 40 per cent. From the point of view of industrialized countries, it is undoubtedly true that the prices of manufactured goods have not increased in real terms; on the contrary, rising wages and money prices of factors of production have been amply compensated by increased efficiency of production.

Yet it is also true that increased efficiency in the production of primary goods has not been absorbed by rising standards and rising prices of factors of production, but by a larger quantum required in exchange for a given volume of manufactured goods. The argument from the point of view of the under-developed countries—and it is a difficult one to answer—is that *if* the labor and other resources employed in the production of manufactured goods had been obtained at a stationary standard of living, these manufactured goods would have been available to the under-developed countries at perhaps a third of the price actually paid for them. In this way, the resources required for economic development, or at least the resources required for the initial stimulus to economic development, could have been supplied by multiplying the imports of capital goods, and no reliance need have been placed on the precarious, insufficient, and awkward process of foreign investment.

The peoples of the industrialized countries have not supported a higher standard of living in the prices which they pay the under-developed countries for their primary goods. Why should it be taken for granted that the people of the under-developed countries should support a higher standard of living in industrialized countries through the prices they pay for manufactured goods? Thinking along these lines, one is bound to conclude that the failure of the under-developed countries to come closer to the levels of the industrialized countries and to approach them more rapidly should not be laid entirely at the door of domestic weaknesses or handicaps implicit in the economic structure of the under-developed countries. Hence, the increasing inequality in the distribution of world income need not be accepted as inevitable, given the present economic structure of under-developed countries. There is little doubt that a sufficient stream of additional capital goods flowing into the under-developed countries to maintain, shall we say, the 1913 quantum relations, over the last two generations could have transformed the economic picture in many of these countries.

There is still another factor in international relations that has had a clogging effect on economic development. In economic development, we may distinguish between the *seeds* of development, such as the accumulation of industrial capital, the spread of modern technological methods, and the rise in standards of education, and the *fruits* of economic development, such as better nutrition, lower death rates, luxury consumption, progress in social security, the development of highly complex administration, multiple state intervention. The awkward fact is that it is very much easier to transplant the fruits of economic development, or at least to go through the motions of doing so, than to transplant the seeds. Such things as medical improvements, low death rates, advanced social legislation, a complex machinery of planning, are the end results of economic development in the industrialized countries, and as such they not only fulfill a definite economic function, but are the things in which economic development finds its meaning and fulfillment. It is fatally easy to transplant them, not as end products but in isolation, divorced from the process which has created them in the industrialized countries. Treated in such fashion, these fruits of economic development have a way of putrefying and even checking development itself. Transplant medical improvements in isolation, and you increase the population which is being maintained at stationary standards rather than raise *per capita* standards; transplant advanced social legislation, and it either remains a dead letter or proves positively detrimental to economic development; create a desire for luxury consumption, and the foreign exchange resources available for the import of capital goods are reduced; set up an elaborate machinery of state planning, and under the conditions obtaining in many under-developed countries, such machinery often becomes absurdly irrelevant to real needs and possibilities. We need not illustrate this point further.

Wherein, then, lies the special difficulty of setting in motion, within the frame of existing exchange relations between primary and manufactured goods, the process of economic development itself? The answer would seem to be that we are faced with a system not only of vicious circles, but of vicious circles within vicious circles, and of interlocking vicious circles. There is, of course, the dominant vicious circle of low production—no surpluses for economic investment—no tools and equipment—low standard of production. An under-developed country is poor because it has no industry; and an under-developed country has no industry because it is poor.

Turning to the next key problem of under-developed countries, namely, the relation of agriculture to industry, we find a new application of this vicious circle. Given a situation where the bulk of the employed population at the start of economic development is engaged in agriculture, it is not difficult to determine two lines of industrialization that would be particularly promising. The first is the manufacture of goods that can serve as incentive goods for farmers and primary producers generally, that is, goods that will induce them to raise their output and to change over from a system of subsistence farming in a non-monetary economy to a system of cash crops in a monetary system. The second type is clearly the production of agricultural tools and equipment suitable for raising agricultural productivity. In both these ways the apparent conflict between industrialization and agricultural improvement could be resolved.

In reality, subsistence farming, lack of division of labor, and pre-monetary arrangements prevail in under-developed countries for lack of supply of incentive goods; and the low output and absence of specialization which go with such subsistence farming in turn prevent the accumulation of food surpluses that could be used for the importation or domestic production of incentive goods. Similarly, low agricultural output prevents the importation or domestic production of improved equipment, and lack of equipment, in turn, prevents higher agricultural output.

Another vicious circle derives from the fact that economic development is an operation characterized by increasing returns. There should be a long period of heavy and seemingly fruitless expenditure prior to the stage when further expenditure brings tangible results. Small scale development (in terms of the amount of total expenditure, not the size of the individual project) is likely to be much more difficult. Continuous development in small doses is apt to be very disappointing. What is needed is a big initial effort to carry through the barren period, and this in itself presents a basic difficulty with many ramifications, three illustrations of which will point up the problem.

1. The most productive form of development is the systematic creation of those indispensable external economies in economic production, especially in the fields of transport and power. The creation of these external economies is not only fruitless in the sense that it is merely a pre-condition, albeit an essential one, of useful production; it also implies activities of a peculiarly high capital intensity. Nevertheless, the soundest type of development is the one requiring you to cast your bread upon the waters by expending an enormous amount of capital in the creation of external economies without immediate return. It would be much easier if it were the other way round, if one could start off with light investments bringing immediate returns, which could then be utilized for heavier investments, gathering strength in the process. But, alas, it is not so. Hence, under-developed countries, with the modest resources at their disposal and with a natural impatience for results, are under constant temptation to skip the necessary external economies and engage in premature projects which fail to attain their full productivity for lack of external economies, or else to sit back hopelessly and do nothing. This is a real dilemma.

2. Under the conditions obtaining in under-developed countries, the immediate effect of slight steady improvement is a bettering of nutrition and sanitary conditions, which lowers the death rate. This results in

an increase in population which uses up the increment in production, leaving no room for investment. It is highly probable, in view of the experience of industrialized countries, that sustained development and industrialization might result in a lowering of birth rates, thus releasing sources of investment. That blissful stage, however, is never reached because the immediate effect of small improvements is such as to throw the under-developed country back to its starting point. Development under such conditions is like trying to run up a downward-moving escalator. If you could only move from your original position, you could get off the escalator and go forward without difficulty; but once on the escalator, you are prevented from obtaining freedom of motion.

3. A further fact, and one frequently noted by economists,[1] is that multiple development is easier to maintain, per unit of expenditure, than development in isolated projects. Provided that reasonable balance is maintained in multiple development, each project will be the market for some other project and the supplier of yet another. In the income sense, too, the incomes generated in projects A, B, C, . . . provide the purchasing power for the product of project X. In turn, each particular project becomes "project X." The advantages of multiple development may make interesting reading for the economists, but they are gloomy news indeed for the under-developed countries. The initial resources for simultaneous development on many fronts are generally lacking. The preferable way, in view of this paucity of resources, would again be to make a start somewhere and gradually increase the rate of investment and the number of directions of expansion. Thus, the most feasible procedure for the under-developed countries is the least desirable and least economical type of all.

Still other choices of evil confront the under-developed countries. Perhaps the most striking of these relates to income distribution. In the historical course of nineteenth-century industrialization, there was sharply unequal income distribution, which lowered consumption and produced savings from the upper income group which could be reinvested. This is not the only means of capital accumulation, but the other methods involve mass taxation, economic controls, rationing, or the like, which are most difficult to organize in under-developed countries. Such countries may try to promote a high rate of domestic savings by an unequal income distribution, but the "savings" of the upper income group are likely to take forms not conducive to economic development, such as luxury consumption, especially of imported commodities, transfer of capital abroad, or hoarding of gold, other precious metals, or foreign currency. The machinery for effective taxation of high incomes is usually lacking. On the other hand, with an equal income distribution, it is futile to hope for a

[1] See P. N. Rosenstein-Rodan, "Problems of Industrialisation of Eastern and South-Eastern Europe," in *Economic Journal*, June–September 1943, pp. 202–11.

volume of domestic voluntary savings sufficient for even a modest start in economic development.

There remains the method of financing development by inflation; but at this point, yet another vicious circle appears. The inflationary method of increasing output and transferring resources from consumption to investment is much more dangerous in the under-developed countries than in the industrialized ones. Output in the former is rigid, and much less likely to increase under the stimulus of increased monetary demand than in the latter. A comparison of wartime development in the under-developed countries compared with that of the United States or the United Kingdom supports this contention. The whole theory of stimulating output by raising effective demand has been developed for industrialized countries, and its application to under-developed countries may do more harm than good. An external identity of the goal—that is, to raise output—conceals a fundamental difference in the techniques required for its achievement.

Although it has been argued that inflation does less harm in the under-developed countries than in the industrialized countries,[2] second thought suggests that this is only superficially true. One of the things essential for under-developed countries is the transition to a fully monetary economy and fully developed specialization of labor; this may be just as indispensable as technological improvements. Inflation delays and may prevent the transition to a monetary economy because it undermines confidence in money, especially among farmers. In this respect, the wartime inflation has been a serious setback to the under-developed countries.

The last and a particularly vicious example of the vicious circles with which we are concerned derives from the political context in which economic development has to be carried out. The desire for economic development may or may not arise from popular feelings and popular pressure; but in under-developed countries, it is always government that has to formulate the desire and translate it into action. A private entrepreneur class either does not exist at all, or finds conditions in the under-developed countries generally unfavorable for its assumption of the major role in determining the course of economic development. This dependence of economic development on government has two significant implications. First, there is a problem of government stability. Where the economic institutions for development are governmental, political instability is reflected in confused, contradictory, or abortive economic policies. Under-developed countries need stability of government far more than industrialized countries, where development has become automatic. At the same time, the very lack of economic development in many countries makes for instability of government. Second, as has been pointed

[2] A. R. Prest, *War Economics of Primary Producing Countries* (Cambridge, Eng., 1948).

out, the soundest advice on economic development would generally be in the direction of patience—that is, waiting to proceed until enough resources for sizable and simultaneous investments and the creation of external economies can be accumulated. To the peoples of under-developed countries, this is highly unpalatable advice, to say the least; to their governments, it is unacceptable. Very few governments can afford to justify their policies over the economist's "long period." For governments, it is indeed true that "in the long run we are all dead." The economist, if he is to render useful service, has to accept the time-table laid down by the governments and the people of under-developed countries. The best is the enemy of the good.

This discussion is by no means exhaustive. The situation of the under-developed countries illustrates, in reverse, the universal interdependence of all things economic, and the prevalence of cumulative processes which economics textbooks stress so heavily. As they point out, in economics "one thing leads to another." The tragedy of the under-developed countries is that the reverse is also true: The failure of one thing to move halts the movement of something else. One thing leads to another, but nothing leads to nothing.

Summarizing our position as it emerges from the above remarks: We are faced with an immensely difficult problem. An important step toward its solution will have been taken once the unfavorable shifts in world price relations over the last two generations have been reversed or countered; then only can the harm they have wrought in the under-developed countries be mitigated. Action of this nature may reduce the problem to such proportions that the remedies which are now beginning to be made available in the form of assistance to under-developed countries can exert a real effect. Some of the under-developed countries will overcome their initial difficulties, just as the United Kingdom, the United States, and the Soviet Union have done in their various ways, and perhaps it will not be those countries which would now seem most likely to do so. It is true that revolutionary changes in technique may help to solve the problem, but such a windfall cannot be counted on. We might far better face the fact that the problem is formidable and that we cannot afford to neglect any line of attack on it. Irresistible forces must be mobilized to meet what may perhaps prove, after all, not to be an immovable object.

20. THE CONFLICT BETWEEN "BALANCED GROWTH" AND INTERNATIONAL SPECIALIZATION*

Ragnar Nurkse

SYNOPSIS

1. The United States, Canada, Argentina, and Australia developed during the nineteenth century by producing raw materials for which they had a comparative advantage, and sending them to Europe in return for manufactured goods. The growth that concurrently took place in Europe was transmitted to these undeveloped areas by a vigorous increase in demand for primary products. International trade was an engine of economic growth.

2. In tropical areas particularly, the trade-induced growth of the nineteenth and early twentieth centuries tended to be lop-sided and of an "outpost" nature, with little secondary investment in home industries.

3. While the undeveloped areas should seize any opportunity available for trade-induced growth, the favorable conditions of the nineteenth century are not present. The developed countries, especially the U.S., are themselves efficient producers of primary products or synthetic substitutes for them. The growth of synthetics has offset the marked reduction in the U.S. tariff during the last twenty years.

4. The bulk of the international trade is between the developed countries. Very little is between the undeveloped countries.

5. The post-war industrial boom did not result in improvements in the terms of trade for the undeveloped countries, as would normally be expected, because imports in the developed countries did not increase as rapidly as production.

6. Hence, it is argued that the poorer countries must expand production for their own domestic markets if they are to develop. This calls for a balanced pattern of investment in those countries.

7. Because the application of capital to one industry is subject to sharply diminishing returns, balanced growth calls for development investment in a number of lines simultaneously, each creating a market for the output of the others.

8. Balanced growth does not necessarily require government direction of investment. But since capital is so limited in undeveloped areas,

* Reprinted by permission, *Lectures on Economic Development*, (Istanbul: Faculty of Economics, Istanbul University; and Ankara: Faculty of Political Science, Ankara University, 1958), pp. 165–82.

state investment may be required to mobilize all possible domestic sources of capital.

9. Balanced growth requires horizontal diversification, with each industry supplying the products demanded by consumers whose incomes are rising as a result of economic development.

10. If the products for which a country has a comparative advantage are price-inelastic and show a sluggish rate of increase in demand, investment in export industries may lead to stagnation.

11. Hence, there is need for two kinds of investment: one to utilize opportunities in export industries, and the other those in domestic industries.

12. Balanced growth need not create balance of payments difficulties because it need not be inflationary.

The idea of balanced growth is playing a prominent role in both the theory and the policy of economic development. My purpose here is to consider whether this idea is compatible with the principle of international specialization or whether, on the contrary, it means throwing away the benefits of specialization. The dominant practical question in some of the less developed countries is whether the available means, limited as they are, should be used to promote activities that (*a*) are specialized along lines of comparative advantage internationally or (*b*) are diversified so as to provide markets for each other locally. In western eyes the pursuit of balanced growth is causing only too often a pathetic misdirection of scarce resources. Some of the under-developed countries, on the other hand, feel that they cannot rely on an external demand for their primary products, a demand which is usually inelastic with respect to price. Is there any guarantee, they ask, that the over-spill of prosperity from the advanced countries, through changes in the volume and terms of trade and possibly, in response thereto, through private foreign investment in primary production for export, will induce a satisfactory rate of development—satisfactory in relation, for instance, to population change? The clash of prescriptions on the policy plane reflects what looks like a clash on the theoretical level also.

I

Before we attack the main problem, it will be instructive to take a look at past experience and see how economic growth in certain areas was induced through international trade in the nineteenth century. The areas involved in this process of "growth through trade" were chiefly the regions of recent settlement in the temperate latitudes outside Europe. These areas (especially the United States, Canada, Argentina, and Australia) received a sizable flow of labor as well as capital from Europe, but the basic inducement that caused them to develop was the tremendous expansion of western Europe's, and especially Great Britain's, demand for the foodstuffs and raw materials which they were well suited to produce. Growth at the periphery was induced, through trade, by growth in the rising industrial center.

It was under the impression of this experience that Marshall, in his *Principles,* made the following significant pronouncement: "The causes which determine the economic progress of nations belong to the study of international trade." In the middle of the twentieth century, this may seem to us a curious statement. It can be understood only in the light of certain historical conditions: It embodies the particular experience of Britain's economic relations with the new countries over-seas. Economic growth in these areas was due not to international specialization alone but more particularly to the fact that the character of international trade was such that the rapid growth which was taking place in the center was transmitted to the outlying new countries. It was transmitted to them through a vigorous increase in the demand for primary products. Trade in the nineteenth century was not simply a device for the optimum allocation of a given stock of resources. It was above all an engine of growth. This profoundly important observation is one which we owe to Sir Dennis Robertson. It helps us to see things in perspective; but in doing so, it serves also to put the classical trade theory in its proper place. The conventional tendency is to explain the spectacular growth of the new countries in the nineteenth century as the result of international specialization as such, when actually it was the result of rather special conditions that made specialization favorable to growth. In the light of Robertson's remark, it can be argued that classical specialization theory, which in the nature of the case is a static analysis, has derived more credit and more prestige from nineteenth-century experience than it has deserved. The dynamic nature of trade as a transmitter of growth was overlooked during an era in which progress was taken for granted, like the air we breathe.

There is no doubt that international trade was peculiarly important in the conditions of the nineteenth century. In real volume, it increased tenfold between 1850 and 1913, twice as fast as world production. Imperialism had very little to do with the expansion of trade. As was shown by J. A. Hobson himself, the tropical colonies took a minor share in the growth of British trade. The new countries, outside as well as within the British empire, were more important. Their development was part of the growth of international trade itself. They were high income countries from the start: effective markets as well as efficient producers.

It is true that, aside from the successful regions of recent settlement, economic growth induced through trade carried with it in some cases features that still are regarded as undesirable. It sometimes led to a lop-sided pattern of growth in which production of primary products for export was carried on with the aid of substantial investment by foreign capital while the domestic economy remained far less developed, if not altogether primitive. This applies especially to tropical areas. It is the familiar picture of the dual economy resulting from trade and from foreign investments induced by trade. An area of outpost investment producing for foreign markets often showed a lack of social as well as economic integration internally. In its export activities, it was subject to the familiar hazards of cyclical instability.

In general, economic growth induced through trade, even when re-inforced through foreign investment in extractive industries working for export, can hardly be expected to narrow the gap in income levels between the center and the periphery. Nevertheless, even "unbalanced" and unsteady growth through foreign trade is surely much better than no growth at all. Foreign capital working for export usually leads to an additional demand for local labor, increased wage incomes, expenditures on local materials, increased sources of taxation, and, especially in the case of mineral concessions, lucrative profit-sharing arrangements. All these benefits should help to promote progress in the domestic economy.

The traditional pattern of development through production for expanding export markets is not to be despised. Any opportunities that present themselves in this direction should be seized. The real trouble is that in the mid-twentieth century, with a few notable exceptions, conditions for this type of growth do not seem to be as promising as they were a hundred years ago.

Since 1913, as we all know, world trade has increased less than world production. To be sure, in the last five or six years, we find the volume of trade in the non-communist world increasing at just about the same pace as production. But when we look closely, we find that it is chiefly among the advanced industrial countries that international trade has been expanding in the recent past. These countries, including above all the U.S., are themselves efficient primary producers, especially of food. Their demand for foreign raw materials like crude rubber, silk, nitrates, jute, and vegetable oils has been, and will almost certainly continue to be, affected by the growth of the chemical industry in the twentieth century. The latest technological casualty among American imports that I have heard of is chicle, which we used to import from Latin America for the manufacture of chewing gum. It appears that the American chemical industry has developed a substitute which is just as good or even better. In his comprehensive study of American imports, Professor Humphrey takes the view that, in its effect on total U.S. imports, the displacement of imported raw materials by synthetic products has more than offset the 75 per cent reduction in the American tariff which has taken place in the last twenty years partly through reductions in rates of duty and partly as a result of the price inflation which has diminished the burden of specific duties.

The growth of synthetic materials is undoubtedly one explanation of the findings which Professor Kindleberger reaches in his recent book on *The Terms of Trade: A European Case Study*. It lends some support to the view that the poorer countries' terms of trade have shown a persistent tendency to deteriorate. Other recent studies have provided evidence that world demand for the poorer countries' exports has tended to rise much less than in proportion to the production and incomes of the advanced countries. For the post-war period, this conclusion is very clearly presented in the last world economic survey of the United Nations (1956) and also in the remarkable report on international trade published by GATT (General Agreement on Trade and Tariffs).

Only for minerals is the prospect favorable, although the demand for metals is being affected by the increasing efficiency of scrap collection and recovery of metals in the industrial countries. Besides, it should not be forgotten that the export of minerals, including petroleum as well as metal ores, involves in an obvious sense an element of living on capital. Professor Cairncross, in his careful statistical study of world exports of manufactured goods since 1900, has shown that the manufactured goods which the industrial countries export to each other have constituted a steadily increasing proportion of their total exports.

It is therefore not surprising that, according to the GATT report mentioned, we find the following distribution of international trade in the non-communist world. The exports of twenty advanced industrial countries to each other (United States, Canada, Japan, and western Europe) constitute as much as 40 per cent of total exports. Exports from these twenty countries to all less developed countries in the non-communist world amount to 25 per cent of the total. Exports from the latter to the former group of countries represent another 25 per cent. Only 10 per cent of the total are exports of the less developed countries to each other, although the more than one hundred countries in this group contain two thirds of the total population. Why is it that so little of the coffee, tea, rubber, and tin produced in the countries of this group goes to other countries in the same group? Obviously, the main explanation is the low purchasing power of the inhabitants of these countries, which in turn is a reflection of their low productivity. The fact that the economically advanced countries are each others' best customers is now more than ever the central feature of world trade. It is chiefly within this small circle of countries that international trade is now expanding. With the exception of petroleum and a few other minerals, subject to the reservation noted, it can hardly be said that primary producing countries are enjoying a dynamic expansion in world demand for their exports. The unprecedented boom which the industrial countries have enjoyed in the last decade has had little or no perceptible effect in improving the terms of trade of primary producing countries. In view of the tremendous growth of the American economy combined with the liberalization of American tariff policy in the last two decades, it is surely an extraordinary fact that, according to an official index, the real volume of American imports of agricultural products in 1956 was almost exactly the same as in the period 1924–29. U.S. imports of all crude materials in 1955 were only about 25 per cent higher in volume than in 1929, whereas the U.S. gross national product at constant prices has more than doubled since 1929. These trends are not confined to the U.S. They affect the trade of other advanced areas as well.

If this is the situation in the mid-twentieth century, the mental habits which economists have inherited from the mid-nineteenth may no longer be adequate. It is no longer so certain that the less developed countries can rely on economic growth being induced from the outside through an expansion of world demand for their exports of primary commodities. In these circumstances, reliance on induced expansion through international trade cannot provide a solution to the problem of economic development. It is not surprising, therefore, that countries should be looking for other solutions. It is important to keep these things in mind, because they form the background to the case for balanced growth which is now so much in vogue.

II

The circumstances indicated do not apply to all under-developed countries today: Kuwait and perhaps Iraq have nothing to worry about. But insofar as these circumstances do exist in reality, it is clear that the poorer countries, even if they are only to keep pace with the richer, to say nothing about catching up with them, must expand production for their own domestic markets or for each others' markets. Now, domestic markets are limited because of mass poverty due to low productivity. Private investment in any single industry considered by itself is discouraged by the smallness of the existing market. The limits set by the small size of local markets for manufactured goods are so plainly visible that we are fully justified in assuming conditions of imperfect competition in those markets.

The solution seems to be a balanced pattern of investment in a number of different industries, so that people working more productively, with more capital and improved techniques, become each others' customers. In the absence of vigorous upward shifts in world demand for exports of primary products, a low income country, through a process of diversified growth, can seek to bring about upward shifts in domestic demand schedules by means of increased productivity and therefore increased real purchasing power. In this way, a pattern of mutually supporting investments in different lines of production can enlarge the size of the market and help to fill the vacuum in the domestic economy of low income areas. This, in brief, is the notion of balanced growth.

Isolated advance is not impossible. A solitary process of investment and increased productivity in one industry alone will certainly have favorable repercussions elsewhere in the economy. There is no denying that through the normal incentives of the price mechanism, other industries will be induced to advance also. But this may be a snail's pace of progress. The price mechanism works, but it may work too slowly. That is one reason for the frequently observed fact that foreign direct investments in extractive export industries have created high productivity islands in low income areas and have had little impact on the level of productivity in the domestic economy.

Within the domestic economy itself, advance in one direction, say in industry A, tends to induce advance in B as well. But if it is only a passive reaction to the stimulus coming from A, the induced advance of B may be slow and uncertain. And B's slowness and passiveness will in turn slow down and discourage the initial advance in A. The application of capital to one industry alone may therefore be subject to sharply diminishing returns. As a way of escape from slowness, if not from stagnation, the balanced growth principle envisages autonomous advance along a number of lines more or less simultaneously.

Viewed in this way, balanced growth is a means to accelerated growth. Some economists treat the problem of achieving balanced growth as quite separate from the problem of speeding up the rate of advance in a backward economy. I admit that this way may be a convenient distinction to draw on other grounds. But in my view, balanced growth is first and foremost a means of getting out of the rut, a means of stepping up the rate of growth when the external forces of advance through trade expansion and foreign capital are sluggish or inoperative.

In the existing state of affairs in low income areas the introduction of capital-using techniques of production in any single industry is inhibited by the small size of the market. Hence the weakness of private investment incentives in such areas. The balanced growth principle points to a way out of the deadlock. New enterprises set up in different industries create increased markets for each other, so that in each of them the installation of capital equipment becomes worth while. As Marshall said, "The efficiency of specialized machinery . . . is but one condition of its economic use; the other is that sufficient work should be found to keep it well employed." The techniques that have been developed in production for mass markets in advanced countries are not well adapted and sometimes not adaptable at all to output on a more limited scale. It is easy to see that the relationship between the size of the market and the amount of investment required for efficient operation is of considerable importance for the theory of balanced growth.

Frequently, the objection is made: But why use machinery? Why adopt capital-using methods in areas where labor is cheap and plentiful? Why not accordingly employ techniques that are labor-intensive instead of capital-intensive?

The answer is obvious. As an adaptation to existing circumstances, including the existing factor proportions, the pursuit of labor-intensive production methods with a view to economizing capital may be perfectly correct. But the study of economic development must concern itself with changing these circumstances, not accepting them as they are. What is wanted is progress, not simply adaptation to present conditions. And progress depends largely on the use of capital, which in turn depends on adequate and growing markets, which in the absence of a strongly rising world demand for the country's exports means a diversified output expansion for domestic use.

Reference has been made to the importance of autonomous advance in a number of mutually supporting lines of production. How is this achieved? Autonomous advance in different branches simultaneously may come about through the infectious influence of business psychology, through the multiplier effects of investment anywhere which can create increased money demand elsewhere, or through deliberate control and planning by public authorities. According to some writers, the balanced growth argument implies that the market mechanism is eliminated and that investments must be effected according to a coordinated plan. This opinion, which is widely held, seems to me dubious. There are many important reasons for government planning, but this is not necessarily one of them. As a means of creating inducements to invest, balanced growth can be said to be relevant primarily to a private enterprise system. State investment can and often does go ahead without any market incentives. Planning authorities can apply capital, if they have any, wherever they may choose, though if they depart too much from balance as dictated by income elasticities of demand, they will end by creating white elephants and intolerable disproportionalities in the structure of production. It is private investment that is attracted by markets and that needs the inducement of growing markets. It is here that the element of mutual support is so useful and, for rapid growth, indispensable.

It is important to note that the doctrine under consideration is not itself concerned with the question of where the capital is to be found for all the balanced investment which it envisages. I have tried to make it clear in my discussion of it that the argument is primarily relevant to the problem of the demand for capital; it takes an increased supply of capital for granted. In my presentation, balanced growth is an exercise in economic development with unlimited supplies of capital, analogous to Professor Lewis' celebrated exercise in development with unlimited labor supplies.

In reality, of course, capital supplies are not unlimited. It may be that the case for state investment stems chiefly from the fact that capital is scarce and that government efforts are necessary to mobilize all possible domestic sources of saving. Measures to check the expansion of consumer demand may be necessary to make resources available for investment but may at the same time weaken the private inducement to invest. This is a famous dilemma to which Malthus first called attention in his *Principles of Political Economy.* A case for state investment may clearly arise if and when the mobilization of capital supplies discourages private investment activity and so destroys the demand for capital. But this case is entirely separate from the principle of balanced growth as such. It might only be added that the capital supply problem alone creates a strong presumption against relying on the indiscriminate use of import restrictions which may reduce a country's real income and therefore make it harder to increase the flow of saving.

Elsewhere, I have tried to explain how the balanced growth idea is related to the classical law of markets. Supply creates its own demand, provided that supply is properly distributed among different commodities in accordance with consumers' wants. An increase in consumable output must provide a balanced diet. Each industry must advance along an expansion path determined by the income elasticity of consumer demand for its product. This simple idea must be the starting point in any expansion of production for domestic markets in the less developed countries, insofar as external demand conditions do not favor the traditional pattern of "growth through trade." Yet, as often happens in economic discussion, critics have tended to dismiss this idea either as a dangerous fallacy or as an obvious platitude. It is hardly necessary to add that the pattern of consumable output cannot be expected to remain the same in successive stages of development. The content of a balanced diet of a man with a thousand dollars a year will differ from that of a man with a hundred dollars.

The relation between agriculture and manufacturing industry offers the clearest and simplest case of balance needed for economic growth. In a country where the peasantry is incapable of producing a surplus of food above its own subsistence needs, there is little or no incentive for industry to establish itself: There is not a sufficient market for manufactured goods. Conversely, agricultural improvements may be inhibited by lack of a market for farm products if the non-farm sector of the economy is backward or undeveloped. Each of the two sectors must try to move forward. If one remains passive, the other is slowed down.

It is important in this connection to make a clear distinction between two concepts that are frequently confused: the marketable surplus and the investable surplus of the farm sector. The farm sector's marketable surplus of farm products determines the volume of non-farm employment, including employment in manufacturing and other activities. It reflects simply the farm sector's demand for non-agricultural commodities. This is the concept that is relevant to the balanced growth principle.

An investable surplus of farm products represents an act of saving in the farm sector. It can conceivably result from a transfer of surplus laborers from the farms to capital construction projects: A food surplus may then arise through forced or voluntary saving in the farm sector for maintaining the workers engaged on capital projects. This is the concept relevant to the problem of capital supply. It is obvious that even a large marketable surplus of food need not involve any saving by the farmers. It presents a very helpful inducement, but does not in itself create the means, for capital investment outside the agricultural sector. A fuller discussion of the inter-relationship between marketable and investable surpluses would take us too far from our present subject. It seemed desirable to mention the distinction here merely for the sake of conceptual clarity. So much for the relation between agriculture and industry.

Within the manufacturing field alone the case for balanced investment implies a horizontal diversification of industrial activities, all pushing ahead, though naturally at varying rates. The objection can be made that such diffusion of effort and resources over many different lines of activity must mean a loss of dynamic momentum in the economy. This is possible. The dispersal of investment over a variety of consumer goods industries can undoubtedly be carried to excess. The balanced growth principle can be and has been interpreted far too literally. Producing a little of everything is not the key to progress. The case for balanced growth is concerned with establishing a pattern of mutually supporting investments over a range of industries wide enough to overcome the frustration of isolated advance, in order precisely to create a forward momentum of growth. The particular factors that determine the optimum pattern of diversification have to do with technology, physical conditions, and other circumstances that vary from country to country. There can be no standard prescription of universal applicability. We are concerned with a point of principle and cannot deal with the precise forms of its implementation in practice. Just as it is possible for manufacturing industry as a whole to languish if farmers produce too little and are too poor to buy anything from factories, so it is possible for a single line of manufacturing to fail for lack of support from other sectors in industry as well as agriculture, that is, for lack of markets.

The case for diversification which emerges from these considerations stands in sharp contrast, first of all, to the great concentrations of capital needed for public overhead facilities such as transport and electric power. This type of investment in public overheads will be reserved for a separate discussion.

Secondly, the diversification argument contrasts with the teaching of the doctrine of comparative advantage, which tends to show that countries gain by concentration of effort on a limited range of activities rather than by trying to do everything at home. The first part of this lecture discussed certain reasons why possibilities of growth induced through international trade may have declined of late. Having considered the argument for balanced investment, we are now ready to tackle the central point of our subject: the apparent conflict between domestic diversification and international specialization.

III

The classical theory of trade shows that at least up to a point a country can benefit by concentrating its effort and resources along lines of international comparative advantage. This is an important and familiar truth which no country that is seeking development can afford to ignore. But once a country has adopted an optimum pattern and optimum degree of specialization along these lines, how is it to achieve *continued* further growth if external demand conditions do not induce it? There is no doubt that the opening-up of trade can bring very sizable gains to a primitive economy; but is there any guarantee that trade alone will thereafter cause a rate of growth that can be regarded as satisfactory in the light, for instance, of population increase at home or of the living levels prevailing abroad? There is no such guarantee, especially if the export products which the comparative advantage principle tells a country to produce face an external demand which (*a*) is generally inelastic with respect to price and (*b*), what may be more important, shows only a sluggish rate of increase in total volume. Granted all the advantages of international specialization, there remains a possibility of deadlock and comparative stagnation.

In the nineteenth century, growth was created through international trade not only because countries previously isolated and self-contained now decided to specialize. This was indeed an important factor in the opening-up of Japan and more generally as a result of the great improvements in transport. But it was not all. Economic development was diffused through international trade because the pattern of advance in the rising industrial centers happened to be such as to cause a rapidly increasing demand for imported foodstuffs and raw materials. Insofar as this was the operating factor, it should be kept distinct from the act of specialization. Much of the conventional theory of trade seems to me to be based on a very understandable, yet analytically illegitimate, generalization of nineteenth-century experience, an experience which in some ways was unique.

The theory of international specialization as such is a static analysis. It assumes a given pattern of comparative advantage, given levels of domestic productivity, and given amounts of productive resources. The theory can be and has been supplemented by considering the way in which factor supplies may react to the opening-up of trade; but even in this form, it remains an exercise in comparative statics.

The transmission of growth from a dynamically expanding center is a rather different story, in which a rapidly rising demand for imports of primary products is the decisive feature, which in its turn generates outflows of productive factors to the peripheral areas to meet this demand. Now, my point is that the case for specialization as such is just as strong as ever, but that the forces making for the transmission of growth from advanced to less developed countries may not be as powerful as they were one hundred years ago. In these circumstances, without giving up the benefits of international specialization, there may be a case for output expansion for the home market in a country where the supply of productive factors, including capital, is increasing. The idea, popular in some quarters, that a single country has to have all industries, including especially capital goods industries, derives no support from the economic concept of balanced growth in the limited sense in which I interpret it. This concept, based on the diversity and hence complementarity of consumers' wants, shows how a number of industries advancing simultaneously can create markets for each others' products. It is not an argument for indiscriminate industrialization. Let us remember that agriculture too is an "industry" in the framework of this concept. At low income levels a large proportion of any addition to income is likely to be spent on food. Consequently, in low income countries, agricultural improvement is bound to be a crucial element in any process of balanced growth.

Nor is this an argument for autarchy. There is plenty of room for home market expansion without interfering with international trade. This becomes clear if we consider in particular the existence of transport costs, a factor often neglected in orthodox trade theory. If transport costs were zero, then a country's production pattern would not depend at all on the pattern of its own consumption and other expenditure. There would be no "localization of demand." Actually, we find very considerable localization: Countries usually spend most of their income on their own output. The presence of transport costs is at least one reason for this and certainly the most basic. It is for this reason that in poor countries, where income is spent mostly on food, the bulk of the labor force works in food production (and this is often true even of countries that are net importers of food).

Transport costs alone constitute an important barrier to complete international specialization. They create in each country a wide range of domestic goods and services within which the notion of balanced growth is applicable without prejudice to international trade. In fact, investment for home market production, so far from hurting international specialization, may lay the foundation for an increase in the volume of trade.

But transport costs are, after all, not a desirable thing but an unfortunate necessity. Is it not foolish to introduce in addition artificial barriers to promote balanced domestic development? The case for and against import restriction is a well-worn subject which I am reluctant to take up but cannot avoid altogether. In my own opinion, the restriction of imports may sometimes help but should never be relied upon. Actually, it is always apt to be over-done because it is a relatively easy thing to do.

The argument for balanced investment stresses the creation of investment incentives through the promotion of mutually supporting domestic activities. In the case of imported products, evidently a market already exists in the country. The restriction or prohibition of imports may stimulate the domestic production of import substitutes.

Now, in the first place, this is an essentially unneighborly thing to do: It hurts your neighbor; and even though he may be comparatively rich and strong, it may weaken his demand for your export products. Moreover, if nothing else is done, it is not at all certain that it will lead to a cumulative growth of the domestic market. The output of a certain commodity is increased until imports are replaced, and at that point the expansion may stop if it is based on nothing broader than import restriction and import substitution.

There is a possibility that import substitution draws resources away from export production, which may force up prices of export products and so improve the country's terms of trade. But this is a risky policy: The world outside may learn to do without those export products. Besides, increased production for the home market need not, in my opinion, impinge on the export sector at all. The purpose of the balanced investment policy is not to draw labor away from export industries but to raise the productivity of people now working in subsistence agriculture and other activities for domestic consumption.

The main disadvantage of import restriction is that it may lead to costly and inefficient production of import substitutes. The market for an imported commodity, small as it may be to start with, becomes even smaller in real volume as the price to the domestic consumer increases. The initial effect on real income is bad and may well lead to a fall in domestic saving. If at the same time it increases investment incentives, the result is likely to be inflationary. It is important to make the fullest use of opportunities for international specialization so as to maximize the real income level and hence the volume of saving available for investment. As we saw, the balanced growth doctrine assumes increased capital supplies. Where are these to come from? A high level of foreign trade may be very useful as a source of saving (as it was, for instance, for Japan).

It is not to be denied that import restrictions can help in a policy of balanced domestic investment, but their unfavorable effect on real income, and hence possibly on saving, should always be remembered. They should therefore be used sparingly. Import restrictions enforced in spite of such unfavorable effects can be justified only on the grounds of greater future benefit, which is the infant industry argument for protection. On this point, I am still inclined to maintain that infant creation is far more important than infant protection. If adequate development is not possible by means of international trade, at least we should take care that expansion of the domestic economy does not involve needless additional cost by destroying such gains as are being obtained from international specialization.

The upshot is that output expansion for domestic consumption can go ahead side by side with international specialization. It need not be a substitute for international specialization. It is a substitute rather for the growth transmission mechanism which for reasons indicated may not be as powerful today as it was in the nineteenth century.

The title of this paper has perhaps brought you here on false pretenses. You may have expected to see a fight between domestic growth and international trade. The fight is not taking place. In fact, if you look at the two protagonists in my piece a little more closely, you find that they are really friends, not enemies. Balanced growth is the best friend that international trade can have. Filling the vacuum in the domestic economy is the best foundation for foreign trade, since it means increasing the level of productivity and real purchasing power. After all, that is why the advanced nations are each others' best customers. That is the best hope for expanding world trade, although it is quite likely that trade will expand less than in proportion to national incomes. Trade as a *proportion* of world income may well decline as the domestic economies of the backward areas become more fully developed.

There is, however, a further problem that worries some economists. If production is pushed for domestic markets, will that not lead to balance of payments difficulties? The belief that it will is expressed in several places in Professor Lewis' book, *The Theory of Economic Growth*. Do we have a conflict here between balanced growth and external equilibrium? If external disequilibrium is inevitable, then this may lead to balance of payments restrictions on imports and so indirectly, after all, to a destruction of foreign trade.

Let me indicate very briefly how I would look at this problem. It is true that a new industry producing something new for the home market is likely to create an increased demand for imports because it may need some imported raw material and because part of the additional incomes earned in this industry may be spent on imported goods. But that is not the whole story; that is only one side of it. If this industry sells its products on the domestic market, the rest of the economy will have to divert its expenditure away from imported products, provided that expenditure is not increased by inflationary means—through a reduction in saving, through dishoarding, or through credit expansion. If inflation can be avoided, then the products sold by the new industry will necessarily act as import substitutes indirectly, even if they look totally different from anything imported previously. If there is a balance of payments deficit, it is a result of inflation, not of output expansion for the home market. If there is no inflation, then the rest of the economy will have to reduce its imports in order to buy the products of the new industry, and this will tend to offset the increase in imports caused by the new industry.

It may seem strange that an expansion of income in this model is not necessarily accompanied by any net increase in imports. It would seem that the marginal propensity to import is zero, which looks like a strange and unnatural result. But there is nothing strange about it if we remember that in this case there has been a structural change in the economy: the creation of a new industry. The usual concepts of income analysis in international trade assume a given economic structure. Economic development means changes in economic structure, and in this dynamic context the functional relationships between income and imports need not behave in the usual way.

There is no time to enlarge on this point. Perhaps I have said enough to suggest that it is not development for the domestic economy as such that creates balance of payments difficulties. It is the excess spending associated with inflation that creates balance of payments difficulties, and inflation is due in its turn to the difficulty which the poorer countries have in living within their means, when there is so much investment to be done and when there are so many temptations to spend on consumer goods as well. This is the great difficulty.

I may have seemed to take a rather optimistic and to some of you perhaps over-optimistic note in regard to the particular subject of this paper. That does not mean that it is all very easy in practice. On this occasion, I have neglected, for instance, the whole problem of capital mobilization. I would not for a moment deny that development on the home front is bound to be a painful and difficult process. But it is in some cases a necessary task and a promising one.

Growth via Specialization

21. STABILITY AND PROGRESS:
THE POORER COUNTRIES' PROBLEM*

Jacob Viner

SYNOPSIS

1. The vicious circle of poverty in undeveloped countries has a hopeful as well as a discouraging aspect. Extreme poverty retards growth, and retarded growth reinforces poverty; but once the circle is broken, growth and rising income reinforce each other.

2. Two factors are ignored in the argument that undeveloped countries are injured by a fall in prices of their raw material exports relative to the price of their manufactured imports: (*a*) the improved quality of manufactured goods and (*b*) the improvements of technology that reduce the cost of producing raw materials.

3. Monopolies and cartels in the richer countries do not necessarily put the poorer countries at a disadvantage in bargaining.

4. It is alleged that the attractiveness of the imports from the richer countries makes it difficult for the poorer countries to save and involves them in balance of payment difficulties. But the attractiveness of the commodities can also be an inducement to work and save.

5. It has been argued by Nurkse and others that "balanced investment" in a wide range of industries is necessary to (*a*) achieve external economies and (*b*) provide domestic markets. Attention must also be paid to external diseconomies and to the markets developed by investment in export industries. Many of the net external economies are equally available in the international market.

6. Attempts to stabilize world market prices of primary products have not been successful. Possibly the only solution to the problem is greater stability in the richer countries.

7. The doctrine of comparative advantage, when considered in connection with long run costs, is still a valid guide to resource allocation in the poorer countries.

8. It is not certain that population grows more slowly in urban areas; and hence, there is no justification for directing investment there artificially. The population problem is critical.

9. But if it is solved, the poorer countries can grow rapidly by drawing on the accumulated knowledge of the richer countries.

There has been assigned to me the general topic of stability and progress as problems for the poorer countries. I hope I will be regarded

* Reprinted and shortened by permission from *Stability and Progress in the World Economy*, ed. Douglas Hague (London: Macmillan, 1958), pp. 41–65.

as being responsive to my assignment if economic instability is dealt with only as it may be an obstacle to economic progress in the poorer countries, if progress is interpreted to mean improvement of the levels of per capita income, and if I make my main topic the causes of and the possible remedies for the poverty of the poorer countries.

Sir Dennis Robertson, who has carried out so brilliantly his corresponding assignment for the richer countries, has surrendered to me, with undisguised alacrity, all of Asia, Africa, and South America. I will neither reject nor accept Sir Dennis' delineation of the boundaries of my territory, provided it is understood that people must be poor to fall within my jurisdiction. But did Sir Dennis intend to exclude from my orbit the Central American and Caribbean countries, which do not happen to be in Asia, or in Africa, or even in South America? And did he unqualifiedly reject as outside his orbit all or any of those communist countries which are not located in South America, Africa, or Asia?

Poverty's Handicaps

In discussions of the problems of national poverty, the slightest gesture toward a general statement is liable to meet the objection that the poorer countries differ greatly among themselves in many relevant respects. It would not be practicable for me, however, even if I had the qualifications to do so competently, to attempt to tailor my remarks to fit closely each of the fifty, or perhaps one hundred, countries with which I have been endowed. Of the making of generalizations, there will, nevertheless, be no end in this paper. I must therefore ask you in advance to interpret them as if they were believed by me to apply to most, or to many, but not necessarily to all the poorer countries.

The question why some countries are much poorer than others presents a challenge to the economist, to which he will respond in a great variety of ways, according to his methodological bent, his interests, skills, and insights, and the uses, if any, to which he expects his answer to be put. It is probable that there is scarcely any branch of human knowledge, useful or ornamental, which cannot be drawn upon for a contribution to the answer; and it is clear beyond dispute that political scientists, historians, sociologists, anthropologists, geographers, geologists, and others can profitably be consulted by the economist in his search for an answer. I can speak only as an economist, however; and if I invoke non-economic causes of poverty as part of the picture, I concede in advance that I do so without claim to the necessary professional qualifications. Disciplines, however, usually prefer encroachment on their territories by outsiders to being ignored. On the other hand, there is almost no economic factor, no matter how important it may seem to most of us, which some economist will not ignore or minimize, either out of inadvertence or honest ignorance, or because recognition of it would get in the way of a desired conclusion, or mar a pretty theory, or complicate the analysis. I have done my best to avoid this danger, but my best may well be not good enough.

The concept of "cause" has its own notorious difficulties. I will assume that we are all agreed that national poverty generally has many causes, and that if our interest is in how the poverty can be relieved, the proper procedure is to seek to identify those causes which are both major and strategic in the sense that their removal or moderation is not beyond the conceivable power of the relevant portion of mankind. But "causes" themselves all have the "causes," and so on, in an infinite regress, and I will assume that the best procedure is to try to identify them and to understand their mode of operation at the critical stage at which there is most chance that they can be removed or moderated. In discussion in this area we are likely to hear much of the "vicious circle" of poverty, with the implication sometimes drawn from it that, since poverty is self-perpetuating, the poverty of the poorer countries can be remedied only by the intervention of a *deus ex machina*, in the guise of aid from outside Asia, Latin America or Africa—or Europe, or Australasia. I do think, with many others, that there is an important element of the vicious circle in the problem of poverty, and that there is therefore good reason for invoking external aid to help break that circle and to help to undermine the defeatism on the part of the poor which recognition of the circle is liable to foster. A part at least, however, of what gives rise to the vicious circle is the fact that some of the most important causes of national poverty reinforce each other by their simultaneous existence. Extreme poverty, for instance, is both caused by the absence of health and vigor and literacy and is a barrier to their attainment, while lack of any of these leads almost inevitably to lack of the others. But this has its hopeful as well as its discouraging aspect, since it warrants the hope that the removal or weakening of any important barrier to economic progress will be of itself a contribution to the removal or weakening of other barriers. Economic progress is not completely indivisible, and its major elements seem to be at least moderately contagious. There may be as much of a beneficent circle in progress toward prosperity as there is a vicious circle in economic deterioration.

* * *

The External Handicaps

I turn now to consideration of obstacles to the economic progress of the poorer countries which may arise out of either the misbehavior of Sir Dennis' part of the world [the richer countries] or of the faulty handling by the poorer countries of such aspects of their economic relations with the richer countries as the poorer countries have it within their power to control.

I will disregard "economic imperialism" and "colonialism," if these are understood to mean resort by richer countries to their political or military power to impose on poorer countries an economic régime which is a barrier to their economic progress. However important these may have been in the past, and whatever contribution to the present poverty of the poorer countries past "imperialism" and "colonialism" may have made, most of the countries within my orbit are today completely free from external political control over their economic policies. Even for those which are still in a "colonial" status, it is in most cases at least a matter for reasonable argument whether complete independence would be to their economic advantage.

The commercial policy of the richer countries can most obviously be an important barrier to the economic improvement of the poorer countries when such policy includes severe barriers to the import of the staple products of the poorer countries. One example, chosen from the many available because it is a particularly glaring one, is the promotion, by import duties, import quotas, or subsidies, of domestic production of sugar by such countries as the United States, Britain, and Canada. Another is the selection by the richer countries of staple products of the poorer countries, such as coffee, tea, tobacco, which have no close domestic competition, for specially heavy excise taxation, some of whose burden is undoubtedly shifted back to the foreign producers. These and other such measures are to be charged in the books, at least if the accountant is in principle an adherent of free trade, as debits against Sir Dennis' countries. Except on the principle, however, that in the economic relations between richer and poorer countries reciprocity should be on one side only, it is only fair to point out that the poorer countries are no longer novices themselves in carrying further than is even in their own interest, no matter how narrowly conceived, the attempt to attain prosperity for one's own people by the impoverishment, or the lessening of the prosperity, of other peoples. I leave the ethical question here to more qualified moral casuists, especially as my personal biases would lead me, with relatively minor qualifications, to invoke a plague on both sets of tariff-fostered hothouses. But spokesmen of and for the poorer countries would insist that this disregards the economic grounds on which what is sinful when practiced by richer countries can be ethically justified when practiced by the poorer countries, even if the richer countries should mend their own ways.

The poorer countries are largely exporters of primary commodities; and under universal free trade, many of them would continue indefinitely to be so. It has been claimed that there is a historical law by virtue of which the prices of industrial products rise relative to the prices of raw materials and foodstuffs, and consequently the commodity or net barter terms of trade move against the poorer countries. The statistical record is appealed to in support of the existence of this law, although I would contend that the relevant statistical record has so far been only superficially and clumsily analyzed, and that even the analysis so far made yields a clear or even plausible confirmation of the law only to those determined in advance to find such confirmation with the aid of judicious selection of base years and of terminal years. I have discussed this issue elsewhere. Here I will confine myself to calling attention to two generally neglected considerations. First, in using national price index numbers in order to calculate terms of trade, it needs to be remembered that such index numbers do not ordinarily, and cannot easily be made to, take into account changes in the quality of commodities over time and the introduction of new commodities. Over the past fifty or one hundred years, it has been the leading exports of the richer countries much more than of the poorer countries which have consisted of commodities improving greatly in quality over time or of commodities newly introduced into trade. Second, those who insist that there has been a secular trend of the commodity terms of trade adverse to the poorer countries should deal with the British economists who have, since early in this century, been contending that for Britain the secular trend of its commodity terms of trade was currently unfavorable, and promised, or rather threatened, for various reasons which they adduce, to continue to be so.

All other things equal, it is, of course, to the advantage of a country that its export prices should be high and should be moving still higher, relative to its import prices. As a rule, however, *caetera non sunt paria* [other things are not equal]. If the real costs per unit of producing a country's exports have been falling, it may be getting more in return per unit of factor input devoted to production for export, even if the prices of its imports are rising compared to its export prices, that is, its "single factoral terms of trade" may be improving even when its commodity terms of trade are deteriorating. No one terms of trade concept can suffice to catch all the subtleties and escape all the ambiguities of the "gain from trade" idea. But I believe that the single factoral terms of trade index, though inconclusive, is clearly and unquestionably superior to the net barter or commodity terms of trade index as representing the trend of national gain from trade.

It has been objected that the factoral terms of trade concept is not useful because it is not susceptible of statistical measurement. I am not even yet, at this late date, prepared to accept statistical measurability as a crucial test of the relevance or usefulness of concepts for economic thinking. In any case, one should not under-estimate the ingenuity of the quantifiers. In a recent publication of that hive of statistical innovation, the National Bureau of Economic Research, series of labor input and property input, per unit of output, and weighted combinations of these, are presented. Construct such a factoral cost index for a country's export commodities and multiply its reciprocal by the index of that country's commodity terms of trade, and you have its singe factoral terms of trade.

It has been claimed, however, that the prevalence in the richer countries of entrepreneurial and trade-union monopoly enables them to

withhold from the poorer countries any share in the benefits of technological improvement in the production of the richer countries' export
commodities. Perhaps so, although it should not be accepted without
more statistical or other testing than it has so far received. The effects,
such as they are, of the cartels and monopolies of the richer countries on
price levels and price trends may be less marked for export prices than
for domestic prices, because of dumping and of competition between
national monopolies. In appraising the effect of monopoly on the level
and on the trend of the terms of trade between rich and poor countries,
there need also to be taken into account the valorization schemes and the
export taxes which the poorer countries use, perhaps unsuccessfully, to
raise *their* export prices. In any case, I am wholly unconvinced by any
arguments I have so far encountered that in the process of trade bargaining, richness is always, or even generally, an advantage and poverty
a handicap. Britain, India, and the United States are all exporters of cotton textiles, and I cannot see how their relative per capita national incomes affect the commodity terms on which they exchange these cot-
tons for imports. Nor can I see why Canada has a bargaining advantage
in buying oranges from the poor West Indies rather than from rich California or Florida. Effectiveness in trade bargaining for a country depends
on bargaining skill, on the will to bargain, and on the availability of alternatives. In all these respects, there seems to me to be no presumption,
and assuredly no certainty, that the advantage will lie with the country
with the higher per capita income.

It has been argued recently that the attractiveness of the products of
the richer countries to poorer peoples may be obstacles to the ecinomic
improvement of the poorer countries, not only by involving them in balance of payments difficulties, but also by lowering their propensities to
save. Having in recent years found myself frantically avoiding being
run down by American Cadillacs on the thoroughfares of three not-so-
poor Latin American countries, I see some point to this extension of
Duesenberry's "demonstration effect" to the relations of poorer with
richer countries. Some difficulties, however, remain to bother me about
just what is the significance of the argument.

In the past, economists and others often attributed the lack of economic ambition they thought they could observe in some at least of the
poorer peoples to lack of sufficient attractiveness to them of the things
they were acquainted with which money could buy. Aside from the
question of incentives to work hard, to acquire skills, and to embark on
new enterprises, may not the first consequence of a new relish for radios,
bicycles, and refrigerators be, not the impulse to spend more (especially
if all was already being spent which was available for spending), but to
save more in order eventually to be able to buy these attractive novelties
now beyond their reach? In the case of the Cadillacs, moreover, it is
conceivable that they do not result in net additions to spending but are

substitutes for older and obsolescing forms of luxurious spending—trips to Paris or large retinues of servants, for example.

The new lures to spending, at least in the Latin American countries, seem to take the form, aside from the case of automobiles, of such things as radios, fountain pens, refrigerators, soft drinks, and monumental office buildings and apartment houses—all of them, apparently, suitable products for the early stages of industrialization. Without the home demand for these products, there would be no scope for the development of facilities for their domestic production.

The same lures to spending also operate, of course, in the countries in which these commodities originated. It is not clear to me why they should be more of a depressant of the propensity to save in the poorer than in the richer countries. The point may be that when the richer countries first began to emerge from *their* poverty, these temptations not to save did not yet exist, or perhaps the point is that, if there is to be any saving at all in the countries in which almost everyone is poor, the temptation to spend must be less for persons of a given level of income in the poorer countries than in the richer countries. I could support this by appeal to American statistics, which purport to show that, with the aid of instalment purchasing, there is net dissaving in the United States up to levels of income much higher than the average levels prevailing in many poorer countries. But it may still be true that in the long run the incentives to increase earning capacity which attractive commodities stimulate into being contribute more to economic progress than the incentives to current spending on these commodities subtract from it.

It is becoming increasingly fashionable to invoke the concept of external economies as providing a fresh argument for protection of new industries against foreign competition in under-developed, that is to say, poor countries. Alfred Marshall coined the term "external economies" primarily to signify the cost reductions, technical and pecuniary, which result to the firms comprising a single industry when the industry expands its output through an expansion of the number of firms within it. It has been extended to include the reductions in cost which accrue to a particular industry from the expansion of other industries in the same country or region; and it is these economies—which might be called the economies of complementarity of industries—which are relevant here. They can be used to support a broadened version of the old infant industry argument, as justification for protection to a whole range of new industries where protection to a single one of these industries might be ineffective or uneconomic.

External economies to industry A from the expansion of industry B can be technical, that is, may consist of reductions in A's technical coefficients of production or units of input required to produce a unit of output. Or they may be pecuniary, that is, reductions in the prices industry A has to pay for its input units. Conceivable instances of technical economies to industry A from the expansion of industry B would be: the availability to A, as a result of the proximity of industry B, of services of a kind which could not otherwise be obtained or which A would have otherwise to provide for itself at greater cost or with less efficiency; the elimination or reduction for industry A of transportation costs and the prompter availability with respect to certain input items when they are produced by a nearby industry B; the general inter-industry diffusion of know-how and skills, both at the managerial level and in the rank and file of the labor force, resulting from the proximity to each other of many industries.

Pecuniary economies to industry A from the expansion of industry B are also national or social economies only if they are the result either of internal economies of scale of plant or firm within industry B or of intra-industry external economies within industry B.

These external economies of complementarity of industries are distinct from, but can reinforce, the advantages which Nurkse has suggested as associated with simultaneous or "balanced" investment in a range of industries, as compared to investment in one industry at a time. According to Nurkse, investment in a single industry may be unprofitable because of the absence of an adequate market for its product, whereas if a number of industries are simultaneously established, each industry by its payroll and other expenditures will help to create a market for the products of the other industries.

All of this seems to me to have unquestionable theoretical validity, but needs careful interpretation for even theoretical purposes, and may call for major qualification if it is presented as having much practical significance.

First, as to the external economies: It is always net, not gross, external economies which are relevant, net external economies being the amount of gross external economies minus the amount of external diseconomies. Examples of pecuniary external diseconomies to industry A from the expansion of industry B would be prices to A, for input items which it purchases elsewhere than from industry B, that are higher as a result of competition between the two industries for a common supply of labor, or power, or transportation services, or other input items. There could also be technical external diseconomies for industry A from the expansion of industry B, as, for example, if internal costs of production in industry A were increased because of air or water pollution, or traffic congestion, or depletion of water supply, as the result of the establishment or expansion of industry B. The pecuniary external diseconomies to industry A resulting from expansion of industry B can, moreover, result, at a second stage, in technical diseconomies to industry A—and to third industries. This can happen when adaptation by A to increased prices of its inputs—these increases constituting the pecuniary diseconomies to A—takes the form of a forced alteration of the proportions in which it uses the various input items and thus brings into play the law of diminishing returns in its variation of the proportions of the factors sense.

Even if the external economies are net economies, for the industries directly involved and for the national economy, this is not sufficient to establish a case for the new industry or industries, since the net economies resulting from this investment have to be compared with the net economies which would result from alternative investments. If it is a question of subsidy or of tariff protection, it should especially be borne in mind that there is no presumption that an investment which would be unprofitable without subsidy or tariff protection to its owner would yield a larger flow of external economies to other industries—or to the community at large—than one which could maintain itself without subsidy or protection.

Other qualifications are applicable to the argument for balanced investment, where the advantage claimed is the mutual provision of a market for the products of the respective industries instead of external economies in the form of reductions in each other's unit costs of production. The argument of an inadequate market for the product of a single new or expanded industry will have no, or less, weight if the investment under consideration (*a*) is cost-reducing instead of output-expanding, (*b*) is import-substituting, (*c*) is for production for export, or (*d*) is some combination of these. A great deal of the investment in poor countries falls into one or the other of these categories.

It needs further to be pointed out that the economic advantages of spatial proximity between plants are subject also to exaggeration, that foreign trade does not necessarily mean distant trade, and that external economies are not by their nature confined to industries close to each other geographically but can flow across national boundaries.

I apologize for the detailed argument which I have imposed upon you. It seemed to me potentially useful to do so, however, if it served to reduce to reasonable proportions the current enthusiasm for the new arguments for protection of industries yielding external economies and for "balanced" investment at the cost of profitable investment in the private sense.

The Economic Stability of the Poorer Countries

I have so far had nothing to say about the problem of economic instability for poorer countries. As far as volume of employment is concerned, instability is less of a problem for them than for richer countries, or at least than it used to be for richer countries when the major business cycle still seemed to be a law of nature. The usual explanation of this seems satisfactory to me. The poorer countries, because of their lower per capita incomes, have investment cycles of smaller amplitude, and these cycles involve smaller fractions of total national income. The export staples of the poorer countries have greater cyclical flexibility of prices than the major exports of the richer countries, and therefore have smaller cyclical variations in volume and in the employment they afford. In many of the poorer economies, a good deal of subsistence farming survives, and the urban population still has important family links with the rural population. When depression comes, therefore, there is a reflux of population from the towns to the farms, which act as a safety valve for urban unemployment. In times of depression, the governments of the poorer countries also resort more readily and more freely to exchange depreciation and to the printing press than do the governments of richer countries, and their national stocks of money are less dependent on the volume of loans made by commercial banks. The poorer countries, therefore, suffer less in depression periods from the conjunction of falling domestic price levels, rigid wage scales, and shrinking supplies of loan funds than do the richer countries. For these reasons, and no doubt for other reasons as well, cyclical unemployment is not a major problem for the poorer countries.

The situation of the poorer countries with respect to the stability of national income, or at least of that part of national income which passes through the market, is not so favorable, however. Receipts from exports play an especially large role in the national incomes of the poorer countries; and, because these exports consist primarily of agricultural commodities and raw materials, their prices, at least in terms of hard currencies, have an amplitude of cyclical swing far exceeding that of the prices of their major imports, of freight costs, and of external debt charges. Where the imports consist largely either of luxuries or of machinery and other supplies associated with investment in durable production facilities, the demand for imports has high income elasticity, and the decline in export receipts during depression therefore does not result in severe pressure on their international balances of payments. But in all the poorer countries the decline in real national income during a world depression presses hard on already low levels of consumption and of capital formation.

The wider the range of primary commodities exported by a country, the greater is the probability that the average cyclical fluctuations in their prices in terms of hard currencies will not greatly exceed the average cyclical fluctuations in the prices of primary commodities, in general, in world markets. The less dependent the country is on exports, the more stable also is its real national income likely to be cyclically—although it should be noted that this has not been the experience of the United States. The desire for economic stability has therefore led poorer countries to seek for a widening of the range of their staple export products, and for diversification of their economies by increased domestic production of manufactured commodities largely obtained by import. However, this may not be a wise procedure, for the reduction in cyclical instability thus obtained may be purchasable only at the cost of a substantial reduction in the national real income for the cycle as a whole.

The poorer countries press hard for assumption by the richer countries of major responsibility for the artificial stabilization of the prices of primary commodities, so far with little or no success except with respect to primary commodities such as wheat and sugar, of which the richer countries are also important producers. Such stabilization, judging from the historical record, is difficult to negotiate and to administer, and the extent to which it is beneficial is at least open to debate. When the countries which are exporters of primary commodities ask for the stabilization, on a world market basis, of their prices, they often mean stabilization at or near the cyclical peaks, rather than at the mean prices of the cycle as a whole, or than at the price levels which would stabilize the *ratio* of these prices for the cycle as a whole to the average prices of their import commodities. The problem, moreover, of how to stabilize cyclically the prices of particular commodities without interfering with their long run trends, may be technically and administratively an insuperable one and, in any case, still awaits a tolerable solution. The experience with wheat stabilization presents a clear-cut illustration of this.

The instability of the prices of primary commodities is largely, though not wholly, the result of the cyclical instability of the richer countries and of their tendency to intensify their import barriers during depression. If the problem of the major business cycle really has been largely solved by the richer countries, then the problem of the instability of the prices of primary products on world markets will not be nearly so serious in the future as it has been in the past. If to general maintenance of economic stability the richer countries were to add stabilization—or still better, reformation in the direction of free trade—of their import policies, I think the poorer countries would have obtained about all that was practicable in the way of international cooperation to stabilize the prices of primary commodities. I once ventured to propose an additional measure in the form of an international investment fund which would operate counter-cyclically. While I still think this in abstract principle has its attractions, I see no practical future for it in a world split by the cold war, and in a world in which the potential major lenders would not be much more than one, and the potential borrowers would be more numerous than one.

"Lord Justice Comparative Cost"

Sir Dennis, having made an appropriate appeal to the richer countries to follow the dictates of "Lord Justice Comparative Cost," presumably both in their own national interests and in the interests of the poorer countries, went on to express confidence that I would extend similar advice to the poorer countries as well. I appreciate his trust in me, and I hope I have already in large part justified it, even if I have not so far been brave enough to use the precise term which so many modern economists find so distasteful, without always making quite clear whether it is its triteness or its error which they dislike.

The doctrine of comparative costs, properly phrased and properly interpreted, would seem to me to go little beyond common sense, were it not that men of intelligence and intellectual integrity have for generations fought it tooth and nail. To some, it has unfortunate associations with a "real cost" theory of value which they do not believe in, and is defective in its implication that either it is "costs" alone, in whatever sense of the term, that need to be compared when guidance is sought as to appropriate allocation of resources, or that "costs" are important above all other considerations. But I, for one, am just as content with the term "comparative advantage" as the label for the doctrine, and would not object strongly to the substitution for both of these terms of the term "comparative income." In any case, what need to be compared are the national real benefits to be derived from alternative patterns of economic behavior; and *all* the benefits—and worsements—that are involved are relevant to a judicious verdict. When private money costs are not closely representative of social real costs, the doctrine ceases to be a doctrine of allocation of resources according to comparative private money costs. External economies and diseconomies need to be explored and accounted for, and allowance made for monopoly elements in prices and for the effects on relative prices of such things as subsidies and discriminatory taxes. But Ricardo himself not only would have conceded all of this, but insisted repeatedly on some of it. I am not salvaging a doctrine by changing its meaning, but restating it in its original form.

It is today often objected against the traditional doctrine of comparative cost that it is a static doctrine and thus affords poor guidance for a dynamic world. Perhaps so, but I am not at all convinced that when the classical economists stated the doctrine, as they did, in long run terms, they did not intend to include in their "long run" all the dynamic factors which could reasonably be foreseen or provided for in advance. It was always costs as they could be presumed to be in the long run, and not costs as they might prevail fortuitously at the moment, which they regarded as the crucial factors to be measured and compared. Their acceptance in principle of the "infant industry" argument cannot otherwise be explained. In any case, this is the only kind of doctrine of comparative cost I can support. I may add that it calls unqualifiedly for free trade only in a world in which market prices can be accepted as close measures of the real long run social costs of production and social worth. When better measures are available, market price should be made to surrender its judicial robe—but not to promiscuous protectionism.

The Population Problem

I have not yet liquidated my indebtedness to Sir Dennis for sound advice as to what to include in my paper. He commented that if he were dealing with my part of the world, he would have to say a great deal about population. Unfortunately, I do not have time or capacity to say a great deal about population, but I will substitute emphasis for quantity.

First, I want to emphasize that the population "problem" arises not only from an excessive rate of increase of population, but also, even in the absence of any increase, from an excessive ratio of present population to natural and other resources, and from a high ratio of present population to labor force or a high ratio of dependents to total population.

Second, confidence in rising prospective levels of income as sufficing to solve the problem of excess population, by operating in some unspecified way to reduce birth rates, seems to me unwarranted. If this has worked in the richer countries, it has worked, despite the more favorable position from which they started, only at a pace too slow to satisfy the poorer countries of today, and too slow to meet their urgent needs. The first essential ingredient in this recipe, moreover, is to catch the hare, or to attain the rise in per capita income of the masses. It took England, as best I can determine, a full two centuries before technological progress brought an unambiguous rise in per capita income for the working classes.

Modern public health activities, moreover, even if welcome on some other humanitarian grounds, can operate in a new way to intensify the population problem. They can, at extraordinarily low costs per capita, and therefore without being dependent on prior economic improvement, reduce mortality rates, while not appreciably reducing, and even while increasing, age-specific fertility rates. The net result may therefore be an increase in over-all population above what it otherwise would have been, an increase, for a generation or longer, in the ratio of dependents to workers; and an adult population unimproved in health and vigor.

It is often taken too much for granted that industrialization means urbanization, that urbanization means higher per capita income levels, and that both the higher per capita income levels and the urbanization per se mean lower fertility. On the basis of these assumptions or affirmations, it has recently been argued that population needs to be introduced into the comparative cost doctrine as an additional variable, and that it then becomes, or can be made, evident that investment in industry is preferable to investment in agriculture, even if the latter yields a higher return to the investor. I do not deny the possible validity of this argument, but I will not concede its general or even probable validity until more supporting evidence or argument is supplied.

Aside from the effects on population growth, the most rewarding investment is often in the countryside and in the villages, not only in agriculture proper, but also in such non-agricultural undertakings as hydro-electric plants, cement plants, mining, tile and brick kilns, cotton gins, seed-crushing plants, bridges and roads and railroads. Second, the public health activities which reduce mortality rates may be concentrated in the cities, partly because the governments of the poor countries often favor the cities in their expenditures, and partly because the per capita costs of given public health activities are much lower in the cities than in the countryside. Third, the higher per capita money incomes in the cities may be subsidized, or parasitic, incomes at the expense of the rural population, and may not be higher real incomes after allowance for the higher cost of living. I wonder if the population experts are still so sure that in poor countries the natural rate of increase of population is slower in the cities than in the rural areas, and I venture to suggest that the reasons I have given suffice to remove warrant for such assurance.

Even if it were true that industrialization and urbanization of themselves would eventually check the rate of increase of population, can they be relied upon to do it soon enough? If the serpent of excess of population will have bitten before the urbanization charm put on it can work its effect, then there is no advantage in the charm (see Ecclesiastes x.11). "The house is crazy," Adam Smith reported a weary traveler as saying to himself, "and it will not stand very long; but it is a chance if it falls tonight, and I will venture, therefore, to sleep in it tonight." For many of the poorer countries, tonight is already dangerously late, as far as facing up to the population question is concerned.

The Promise of Better Things to Come

My emphasis, so far, has been on the obstacles to economic improvement, and on the need for self-discipline, for temporary sacrifice, for the prudent husbanding of scarce resources, if these obstacles are not to prove decisive. This, I fear, has given my paper an excessively pessimistic and austere tone. Let me, therefore, redress the balance somewhat by devoting the conclusion of my paper to the more cheerful side of the picture.

The poorer countries have today one great advantage which the richer countries did not have when they began to emerge from deep and pervasive poverty, and which the richer countries do not have today despite their prosperity. There is available today to the poorer countries a great stock of scientific and technical knowledge which they have not yet exploited for the purposes of economic progress. The richer countries must in the main rely for further economic improvement, aside from further accumulation of capital, on new scientific and technical discovery, whereas the poorer countries have in large measure still available for borrowing the existing stock of knowledge. This knowledge will not flow to them automatically, and it may not be precisely what they need. Progress in education, immigration of skilled personnel, foreign capital and technical aid, the traveling merchant and the foreign entrepreneur in search of profit, all of these, however, promote the international sharing of knowledge and its adaptation to local needs.

The poorer countries also can reasonably count on some supplement from outside to their own capital formation, even if they must reconcile themselves to the prospect that they themselves will have to finance most of the facilities, the tools, and the implements necessary for increased productivity, out of savings from their own meager earnings.

Some of the poorer countries have favorable prospects of the discovery of new mineral resources, and others still have empty or sparsely settled areas which in time there will be the capital to open up to profitable settlement. The growth in income and in population of the richer countries, and the progressive depletion of their own mineral resources, are operating to make them better markets for the export staples of the poorer countries, and it is conceivable also that more liberal commercial policy on the part of the richer countries will make an important contribution here.

If population increase is checked, the improvements in public health techniques will have their major effect in improving the health and vigor of the population as a whole, and in providing the incentives and the financial resources for making what is for most of them the most productive in the long run of all investments, investment in education for modern production and for good citizenship.

I do not regard this as merely a ceremonial balancing of utopian aspirations for the future against wholly grim realities of the present. Some of the poorer countries are today outpacing many of the richer countries in their annual rates of increase of per capita income. I have recently visited three under-developed countries where, superficially at least, there is all the evidence of economic progress proceeding at a spectacular rate. I am sure that if only they seek and find a solution of their population problem, most of the poorer countries of the world can have good prospects of substantial and sustained improvement in their levels of living, without need of recourse to forced labor, to forced saving, or to subjection to dictatorship, whether personal or collective.

POLICIES FOR TRADE AND DEVELOPMENT

Tariffs, sugar and crude-oil quotas, foreign travel regulations, support or opposition to the International Monetary Fund, and other international economic measures combine to form a country's policy for trade and development. International economic policies, like others, in a democratic society, are the result of compromises between different social goals and differing special interest groups. It is doubtful, however, that any other set of economic policies is subject to as many conflicting forces as are international economic policies.

In the first place, there are pressure group considerations which prompt a nation to set up tariffs, quotas, and other restraints on trade in order to benefit particular producers. The bicycle producers are well organized; the newsboys who buy the bicycles are not. There is then, a tendency for Congress, the Tariff Commission, and the President to respond to these pressures for protection even though it can be demonstrated that consumers as a group—and the economy in its entirety—have a lower real income as a result.

In the second place, military considerations are important. Nations have protected their machine-tool industries, their dye industries, and their transportation equipment industries, to mention only a few, because it has been argued the economy must maintain these skills and organizations during peacetime in order to have them during a war. If the next war is to be a nuclear war, rather than a prolonged industrial struggle, it is doubtful that this argument is very powerful. But it is used.

In the third place, it is widely thought that a country should be able to deal with its problems—such as unemployment, rising prices, agricultural surpluses, and the like—without being hampered by their international implications. The depression during the thirties strengthened economic nationalism (as this attitude is called) because it made full employment the responsibility of national governments. International organizations, on the other hand, have been slow to deal with the problem of instability.

And in the last place, and possibly most important, there are external forces which have to be taken into account. The cold war is one, and no country in the west can ignore it in the making of its international economic policies. The post-war economic recovery of western Europe and Japan and the capacity of Russia and other communist countries to sell in the world markets must be considered. Finally, every nation must take into account the needs of the undeveloped countries as they turn to industrialization as a means of breaking the vicious circle of poverty and excessive population.

The readings in this section analyze these external forces and examine their implications for the United States in the formulation of its international economic policies.

America's Prospects in the World Economy

Starting from the proposition that foreign trade and payments are largely transmission belts connecting the political as well as economic developments of the countries involved, William Diebold, Jr., concentrates his attention on the broad strategic considerations involved in formulating international trade policies for a world dominated by a power struggle between the communist countries and the west. What are the economic aspects of the power struggle?

1. Military expenditures are likely to continue to be high. This means for the U.S. the continuation of large expenditures abroad for NATO and other military purposes.

2. The U.S. and other western countries must accept the responsibility for formulating international trade policies in the light of the needs of the undeveloped countries of the world if they are going to win the allegiance of these countries. Economic development is a long and complex problem, and this means that the west must expect to be involved with it for a long time. Not only is economic assistance involved—trade policy is also. The undeveloped countries need stable markets for the raw materials they produce—sugar, rice, minerals, etc.—many of which are also produced by the U.S. They need a market for the light manufactured goods they will soon start producing with low cost labor.

3. The post-war recovery of western Europe has brought an end to the dollar shortage. The Marshall Plan and other forms of economic assistance helped to rebuild its industrial plants, and its countries can now compete effectively in world markets.

4. The European Economic Community has moved toward a common market in which tariffs are being reduced. This means the U.S. will probably have to offer additional tariff concessions in order to compete in the Common Market on the same terms as the countries that are a part of it. The Common Market may induce other countries also to move in the direction of regionalism.

The Balance of Payments Problem and a Solution

It is against the background of these international political developments that Robert Triffin explains the long term problems the U.S. faces in formulating its international trade and monetary policies. The recovery of western Europe has made it possible for the central banks of these countries to build up their monetary reserves. Because of the U.S. balance of payments deficits, these central banks have been able to acquire dollar balances and gold from the U.S. In 1949 the U.S. gold stock exceeded foreign short term claims against the U.S. by about $18 billion, but in 1959 the excess had been reduced to about $3 billion. These increases in foreign monetary reserves are probably necessary if foreign currencies are to be fully convertible. And since increases in the world's gold stock during this period could supply only about one third of the desired increases in monetary reserves, the other two thirds had to be provided by the U.S., which it did by buying more goods and services than it sold. The net effect was to make the U.S. vulnerable to a "flight from the dollar," and the consequent loss of gold and monetary reserves. And this in turn means that the U.S. must formulate its domestic policies in the light of what foreign countries will do with their dollar balances and short term claims. The days of fiscal and monetary independence from the discipline of international monetary developments are apparently past.

Can the U.S. regain its independence of action and protect itself against a further deterioration of its international monetary position by cutting down on its capital exports, both private and governmental? The answer is that it cannot. The bulk of its capital exports and economic assistance is going to the undeveloped countries. There are, as we have seen, strategic reasons for avoiding this course of action. Furthermore, to reduce these payments would reduce U.S. exports and thus not markedly help its balance of payments position.

To remedy its situation, the U.S. could (*a*) cut its large defense expenditures abroad, (*b*) press for the elimination of foreign tariffs on U.S. exports, (*c*) encourage European countries to assume a larger share of the financing of undeveloped countries, (*d*) arrest creeping inflation at home, and (*e*) maintain fairly high rates of interest. These measures, it is interesting to note, involve both changing some of our foreign *political* policy and giving up some portion of our independence in fiscal and monetary affairs. Neither, we have seen, is easy to accomplish.

Another remedy is to reverse our policy of lowering trade barriers, but this would lead to special difficulties. Other countries probably would retaliate, further reducing our exports. And the U.S. would weaken its position as the leader of the west and as a source of dollar earnings necessary to the growth of the undeveloped areas.

To ease the situation, Triffin proposes that the International Monetary Fund hold the bulk of monetary reserves of the countries participating in world trade. The IMF could then act as a supra-national central bank, eliminating the need to use foreign currencies as reserves and conserving the use of gold. The IMF, by lending and by investing in short term securities in the financial markets of the world, could expand the supply of bank reserves by open market operations. While this would avoid the special difficulties arising out of a shortage of gold and also the danger of a flight from the dollar, it still would leave the U.S. with a troublesome matter. If it is to provide economic assistance to—as well as a market for—the undeveloped countries, it must adopt such policies as will make its exports competitive with those of the economies of western Europe. It is against this background that the plight of the undeveloped countries needs to be examined.

The Dilemmas of Undeveloped Countries

The perverse problems of the poorer countries are described by H. W. Singer. Their population has increased more than those of the developed countries, giving them an increasing majority of the world's people, while their income has risen less or (as of 1949) not at all. The median income of the world is (or in 1949 was) therefore probably less than in 1913. What they need to increase their income is enormous investment, especially outside agriculture, higher prices for their exports in relation to the prices of their imports, and stability in the receipt of income and capital.

In the two generations before the second world war, there was a decline of 40 per cent in the quantity of imports which undeveloped countries could obtain for a given quantity of exports, because the prices of their exports fell relative to those of imports. If the relative prices of exports had not fallen, the countries could have obtained manufactured imports cheaper and could have used the difference to buy the capital goods needed for initial investment. By paying higher prices for imports, the poorer countries have helped to increase the real income of the developed countries.

The undeveloped countries are poor because they did not invest in manufacturing industries in the past; and being poor, they are unable to invest now. What they need is a great spurt of investment that will produce external economies in order that subsequent light investment will be as productive as possible. But the returns are slow from investment that yields external economies—like road building and power installations—and the countries are tempted to make light investments in the hope of prompt returns, like the building of light manufacturing plants. But the latter cannot operate efficiently until there is power, transportation, and the other means to external economies that heavy investment yields. Meanwhile, they introduce public health measures, improve nutrition, and in other ways cause the population to increase faster than total income, so that the living standard falls. It is dangerous, Singer states, for undeveloped countries to import the end products of industrialization because that can stifle growth.

Growth versus Specialization

To the debate over how the perverse mesh of poverty can be broken in the undeveloped countries, two points of view have emerged. One, presented by Ragnar Nurkse, maintains that economic growth in the undeveloped areas is not likely to be based on international specialization, with the undeveloped countries exporting raw materials to the developed nations and importing manufactured goods from them. Instead, growth is likely to arise out of simultaneous investment in a variety of industries producing for home consumption. The other viewpoint, presented by Jacob Viner, is that there still is room for a great deal of international specialization and that the principle of comparative advantage should guide the poorer countries in their development programs. The former view would lend credence to the proposition that industrialization is the only hope for the poorer countries, while the latter leads to the conclusion that industrialization should come only when a country is not at a comparative disadvantage in the production of industrial goods.

Nurkse points out that the U.S., Canada, Argentina, and Australia developed by producing raw materials and sending them to Europe in return for manufactured goods. The rapid industrial growth in Europe in the nineteenth century produced a large demand at favorable prices for primary products. International trade was the engine of economic growth. The countries which then were undeveloped, such as the U.S., were beneficiaries of the vigorous growth that was occurring in the industrial countries. However, Nurkse argues, the favorable conditions of the nineteenth century are not present today. The U.S. is itself an important producer of primary products or synthetic substitutes for them. Despite tariff reductions, U.S. imports of raw materials have not risen in the same proportion as its gross national product. The poorer countries' terms of trade have shown a chronic tendency to deteriorate. The bulk of international trade is now between the developed countries themselves, and not between them and the undeveloped countries. The latter can no longer depend on their growth being induced from the outside through an expansion of the world demand for their primary products.

In place of relying on expanding international markets, Nurkse proposes that the undeveloped countries should invest in a number of different industries so that each of them provides a market for the output of the others. In this way, a country can secure the external economies that are not available to each of the industries taken separately. While this process of industrialization can occur within the framework of an enterprise economy—once such an economy has established itself—state control may be needed at the start because of the difficulty of mobilizing domestic as well as international capital. The policy of balanced growth has the purpose of establishing a pattern of mutually supporting investments over a range of industries wide enough to overcome the frustration of isolated advance and to create a momentum of growth.

Nurkse does state, however, that balanced growth need not always mean tariff protection or the drawing-away of resources from the export industries in which the country has a comparative advantage. Rather, it is a way to use the excess labor now found in agriculture. It is, then, not a substitute for international specialization but a substitute for the mechanism by which the nineteenth century transmitted growth.

Growth via Specialization

Jacob Viner, while agreeing that it is difficult to start the processes of growth without a push from the richer countries, states that it has not been demonstrated that specializing in the export of primary products necessarily puts an undeveloped country at a disadvantage. The argument that the prices of raw materials (their exports) tend to fall relative to the prices of manufactured goods (their imports) ignores reductions in the costs of producing exports and ignores improvements in the quality of imports. Nor has it been demonstrated that there are net (as distinct from gross) external economies arising out of balanced investment in complementary domestic industries, he states. There may be external diseconomies also. The argument is sometimes advanced that the industrial products imported by the undeveloped countries are so attractive as to reduce savings in these countries. That too is questionable, he states. The presence of such imports in the markets of the undeveloped countries may provide incentives to work, and thus lead to a larger income and larger savings. In summary, Viner finds no certain proof in logic or fact for the balanced growth doctrine.

He does acknowledge that the poorer countries face problems arising out of the instability of the prices of primary products. The resulting declines in the real incomes of the poorer countries during industrial recessions are particularly galling, since many of the countries are already at a subsistence income. And it is not surprising that many of them have sought relief by increasing the number of different staple exports and by increasing their production of manufactured commodities. The solution to price instability is not for a poorer country to move toward self-sufficiency—which would reduce its real income over the entire period of the cycle—but to find a way to stabilize the demand for primary products. And this is largely a problem for the developed countries.

Viner's solution is for the poorer countries to specialize in the production of those commodities for which they have a comparative advantage, leaving it to the richer countries to find ways, through the liberalization of trade policies and through stabilization measures, to provide stable markets for the products of the poorer countries. The latter, if they are willing to save and use their resources wisely, particularly if they receive aid from the richer countries, can expect marked increases in real income. They have an additional advantage in being able to use the newer techniques of production that were not available to the richer countries when they were developing.

Policies for Trade and Development: A Summary Statement

The realities of the cold war, the loss of competitive advantage vis-à-vis Europe in international markets, the loss of gold and of independence in determining domestic monetary and fiscal policies, the desirability of giving economic assistance to and providing a market for the undeveloped countries of the world—all of these present serious problems for the U.S. Should it encourage the further liberalization of international trade, or should it move—and encourage the undeveloped countries also to move—toward self-sufficiency and nationalism? There is no quick answer to these questions. The answer, when it comes, will be a composite that tries to satisfy the interests of particular economic groups at home and abroad, and it will be an answer very much affected by national political interest.

PART 5

The Planned Economy

Editorial Introduction

PLANNING AND POLICY

Policy in a planned economy takes its purpose and methods from the doctrine on which the political system is based, whether philosophical liberalism or idealism. The first assumes that society is a collection of individuals who know, or are capable of knowing, what they want and how it should be gotten. That doctrine is the basis of representative government, or democracy. Its economic policy is to allow individuals to decide what is to be produced, how it is to be produced, and who is to get it. A free market is a large part of the policy; but the policy does not prevent considerable, even complete, state control so long as control is what the people want. The second assumes society is the creature of immanent forces or of powers beyond human control, such as great historical movements, and individuals are free only to act consistently with them or to be cast aside by them. Accordingly, economic policy is determined by necessity, and cannot be affected by individual choices.

The most important form of planning today is socialism, and there are two kinds: democratic socialism, which derives its values from philosophical liberalism; and authoritarian socialism, which comes from philosophic idealism and in its most consequential form is communism, or Marxian socialism. The difference between democratic socialism and liberal economic policy (the subject of the preceding sections of this book) is a difference in the extent to which measures common to both are applied. The difference between liberal policy and communism is a difference of substance, and comes from their different philosophic premises.

The distinction between the kinds of socialism is explained by H. D. Dickinson, and he argues the democratic socialists' case against capitalism and against authoritarian socialism. The purposes and premises of democratic socialism have not changed since Dickinson wrote, but some of its methods have.

There is a new view of nationalization, and it is explained by R. A. S. Crosland. The major forms of communist planning were developed in the Soviet Union before the second world war and influenced the communist states established after it. That planning is described by Paul A. Baran. After the death of Stalin, it changed in important ways in

Russia and in some of the other communist countries. Oskar Lange describes some of the changes and proposes a new theory of communist policy.

The communist economies have a high rate of economic growth. It has impressed the undeveloped countries, and has made the west anxious. A policy by which the west may match the growth rate of communism is proposed by P. J. D. Wiles.

22. THE ECONOMICS OF SOCIALISM: INTRODUCTORY*

H. D. Dickinson

SYNOPSIS

1. The price system under capitalism does not direct resources to their most needed uses because of income inequality, monopoly, consumer deception and ignorance, and because money cost does not measure all costs of production.

2. The private ownership of all the means of production is the root of the disharmonies of capitalism, leading to inefficiency, monopoly, cumulative inequality, and class stratification.

3. Socialism is the social ownership of the means of production, which are used according to a general plan for the equal benefit of all.

4. Its opponents contend it would destroy incentive, provide no guide to the efficient use of resources, and deprive consumers of their freedom.

5. Socialist planning is the deliberate control of the entire economy by a central authority acting with complete information. Though conceivable, unplanned socialism is unlikely.

6. Planned capitalism can mean limited kinds of intervention or the complete control of all economic affairs. If the latter, the government would be led to dictatorship in order to protect the income of property owners.

7. The economic problem is the same under socialism as under capitalism and can be solved by directing resources either according to what the government thinks are their best uses, *authoritarian socialism,* or in response to individual choices, *libertarian socialism*—the latter being the author's.

8. Libertarian socialism requires (*a*) the measuring of demand in order that the right goods be produced, (*b*) the measuring of costs in order that resources will be used efficiently, and (*c*) the distribution of the product.

9. It can use the price system for any or all of the three and need not use the same method of pricing for all of them.

The fundamental problem of every economic society is the allotment of limited resources (including human labor power) to the satis-

* Reprinted by permission and shortened from *The Economics of Socialism* (Oxford: Oxford University Press, 1939), pp. 2–29.

faction of needs (including the need for leisure), so as to secure the maximum of satisfaction. It is essentially a quantitative problem as well as a qualitative one. It is not only a question of what needs are to be satisfied, but to what extent, as compared with other needs requiring satisfaction; not only a question of what resources are to be made use of, but the proportions in which a given quantity of resources is to be divided among different uses, all yielding different and competing satisfactions. It is this quantitative problem that is the essential economic problem.

It is here that we must distinguish between technology and economics. The agronomist can tell us the most efficient method of growing wheat under given conditions, and, given the quantity of wheat desired, can tell us the quantity of land and labor required for the production of that quantity. He can tell us the same for the growing of cotton and the rearing of cattle. But the determination of the quantity of wheat, cotton, and meat required for a certain population, with certain tastes and standards of living, balancing the relative satisfactions afforded by wheat, cotton, and meat as against the quantities of land and labor required for their production—this is the problem of the economist. We may say that the proper work of the economist begins after that of the technician has been done.

Any society must have a method of determining what and how much is to be produced, of choosing between alternatives, and of achieving its ends with the greatest economy of means. The method of a capitalist society is the system of production for profit and exchange upon the market,[1] modified by monopolistic combinations of capitalists, by trade-unions, and by such occasional and irregular intrusions of deliberate social intervention as tariffs, marketing boards, railway rate regulation, factory acts, social insurance, etc. The productive energies of society are continually being diverted by the motive of private gain into the channels in which they will yield most profit to those who control them— that is to say, the greatest surplus of selling price over cost of production. Meanwhile, competition, even if imperfect, is tending to equalize selling price and cost. Therefore, in theory, since sale price is determined by the consumer's effective demand, and cost depends upon the capacity of productive resources to satisfy demand in alternative uses, there should emerge the maximum satisfaction of needs with the minimum expenditure of resources. In reality, this desirable result is attained only very imperfectly. Under capitalism, four causes contribute to falsify the readings of the price index and hence to pervert the allocation of resources to production.

---

[1] It is also the method of an economic system without large scale production or large scale marketing, but having private property and division of labor, in which goods are produced by small independent producers directly for a local market. This system is what Marx calls "simple commodity production."

a) The inequality of consumers' incomes systematically distorts the measurement of social needs. A rich man wanting a country cottage for a few week ends in summer can outbid two farm laborers who need shelter all the year round; two cottages are thrown together to make one week-end dwelling, and two breadwinners have to seek work elsewhere at grave risk of unemployment or else add a six-mile tramp to their already fatiguing labors.

b) Another all-pervasive cause of the falsification of the price and cost calculus is monopoly. The "invisible hand" which is presumed to maximize satisfaction operates only under conditions of perfect competition. But perfect competition is not a real entity; it is an abstraction born of the economist's urge to rationalize the working of the economic system. Even that degree of competition which, in John Stuart Mill's day, was enough to give the "invisible hand" good scope for its beneficent work, only exists during a period of exceptionally rapid technical development: It is a fleeting transitional phase between one period of monopoly (mercantilism) and another period of monopoly (imperialism). Monopoly is the natural offspring of competition. Once it is established, the presumption no longer holds good that the distribution of resources produced by the self-interest of private entrepreneurs corresponds to the maximum satisfaction of consumers.

c) The meretricious modern art of publicity makes it often more profitable for the manufacturer to spend money in making people want to buy the things that he produces, rather than on producing the things that people want to buy. This tendency is reinforced by the inevitable ignorance of the consumer, called upon to discriminate between the properties of rival brands of tooth paste, vacuum cleaners, canned peaches, and radio sets. It is often more profitable to advertise poor goods than to improve their quality.

d) On the production side, money costs not infrequently fail to correspond to true social costs. Cheap goods can be made out of sweated labor, the costs of salvaging the human wreckage of industry being thrown on the relatives of the workers or on the general tax or rate payer. Costs can be cut by means involving the neglect of safety precautions, the pollution of the air by smoke, the contamination of rivers by noxious affluents, or the sacrifice of human life on the roads.

Nevertheless, the price and market system does give some sort of a solution, even though it be distorted and perverted by class privilege and exploitation, to the problem of the economic allocation of resources to the satisfaction of various and competing needs. However much this solution may be criticized, it is urged that some solution, even an imperfect one, is better than none.

Socialism

1. *General Notion of Socialism.* Ever since the early days of industrial capitalism, men have sought a remedy for its abuses and defects in some material re-organization of the economic system. In particular, the private ownership of the means of production has appeared to many reformers as the fundamental source of evil in the system. To some, such as James Mill and Henry George, it is the private ownership only of land and natural resources; to others, such as Major Douglas and Professor Soddy, it is the private ownership only of credit, that is the source of evil; but to the majority, the private ownership of *all* non-human means

of production—factories, railways, machinery, and raw materials, as well as land and natural materials, and credit—has appeared as a barrier to the full utilization of the resources of the world in the service of the needs of mankind. The author holds this last-expressed view. However important historically may have been the special role played by private property in land and minerals, or in credit facilities, as a factor in the evolution of class privilege, in the present stage of development of capitalism all forms of land and capital have become merged in a single mass of privately owned means of production. The concrete goods of which this is composed have become interchangeable with one another; their special nature —whether land, produced means of production, or intangible "productive relations" such as credit—has become irrelevant. The ownership of a portion of this mass confers the right to appropriate a certain part of the income of society. If private ownership of productive resources is to blame for the disharmonies of capitalism, it is private ownership of *all* means of production, and not of land, or credit, or some other part of the whole, that must be set in order.

Nor, in view of the intimate interlocking of share capital and loan capital in modern business organization (especially that effected by holding companies, so that loan capital controls share capital and vice versa), it is possible to establish a distinction, such as the theorists of "National Socialism" do, between creative capital (*schaffendes Kapital*) and predatory capital (*raffendes Kapital*), and to make of the latter (generally loan capital: hence the "tyranny of interest"—*Zinsknechtschaft*) a scapegoat for the sins of the twain.

Once private property in land and capital is established, there is a constant tendency for its ownership to become concentrated in fewer hands, until a definite class of owners of means of production ("capitalists") emerges. The interests of this class are distinct from, and in many ways antagonistic to, those of the rest of the community. The class division between owners and workers begins.

The distribution of property tends to inequality, and therefore the distribution of incomes derived from property tends to inequality. On the other hand, the distribution of incomes derived from work tends to be much less unequal. The reasons for this are legion. A few are:

1. Owing to the diminishing marginal utility of income, the larger one's income, the easier it is to save out of it or otherwise use portions of it for the purpose of adding to one's property. The marginal disutility of labor, however, increases steeply after a certain point. Thus, while it is progressively easier to add to a property income, it is progressively harder to add to a work income.[2]

2. Owing to the working of the law of averages, the chances of total loss of capital diminish the greater the number of different portions into which it is divided for purposes of investment. The "small man" cannot easily or cheaply spread his risks in this way, and is thus more subject than the big investor to loss due to the vagaries of the market. (This is particularly noticeable in the

[2] See the present author's *Institutional Revenue*, chap. v, § 26.

general depressions that, under capitalism, periodically devastate the market economy.) If the "small man" seeks safety in gilt-edged securities or in conservatively managed investment trusts, he has to put up with a distinctly lower rate of return than the big operator can get on his capital with equal safety.

3. Exclusive market information and exclusive opportunities for investment on profitable terms are more likely to come to those who are already rich than to men of small means. Similarly, employment at a high remuneration is more readily obtained by those who are already well-to-do or who are connected by birth, education, or social ties with the rich than it is by poor men.

4. Once a society has begun to be stratified into classes on the basis of differences in income, the wealthier sections of the community in general contrive to monopolize the educational machine so that the necessary training and equipment for the better paid employments can only be acquired by those who already belong to the higher income classes.[3]

All these (and other) influences are cumulative in effect. There are, of course, counteracting influences, such as the tendency of the rich to relative sterility, extravagance, and spendthrift behavior (Veblen's "conspicuous waste"), the voluntary endowment of public institutions by the rich, and progressive taxation. But the general tendency, in a system of private free enterprise and private ownership of the means of production, is toward greater inequality and toward the stratification of society into antagonistic classes on the basis of wealth and of the origin of wealth. While minor divisions may be important, the division that dominates social life is that between the owners and the non-owners of the material means of production.

Socialism thus arises as the political objective of the non-owning class. In order to diminish inequality of wealth and to abolish the class stratification of society, socialists propose to abolish private ownership of the material means of production. Some method must be devised of administering the economic system after the expropriation of the existing private owners. This is the problem of the economics of a socialist community.

2. *Definition of Socialism.* The definition of socialism that was generally accepted during the half-century between 1875 and 1925 is "social ownership of the means of production." Since that time the phrase "planned production" has been tending to take its place. There is a close connection between these two definitions. On the one hand, one of the chief advantages claimed for the socialization of the means of production is the elimination of the waste due to unplanned, chaotic, individualistic production. Individualistic production is coordinated, it is true, by the mechanism of price and the market; but it is subject to gross disturbances even in this sphere, and it is fundamentally blind, purposeless, irrational, and incapable of satisfying many of the most urgent of human needs. On the other hand, so it is claimed by socialists, the planning of production is impossible on any basis less radical than the complete elimination of

---

[3] See E. Ll. Lewis, *The Children of the Unskilled: Institutional Revenue*, pp. 58, 156; and *Political Arithmetic* (ed. L. Hogben), chaps. viii, ix, x.

individual property rights in the means of production, at least in all the major branches of economic activity, and the transfer of these means of production to organs of collective economy. Only so can the community sweep away the secrecy, arbitrary boundary lines, vested interests, overlapping of functions, waste, and monopoly that characterize private enterprise. One fundamental difference between socialism and capitalism will be the existence of an authority able to view the economic system as a whole and with power to make decisions involving the system as a whole. Another fundamental difference will be the fullest publicity of all relevant economic statistics throughout the whole system. All organs of a socialist economy will work, so to speak, within glass walls.

Socialism has also been defined *tout court* as equality of income,[4] and, although few socialists would adopt this definition without reserve, socialism of nearly all schools has been held to imply equality in one or other of the following senses:

a) A greater approach to equality in the distribution of wealth;
b) Equality of economic opportunity, in a more genuine sense than that of bourgeois liberalism;
c) Distribution according to need rather than according to effort or product.

In effect, these three tend to the same result, since both equality of opportunity and distribution according to need would lead to greater equality of actual income than exists under capitalism, although not to an absolute arithmetical equality. Nor is the concept of greater equality unrelated to the definitions in terms of social ownership or of planned production. Since the most glaring inequalities of actual income and nearly all the inequalities of opportunity are based on the private ownership of land and capital, social ownership will almost certainly tend to greater equality. Also, since the object of genuine economic planning (as opposed to the sham "planning" which, like so-called "rationalization," is simply a euphemism for the restriction of production and the destruction of machinery organized by monopoly capitalism) is to substitute a conscious and direct relation of production to human needs for a relation arrived at by an indirect mechanism through the unconscious pushes and pulls of innumerable private interests in the market, a true planned economy would approach to some extent the ideal of distribution according to need.

The formal definition of socialism that will be used in this book is as follows:

Socialism is an economic organization of society in which the material means of production are owned by the whole community and operated by organs representative of and responsible to the community according to a general economic plan, all members of the community being entitled to benefit from the results of such socialized planned production on the basis of equal rights.

[4] G. Bernard Shaw, *The Intelligent Woman's Guide to Socialism and Capitalism*, pp. 19, 49, 68, 94, 297, 343.

This definition includes the three elements of

i. Social ownership of the means of production,
ii. Economic planning,
iii. Equality.

It purposely, however, leaves vague two points:

a) How society is to work the productive equipment that it owns, whether through government departments, public utility corporations, national guilds, cooperative societies, or what not;
b) Exactly how the social product is to be distributed, whether according to service or need, whether in separate shares to individuals, or in communal supplies and services.

But it does explicitly rule out irresponsible private enterprise, and the continuance of any form of privileged income or of class inequality in the division of the social product.

3. *Criticisms of Socialism.* Criticisms of socialism have their fashions just as socialism itself appears from time to time in various guises. During the first half of the nineteenth century the Malthusian bogy was most consistently invoked by opponents of communistic schemes. It was held that population was always pressing upon the means of subsistence and that only private property coupled with individual responsibility for the support of offspring could prevent an increase of population up to the point of famine. Communism might establish equality, but it would be an equality of misery. As the *bourgeoisie* lost their fear of over-population, new arguments against socialism had to be found; and thus, until recently, the question of incentives has occupied the front place in discussions on the possibility of collectivist socialism. It was held that socialism would lack the incentives to work and efficiency that under capitalism force men to give of their best in the service of the community—the magic of ownership, the ambition of making a pile, or, for those not fortunate enough to inherit or win an independent business command, the hope of promotion and the fear of dismissal. Socialism might eliminate exploitation, but it would be at the price of universal mediocrity and inefficiency. But this has not happened in such public enterprises as the Post Office, the B.B.C., and the Central Electricity Board in Britain; nor has it in the Soviet Union, where, under a collectivist economy, there have taken place an unprecedented rise in productivity and a spectacular outpouring of human energies and enthusiasm. Thus, the "incentive" argument appears less convincing. Accordingly, there appears in orthodox economic circles a new critique of socialism, more subtle and technical than the previous ones, based on the supposed inability of a socialist community to solve purely economic problems. It is admitted that such a community might acquire a mastery over technique not inferior to that achieved under capitalism; that new psychological incentives to do and give of one's best might be developed, as powerful as the love of gain or the fear of destitu-

tion; that, even though every child born were guaranteed a share in the resources at the disposal of the community, philoprogenitiveness would not necessarily bring the law of diminishing returns into rapid and fatal action. What is asserted is that, even with highly developed technique, adequate incentives to activity, and rational control of population, the economic directors of a socialist commonwealth would be unable to balance against each other the worth-whileness of different lines of production or the relative advantages of different ways of producing the same good. L. von Mises, in his *Gemeinwirtschaft*[5] makes two definite charges against socialist economy:

1. Where the state is the sole owner of intermediate or instrumental goods, there can be no price formation for such goods, hence no rational reckoning of cost and hence no rational economy;
2. Under planned economy the managers of industry can have no discretionary power and no pecuniary responsibility for production; therefore, rational risk bearing becomes impossible.

The conclusion to be drawn from these two propositions is that a socialist economy would have no guiding principles and would, as soon as it lost any parasitic support that it might get from comparison with neighboring capitalist economies, degenerate into an affair of wild guesses and random decisions.[6] One of the objects of this work is to refute this criticism of socialism and to show that, as far as pure economics is concerned, a socialist economy is at least theoretically possible.[7]

Another line of criticism, which was run in double harness with the incentive arguments by such critics of socialism as Mallock, and is paraded today by Mises and Gregory alongside of the "rational calculation" argument, is that planned collective economy is inconsistent with any kind of freedom of choice for consumers or freedom of employment for workers. This point, too, will receive attention in this work.

Planning

1. General Notion of Planning. The words "planned production" and "economic planning" have been used in section 1 of this chapter. It is time to give a more precise definition to the concept. For the purpose of this book the following definition is adopted:

Economic planning is the making of major economic decisions—what and how much is to be produced, how, when and where it is to be produced, and to whom it is to be allocated—by the conscious decision of a determinate au-

[5] Translated as *Socialism*, 1936.

[6] For other critiques along these lines, see F. A. Hayek, *Collectivist Economic Planning;* B. Brutzkus, *Die Lehren des Marxismus im Lichte der russischen Revolution;* G. Halm, *Ist der Sozialismus wirtschaftlich möglich?*

[7] For slightly different solutions of the problems, see F. M. Taylor, "Production in a Socialist State," *The American Economic Review*, March 1929; G. Morreau, "De Economische Structuur eener Socialistische Volkshuishouding," *De Economist*, June, July–August, September, 1931.

thority, on the basis of a comprehensive survey of the economic system as a whole.

This definition emphasizes three characteristics of planned economy:

    i. Conscious nature of economic decisions,
    ii. Unity of control,
    iii. Basing decisions on survey of economy as a whole.

Item i restricts the designation "planning" to forms of deliberate conscious control of economic life. An economic plan involves more than an economic system or an ordered scheme of economic life. A pure market economy gives rise to an ordered scheme of economic activity, in the sense that definite laws of economic behavior are discoverable in it; but the order that exists under it is not one that is consciously willed by any economic agent; it emerges as the resultant of the separate and independent wills of a large number of economic agents, each of which makes his decision in ignorance of all the others. Such an economy exhibits orders of a sort, but no plan.

Under ii, the possibility of deputed or federal authority is not excluded, nor is the existence of a field of minor economic decisions that need not be made in detail according to plan, but simply fitted into the plan in their totality. In the ultimate analysis, however, the responsibility for economic decisions must be single and undivided.

Under iii, partial planning of particular industries and enterprises is excluded. Planning must be general if it is to deserve the word. However, we may apply the term "planning" to schemes of economic control that deal with the broad outline of economic activity, without regulating details, provided that, so far as they go, they treat the economic system as a whole. Thus, schemes for deliberate control of the price level, of the proportion between consumption goods industries and capital goods industries, or of the distribution of the national income between different classes might all be referred to as examples of economic planning.

In this connection it is convenient to give more exact and specialized denotations to certain terms in common use, to wit: "planning," "rationalization," and "scientific management." The meanings of all three terms contain a common element: the idea of rational coordination of means and ends. It would be convenient, and would agree with common usage, if we used the word "planning" to denote such rational coordination in the economy as a whole, "rationalization" to denote rational coordination in an industry or group of industries, and "scientific management" to denote the same in an enterprise or group of enterprises.

We must also distinguish planning from intervention. Intervention involves some degree of deliberate interference with the working of the free-market system of economic coordination, but need not involve planning the system as a whole. Intervention may be exercised by the state, as by protective duties, quotas, marketing boards, factory acts, minimum-wage laws, and regulation of the hours of labor; or it may be exercised by private associations, such as trade-unions or manufacturers' associations, and take the form of collective wage bargains, of price and output control, of delimination of sales territory, and of other restrictive covenants that modify the normal working of market equilibrium. The point about intervention of this type is that, while it modifies the conditions under which the market system works itself out, it still leaves the ultimate result of the economic process to be determined by the mutual interaction of a large number of independent economic agents. It does not create a deliberate, conscious control of economic life.

It is clear that economic planning, in the sense in which the word is used here, implies the unification of property rights in the means of production. The powers of control over the land and capital of the community that must be vested in the planning authority will give the latter the effective substance of ownership. It may be that individual proprietors of means of production may be allowed to retain nominal titles of ownership; but, if so, this will amount to little more than a vested right to receive certain incomes secured on the general product of planned industry. Planning thus, by its nature, implies *unified* ownership of the means of production. This does not of logical necessity mean *public* ownership: We shall examine later whether there are reasons for believing that, in fact, planning must involve public ownership of the means of production.

2. *Planning and Socialism.* The terms "socialism" and "planning" have been defined. It remains to examine the relation between them. Although socialism has been defined so as to include planning, let us for a moment take it to mean only public ownership and control of the means of production (better called collectivism) and consider whether it necessarily involves planning. We must also consider whether planning necessarily implies public (as distinct from unified) ownership. In other words, can unplanned socialism or planned capitalism exist?

1. *Unplanned Socialism.* We can, in abstract theory, conceive the transformation of an unplanned capitalist economy into collectivism in the following way: (*a*) All the separate enterprises existing under capitalism are converted into public bodies *without further unification or coordination*, in such wise that each trades on the basis of market prices as an autonomous concern, having no connection, except through the market, with any other undertaking; (*b*) all rights of property in land and capital are transferred to the community in such wise that the latter appropriates the shares of the national income imputed to these factors by the process of price determination in the market and redistributes these shares to its members as individual income. Such an economy would be unplanned collectivism. It is easy to see, however, that it would almost inevitably slide into a planned system. The separateness of the various

enterprises and the mutual blindness of those who conduct them, while natural under private ownership, would be a highly artificial state of affairs under public ownership. The organs of public economy would have every reason for mutual consultation and publicity, none for separateness and secrecy. In particular, the organs responsible for the investment of savings and the creation of new capital would, by the very nature of their functions, tend to envisage their task from the viewpoint of the social economy as a whole, and thus become, whether they would or not, planning organs. Thus, unplanned collectivism, although logically thinkable, is unlikely to occur in practice.

2. *Planned Capitalism.* Can a planned organization of economic activity be combined with private ownership of the means of production? As we have seen, planning involves a *de facto* unification of property rights in the means of production. Must this unification lead to public ownership and to the abolition of income from property, i.e. to socialism, or is it possible that a planned economy would continue to hand over a large proportion of its total product to a small class of *rentiers?* This question is so important that a separate section has been allotted to its discussion. The broad conclusions that emerge from the discussion are that planned capitalism, although a possible form of economic organization, is unlikely to be durable, because of its social and political consequences.

3. *The Consequences of Planned Capitalism.* It now remains to consider the reasons which, in the present writer's opinion, render impracticable any mixed system of public and private enterprise or combination of planning with private property in the means of production. Mixed systems may be divided into two classes: (1) those of which unplanned private enterprise forms the essential basis and fundamental pattern, but which have been extensively invaded and infiltrated by various kinds of state intervention in particular industries, such as public ownership, public control of prices and profits (e.g., in public utilities), or tariff privileges and subsidies from public funds granted to industries which remain in private ownership; (2) those which consist of a system of planning superimposed upon and coordinating a system of private enterprise and individual ownership. Into this class come the various projects of planned capitalism, including the Corporate State in its various forms, Sir Arthur Salter's Ordered Society,[8] Mr. Harold Macmillan's Industrial Self-Government,[9] and Mr. Walter Elliot's Bucolic Utopia.

1. Intervention, whether in the form of state ownership, of state control, or of fiscal manipulation, which is confined to particular industries and stops short of planning the national economy as a whole, suffers from all the defects of unplanned economy and from some pe-

---

[8] A. Salter, *Recovery* and *Framework of an Ordered Society.*
[9] H. Macmillan, *Reconstruction* and *The Middle Way.*

culiar to itself. As in a completely unplanned economy it is liable to cyclical fluctuations and to unexpected variations in economic data. The state, if it runs an enterprise, is simply one entrepreneur among many, competing with the others in the capital market and in the labor market. It is as much at the mercy of fluctuations in the supply of capital as a private entrepreneur, and in its relations with labor it is forced willy-nilly into the role of the exploiting employer. This is the position of the London Passenger Transport Board vis-à-vis its employees. In a capitalist society even a socialist government has to consider the interests of *rentiers* and to resist "unreasonable" wage demands from its employees. An example of this is afforded by successive "Front Populaire" governments in France. If the state does attempt any different policy, it is as likely as not, working in an unplanned economy in ignorance of many of the relevant data, to do things which defeat its own ends. A case in point is the dilemma of a socialist government in a capitalist state trying to deal with unemployment under the stipulation, imposed by capitalist interests, that it will not compete with potential private enterprise and that it will do nothing to disturb "confidence."

Unless the state can consider the economic system as a whole—i.e., unless it plans—intervention is likely to do more harm than good. As an example, we may adduce the usual consequences of tariff protection: One industry is benefited, and a number of others are harmed. Moreover, such piecemeal intervention can rarely envisage the true objectives of economic policy. Thus, the natural attempt of the state, dealing with unemployment in a fundamentally unplanned economy, is to give help of some kind, financial or administrative, to declining industries and obsolete processes, thereby prolonging their uneconomic existence, rather than to develop new and more efficient processes and new industries satisfying hitherto latent wants.

Finally, the peculiar bane of all state intervention that falls short of complete socialism is political interference by sectional interests. Once the state deviates from the policy of *laisser faire* (or more precisely from the individualistic minimum of intervention[10]), it immediately puts a premium on political corruption. It becomes advantageous for any compact economic interest to capture the machinery of the state and to use it to further its own private purposes. The tariff history of all protectionist countries[11] and the annals of economic imperialism[12] offer ample illustration of this.

2. A completely planned capitalist economy[13] could avoid most of

[10] See H. Sidgwick, *Elements of Politics*, chap. iv; *Principles of Political Economy*, Book III, chaps. ii, iii, iv.

[11] F. W. Taussig, *Tariff History of the United States*.

[12] J. A. Hobson, *Imperialism*; V. I. Lenin, *Imperialism*; P. T. Moon, *Imperialism and World Politics*; L. Woolf, *Economic Imperialism*.

[13] Completely planned in the sense that the planning authority would be in a position to review the economic system as a whole, not in the sense that every detail of economic life must be regulated by it.

these difficulties. It would be free from the defects of piecemeal intervention. Through the glass walls of a planned economy the consequences of favoring one section at the expense of another could be clearly seen —so clearly seen, in fact, that inequalities of personal advantage, not based on functional differences of generally accepted utility, would soon cease to be tolerated in a politically democratic community. Moreover, the economic functions of the capitalist—the provision of new capital, the assumption of risk, the introduction of new materials and processes—that in an unplanned economy afford some sort of social justification for his existence would be wholly or largely superseded in a planned capitalism by the planning authority, leaving the capitalist as a mere *rentier*, a receiver of socially unjustified and therefore privileged income.

Thus, a planned capitalist economy would come up against one almost insuperable difficulty. This is the division of the product of industry, not only between the owning class and the working class, but among different sections of the owning class. As long as the market is the ultimate arbiter between the claims of the different parties to the production process, so long can the illusion be maintained that the division of the product is governed by forces as impersonal and inevitable as those which govern the weather. Even in a society where many industries are in fact carried on by the public, but as isolated enterprises not part of a general social plan, this illusion of inevitability may persist. But as soon as the state, through a definite planning organ, makes itself responsible for the consideration of economic activity as a whole, this illusion is destroyed, and the essentially social nature of all economic relations is revealed.

If, under private enterprise or under unplanned piecemeal state enterprise, the coal miners ask for an advance in wages, they may be told that their demands cannot be granted because they go beyond the capacity of the industry to bear. If they ask why the industry cannot afford to pay higher wages, they will be told that it is because the price of coal is too low. If they ask why the price of coal is as low as it is, they will be told that it is because the demand for coal is small; and so on. But in a planned economy the whole system of quantities, prices, wages, etc., is the result of the deliberate decisions of a responsible planning organ. If wages are too low in any one industry, it is the duty of the planning organ to adjust prices and quantities produced, so as to yield equal wages to work of equal skill, responsibility, and difficulty in every industry. If, then, wages are low in all industries, it is either because productivity per head is low, or because factors other than labor are taking a large proportion of the total social product. But the proportions in which the social product is divided between labor and other factors, while in an unplanned economy they are the apparently fortuitous result of the interaction of innumerable uncontrollable factors, are, in a planned economy, the result of decisions for which the planning authorities are directly responsible. The illusion of objectivity thus stripped from the process of income formation, the non-wage elements in distribution will be seen clearly for what they always have been in essence—the fruits of exploitation (Marx's *Surplus Value*, Veblen's *Free Income*, my *Institutional Revenue*). Once this occurs, the pressure of the organized working class for a continually increased share of the social product, leading ultimately to a complete expropriation of the property owner, can only be resisted by the destruction of the organized working class movement and the abolition of all democratic institutions. In other words, capitalist planning can exist only on the basis of fascism.

Not only the distribution of the product between labor and property, but also the division of the share of property among the various groups of property owners will be attended by a similar difficulty. In a planless economy, a ceaseless process of competition, modified by partial and usually temporary monopoly, allocates varying amounts of surplus value to one group and another in a manner that seems inevitable and "natural." Once planning is complete, the share of each section has to be determined by a deliberate decision of the planning organ. Unless the property-owning class is content to accept once and for all an allocation of shares in the surplus product according to the relative competitive strength of different sections at some definite moment before full planning was established, the planning organization will be the object of ceaseless attempts on the part of vested interests to seize control of it for their own profit. (Observe that this is equally true of national groups—e.g., British finance capital as against French finance capital—and of industrial groups within a country—e.g., export industries against home market industries, capital goods industries as against consumption goods industries.) It is in the highest degree unlikely that conflicting interests—whether national or industrial—within the owning class will acquiesce in such a stabilization of any particular *status quo*. On the international scale war and on the national scale organized political corruption will be the result. Planned capitalism will not only be a fascist society but a gangster fascist society. A socialist society can avoid this difficulty by distributing the surplus product on a basis of equality. Capitalism, however, is based on the creation and preservation of privileged income for a particular class. Since its essence is the denial of equity, it is impossible for it to find any "equitable" formula for the division of the social product either between labor and property or among the different sections of property.

In this connection it is interesting to note the objection made by defenders of the existing system to "bring economics into politics." In truth, economics have been in politics all the time, but in a concealed form. What the supporters of capitalism object to is the making manifest of the economic implications of existing social institutions of property, inheritance, and educational inequality. They attempt to divert the workers' interest from fundamental social institutions—the true subject of politics—to the superficial inanities of party-political sham fights. It is to their interest to prolong the illusion of a "natural" economic order, working by impersonal and irresistible economic laws; it is to their interest to conceal the exploitation of the worker behind the veils of a system of objective market relations which allot wages to the worker and interest to the capitalist equally in the form of the price of a "service."

Of all forms of piecemeal nationalization or state control, that of the banking system would come closest to setting up a planned economy at one stroke. Once the state was responsible for the conduct of the banking system, it would be obliged to look beyond the purely commercial criteria of banking practice (reserve ratios, liquidity of assets, etc.) and consider demands for credit from a social-economic point of view. It would have to consider the balance of saving and investment, the proportion between consumption goods and production goods industries, the volume of speculative compared with productive transactions, etc. In other words, a state-controlled banking system would be obliged to consider the economic activity of the community as an organic whole; thus, it would already be in embryo a planning organ. Ultimately, therefore, the nationalization of banks would make manifest that fundamental conflict of classes which is latent all the time in the system of market economy. This probably accounts for the fact that proposals for the nationalization of the banks arouse much more bitter opposition from the capitalist ranks than proposals for the nationalization of any other industry.

The Economic Problem under Socialism

1. In General. A socialist society will have to solve the problems that are solved in a capitalist society, however imperfectly, by the method of production for sale in the market at a price. Must it work out a brand-new solution *ab origine* for these problems, or may it make use of some of the machinery evolved during the period of petty commodity production that preceded capitalism and perfected under capitalism itself? In other words, the field of our investigation is the extent to which price and its correlates, money and the market, can be adapted to a planned socialist economy.

With regard to the significance of pricing for a socialist economy, socialists are divided into two schools of thought: those who hold that the individualistic assumptions behind the pricing process have no relevance for a socialist community, and those who hold that they have.

a) The first school would reject in principle the notion that the demand schedules of individual consumers give any adequate indication of human needs. The most brilliant exposition of this view is probably Lancelot Hogben's *Retreat from Reason*. It rejects the two corner-stones of individualistic economies: the doctrine that the individual knows best what is good for him, and the doctrine of the insatiability of human wants. It asserts rather that the basic needs of humanity can be ascertained better by scientific study than by offering people a choice of goods in the market place, and that non-basic needs are the result either of class standards of consumption (Veblen's "conspicuous waste" and "pecuniary emulation") or of profit-mongering advertising campaigns, which multiply satisfactions without increasing satisfaction. If these views be accepted, social production will be carried out not in response to the indications of the market but according to a planned survey of human needs.

A further point made by these theorists is that the normalizing of consumption, following on the scientific study of human needs, would make possible standardization in production to an extent previously unheard of, and thus reduce greatly the cost of satisfying those needs. In this way, it is hoped, the goods that are required for human consumption can be so few and so easily produced that they will become free goods and the economic problem as such will disappear. Meanwhile, however, we shall adhere to the more orthodox views.

b) The second school of socialists starts off with the liberal individualistic conception of welfare as consisting in the satisfaction of particular individuals' particular wants, interpreted by those individuals themselves by an act of deliberate conscious choice. It entrusts the satisfaction of those wants to a collectivist economic organization rather than to private enterprise, because it believes that collectivism can, when the distribution of income as well as the organization of production is taken into account, provide a greater aggregate of individual satisfaction than private enterprise can. A social order of this type may be called libertarian socialism. Adherents of this school desire socialism in order that they may establish, for the first time in human history, an effective individualism.

2. *Pricing under Socialism.* Whichever view, therefore, be taken of the process of satisfying human wants—whether we accept or reject the relevance of the individual's demand schedule—there remains the economic problem, the problem of disposing of limited resources so as to provide the maximum satisfaction of human needs, which needs are, if we interpret the word "needs" in its widest sense, capable of indefinite expansion. This implies that the economic organizers of the community must adopt some system of valuation. That is to say, there must be established a scale of relative importance (in other words, "value") among the different possible ends of economic activity; resources must be valued according as they contribute to these ends; the most advantageous uses of resources must be discovered, and scarce resources must be husbanded ("costing" and "principle of substitution"). According to the first school of socialists, the alternative ends of economic activity will be comparatively few and will be laid down by some authority acting on behalf of the community as a whole. According to the second school, they will

be determined by the individual preferences of millions of separate economic subjects; in this case the problem of balancing one man's preference against another's will arise.

Analogous to the problem of consumers' preferences for goods is that of workers' preferences for jobs. Here, too, two solutions are possible. Either people can be allocated to different occupations in accordance with some objective test of capacity (e.g., by some development of industrial psychology), or they can be allowed to choose according to their own preferences. In both cases the fact that some kinds of labor are scarcer than others must be taken into account in the social cost-accounting scheme; in both cases it will be economically desirable to increase the supply of the scarcer types of labor. In the first case, however, the only problem will be the balancing of the cost of training against the productivity of the factor; in the second case an additional problem arises of offering inducements to workers to move into occupations where labor is relatively scarce out of occupations where it is relatively superfluous. A libertarian socialist community cannot dispose of human factors of production by administrative order as it can dispose of non-human factors. It must respect individual workers' preferences for one job over another.

In what follows, we will assume a libertarian form of socialist community; not because it is necessarily the best or the only possible form of socialism, but because it raises in the most acute form the economic problem. If it is soluble under libertarian socialism, it is *a fortiori* soluble under authoritarian socialism.

The problem before a libertarian socialist economy is threefold. First, there is the measurement of demand, in order that production may be directed so as to yield the maximum of satisfaction. Second, there is the measurement of cost, in order that the satisfactions that are procured may be procured with the minimum expenditure of resources; the calculation of costs affords a criterion for deciding between alternative plans of production. Third, there is the problem of distribution—that of allotting to particular members of society definite shares in the goods produced.

In capitalist society the price system solves, after a fashion, all three of these problems at once.[14] Thus, the pricing process has a threefold function in the individualistic system, corresponding to the pricing of consumption goods, of intermediate goods, and of ultimate factors of production.[15]

---

[14] Price also is a means of comparing physically and technically dissimilar goods, and hence of calculating a measure of aggregate production. This function of price is derived from those numbered 1 and 2 following.

[15] The phrase "ultimate factors of production" is used to designate production goods (such as land and human labor) that cannot be resolved into other production goods.

1. The pricing of consumption goods acts as a regulator of demand. Hence, it (i) allocates already produced goods to consumers according to the scarcity of the goods and the intensity of the consumers' demand; and (ii) indicates the kind and number of goods that should be most worth while to produce in the future.
2. The pricing of intermediate goods (and of ultimate factors of production) yields a measure of relative cost and hence acts as a guide to the worth-whileness of production, as well as to the best method of production.
3. The pricing of ultimate factors of production affords an automatic method of distribution. By allowing owners of such factors to appropriate their economic value as personal income, the value of the whole mass of the social product is allocated without residue and without deficit, among the collective producers of it, according to a process that, apparently, takes place independently of the wills and preferences of any individual in authority.

A socialist society that adopts the price system may also use the same device for all three purposes. If, however, the socialist community jettisons the system of sale at a price in a free market, then it will have to develop new machinery to deal with these three problems. It is possible that three different kinds of machinery will be necessary for these three separate purposes. In other words, there is no necessity in the nature of things that a device for the measurement of consumers' preferences should serve at the same time for the allocation of producers' shares in a collective product.

A socialist community might adopt the price system for function 1 only, or for functions 1 and 2, or for all three functions. That is to say, it might price finished goods and allow the consumer free choice of goods already produced at the prices fixed, but might adopt a completely separate and distinct method for the calculation of costs and a third system for the distribution of individual income. Alternatively, it might extend the pricing process to include a costing system based on imputed prices of intermediate goods and ultimate factors of production, while completely divorcing individual earnings from the value of factors of production. Finally, it might adopt the price system in its entirety, thus setting up within the socialist community a simulacrum of capitalist economy.

23. THE ECONOMICS OF NATIONALIZATION*

R. A. S. Crosland

SYNOPSIS

1. Pre-war socialists argued on economic grounds that an industry should be nationalized if it is a public utility, a monopoly, if it is basic to the economy, if it is wastefully competitive, or if planning requires public ownership.

2. On social grounds, they argued that nationalization promotes industrial democracy and equality, and does away with the immorality of private profit.

3. British experience has shown that the nationalized industries are not always well planned and that planning does not always require nationalization, that their pricing policies increased instead of reduced private relative to total saving, that publicly owned monopoly is not entirely good and that competition has some merit, that the technical economies of large scale enterprise can be offset by managerial diseconomies, that labor relations have improved less than hoped, and that nationalization has created many problems of organization.

4. In deciding which industries to nationalize next, socialists find their economic arguments do not provide a clear guide because there are few private monopolies left, much private enterprise is reasonably efficient, multi-product firms operate in industries which might be nationalized and in others which should not be, managerial problems are more complex than in the industries already nationalized, and the increased efficiency of the entire economy has lessened the need for nationalization.

5. Policy in the future should be (*a*) to nationalize an industry only if an increase in efficiency can be expected by no other means and if nationalization will not itself produce compensating disadvantages, and (*b*) preferably to nationalize firms rather than industries and operate them in competition with private firms.

6. The efficiency of enterprise depends on the quality of its leading management and its technical structure, and there is no necessary relationship between them and ownership.

The Pre-war Case for Nationalization

In the 1930's, the central importance of nationalization was taken for granted in the Labour Party. It was desired partly for reasons specific to

* Reprinted by permission and shortened from *The Future of Socialism* (New York: Macmillan, 1957), chap. xxii.

particular industries, that is, in order to control the use of particular capital assets; and partly for reasons common to all industries, that is, because it was thought that "socialism" was ultimately consistent only with the public ownership of all (major) capital assets. The specific reasons, which naturally determined the order in which industries were to be nationalized, were as follows.

First, the Public Utility argument. It is a characteristic of certain industries providing essential services either that the basic size of plant is very large in relation to the market (gas, electricity), or that an elaborate "octopoid" system of distribution (by piping, cabling, wiring, railway lines, etc.) involves extremely heavy capital costs. Any duplication of such equipment would be clearly wasteful, and simply cause under-utilization of the competing capital assets. It has therefore long been recognized that such public utility industries were unsuitable for competition, and that monopoly must be permitted. But all governments have insisted, as a safeguard, on elaborate supervision of such monopolies; and the tradition of public regulation had grown to the point where outright public ownership seemed a simpler and more logical solution.

Secondly, the Monopoly argument. While it was conceded that cartels might be disrupted by legislation, it was argued that large single firm monopolies, or trusts, were often justified by technical economies of scale which would be lost, to the disadvantage of the consumer, if competition were to be forcibly restored. Since it appeared, to most economists as well as to socialists, that private monopoly inevitably constituted a threat of exploitation (political and social even if not economic), the natural solution seemed to be to substitute public for private monopoly by means of nationalization.

Thirdly, the Basic Industry argument. There are certain commodities, used normally by a wide variety of other industries, on which the prosperity of the community depends to an especially marked degree, so that any breakdown or weakness in their production, and indeed generally the level of their output and prices, is a matter of particular public concern—to such an extent as to require the extreme solution of public ownership.

These three arguments all relate to certain inescapable characteristics of an industry which make it a natural candidate for state monopoly. The Efficiency argument, however, which comes fourth, has a more general application. It was most commonly based on the economies of large scale organization. These were thought to apply almost universally and without limit, and to provide a general argument for unification such as would be possible only under a single ownership. The word "competition" was always preceded by the epithet "wasteful," and efficiency was held to be largely a function of monopoly control.

There were some industries in particular where the advantages of unification seemed likely to be overwhelming—industries, for ex-

ample, where the optimum size of plant was larger than the average existing size (electricity, gas), or where redundancy clearly demanded large
scale reorganization (coal and steel, as it seemed in the 1930's), or where
wide differences in efficiency separated the best and worst plants, pointing to a redistribution of output within the industry (coal and steel
again), or where overheads were so high that competition must lead to a
wasteful under-utilization of capital equipment (road versus rail). It was,
in theory, admitted that there were industries to which these strictures
did not apply, and which might be well served by a purely competitive
solution. But this was thought to be an academic point.

Thus, the efficiency argument came to be bound up with a justification of monopoly control. Naturally, existing single firm monopolies were
to be taken over—but because they represented a dangerous concentration of power, not because they were inefficient. Indeed, they represented, so far as their organization was concerned, the ideal to which
large scale industry ought to conform; where it failed to do so under the
spur of market forces, it must be compelled to do so under the aegis of
state enterprise.

Lastly, the Planning argument. Generally, this was based on the
belief that the profit motive and the national interest must always be in
conflict. It was applied most commonly to the basic heavy investment
industries, in which the level of investment dictated by profit maximizing
was both on the average too low to ensure full employment and too
fluctuating. These were also the industries in which private and public
interest were most liable to clash when it came to questions of the loca-
tion of new plant or the shut-down of old.

In addition to these economic arguments for nationalizing particular
industries, there were also the wider (and older) social arguments.
First, it was thought that the profit motive was ethically wrong and
could be eliminated only by nationalization. Secondly, it was thought
that harmonious labor relations and the creation of industrial democracy
could be achieved only under public ownership. Thirdly, it was assumed
that equality required the extinction of incomes from private property.
Originally, this was conceived as occurring automatically with the
transfer of ownership. But later, it was realized that complete confiscation
of private property by nationalization was neither just nor politic, and
that reasonable compensation must be paid. The argument was then that
nationalization, although it would not destroy, would yet diminish property incomes, since equity holdings, carrying with them the likelihood of
a gradual rise in dividends and capital values, would be replaced by
fixed interest compensation stock, carrying with it no such long run prospect, and even in the short run generating an income that was smaller because the risk was smaller.

When it came to deciding what industries to nationalize, these arguments all pointed in broadly the same direction. The wider social argu-

ments pointed to taking industries over in order of size. And the largest industries were in fact either public utilities (gas, electricity, railways), effective monopolies (coal, steel), basic (coal, transport, steel, electricity), notably inefficient under private enterprise (coal), apparently in need of larger scale or central reorganization (coal, gas), heavy capital users (electricity, steel, transport), or subject to exceptionally bad labor relations (coal). Other, less important industries were added for special post-war reasons (raw cotton purchasing, civil aviation, cable and wireless). But broadly, the 1945–50 list seemed obviously dictated by these various criteria. Indeed, it was so far accepted by public opinion that the greater part of it is still in public ownership after several years of Tory rule.

Post-war Experience of Nationalization

But do we now simply go on, and in our next period of office take over the next five largest industries, and so on ad infinitum? Not many socialists would now definitely answer yes; and for the first time in a century, there is equivocation on the Left about the future of nationalization.

For this there are several reasons. The most obvious is that the reality proved rather different from the blueprints. Some of the anticipated advantages did not materialize, while certain unexpected disadvantages emerged.

The planning argument, for example, looks a good deal less clearcut than it used to. I am not thinking simply of the considerations (sufficiently discussed elsewhere in this book), first, that the distinction between public production for use and private production for profit has in any case lost much of its force at present levels and distribution of purchasing power and, secondly, that one can scarcely argue, after the experience of the last ten years, that full employment requires as an absolute condition a much larger public sector: but of the fact that even where planning was admitted to be desirable, it proved scarcely easier to achieve under public than private ownership.

This was due to changes on both sides. On the side of private ownership, whereas before the war it was assumed that a change in ownership was a condition of state control, today it is realized that planning can be made effective even in the private sector. The government has access to a wide variety of fiscal, physical, and monetary controls that enable the government broadly to impose its will on private industry.

While control over the private sector thus exceeded expectations, control over the public sector fell short of them. Chapter I has already drawn attention to the independence of some of the nationalized boards and their lack of public accountability. Indeed, it was a common saying that the government had less power over Lord Citrine than over I.C.I., and the quip was not without force. The Bank of England, for example, continued to pursue a highly independent policy, especially in the field of the foreign exchanges. In the crucial fuel and power industries, control was almost non-existent. The three industries were allowed to go their own way: each competing and advertising against the other; each charging the lowest price it could (and indeed encouraged, and in the case of coal compelled, to do so by the government itself); each unrestrictedly pushing sales in every direction, oblivious of the fact that coal was desperately scarce and large economies clearly possible if policy were only unified. It was a situation which cried out for government co-ordination, either through prices or physical controls, but none was forth-coming.

Investment policy was similarly uncoordinated. It was argued before the war that one of the advantages of nationalizing heavy investing industries was that their large investment plans would become a stabilizing factor in the trade cycle—to be retarded when private investment was booming, accelerated when private investment was lagging. This never in fact occurred; and fluctuations in private investment simply increased or diminished the degree of inflation, with little effective attempt at countervailing action.

The reasons for this outcome were twofold. First, the planning issues which arose had not been properly anticipated, nor were they always clarified even as time went on. The ministers themselves, therefore, often had no clear policy which they *wanted* to impose on the boards; and so they took the line of least resistance, which was to allow the boards to do more or less as they wished.

Secondly, however, even when ministers held clear views, they were often reluctant to impose them on account of a rather dogmatic attachment to the theory of the independent public board. Insofar as this helped to ward off detailed parliamentary supervision, or even state department nationalization, it was thoroughly healthy. But it was often pressed to an undesirable extreme.

Of course, this is largely a question of politics. The truth is that there is now no insuperable *economic* difficulty about the government imposing its will, provided it has one, on either public of private industry. Indeed, post-1945 experience in the planning field strongly underlines one of the main arguments of Part One, namely, that ownership is not now an important determinant of economic power. The planning argument for more nationalization has, for the moment, fallen into some disrepute. It can now only be held to apply if three conditions are fulfilled: first, that ministers have a clear idea of what their planning objectives are; secondly, that these objectives cannot be achieved by fiscal or physical controls; thirdly, that ministers are in fact prepared to plan for their achievement under nationalization.

Allied to the planning failure was a pricing policy which prevented the full achievement of another of the objects of nationalization, the transfer of wealth from private to public hands. Briefly, the refusal to allow the boards to build up large surpluses (besides often leading, as in the case of coal, to a serious misallocation of resources) meant that savings in the public sector were zero or negative, and hence that total savings were more heavily concentrated than they need have been in private hands. A quite different pricing policy would have been required to increase greatly public relative to private capital.

These two failures are in principle remediable, in the sense of having been due to freely chosen government policies (for which, to be fair, there were some strong practical arguments). But other difficulties emerged which appear to be inseparable from nationalization as so far envisaged; that is, they are inseparable from monopoly and large (indeed, enormous) scale.

We now understand rather better that monopoly, even when it is public, has definite drawbacks. Not only is there a genuine restriction of freedom in forbidding the citizen by law to produce certain goods, and an even more dangerous restriction, notably in those cases (such as the B.B.C.) which call on highly specialized talent, in having only one employer: but competition is seen to bring greater advantages than pre-war socialists realized—in preventing sloth and encouraging initiative, and in increasing the sense of consumer welfare by allowing a free choice of goods and suppliers. Naturally, this does not mean that monopoly has no advantages and competition no faults, but only that the balance of advantage now looks rather different. Nor, of course, does it mean that competition is always physically possible; on the other hand, pre-war Marxist prophecies of its inexorable decline have not been fulfilled, and we have a wider choice between competition and monopoly than was once supposed.

But perhaps the biggest change of view has occurred on the subject of large scale. Before the war, it was treated as axiomatic that, in the words of a typical and well-known judgment, "large-scale production, especially when conducted in large-size firms and plants, results in maximum efficiency."[1] Today, we are not so sure—at least beyond a certain size. It is not that the technical economies of scale are in dispute, but that doubts have arisen as to whether these may not be offset by diseconomies in other spheres, such as labor morale (leading to a higher accident rate, more absenteeism, and a less willing attitude to work), or managerial responsibility and control, with the risk that decision making may become over-centralized and hence slowed down. So far, none of these points is proved one way or another. But it seems clear, at any rate, that enormous scale is not an unmixed blessing, and in particular that it must bring with it at least the danger of over-centralization.

This danger has not in practice always been avoided; and this is one of the reasons (though there are others) for the disappointment of yet another of the hopes of nationalization, namely, that it would rapidly and

[1] P. Sargant Florence, *The Logic of Industrial Organisation* (Kegan Paul, 1933), p. 11.

significantly improve labor relations, offering at the same time the hope of a steady advance toward industrial democracy.

Some of these problems may recede as we gain a clearer idea of how to run these vast organizations. At the moment, we have a huge area of disagreement: about the degree of public accountability required; on the issue of centralization or decentralization of management, and how much latitude to allow operational management; about how to make joint consultation effective; on what role (if any) to allot to consumer councils; on promotion policy, on which the unions lean to seniority and the management to merit, with no agreement about the recruitment of university graduates; and so on.

The Case against a Proliferation of State Monopolies

Even if these difficulties had not arisen, we should still face the fact that the specific economic as opposed to the wider social criteria do not now point unequivocally to a particular list of industries. There are no more public utilities (except for water) and no more industries (except for steel) which can be described as basic in the sense that coal or railways are basic. And if we adopt the policy of simply tackling industries in order of size, we find that the next most obvious candidates—chemicals, motor-cars, aircraft, shipbuilding, radio, electrical equipment, and so on—are not for the most part monopolies, nor in need of centralized planning, nor obviously inefficient, nor indeed suitable for organizing on a national scale. There are industries quite different in kind from the 1945–50 list, above all in respect of their suitability for monopoly control and their level of efficiency.

On the first point, they are not (with the exception of certain heavy chemicals) monopolies, but competitive oligopolies. Nor are they "ripe" for nationalization in the sense that although not yet monopolies, they would be improved by becoming monopolies. On the contrary, the element of competition is essential to their efficiency, the units are not obviously of less than optimum size, and their type of product and market is such that centralized control would be disadvantageous. Old-model nationalization would mean imposing a state monopoly on unsuitable and competitive industries, with the corollary of a large increase in the area of unitary control.

They are unsuitable for old-model nationalization for other reasons also. The 1945–50 industries had, for the most part, clearly defined boundaries, a relatively homogeneous output normally consisting of a service or raw material, few marketing problems, and a fairly predictable (in the short run) demand. These industries, on the other hand, have indistinct boundaries, a diversified range of output, and a much less stable final demand. Thus, once we move from the basic industries into the sphere of manufacturing, an industry becomes extremely hard to define. As multi-line production has spread, over-lapping has become general; and most large firms today sprawl over several "industries" at once. The lack of coincidence in the boundaries between firms and those between industries faces the would-be nationalizer with problems of definition far more intricate than those which caused such difficulty even in the relatively simple case of steel.

The fact of multi-line production, moreover, elevates sales and marketing policy to a position of much greater importance than it occupies in the existing public sector. The demand for manufactures tends in any case to be less predictable than that for basic services. But, in addition, the more variegated the output (and the more products are "branded"), the more central becomes the role of sales policy. This would be so even in an industry catering solely to the home market. But the metal, engineering, and chemical industries are also producing for the export market, where the competition is fiercer, the risks greater, and the fluctuations much more marked. Here the marketing problem, and the need for continuous rapid adaptation to the vagaries of a buyer's market, assume an even greater importance; and it is not clear that the routine type of management which appears to be characteristic of centralized public boards, suitable though it may be for the basic utilities, would be flexible and dynamic enough for this quite different task.

Quite apart from their *structural* suitability or otherwise for nationalization, it cannot be said that these industries are so patently inefficient or unprogressive (as one could have said of coal before the war) as imperatively to demand a change of ownership. Whether judged by output, productivity, exports, or investment, their post-war record has been at least a reasonable one—indeed, the metal, engineering, and chemical industries have been responsible for by far the greater part of the rise in production and exports since the war.

This does not mean that they are of perfect efficiency, or that serious flaws cannot be found. Naturally, being human organizations, they fall very much short of perfection. It simply means that a reasonable man would judge their economic record to be better than the average, and would doubt whether it was likely to be improved by a transfer to public ownership.

The economic arguments do not give the same clear answer when applied to the next group of industries as they did when applied to coal and railways. And this is not due solely to specific factors, but also to the more general fact that British industry, working under conditions of full employment and in a healthier social climate, is significantly more efficient, competitive, and expansionist than it was before the war. The Labour Government can take some credit for this; but it inevitably weakens the case for further major structural changes.

The Criteria and Conditions for Successful Nationalization

The diminished importance of nationalization on economic grounds is only one aspect of the diminished importance, analyzed in Chapter III, of industrial ownership for social relations as a whole. Socialism, whether viewed in social or ethical or economic terms, will not be brought much nearer by nationalizing the aircraft industry. A higher working class standard of living, more effective joint consultation, better labor relations, a proper use of economic resources, a wider diffusion of power, a greater degree of cooperation, or more social and economic equality—none of these now primarily require a large scale change in ownership for their fulfillment; still less is such a change a *sufficient* condition of their fulfillment.

The gradual (though still often subconscious) realization of this truth[2] has brought a reaction against making state monopoly the central feature of Labour policy. In this new situation, probably most thoughtful socialists would agree on two points. First, any nationalization proposals must be capable, given the present climate of public opinion, of being justified to the electorate as likely to lead to an economic improvement. The approach must therefore be precise and selective, concentrating not on the next industries in order of size, or on those which happen to be in the public eye, but on those where a genuine economic case can be made out. Secondly, in the light of the evident disadvantages, outside the public utility field, of state monopoly and enormous scale, the method should be to take over not whole industries, but individual firms, leaving others still in private hands; or to set up new government-owned plants to compete with existing private firms. This is the "competitive public enterprise" approach. It need not rule out occasionally nationalizing whole industries where the arguments for doing so seem overwhelming, but it should have a preference wherever possible.

An economic improvement may follow from public ownership where the existing industry is clearly performing poorly, where competition either cannot or is not permitted to enforce an improvement, where physical or fiscal controls are incapable of curing the situation, and where public ownership will not bring attendant disadvantages of its own.

The first three conditions may be fulfilled where an industry is clearly failing to expand in line with national requirements. The steel industry, for example, consistently under-rates the expansion in its capacity required to accommodate the sustained rise in metal-using output; and the consequence is recurrent periods of strain on the balance of payments as marginal supplies have to be imported (often for dollars, and at a heavy cost), and steel exports cut back below their potential level. This constant lag in British steel capacity (which appears to be rooted in the psychology of the British industry, since it does not occur in Germany, the United States, or Russia) is not automatically corrected by the mar-

---

[2] Or rather, of most of this truth. The exception is the still widespread belief, which is discussed fully in the next chapter, that nationalization is essential to the diminution of property incomes, and hence to equality.

ket mechanism. Nor is it easily curable by government controls, which are naturally more effective in preventing than encouraging particular lines of conduct: One cannot compel businessmen to spend large sums of their own capital if they do not wish to. There is here an over-whelming argument for public ownership.

There may be other industries where sufficient expansion fails to occur under the influence of market pressures. Industrial investment has been constantly held back since the end of the war (and the balance of payments again worsened by the consequent need for imports) by the slow rate of expansion of the machine-tool industry. There is surely an argument for some public ownership here to hurry things along. Outside the industrial sphere, the "municipalization" of blocks of private rented property is justified by the fact that landlords are unwilling at current controlled rents to spend the necessary sums on repairs and improve-ments; that governments are reluctant, for social reasons, to allow rents to rise to the point where they might be so willing; and that in consequence a glaring social inequality is emerging between those who live in new houses and those who live in old.

The most successful example in practice of state action in a sphere in which the risks were too heavy for private enterprise is, of course, atomic energy. This has been a spectacular instance of public initiative, efficiency, and risk taking (though the display of these qualities has prob-ably been aided by the secrecy surrounding atomic development, and the consequent immunity from parliamentary questions and press cam-paigns).

A slightly oblique case is that of the insurance companies. Chapter XX made the point that these and other financial institutions must now logically fill the role of the erstwhile rich investor, and become a source of risk capital to a greater extent than they have yet been willing. This consideration, allied to the fact that a great deal of wasteful over-lapping between the companies is known to occur, should encourage the Labour Party to re-examine the question of public ownership.

There may also still be a few cases where public ownership is the simplest answer to the problem of monopoly. This will rarely be the case with trade association cartels, which are much better simply broken up, but might occasionally be the case with a single firm monopoly. The Monopolies Commission found, for example, that the British Match Corporation had a complete and integrated monopoly of match produc-tion, which operated against the public interest. But since the B.M.C. already owned ample capacity, and match making appears to be a "natu-ral" monopoly in almost every country, it seemed pointless either to en-courage or to create a new competing company; while to have split the B.M.C. itself up into independent competing concerns would have in-volved the sacrifice of important advantages of scale. The majority and minority reports therefore recommended, respectively, government price control and a government wholesaling agency. But neither seemed happy with its recommendations, and nationalization might have been a simpler solution. A few such cases may occur, though normally the problem of monopoly can be dealt with quite well by government controls—if only the will is there, which it has not always been in the past.

So far as efficiency is concerned, it will already be clear that no general statements about public versus private ownership can ever be justified. Examples have been quoted of efficient private industries; they could equally be quoted of efficient nationalized industries—e.g., the civil air corporations, the trunk fleet of British Road Services, or the electricity industry (except for its pricing policies).

On the other hand, some public industries have done less well; not many people are satisfied with the performance of the railways, and the Fleck Committee found much to criticize in the management structure of the coal industry. But there are also plenty of less efficient private industries.

Efficiency has little to do with ownership because in the modern corporation, ownership has little to do with control. Thus, a change of ownership, by itself, makes little difference. The steel industry in recent years has undergone the most kaleidoscopic changes: first private ownership, then the Iron and Steel Corporation, later an anomalous period of ownership by the Realisation Agency, and now back to a (different) private ownership again. Yet management was hardly affected by all these changes in Whitehall; and output continued to rise (though never fast enough, since public ownership never had time to compel a better view of the long term optimum capacity).

The basic fact is the large corporation, facing fundamentally similar problems and acting in fundamentally the same way whether publicly or privately owned. Its efficiency depends simply on the quality of its top management, and on whether the firm or industry is structurally well adapted from a technical point of view. There are, of course, exceptions—as when a dynamic and progressive top management (or an all-important research team) has a strongly marked private enterprise outlook, and is very allergic to Whitehall; or where the whole enterprise revolves round a refractory individual genius; or, in the opposite case, where the workers would simply refuse to cooperate with private owners (as they would in coal). But with these exceptions, ownership as such makes little difference; and a transfer to public ownership will improve efficiency only if either (1) the government puts in a better management, or compels the existing management to take greater long term risks, or (2) it is able to adapt the structure of the industry (e.g., by amalgamations) in a manner obviously required by productive efficiency. Conversely, it will make things worse if it does the opposite.

In certain cases, it might easily do the opposite. Thus, the imposition of centralized monopoly control on an efficient competitive industry would certainly lead to a fall in efficiency. This danger is now well under-stood. But a further danger is not—that nationalization might actually lower the caliber of management. This will occur if we continue to pay such stingy salaries in the public sector. We have heard too much ob-jection to the allegedly high, but in fact relatively low, level of salaries in nationalized industry; we can begin to worry about these when we have removed many far more glaring (and socially unjustified) sources of inequality. As it is, we simply place nationalized concerns under a hope-less handicap in competing with private enterprise.

The second condition is that we give the industry a more efficient structure that it had before. There are certainly cases where this is in theory possible—cases, that is, where larger scale would be a positive advantage; where the average existing scale is too small for maximum technical efficiency; where there are too many small, non-specialized firms, each producing a wide range of output, and consequently gaining no advantages of scale; and where competition is too imperfect to com-pel a greater concentration. In such cases the public acquisition and sub-sequent amalgamation of a number of separate firms might greatly im-prove the structural fitness of the industry.

I have no intention of drawing up a detailed list of industries where such improvements might occur, having always thought this a task for industrial experts rather than for laymen. Whatever industries are chosen, we should now have a definite preference for the "competitive public enterprise" approach,[3] although there will occasionally be cases (such as steel) where state monopoly still provides the right answer. There are, it is true, some difficulties about the form of competitive public enterprise which is usually envisaged. But I leave a detailed discussion of the ap-propriate forms until after a consideration of the one remaining popular argument for rapid and large scale nationalization.[4]

[3] Which is in any case a good Fabian concept. G. B. Shaw wrote in Fabian Tract No. 2, in 1884, that "since Competition among producers admittedly secures to the public the most satisfactory products, the State should compete with all its might in every department of production." This is the tract which also contains his acid phrase about "the division of society into hostile classes, with large appe-tites and no dinners at one extreme, and large dinners and no appetites at the other."

[4] [See above, n. 2.]

24. NATIONAL ECONOMIC PLANNING: THE SOVIET EXPERIENCE*

Paul A. Baran

SYNOPSIS

1. A general theory of planning is impossible, because the planning authority cannot predict all the problems which it will confront, including those it creates itself.

2. After the failure of the revolutions outside Russia in the twenties, planning had to be directed to the survival of Russia, which required rapid economic development, immunity to blockade and invasion, and an increase in consumption.

3. The rate of attaining the long run goals was set by the technical coordination of capital outlays, defense, and need to increase popular support. They required dividing the national product between the government's share—for investment, defense, social services, etc.—and consumption, the difference between consumption and the total product being the "economic surplus."

4. Consumption had to be limited in the interest of investment and defense, and the burden divided between city and country. The main reason for collectivizing agriculture was to prevent farmers from increasing their consumption or reducing their output.

5. Total wages (including agricultural income) are set equal to the value of consumer goods, and the remainder of the national product is the profit of state enterprises, of which most is collected by the turnover tax.

6. The proceeds are used for investment, defense, social services, etc., and the government must decide (*a*) how to allocate the total among different industries and (*b*) the technical form of each investment.

7. Decision (*a*) has the object of eliminating critical scarcities of particular kinds of capital. Decision (*b*) is based on the government's estimate of present and future resource supplies, their value in present and alternative uses, the cost of re-allocating them, and the effect of re-allocation on the distribution of the marketed share of agricultural output.

8. Plans for production are brought together in three national-economic balance sheets, showing (*a*) the input and output of consumer and investment goods, (*b*) the income and expenditure of individuals and the government, and (*c*) the demand for labor and sources of additional labor.

* Reprinted by permission from *A Survey of Contemporary Economics,* Vol. II, ed. Bernard F. Haley (Homewood, Ill.: Richard D. Irwin, Inc., 1952), pp. 387–403.

9. The success of planning depends on the accuracy of the estimates in the balance sheets, and mistakes mean disproportionalities and waste. They are less serious the more the economy develops and accumulates reserves.

It is perhaps the very limited extent to which economic theory can offer help to a Central Planning Board engaged in the administration of a system in the throes of economic development and in transition from capitalism to socialism that accounts for the conspicuous paucity of theoretic publications on economic planning on the part of Soviet economists. Indeed, an economic science that has drawn its inspiration from the study of the "coordinating operation of the market and at times the failure of the market to achieve a coordination of decisions"[1] is not geared to deal with problems confronting an economy in which the "coordination of decisions" is a function of a central political body. Nor are possibly other branches of social sciences which are designed to study the processes taking place in capitalist (and pre-capitalist) societies as yet in the position to provide insight as to the regularities characterizing the behavior of such an authority.[2]

It could hardly be otherwise. Although the basic philosophy of the Central Authority may determine the goal of its activities, its concrete policies are shaped by the specific circumstances prevailing at any given time. Even if it were possible to establish some regular pattern of the authority's reaction to any set of specifiable economic and political conditions, an attempt at a general theory of its policies would be necessarily jeopardized by the impossibility of anticipating adequately domestic and international developments determining, and *themselves determined by*, its actions.

Thus the experience of Soviet planning has lent itself very little to theoretical summaries; and most useful writing on the subject has been by necessity of a historical character.[3] Whether in monographs dealing with relatively short periods and with special aspects of the Russian planning effort or in larger treatises seeking to encompass the entire period since the revolution—students of Soviet planning have had to analyze the policies of the Russian government as caused by, or them-

[1] Oskar Lange, "The Scope and Method of Economics," *Review of Economic Studies*, Vol. XIII, (1945–46), p. 26.

[2] See, however, Nathan Leites, *The Operational Code of the Politburo* (New York, 1951), for an attempt to establish a pattern of *political* conduct of the Soviet leadership, an attempt that illustrates, if anything, the sterility of the generalizing formalism characteristic of much of modern social sciences.

[3] "The methodology of Soviet planning has grown with the practise of administering the socialized economy. This discipline is not taught in a single university in the world. One cannot find it in any text. The Soviet practitioners have had to learn the science of planning from their errors and omissions which they have had to discover and rectify." Stanislas Stroumiline, *La Planification en U.R.S.S.* (Paris, 1947), p. 29.

selves causing, specific economic and political constellations. It is by no means fortuitous therefore that efforts at a comprehension of Soviet economic reality in terms of conventional economic theory reached their apex in the years of the New Economic Policy, i.e., at a time when the "coordination of economic decisions" was still largely entrusted to the market mechanism, and have become increasingly rare and unrewarding in the ensuing two decades, in the years in which economic planning has become the effectively governing principle of Soviet economic life.

A brief consideration of the problems that the Soviet planners are called upon to solve may serve to render the foregoing more explicit.

1. *The Determination of the Long Run Goal of Economic and Social Development.* It goes without saying that decisions under this heading represent the bases of all plans and policies pursued by the Soviet government. Although strongly affected by the ideology (and social basis) of the ruling party—and to that extent explicable in its terms—they are powerfully influenced by the specific conditions under which they have to be made. The tasks confronting the Soviet government have turned out to be quite different from what was anticipated in earlier Marxist thought. Indeed, although political developments in Russia permitted the seizure of political power by a socialist party, the economic and social prerequisites for a socialist order were entirely absent. Fully aware of this contradiction, the Bolsheviks had no intention of immediately establishing socialism (and comprehensive economic planning) in their hungry and devastated country.[4]

Their plan was rather to resist all internal and external attempts to overthrow the socialist regime and to preserve political power until the victory of socialism in Europe's leading industrial nations. All economic measures in the years immediately following the revolution were subordinated to this basic purpose.[5] Once socialism had prevailed in the advanced countries of the world, the fortress of Russia's economic and so-

---

[4] "Not 'introduction' of socialism is our *immediate* task, but *immediate* transition merely to control by the Soviets of Workers' Deputies over the social production and distribution of products." Lenin, "On the Tasks of the Proletariat in the Present Revolution" (April 7, 1917), as translated in E. H. Carr, *The Bolshevik Revolution 1917–1923* (London, 1950), p. 80.

[5] "The Party proclaimed the country an armed camp and placed its economic, cultural and political life on a war footing. . . . It took under its control the middle-sized and small industries in addition to large-scale industry, so as to accumulate goods for the supply of the army and the agricultural population. It introduced a state monopoly of the grain trade, prohibited private trading in grain and established the surplus-appropriation system under which all surplus produce in the hands of the peasants was to be registered and acquired by the state at fixed prices, so as to accumulate stores of grain for the provisioning of the army and workers. Lastly it introduced universal labor service for all classes. . . . All these measures which were necessitated by the exceptionally difficult conditions of national defense and bore a temporary character were in their entirety known as War Communism." *History of the Communist Party of the Soviet Union (Bolsheviks): Short Course* (Moscow, 1949), pp. 282 ff.

cial backwardness was expected not to be stormed by a frontal assault but to succumb to a carefully planned flanking operation. Aided by highly developed socialist countries such as Germany and Great Britain, socialist Russia was to approach slowly, although much faster than before, the levels of productivity and welfare attained in the western world. "The achievement of socialism was . . . thought of by Lenin at this time primarily in terms of world revolution."[6]

The New Economic Policy that followed the phase of War Communism was still merely a set of temporary measures, designed to promote a recovery of the national economy from the catastrophic depths into which it had been plunged by war, foreign intervention, and revolution. The purpose of those policies was not, any more than that of the earlier ones, the introduction of a socialist economic system, but the creation of transitional conditions that would permit the socialist government to retain political power until the triumph of socialism in the west.

The picture changed drastically in 1924. The failure of the last revolutionary attempt in Germany (the Hamburg uprising in the fall of 1923) placed the Soviet government face to face with an essentially new situation. It had become clear that the expectation of an early victory of western socialism was erroneous, that socialism in Russia was isolated. This implied, however, that the Soviet regime in Russia, considered earlier as an essentially provisional arrangement for the duration of the "holding out" phase, had to stabilize itself for an indefinite period separating it from the world revolution, and to build "socialism in one country."[7]

Such stabilization was predicated upon a number of crucial conditions. First, the regime had to be able to meet Russia's urgent need for economic development—without any significant foreign assistance;[8] secondly, the economic growth of the country had to be so directed as to render it as immune as possible to economic blockade or outright military aggression deemed probable under conditions of "capitalist encirclement"; and third, the living standards of the population had to be improved and the internal political and economic basis of the socialist regime strengthened and broadened.

[6] Carr, *op. cit.*, p. 107.

[7] Cf. Stalin's *Report to the XVIII-th Congress of the CPSU* on March 10, 1939, where he developed also his modification of the theory of the "withering-away" of the state under socialism. The meaning of that new orientation is frequently misunderstood. As Rudolf Schlesinger points out, "What was really discussed was not whether it was possible to build an ideal type of Socialism in one country but whether what could be built in one country should be supported or opposed." *The Spirit of Postwar Russia, Soviet Ideology 1916–1946* (London, 1947), p. 103.

[8] For a short review of the foreign economic relations of the U.S.S.R., cf. P. A. Baran, "The U.S.S.R. in the World Economy," *Foreign Economic Policy for the United States*, ed. S. E. Harris (Cambridge, Mass., 1948).

These objectives became the guiding principles of the Five Year Plans of which the first was enacted in the spring of 1929.[9]

2. *The Determination of the Speed of Attainment.* The policies followed at any given time are only partly determined by long term goals. The other coordinate is provided by the decision concerning the *tempo* at which the realization of these ends is sought. To be sure, the speed with which the long term goals are to be attained is far from independent of the nature of the goals themselves. Indeed, the development of an integrated economy independent of foreign markets and able to support technically no less than economically its own further growth calls primarily for expansion of basic industries. This in itself necessitates certain minimum rates of advance. In the absence of an already existing elaborate framework of an industrial economy, every major industrial project requires outlays far in excess of its own cost. These outlays have to be synchronized if waste is to be avoided; plants consuming electric power have to be built at the same time as power stations are erected, coal mining has to be expanded simultaneously with the construction of blast furnaces, and dwellings for workers have to be built where new factories are established.[10]

What is more, prevailing technological standards impose indivisibilities that have to be taken into account in the determination of the investment program of any given year. Neither automobile factories nor hydro-electric plants can be acquired piecemeal or in such sizes as might be convenient. Even if adoption of units smaller than technologically optimal or of a technology less capital-intensive than the most advanced should appear rational at any particular moment, such policy might prove to have been myopic in the longer run.

At the same time, the nature and the rate of investment decided upon for the initial period of the program exercises a powerful influence upon the speed of expansion in ensuing periods. The basic industries constructed during the first period produce the investment goods to be used in the next; the volume of saving needed in the next period is thus greatly influenced by investment decisions made earlier.[11]

If the goal of expansion of basic industries necessarily implied rather high rates of speed in the execution of the development program, the Soviet government's appraisal of the international situation and of the

---

[9] For the history of the planning effort at that time, see Friedrich Pollock, *Die Planwirtschaftlichen Versuche in der Sowjetunion, 1917–1927* (Leipzig, 1929), *passim;* and Maurice Dobb, *Soviet Economic Development since 1917* (London, 1948), pp. 230 ff.

[10] Cf. Dobb, *loc. cit.*

[11] Correspondingly, a program directed toward economic development via consumers' goods industries implies automatically not only smaller initial investment but also much lower rates of subsequent growth.

dangers threatening Russia's external security suggested even higher *tempi* of growth.[12]

To some extent the accelerated preparation for defense coincided with the general industrialization program. Calling for emphasis on basic industries and mining as the essential prerequisites for current and potential expansion of military output, it reinforced the reasoning underlying the Soviet broad plan of economic development. On the other hand, suggesting dispersal of industry, erection of parallel plants, and the industrialization of the more distant areas of the Soviet Union, it prevented full utilization of available "external economies" and thus increased the magnitude of the required investment. It stimulated, however, the development of the backward regions of the U.S.S.R.—highly desirable on its own account.

No such harmony, tentative as it may have been, existed with regard to the third fundamental objective: strengthening of the internal basis of the regime and improvement of the standard of life. That goal would have pointed to an altogether different strategy and to altogether different rates of development.

What is necessary in such a situation is a decision on the magnitude of the "economic surplus" that can be used for investment (and defense) purposes in any given period. If great urgency is attached to the attainment of the developmental (and/or defense) goals, consumption standards may be fixed at "rock bottom." This "rock bottom" is indicated by the need to preserve health and productive efficiency of the population and to maintain political stability.

It goes without saying that the reduction of current consumption to such "rock-bottom" levels is highly undesirable. Under conditions of strain that would inevitably result from such "belt-tightening," even small hitches in production, let alone crop failures, may easily give rise to major difficulties.[13] Moreover, the political and economic costs of mobilizing the marginal amount of the "surplus" may be entirely out of proportion to the advantages that can be derived from it for the developmental program. Thus the First Five Year Plan, although programming extremely high rates of expansion, was very far from scheduling a reduction of consumption to "rock-bottom" levels. In actual fact it anticipated

---

[12] "We are 50–100 years behind the advanced countries. We have to traverse this distance in ten years. We will either accomplish it or else we will be crushed." Joseph Stalin, *Problems of Leninism* (11th ed.; Moscow, 1939), p. 329. (Translated from the Russian by the writer.) It is interesting to note that this statement was made on February 4, 1931, i.e., exactly ten years prior to Germany's invasion of Russia.

[13] This is the reason for the stress placed by the Soviet authorities on the accumulation of sizable reserves of all important consumers' goods. Cf. G. Sorokin, *Sotsialisticheskoie Planirovanie Narodnogo Khosiaistva SSSR* (*Socialist Planning of the National Economy of the U.S.S.R.*) (Moscow, 1946), p. 24.

an increase of consumption by as much as 40 per cent over the quinquennium.[14]

The decision on the magnitude of the "economic surplus" extractable from the economy for investment purposes is thus of an eminently political and socio-psychological nature. It has to take into account not only the "margin of social and political tolerance" but also the effect of any level of consumption on incentives and efficiency. It has to depend, moreover, on the possibility and the cost of securing control over the "economic surplus" by the governmental authorities.[15]

3. *The Mobilization of the "Economic Surplus."* The authorities can secure the resources needed for investment, defense, social services, administration, and the like in a number of alternative ways. Some of the criteria by which the choice has to be made are purely technical—the reliability, convenience, and cost of various procedures. Where the resources involved represent a large share of an absolutely low aggregate income, as is the case in the Soviet Union, political considerations assume prime importance. The mobilization of the "surplus" has to be so organized as to minimize the political resistance to what is bound to be an unpopular policy. At the same time, the distribution of the burden of the program among various social groups and classes has to be calculated so as to strengthen the social and political basis of the regime. Much of the controversy in Russia in the late twenties and early thirties centered around this issue.

The best procedure for withdrawing from the population the share of its money income which is required to meet the government's outlay is an income tax. Under the conditions prevailing in the Soviet Union prior to the industrialization period, this method of raising revenue was beset with considerable difficulties. As far as the urban population was concerned, the tax could be readily assessed and collected. Matters were much less simple with regard to the rural sector of the economy. Neither the assessment of income accruing in agriculture nor the collection of the tax from subsistence farmers appeared to be a manageable task. The fiscal authorities were confronted with strong resistance from peasants— only recently freed of czarist tax and rent burdens of the czarist days— and measures of enforcement of the tax assessments, such as removal of produce in kind or confiscation of livestock, were bound to provoke profound hostility against the government and were politically intolerable.

---

[14] Dobb, *Soviet Economic Development*, p. 235. This increase did not materialize in view of unexpected difficulties associated mainly with the peasants' resistance to collectivization.

[15] On the share of national product devoted to investment, cf. Abram Bergson, "Soviet National Income and Product in 1937," *Quarterly Journal of Economics*, May and August 1950, pp. 208–41, 408–41; also P. A. Baran, "National Income and Product of the U.S.S.R. in 1940," *Review of Economics and Statistics*, November 1947, pp. 226–34.

Another method of securing the resources needed for the realization of the governmental program is the expansion of the earnings of the government-owned and -operated sector of the economy (industry, transportation, trade, etc.). This could be accomplished by keeping industrial prices low in relation to prices of agricultural products—combining, however, such a price policy with a wage policy leaving large profits in the hands of the nationalized enterprises. Such a course, favoring the agricultural population, would place the burden of the program upon the shoulders of industrial workers. Even if it could have been made to yield sufficient revenue—a doubtful assumption in view of the relative smallness of the government sector of the economy prior to its expansion under the Five Year Plans—it would have been politically wholly unacceptable.

The accumulation of profits in the governmental sector of the economy could be brought about not merely by an appropriate wage policy but also by raising the prices charged for its output. The obvious advantage of this procedure as compared with relying on industrial wage policy alone is that it distributes the burden of the accumulation process between the urban and the rural sectors of the population.[16]

Yet this strategy, involving the "opening of the scissors," i.e., a shift in relative prices in favor of industry, could be and was effectively counteracted by the "kulaks," i.e., peasants in possession of marketable surpluses, who refused to exchange on terms proposed by the government. While rural demand for some products of the nationalized sector was sufficiently inelastic to enable the government to obtain for them certain quantities of agricultural produce, the general tendency of those agricultural producers that mattered was either to reduce their output or to increase their own consumption of agricultural produce, rather than to trade on terms below what they considered to be a "parity" ratio.

At the peril of over-emphasizing one aspect of the problem at the expense of others, it may be said that the collectivization of Soviet agriculture was motivated to a large extent by the necessity of overcoming this crucial hurdle. To be sure, expansion of agricultural output and release of agricultural man power for industrial employment—possible only through transition to large scale farming and mechanization of agriculture—were by themselves objectives of tremendous importance. However, without a reorganization of the agricultural economy assuring the possibility of "syphoning off" agricultural surpluses, progress in agricultural production would have only slowly affected the volume of agricultural output available for non-rural consumption.

By transferring the disposal of agricultural output from individual peasants to government-supervised collective farm managements, collec-

---

[16] This policy could be and was—actually not according to plan—reinforced by inflationary developments accompanying almost the entire period of the first two five-year plans.

tivization destroyed the basis for the peasants' resistance to the accumulation policy. From now on the share of agricultural output consumed on the farm could be fixed by direct apportionment to collective farm members, while farm consumption of non-agricultural commodities could be regulated by fixing the prices paid by the government for the marketed share of agricultural output and charged by the urban sector of the economy for goods supplied to the farm population. The way was thus open for wage and price policies to become the main instruments for mobilization of the "economic surplus." The total of wages paid (including the apportionment in kind to collective farm members) is calculated to absorb the share of total product allotted to consumption, while the government secures control over the part of national income to be devoted to investment, defense, social services, administration, etc., through the profits of the government-controlled enterprises.

These profits could be transferred in their entirety to the government, which could use them to defray its planned outlays. In fact, a more complicated procedure is employed. A large share of the profits is paid over to the government in the form of an "advance." This "advance," called "turnover tax," is contributed to the state budget immediately following the marketing of the factory's products, *independent of cost accounting*.[17] The balance of the profits—the difference between the wholesale price net of turnover tax and cost—appears as profits *sensu strictu*. A share of these profits is paid to the government at the end of the accounting period as "deductions from profits," while the remainder is left with the enterprises for various stipulated purposes.[18]

There are a number of reasons for the employment of this cumbersome device. One is that "the State cannot wait for periodical balance sheets to be issued in order to determine how much a given establishment has accumulated."[19] Payment (or non-payment) of the turnover tax serves thus as a rapidly reacting indicator of the extent to which productive plans are fulfilled by the individual enterprise. Equally important perhaps is the consideration that "flooding" of individual enterprises with vast profits not to be surrendered until the end of an accounting period would generate an atmosphere of "quasi prosperity" in their managerial offices and exercise an adverse effect upon the effort to assure economical conduct of plant operations. Moreover, this arrangement prevents accumulation of "artificial" profits generated *within* the industrial system and not representing a withdrawal of "economic surplus." ". . . Since a very large part of what is produced by heavy industry is consumed by State-

[17] M. I. Bogolepov, *The Soviet Financial System* (London, 1945), p. 9 (italics supplied).

[18] Approved local investment, payment of bonuses to employees, erection of welfare establishments (work canteens, rest homes, etc.).

[19] Bogolepov, *loc. cit.*

owned industry . . . prices of industrial equipment either do not include the turnover tax or only at a very low rate. . . ."[20]

This is not the place for a detailed description of the Soviet financial system.[21] Suffice it to add that the "turnover tax" and the "deductions from profits" account for the bulk of the "economic surplus" generated in the country. The balance appears in the form of small amounts of profits reinvested locally, the even less significant income taxes, various minor business taxes, loans from the public, and the like.

4. *The Allocation of the "Economic Surplus."* Most of the "economic surplus" is channeled through the government budget into a variety of purposes. While a share of it serves to support the military establishment, governmental administration, and social and cultural undertakings, the balance is used to carry out the investment program.

Two types of problems have to be solved in determining the use of these investment funds. The *total* must be divided among different industries, and a choice has to be made concerning the technical form that investment should take in any particular case.[22] The former issue is to a large extent pre-judged by the decisions concerning the goal and tempo of the developmental program. Once these decisions are made, "the problems of economic planning seem to acquire a resemblance to the problems of military strategy, where in practice the choice lies between a relatively small number of plans, which have in the main to be treated and chosen between as organic wholes, and which for a variety of reasons do not easily permit of intermediate combinations."[23] This choice between "a relatively small number of plans" seems to be made by an appraisal of the feasibilities and implications of the available alternatives. Certain specific bottlenecks—shortages of steel or machine tools or transportation facilities—may dictate the selection of a plan calling for the least quantity of the critical item. The need to concentrate scarce talent on one construction project rather than dissipating it on a number of undertakings may dictate the preference for a certain technological process.

Such a preference, in turn, may temporarily preclude investment even of relatively small quantities of resources in other branches of the

[20] *Ibid.*, p. 10.

[21] Good treatments of the subject will be found in Bogolepov, *op. cit.;* Dobb, *Soviet Economic Development;* Alexander Baykov, *Soviet Economic System* (Cambridge–New York, 1947); and in the Russian language in K. N. Plotnikov, *Budzet Sotsialisticheskogo Gosudarstva* (*The Budget of the Socialist State*) (Moscow, 1948); and N. N. Rovinski, *Gosudarstvenny Budzet SSSR* (*The State Budget of the U.S.S.R.*) (Moscow, 1949).

[22] Maurice Dobb, "A Note on the Discussion of the Problem of Choice between Alternative Investment Projects," *Soviet Studies*, Vol. II, January 1951, p. 291.

[23] Dobb, *Soviet Economic Development*, p. 6. "Much substitution in production arises through shifts in the extent to which alternative processes are used, rather than through variation in factor combinations in the individual process." T. C. Koopmans, "Efficient Allocation of Resources," *Econometrica*, October 1951, pp. 455 ff.

economy, although the advantages that such investment may promise could be large. "The economic plan singles out each time the leading branches of the national economy, the crucial links that have to be grasped for the entire chain of economic development to be pulled up."[24]

The consecutive plans are thus characterized by the nature of the "link" singled out. "The crucial link of the first Five Year Plan was the heavy industry with its heart piece—machine building. The decisive links in the second and third Five Year Plans were the leading branches of the heavy industry—metallurgy, machine building, fuel, energetics, chemistry. Under the conditions of the Patriotic War the crucial link in the plan was military production."[25] It is this concentration upon the highest priority tasks that gives the Soviet economy the character of a "target economy." At any particular time, certain highest priority objectives command exceptional attention. This frequently results in transitory "disproportionalities." The fulfillment of one target is accompanied by lags in the attainment of others. The next period witnesses, then, a shift of emphasis to the backward "links" that have to be pulled up for the "chain" to be straightened out.

This strategy of local advances followed by a subsequent consolidation of the conquered terrain is dictated, however, by the specific conditions of the Russian economy, and may well represent a particularly effective method for a rapid development of under-developed countries. Where slow growth rather than urgent structural change should constitute the guiding principle of the economic effort, the pattern of "campaigns" and "targets" may be inappropriate, and investment could be allocated in relatively small portions among different branches of the economy with a view to equating their productivities on the margin.

However, the decision about the production targets and the distribution of the investment funds among different *branches* of the economy leaves unanswered the question how to choose between different *modes* of producing the desired output. The solution of this problem suggested by conventional theory (the ratios of costs of factors to their respective marginal value products should be the same for all factors) would provide no succor to the planning authority. Even if sufficient continuity of substitution could be assumed, the planning board would have to consider not only the *social* costs involved in the employment of an additional quantity of a factor, but also—and this is most important—take into account the impact of its own activities on the future relative scarcities of factors.

Thus, the existence of a large rural surplus population may have suggested (and still suggests) that in Russia strong preference should be given to techniques employing much labor and little capital. Yet, such advice would overlook the large social cost of transferring a man from

[24] Sorokin, *op. cit.*, p. 22 (translated from the Russian by the writer).
[25] *Ibid.*, p. 23.

the village into industrial occupation. The additional industrial worker must be provided with urban dwelling space. Paid the going industrial wage, he must be assured of the quantity of food, clothing, etc., that is usually consumed by industrial workers.[26] Even if his product in the new occupation should exceed the cost of his sustenance in the city, it may be impossible for technical and/or political reasons to extract the requisite additional food from agriculture. True, the "disguised unemployed" had contributed previously nothing or little to total agricultural output while consuming a certain quantity of food. That food came, however, from his family's table and constituted no drain on the sparse "marketed share" of agricultural output.

Since the expansion of agricultural output and the increase of agricultural supplies available to the cities require not only large scale investment but also a considerable amount of time, the physical limitations on the amount of food that could be placed at the disposal of the urban population may by themselves call for the selection of capital-intensive rather than labor-intensive techniques of production.

The same conclusion may be arrived at if it is considered that the abundance and "cheapness" of currently available labor is only a temporary condition *preceding* the realization of any given stretch of the developmental program. The Planning Board, aware of the aggregate demand for labor entailed by its own plans, has to bear in mind therefore that relatively soon, during the life span of the equipment that is to be installed, labor may turn from a relatively ample to a relatively scarce factor.

These very general considerations may suffice in the present context. A lively and extensive discussion of possible formal criteria to be followed in making specific investment decisions has been taking place in the recent Soviet literature; it would exceed by far the available space to present here a detailed account of its contents.[27] The Planning Board itself has not yet stated, to my knowledge, what principles it follows in making the relevant decisions. It is most likely, however, that the Soviet economist Chernomordik expresses the official view:

Our advocates of the employment of a coefficient of effectiveness to solve the problem of comparing alternatives try to equip themselves with some kind of a slide rule to mechanize the labor of project-making. This mathematical method only serves, in the last analysis, to divert attention from the real problem: the comprehensive study of the basic processes of the economy; ascertainment of the effect on the national economy of any particular capital construction.[28]

[26] This quantity itself is largely influenced by political considerations!

[27] Condensed translations of the relevant articles are published in *Soviet Studies* as well as in the *Current Digest of the Soviet Press*. Norman Kaplan has presented an excellent summary and analysis of the debate in "Investment Alternatives in Soviet Economic Theory," *Journal of Political Economy*, April 1952, pp. 133–44.

[28] D. I. Chernomordik, "Effectiveness of Capital Investment and the Theory of Reproduction: Towards a Statement of the Problem," *Voprosy Ekonomiki*, June 1949, pp. 78–95, translated in *Soviet Studies*, Vol. I, April 1950, pp. 359–63.

5. The Balance Sheet. The investment decisions of the Central Authority as well as of managements on lower (plant and regional) levels are combined with the estimates of the magnitude and composition of consumers' goods supply and checked for mutual consistency in the so-called "national-economic balance sheets." To describe the procedure involved, it may be best to present an extensive quotation from the work of a Soviet economist:

The balance sheets and distribution plans as drawn up at the present time include: firstly, material balance sheets (in kind) showing the proportions of the material elements of reproduction; secondly, value (price) balance sheets showing the proportions in the distribution of financial resources and ensuring proper proportion in the distribution of the social product in respect of its material form and its value; thirdly, balance sheets for labour power.

Material balance sheets (in kind) consist of the following: (1) balance sheets of industrial products which, considering the main purpose for which they are to be used, represent the elements of the fixed funds of the national economy that ensure fulfillment of the construction program of the national-economic plan (equipment and building materials), (2) balance sheets of industrial and agricultural products, which considering the main purpose for which they are to be used, represent the elements of the circulating funds of the national economy that ensure fulfillment of the production program of the national-economic plan (metals, fuel, electric power, chemicals, agricultural raw materials), (3) balance sheets of industrial and agricultural products, which, considering the main purpose for which they are to be used, represent articles of individual consumption.

The material balance sheets and distribution plans, which are approved by the Government, cover products of national-economic importance as well as products which require centralized distribution because of their shortage. During the war the number of items of funded products, i.e. products distributed by the centre, had to be considerably enlarged.

Value balance sheets consist of the following: (1) balance sheet of the population's money income and expenditure, (2) the State Bank's cash plan, and (3) the state budget.

The income side of the balance sheet of the population's money income and expenditures covers the wage fund of the workers and office employees and other incomes of the urban population; the expenditure side covers expenditure by the population in buying goods at state and cooperative stores, paying for services and other money expenditures. The chief purpose of this balance sheet of the population's money income and expenditure is to ensure proper proportion in planning the volume of trade, the wage fund and the money income of collective farmers. This balance sheet serves as a basis for drafting the trade plan and also for planning the wage fund in the national economy.

The State Bank's cash plan serves as an important means for planning money circulation. The income side accounts for money received by the State Bank from trade turnover and payments by state organization; the expenditure side accounts for payments made against the wage fund and other money expenditures. The State Bank's cash plan makes it possible to determine the volume of currency emissions required for the ensuing period.

The state budget is a most important financial balance sheet which determines the distribution of the bulk of the national income. The main items of revenue in the state budget are accumulations of the socialist economy in the form of profits and turnover tax, and money received from the population in payment of taxes, subscriptions to state loans, etc. The expenditure side of the state budget consists of disbursements made in financing the national economy (production and capital construction), social and cultural development, administrative expenses and expenditures on defence. The function of the state budget is to ensure the financing without deficit of the national economy with the aid of the country's internal financial resources.

The labour power balance sheets include: (1) the balance sheet for labour power in the state economy, which determines the demand for labour power and skilled personnel in the various branches of the national economy, and the principal sources for recruiting labour for it (training, the state labour reserve schools, organized hiring of labour), (2) the balance sheet of labour power in the collective farms, which determines the utilization of collective-farm labour resources for carrying out the plan of agricultural production and for work in industry.

The balance sheets system in the national-economic plan makes it possible correctly to solve the problem of planning resources, consumption and distribution in the national economy.[29]

The method thus briefly sketched represents a merely formal solution of the task of maintaining a general dynamic equilibrium of the Soviet economy. Whether it assures a smooth functioning of the economic system depends obviously on the magnitudes that are entered in that generalized "input-output" matrix.[30] The degree of accuracy that is attained in the estimation of the shape of the technological transformation functions, of the volume of actual production in individual plants, and of consumption of various goods by the consumers, determines the extent to which the plan is able to avoid disproportionalities and waste.

There can be no doubt that both have characterized the working of Soviet planning—particularly in its earlier phases. Yet the causes of these deficiencies may have been primarily associated with the historical setting of the Russian planning effort rather than with the principles underlying it. The breakneck speed of the "target economy" calling for the "leading links" strategy accounted for continuous occurrence and recurrence of major successes in some parts of the economy and equally serious "gaps" in others; the poverty of the country made it impossible until the late thirties to accumulate sufficient reserves to permit a rapid plugging of those "gaps"; and the lack of personnel scientifically trained for planning work on all levels caused avoidable mistakes in the preparation of the estimates determining the relationships embodied in the plan.

The "hitches" that occur in the functioning of the system become

[29] A. D. Kursky, *The Planning of the National Economy of the U.S.S.R.* (Moscow, 1949), pp. 129 ff. The remainder of the chapter from which the above is cited contains additional valuable information on the methodology of Soviet planning. Cf. also Sorokin, *op. cit.*, *passim*.

[30] The problems involved in elaborating such a matrix are akin to those discussed in W. W. Leontief, *The Structure of the American Economy, 1919–1929* (Cambridge, Mass., 1941), in particular p. 34, although the difficulties that have to be overcome in the planning practice may not be quite as stupendous as suggested by Leontief's analysis. It may be sufficient for the "central" matrix to include only the "leading links" of the economy, leaving a great deal to the functioning of the decentralized economic units.

less frequent and less costly as their causes gradually disappear. Slowing down the speed of industrialization, filling the "pipe lines" of the economy with the indispensable stocks of food, raw materials, fuel, etc., the availability of adequately prepared planning officials, combined with growing levels of literacy and civic responsibility on the part of the population, lead to a progressive improvement of the actual performance of the economic system.[31]

As Maurice Dobb points out, ". . . the notion that successful development from one economic situation, with its given combination of resources and configuration of demand, to another might be a more crucial test of the contribution made by an economic system to human welfare than the attainment of perfect equilibrium in any given situation seldom commanded attention."[32] Such attention on the part of social scientists is, however, urgently called for by the problems faced by many relatively advanced nations, but faced especially by the multitudes living in the world's under-developed countries.

Very little of what constitutes the main body of our customary economic theorizing would seem to be of much help in solving these perplexities. What the Soviet experience strongly suggests is the need for concrete historical research into the social and political prerequisites for economic growth and development. The "standards of perfection" evolved in the writings on "economics of socialism" offer no guidance in the effort to conquer backwardness, squalor, and oppression. "The advocacy of impossible changes is advocacy of no changes at all." The contribution that economic science can make to the solution of the problems of a planned economy is more likely to be found on the lines suggested by Wassily Leontief and "linear programming" than in the refinements of "optimum conditions" pertaining to an imaginary world. This contribution would be amply rewarded—by the continuous "feedback" linking realistic economics with the demands and issues of reality. What this implies, however, is that in a rationally organized society the economist of our days would be one of the "disguised unemployed" to be transferred to the position of "social engineer" helping to understand and to create the conditions for economic and social progress.

[31] An impressive testimonial of efficiency was the rapid conversion and reallocation of the Russian industry during the war, as well as its reconversion and growth during the post-war years. On the latter, cf. Abram Bergson, J. H. Blackman, and Alexander Erlich, "Postwar Economic Reconstruction and Development in the U.S.S.R.," *Annals of the American Academy of Political and Social Science*, May 1949, pp. 52 ff., as well as the more recent statements on the "Results of the Fourth (Postwar) Five Year Plan," *New Times*, April 25, 1951 (Suppl.).

[32] *Soviet Economic Development*, p. 3.

The New Forms of Communist Planning

25. THE ROLE OF PLANNING IN SOCIALIST ECONOMY*

Oskar Lange

SYNOPSIS

1. The initial purpose of (Marxian) socialist planning is to liquidate what remains of capitalist institutions and to control the non-socialist sector of the economy, the latter being facilitated by nationalization of the basic industries.

2. In the first stage of the socialist revolution the state makes all of the decisions and supervises the detailed management of the economy, using political as well as economic force.

3. Such centralization of power is necessary because the state must defend the revolution and industrialize rapidly, the latter requiring maximum efficiency of investment and the formation of a working class.

4. But as socialism matures, planning becomes less centralized, relies more on economic incentives and less on political force. This change is now occurring in almost all socialist countries.

5. Planning should be active in the sense of directing production and distribution to pre-established goals as well as of coordinating its physical and financial aspects.

6. Active planning determines how the national income shall be divided between investment and consumption and what the principal kinds of investment shall be. It does not determine the kind and quantity of particular consumer goods or of all investment goods.

7. In executing the plan, the state should rely on economic incentives (which it may itself create) and use administrative means only in exceptional circumstances.

8. But the formulation of the plan is a political decision and is supported by political power, unlike the decisions made under capitalism, which are economically motivated and enforced.

9. The basic decisions of the plan must be made by the central authority. Decentralized units (e.g., the firm) should make subsidiary decisions if the incentives in the plan make those decisions the same as the central authority itself would make. The decentralized units also should make decisions whenever the central authority cannot act in time.

10. Decentralization is necessary in order to fulfill the aims of the plan, to prevent elemental (market) behavior, and to assure prompt and sensible decisions.

* Reprinted by permission from *The Political Economy of Socialism*, Publications on Social Change, Institute of Social Studies, No. 16 (The Hague: van Keulen, 1958), pp. 16–28.

11. The production plan should fix the physical output only of those firms producing basic commodities and the money value of output of all others, leaving them to determine the kind and quantity of goods they will produce.

12. There are two kinds of prices in a socialist economy: market prices, which distribute output by equalizing the quantities supplied and demanded; and normal prices, which measure total costs. An excess (or deficiency) of market over normal price indicates that output should be increased (or decreased).

13. The marginal cost principle can be used to set normal price by relating that price to (a) average variable costs of the highest cost firms, (b) fixed costs for the entire industry, (c) the cost of additional investment for the entire economy, and (d) the cost of total collective consumption—the last three being allocated in a way that keeps all prices proportional to average variable costs.

Economic planning, or, more precisely, the planning of economic development, is an essential feature of socialism. It expresses the fact that socialist economy does not develop in an elemental way but that its development is guided and directed by the conscious will of organized society. Planning is the means of subjecting the operation of economic laws and the economic development of society to the direction of human will.

The experience of the construction of socialism in various countries indicates that the establishment of planned economy is one of the first achievements of the socialist revolution. It precedes the full development of socialist relations of production, though it requires a certain minimum of such relations. In the transitional period, when non-socialist modes of production still play an important role, the economy becomes already subject to planned direction of its development. This is made possible by the existence in the economy of a large socialist sector which controls, as one frequently says, the "commanding outposts" of economic life. This is the minimum requirement of establishing planned economy.

Economic planning starts with the direct intervention of the state in economic relations. This intervention has for its objectives the liquidation of capitalist relations of production and the control of the non-socialist sectors of economy which still remain. The basis which makes control of the non-socialist sectors possible is the existence of a socialist sector, particularly that part of the socialist sector which is nationalized, and which controls the commanding outposts of the economy.

In this first, transitional phase the new revolutionary state is not neutral with regard to the various sectors of the economy. It consciously utilizes the nationalized socialist sector as an instrument of controlling the development of the whole economy. The means it utilizes consist of economic instruments which result from the existence of the nationalized sector comprising the decisive controlling part of the economy, and also of intervention by political force, i.e., non-economic force. In the first revolutionary period, intervention into economic processes by political force plays a decisive role.

In the first period of development of a socialist economy, both the planning of economic development and the day-to-day management of the socialist sector are highly centralized.

There may be some doubts of how far this represents a universal necessity. For instance, in Poland, we had some discussions whether such a period of highly centralized planning and management was a historical necessity or a great political mistake. Personally, I hold the view that it was a historical necessity.

It seems to me that, first, the very process of the social revolution which liquidates one social system and establishes another requires centralized disposal of resources by the new revolutionary state, and consequently centralized management and planning. This holds, in my opinion, for any socialist revolution.

In under-developed countries, there is a further consideration. Socialist industrialization, and particularly very rapid industrialization, which was necessary in the first socialist countries, particularly in the Soviet Union, as a political requirement of national defense and of the solution of all kinds of political and social problems, due to backwardness, requires centralized disposal of resources. Thus, the very process of transformation of the social system and in addition, in under-developed countries, the need of rapid industrialization, impose the necessity of high centralization of planning and management.

The process of rapid industrialization requires such centralized disposal of resources for two reasons. First, it is necessary to concentrate all resources on certain objectives and avoid dissipation of resources on other objectives which would divert resources from the purpose of rapid industrialization. This is one of the reasons which leads to highly centralized planning and management and also to the allocation of resources by means of administrative establishment of priorities. The second reason why rapid industrialization demands centralized planning and management is the lack and weakness of industrial cadres. With the rapid growth of industry the cadres are new and inexperienced. Such old cadres which had some experience in management of industry and other economic activities are frequently politically alien to the socialist objectives. In consequence high centralization of managerial decisions becomes necessary.

Thus, the first period of planning and management in a socialist economy, at least according to our present experience, has always been characterized by administrative management and administrative allocation of resources on the basis of priorities centrally established. Economic incentives are in this period replaced by moral and political appeals to the workers, by appeals to their patriotism and socialist consciousness. This is, so to speak, a highly politicalized economy, both with regard to the means of planning and management and with regard to the incentives it utilizes.

I think that, essentially, it can be described as a *sui generis* war economy. Such methods of war economy are not peculiar to socialism because they are also used in capitalist countries in wartime. They were developed in the first and the second world wars. In capitalist countries, similar methods were used during the war, namely, concentration of all resources on one basic purpose, which is the production of war material, centralization of disposal of resources in order to avoid leakages of resources to what was considered non-essential utilization (everything which was not connected with the prosecution of the war). Allocation of resources by administrative decision according to administratively established priorities and wide scale use of political incentives to maintain the productivity and discipline of labor through patriotic appeals were characteristic of war economy. This was the case in all capitalist countries during the war.

It shows clearly that such methods of centralized planning and management are not peculiar to socialism, that they are rather certain techniques of war economy. The difficulty starts when these methods of war economy are identified with the essence of socialism and considered as being essential to socialism.

One of the methods of war economy, which most of the socialist countries used at one stage or another, was compulsory deliveries by peasants of part of their produce. Many comrades in my country feel rather upset by the present program of our government of abolishing such deliveries. They fear that this implies giving up some socialist principle. I usually answer them by asking whether they remember who in Poland first introduced compulsory deliveries by peasants. Such deliveries were first introduced during the first world war by the occupation army of Kaiser Wilhelm the Second, whom I do not think anybody regards as a champion of socialism. These methods cannot be considered as an essential aspect of socialism; they are simply methods of war economy necessary in a revolutionary period of transition.

The fate and history of these methods is a classical example of the dialectical character of the development of socialist society. Methods which are necessary and useful in the period of social revolution and of intensive industrialization become an obstacle to further economic progress when they are perpetuated beyond their historic justification. They become obstacles because they are characterized by lack of flexibility. They are rigid; they lead, therefore, to waste of resources resulting from this inflexibility; they require a wasteful bureaucratic apparatus and make it difficult to adjust production to the needs of the population. However, it seems that the greatest obstacle to further progress results from the lack of proper economic incentives in this bureaucratic centralistic type of management. This hampers proper economic utilization of resources, encourages waste, and also hinders technical progress.

Therefore, when the socialist society starts to overcome these centralistic, bureaucratic methods of administrative planning and management, it indicates, so to speak, that it is maturing. I would not want to make this a final definition of the period of transition. But I might say that substituting for the methods of administrative and centralized management new methods based on the utilization of economic laws indicates the end of the period of transition and the beginning of the functioning of an established socialist economy. I would not say that this is the only aspect of the problem of the period of transition, but it is certainly an important aspect of it.

The period of centralized planning and management, as I said, is the result partly of the necessities of the revolutionary transformation of society and, in under-developed countries, also of the needs of rapid industrialization. In studying this period, a certain important sociological factor has to be taken into account, which is the weakness of the working class in an under-developed country. It seems to me that it is on the basis of this weakness, under conditions of under-development, that the bureaucratic state machine gains great importance, and phenomena like the "cult of personality" develop. It, so to speak, in a way substitutes for the spontaneous activity of the working class.

But here again, the dialectics of the processes of construction of socialism becomes apparent. The centralistic methods are successful in achieving rapid industrialization and, as a consequence, cause a rapid growth of the working class. The working class grows in numbers as well as in consciousness and political maturity. Next to the growth of the working class, another important sociological element appears. This is the growth of a new socialist intelligentsia which largely comes from the ranks of the workers and peasants. When it becomes clear that the highly centralized administrative and bureaucratic methods of management create obstacles to further progress, a part of the political and state apparatus becomes convinced that a change of methods of administration and management is needed. Thus, new social forces mature which require and also make possible a change of these methods.

This precisely is the basic difference between the development of a socialist society and a society which is based on antagonistic class relations. There is no ruling class which may oppose these changes. There may be certain strata or groups which have a vested interest in the old methods and create obstacles, but these obstacles can never become of such importance as to make impossible the changes required by new historical circumstances.

This is very clear if you take, for instance, the experience of Poland, where the industrialization by means of centralized administrative planning and management has led to a great increase of the working class. Our working class is now more than three times what it was before the war. The working class has got experience in large industrial establishments. It was at first to a large extent of peasant origin and that, of course, weighed on its psychology. But that was only a transitional phase. Industrialization and the social revolution have created a new intelligentsia—

largely coming from workers and peasants. All that led to a maturing of the forces of the new socialist society. In consequence, we got such a phenomenon as the great movement of workers' councils demanding self-government of workers in industry—the general demand to change the methods of management of the national economy. The party has accepted these demands of the people and given them organized expression.

Changes in the methods of planning and the management of the economy are taking place today in practically all socialist countries. Forms and contents are different, but all these changes imply a certain decentralization or deconcentration of management. I do not want to enter into a description of what is happening in the various socialist countries. I shall rather present to you what I personally believe is the proper formulation of the role and methods of planning in a socialist economy.

First, it must be stated that in a socialist society, planning of the economy is active planning. Some of the economists in Poland use the term "directive planning," but this term is ambiguous; therefore, I shall rather use the term "active planning." By this, I mean that planning does not consist only of coordination of the activities of various branches of the economy. It is something more: namely, it is an active determination of the main lines of development of the national economy. Otherwise, if planning were mere coordination, the development of socialist economy would be elemental; it would not really be directed by the will of organized society. If economic development is not to be elemental but is to be directed by organized society, then planning must be active economic planning.

Two problems arise with regard to active economic planning. First, what is its scope; what activities in the economy have to be planned? And second, what are the methods of securing the realization of the plan?

The active character of planning does not require that it go into each detail of economic life. We actually had a period in the socialist countries (perhaps with the exception of China, which started at a later level and profited by the experience of other socialist countries) when the output of even the least important commodity was planned. There was the famous joke in Poland—really, it was not a joke, but it was true—that the production of pickled cucumbers was in the national-economic plan. Another case, which again was not a joke but a fact, was that the State Planning Commission made a plan of the number of hares which were to be shot during the year by hunters. At the same time, you could not get, for instance, buttons or hairpins for ladies, simply because they had been forgotten in the plan.

Active planning and effective direction of the development of the economy are quite possible without planning such details. Even more, planning such details hampers really effective direction of the economy. Actually, I think it may be said that controlling such details had nothing to do with planning. It was a part of the high centralization of day-to-day management of the economy by means of administrative measures. This is a different thing than planning.

However, the plan which is to determine the development of the economy must include at least two things: first, the division of national income between accumulation and consumption; second, the distribution of investments among the different branches of the economy. The first determines the general rate of economic growth; the second determines the direction of the development.

Unless these two things are in the plan, there is no active guidance of the development of the economy. This is, therefore, the minimum requirement of the plan. In addition, it may or may not include the targets for the production of certain basic commodities, like basic raw materials, basic means of production, and so on. These are technical problems, not fundamental problems.

These are the fundamental aspects of the plan which determine the pace and the direction of development of the economy. In addition, economic planning must be concerned with coordination of the activities of the various branches of the economy—first of all, with coordination of the financial aspects of the plan and of its real aspects, in particular coordination of the total purchasing power at the disposal of the population and the amounts of consumer goods which are provided for distribution to individuals. The plan must also in some way and by some means be interested in the coordination of the output of the various branches of the national economy. Otherwise, the determination of the directions of development established by the plan may not be realized. If there is no proper coordination between the output of the various branches, investments may not be realized because the necessary investment goods are not produced. All kinds of bottlenecks appear and cause difficulties which may make it impossible to carry out the investment plan. So much for the content of the plan.

The second problem is that of the methods of securing the realization of the plan. Here, we have basically two possible methods. One consists of administrative orders and administrative allocation of resources. The various units in the socialist economy are ordered to do certain things —for instance, to produce so much of something. The resources which are necessary for that purpose, both material and financial, are allocated in an administrative way. This was the traditional method of realizing the plan in the past period. The second method consists in the use of what we call "economic means," namely, of setting up a system of incentives which induces people to do exactly the things which are required by the plan. It seems to me that in effective planning, both methods have to be used, though in different proportions.

Preference should be given to the use of economic means. Administrative methods should be limited to those fields where, for some reason or other, economic means are ineffective. Such situations, where economic means are not effective, always do exist. They exist, of course, particu- larly in periods of very great changes, because economic means are rather subtle instruments responding to "normal" changes in the situation and frequently breaking down when very fundamental or revolutionary changes are needed. In such cases the use of administrative means must be accepted. Even in a capitalist economy, in situations of profound change, the state uses measures of administrative control, because the nor- mal kind of economic means is not sufficient to provoke the responses which are necessary.

The fundamental decisions of the plan—the division of national in- come between accumulation and consumption and the basic direction of investments—are really of a political character, and the means of imple- mentation must be partly administrative. The decision of the plan con- cerning the rate of accumulation is basically realized by administrative measures. Part of the national income produced is not paid out in the form of individual incomes; part of the profits of the socialist enterprises are held back by the state, and this is an administrative measure. So also are all forms of taxation of enterprises and individuals. The basic directions of investments—for instance, the decision to build an electric power plant —are usually not made as a reaction to market situations, but are made as basic decisions of economic policy, though in this case the realization of the decisions may make use of all kinds of economic instruments.

We may ask in what sense the economic plans must take account of economic laws. Even when the realization of the plan is achieved by ad- ministrative measures, the plan must observe the general economic laws concerning the proportions necessary in the process of production and reproduction. For instance, if the plan provides for an increase of the pro- duction of steel, it must provide for a certain additional output of coal which is needed to produce the additional steel. *Any* kind of planning has to take care of such objective kinds of relationships.

There are also other economic laws which must be observed by the plan. These are the laws which result from the operation of economic in- centives under the circumstances created by the plan. The process of realization of the plan sets into motion definite economic incentives to which the people react in a certain way which can be calculated. Even in the period of administrative planning, certain economic incentives were operative, and their consequences had to be taken into account. In this period, however, economic means were only subsidiary in relation to ad- ministrative means. I would say that now the situation has to change in the sense that the economic means are the rule and administrative means be- come subsidiary to the economic means. Thus, the plan has to observe the laws of production and reproduction; and insofar as the realization is based on the use of economic means, i.e., the operation of economic laws, it also has to consider these laws.

By utilizing economic means, planning makes use of the automatic character of people's responses to given incentives. Thus, certain automatic processes in the economy are established. However, these automatic processes are not elemental. These two things should be distinguished. The difference is that in a socialist society, where the automatic processes are part of the method of realization of the plan, the conditions establishing incentives are set up by economic policy; whereas in capitalist society, these conditions develop in an elemental way. There is a basic difference: In one case (capitalism), the incentives develop in an elemental way and are not subject to conscious control of society; in the other case (socialism), they are consciously established by organized society in such a way as to produce the desired results. As Engels said: "The social causes set into motion will produce to an ever-increasing extent the results desired by man."

I shall illustrate this by an analogy. The capitalist economy may be compared to an old-fashioned balloon which is moved by the currents of the air in the direction in which the wind pushes it. Man has no control whatever over the direction in which the balloon is moving. The socialist economy in the period of realization of its plan by administrative measures can be compared to an old-fashioned airplane, in which the pilot with his hands moves the steering gear. By always attending to the steering gear, the pilot directs the plane in the direction he chooses; whenever the current of the air changes, he moves the gear in such a way as to keep in his chosen direction. Planning in which the realization is based on economic means I would compare to a modern plane which has an automatic steering mechanism. The pilot sets the mechanism in the direction in which he wants the plane to go, and the automatic mechanism keeps the plane in the desired direction. The pilot can read a book or a newspaper in the meantime, and the plane by itself keeps the desired direction. But it is not the direction where the wind pushes the plane, but the direction which the pilot has chosen—consciously chosen. It is the pilot who determines the direction of the plane; if he wishes, he can change the direction by re-setting the automatic mechanism.

If I were to carry the analogy to the end, I would say that the pilot must, of course, from time to time determine whether the automatic steering mechanism is working. As a rule, experience shows that when the wind is very strong, the automatic mechanism does not work, and the pilot has to take the steering gear in his hand and steer himself. When the wind again becomes quiet, he can once more let the automatic mechanism work. In sudden upsetting situations, administrative measures have to be used in managing a socialist economy.

The next problem is to what extent the decisions implied in the plan, (not their realization, but the decisions themselves) can be centralized, or can or even must be decentralized. The need for centralized decisions obviously results from the need for coordination. Such decisions as the basic direction of investments, since they also must be coordinated through the coordination of various branches of economy, must be centrally planned. Each plan must have centralistic elements. I would say that the basic decisions of the plan must be made centrally. In addition to that, the plan may have as subsidiary parts certain decentralized subsidiary plans, in order to secure the proper flexibility. There are two criteria which determine the decentralization which economic planning can or must have. One determines the possibility of decentralization and the other the necessity of decentralization.

Economic planning should be decentralized so far as it is possible to set up economic incentives such that the decisions of the decentralized units are the same as the decisions which would be made centrally. Second, economic planning *must* be decentralized in all cases where the central decision responds to a situation too late because in such cases, unless there is decentralization, central planning becomes fictitious. What actually is obtained is an elemental development. It is important to notice that in all socialist countries, in the period of highly centralized planning and management, there were many elemental processes of this type.

For instance, in Poland in a certain period the elemental processes were so common that one could have asked whether a planned economy still existed. On the one hand, there was a plan; but on the other, the economy produced results in a very elemental way. The elemental character of this process was the result of two facts. One was the over-centralization of the plan. Before processes that took place in various branches of the economy came to the attention of the central authority, and before the central authority took action, irreversible things had already happened. The result was purely elemental. The other fact was the existence of "wrong" economic incentives. When the old moral and political incentives stopped working (they can only work for a certain period), it was discovered that all kinds of incentives were implicit in the plan of which the central authority was not aware and which hampered the realization of the plan.

Thus, it is a practical and important question to know how many of the decisions are made in the central economic plan, and how many decisions are delegated to lower economic units, e.g., enterprises or organizations of enterprises in the industry, etc. This is particularly important with regard to the investment plans. In Poland, for instance, we are now developing a scheme which provides central planning of what we call fundamental investments, for instance, building a new plant or substantially enlarging an existing plant. We give the enterprises the right to undertake the subsidiary investments autonomously, without asking anybody for approval.

The latter has proved to be necessary in order to assure greater flexibility of investment decisions. For instance, if the enterprise needs to put up funds for unforeseen repairs, or if it wants to buy machines to increase output quickly, or to make some technical improvement, it must have the power to do so. Our experience was that before it got the approval of the central authority to make the necessary investments, the whole situation was already different. Thus, the situation was utterly inflexible. The financial resources for such subsidiary investment would consist of a part of the amortization fund of the enterprise and of bank credits it could take up for the purpose of such investments. Investments of small enterprises are to be entirely financed by bank credits without appearing at all in the central economic plan.

Now, of course, one thing should be kept in mind. The fact that a part of that investment is financed by bank credits does subject them in an indirect way to central planning, because obviously the bank can refuse to give the credit. The bank acts on the basis of a certain general economic policy in deciding how much credit it is going to give, for what purpose it is going to give it, and on what conditions it will give it. These are indirect ways by which the central authority influences the subsidiary investments.

A similar economic problem, and a more acute one, exists with regard to the planning of production. In the former period, even the smallest product had to be in the central economic plan. Now, however, only the basic production of enterprises is in it. The enterprise has the right to undertake what is called subsidiary production, which is not in the plan. There is quite a discussion among Polish economists as to whether production should be in the economic plan. There are a few economists who think that production should not be in the economic plan at all, but that it should respond only to the economic incentives of the market. The practical solution which will probably be adopted in Poland will be to put in the central economic plan the output of certain basic commodities, like coal, steel, raw materials, certain means of production, and textiles of mass production, i.e., commodities of a particular significance for the national economy. As to the rest, the enterprises will have a plan of output in terms of its total net value without prescribing the detailed assortment. A shoe factory, for instance, will have a total value plan of output but be able to produce any assortment of men's shoes, ladies' shoes, and children's shoes, according to its own decision.

All these are problems of technique and not of principle. I think that the one essential thing in the socialist economy is that the plan has to be an active one which determines the pace and the direction of development of the national economy. The other things are really questions of technique, which may change under different conditions. There is, however, one more problem which I want to mention in this connection. This is an essential and not a technical thing—the plan must be based on correct economic accounting. Correct accounting of economic costs and economic benefits, and consequently a correct price system, are indispensable.

In a socialist economy, prices have two purposes: One is as a means of distribution, and the other as a means of economic accounting. Therefore, there are two principles which must be taken into account in the formation of prices. This requires a calculation, at least as we see it now in our work in Poland, of two kinds of prices, namely, market prices and accounting prices.

Unless distribution of consumers' goods is done by rationing, the market price must obviously be such as to establish equilibrium on the market, to equalize demand and supply. The same holds also for prices of the means of production when administrative allocation is removed and enterprises freely buy and sell their products. Market conditions determine the equilibrium prices which equalize demand and supply. The principle of determining the market prices is very simple. They simply must equalize demand and supply.

However, market prices are not sufficient. In addition, there must be calculated accounting prices, which reflect the social cost of production of the various products. The accounting prices, of course, may strongly differ from the market prices. In Poland, we propose now to calculate what we call the initial or normal prices, which would be the cost of production plus a profit, which serves to cover accumulation and the collective consumption of society. To these normal prices, we propose to add a (positive or negative) markup in order to obtain the market prices which equalize demand and supply. Then the (positive or negative) differences between the market prices and the normal prices would be an indicator for economic planning.

The indication for the next plan would be to increase output (by making the necessary investments) where the market price is high above the normal price, and to stop expansion or even diminish output where the market prices does not cover the normal price.

The great controversy at this moment among Polish economists is what cost should be included in the normal price: whether it should be average cost of the enterprises in a given industry or marginal cost. The majority of economists take the view that it should be marginal cost. Those who are in favor of average cost really consist of two groups: one is in principle in favor of average cost, and the other is in principle in favor of marginal cost but believes that this would in practice be a very difficult system of calculation and so takes average cost simply because the other solution, though theoretically better, is very difficult to realize in practice.

The proponents of marginal cost, of course, propose to use a practical approximation to marginal cost. The cost on the basis of which the normal price is to be calculated is the average variable cost of the group of enterprises which have the highest cost in the industry. The method proposed is to classify the enterprises in several groups (not too many, because it has to be practically easy), and then to take the group of enterprises which have the highest cost as the pilot group. It serves as the indicator. There is a reason for using average variable cost of the group. If we take just one enterprise, we may get a very unrepresentative figure. We want to have something which represents the real cost structure of the industry. Therefore, we take the average variable cost of the enterprises in that last group.

The argument in favor of marginal cost and of this procedure of practical interpretation of marginal cost is this: We have, for instance, electric power plants. Each plant produces at a different cost. Suppose we can save electric power. What is the diminution of cost to society? Obviously, when we save electric power, we still stop or diminish production not in the plants which have the lowest cost, but in the plants which have the highest cost. The cost in the latter plants represents the resources we save; it represents the saving to society. If we have to expand the output of electricity, the cost to society is the cost of operation of electric power plants which produce at the highest cost. Consequently, if changes in the use of electric power take place, the effect on the cost to society is determined in the most costly plants, and that change is marginal cost. We consider only variable cost in the highest cost plants, because the fixed cost is given and does not change in consequence of a change of utilization of electricity.

This is basically the system which a majority of Polish economists propose. To the marginal cost, there must be added something to cover all the fixed costs in the industry. This may be zero, because the larger profits of the enterprises which produce at lower cost may be sufficient for this purpose. If not, we must add something to marginal cost. Such additions would have everywhere to be proportional to the marginal cost so that the normal prices would be proportional to the marginal costs of the various products and cover the fixed cost.

The indicator for the plan would be whether the market price is higher or lower than this normal price, i.e., whether it socially pays to expand or reduce the output of a product. I have to add that this normal cost would also have to include a surcharge to cover capital accumulation and collective consumption, e.g., non-productive expenses of the state, etc. Such additions would have to be in the same proportion in all branches of the economy so as not to affect the proportions between the normal prices and marginal costs.

So much on this subject. It is clear that good and effective economic planning requires a development of economic science and that it must be based on scientific economic analysis. This is one of the basic differences between a socialist and a capitalist economy. In a capitalist economy, the economic processes are elemental; whereas under socialism, they can be directed on the basis of scientific knowledge of the needs and possibilities of the whole national economy.

26. WHAT IS TO BE DONE ABOUT THE SUCCESS OF SOVIET INDUSTRY?*

P. J. D. Wiles

SYNOPSIS

1. The most important comparisons between economic systems are output per person and the rate of growth. The growth rate of the Soviet Union exceeds that of any free country and, if maintained, will enable it to surpass the United States in output per person.

2. The reasons for communist efficiency are planning, income inequality, nationalization, powerless unions, rapid innovation, constructive competition, control of savings, and the ideology of abundance.

3. The high growth rate of communism makes its promise of abundance plausible to poor countries. Their people prefer bread to freedom when they must choose, and usually believe they can have both under communism.

4. The western countries must increase their growth rate in order to compete with communism and to improve the condition of their own people.

5. They can do it by maintaining full employment even if moderate inflation is the cost; by making income taxes less progressive; by generating enthusiasm for economic expansion; by reducing the power of unions; by the state's rationalizing industry, compelling the sharing of technical information, and establishing a central efficiency audit; and by the financing of heavy investment with taxes if necessary.

6. Such measures increase the power of the state, but that danger is moderated by parliamentary safeguards, an enlightened electorate, the unpopularity of planning, and by commerce and agriculture being outside state control.

It is a great mistake to compare economic systems only, or even mainly, by the justice or injustice with which they distribute income among individuals and classes, by their adaptibility to consumer demand or their economic "rationality," or by the political and social relationships to which they give rise. The most important criterion is coarser, more materialistic, and much less sophisticated: *How much* does each

* Reprinted by permission from *The Soviet Economy: A Discussion* by P. J. D. Wiles *et al.* (London: Secker and Warburg and the Congress for Cultural Freedom, 1956), pp. 27–40.

economic system produce per head? For the principal object, curiously enough, of economic activity is to satisfy human wants; and these being almost limitless, the best way to satisfy them is to produce a great deal of everything.

Now, countries begin to industrialize and modernize at different times and from different levels of prosperity. We are not interested, then, only in how much per head is produced today, but more in the rate of growth of productivity, and especially in the rate of growth in roughly comparable circumstances (e.g., during industrial maturity or during the first phase of industrialization). Perhaps the most important fact in all modern economics is that this rate of growth is higher in the manufacturing industry of the Soviet Union than in that of any free country at the period of its maximum development, let alone now (see [Table 1]).

TABLE 1

	Percentage Rate of Growth per Annum in:		
	Industrial Production	Industrial Productivity	Real National Product per Head
U.S.S.R., 1928–40	c. 12.5	c. 0.2	c. 7.0*
U.S.S.R., 1949–54	c. 12.0	c. 5.0	c. 6.0†
U.S., 1860–1914	5.3	1.9	2.6‡
Japan, 1910–14—1935–38	7.2	3.8	c. 3.0§
Sweden, 1881–83—1911–13	. . . .	. . .	2.5

* 1928–37.
† 1948–53.
‡ 1869–78—1903–14.
§ 1913–17—1933–37.

We perceive that the overwhelming communist superiority in industry alone leads to a great over-all superiority (in the whole national income). The effect of compound interest is very great over a few decades. Thus, growing 3 per cent per annum faster than the U.S., the U.S.S.R. could catch up from a starting point of half the U.S. national income per head in 23 years, and, growing 4 per cent faster, in 18 years.

What are the causes of this superiority? Nothing comforting to the anti-communist. It is not just because the satellites have been exploited: Their own economies are expanding at an almost equal rate, and Soviet exploitation here is offset by Soviet subsidies to China. And in any case, this would not explain pre-war Soviet growth. Again, it is not that, technically stagnant until well into the twentieth century, the Soviet economy has only had to apply methods known elsewhere to cover in one easy technical leap a century of hard-won western progress. For such a leap is beset with every social and economic difficulty: All backward economies stand equally at the brink of it, but only those under communist rule have achieved it.

The reasons for communist industrial progress are to be sought in communist industrial efficiency. First there is the planning system itself: Targets are set, in physical or financial terms, which each ministry, trust, factory, and individual worker must beat. The targets are raised year by year, and the obligation to beat them has quasi-legal force. This is the principal aim and result of the whole planning system. Nor, secondly, does the legal stick exclude the monetary carrot. Anyone from director to laborer can enormously increase his income by over-fulfilling his plan or norm. Various privileges in kind also follow; and for these good economic citizens, promotion to a higher grade is also open, the steps of this promotion being steeper than in free countries. Taxes are not highly progressive: The highest marginal rate of income tax is only 13 per cent; and direct taxes fall most heavily on food, not manufactured luxuries. Then, thirdly, the system of ownership helps efficiency. Factories can be combined, processes transferred from one to another, and specialization and standardization imposed by mere fiat. There are no obstacles of property law, shareholders' vested interests, etc.: All industry is treated as one big trust.

It is a further peculiarity of communism wholly to emasculate its trade-unions. This is indispensable anywhere if production is to be maximized. The influence exercised by a labor monopoly over wages, hours, conditions of work, apprenticeship, hiring, craft demarcations, indeed over almost everything, is restrictive. At almost no point can a union raise efficiency: It can at most—with insignificant exceptions in the U.S. garment trades—not hinder it. All these heavy obstacles are swept aside under communism. The union follows mechanically the party line on industrial matters. It loses all bargaining power except in the field of welfare; it becomes a cheer leader, an organizer of productivity, and a promoter of enthusiasm. If the authorities want the norms raised (i.e., real wage rates reduced), they get the "trade-unions" to get the "workers" to propose it "spontaneously."

Fifthly, new techniques cannot be resisted by deliberate inertia or willful ignorance, as so often is done by trade-unions or small capitalists in free countries. There is but one authority to be cajoled into experiment, and browbeaten by demonstration. Admittedly, this one authority may be obstinate and thus suppress a good new method altogether. But the more serious danger in practice is the very slow spread of methods proved correct by the best firms. This danger the system of central direction minimizes. Also, trade secrets are forbidden: It is sabotage to conceal a technical discovery from the authorities or those whom, in other circumstances, one would call competitors. The inventor is liberally rewarded from state funds, and may not in practice take out a patent. Technical education, too, equals in quality and far surpasses in quantity the best western examples. Technical education is an absolutely vital object of capital expenditure (for it is capital expenditure as surely as money put into machines and buildings). The mere superiority of the number of Soviet technicians is as great a threat to our economic supremacy as any other single factor.

But of course, sixthly, there are still competitors, only the object now is not to divert profits from the other man to oneself (and not every measure conducive to this end benefits the community), but to be more efficient and productive than the other man. "Socialist competition" is not a fight but a race; and greater production is a direct, not an accidental or circuitous, result. This competition is financed and run by the state, for both organizations and individuals. On these latter the pressure is particularly great. The successful hero of socialist competition, the Stakhanovite, is immensely well paid, honored, and privileged; and output norms for the vast majority are continually raised toward the level of his attainment.

Again, savings are extracted much more successfully from the population by taxes than by the lure of interest rates in a free economy. But when the armed forces and the police have had their due, not very much more is left for investment than elsewhere. The U.S.S.R. invests a fifth or more, the U.S. and Great Britain about a sixth, of their national incomes. The sheer accumulation of capital may not be so important as technical progress, but it still plays an undoubted role—not least in financing the research that makes technical progress possible. It is true that industry gets a much larger share and construction a much smaller share of the capital available than in other countries, so that, to some extent, Soviet industrial growth is the obverse of the Soviet housing shortage; but this does not remove the Soviet system's superiority in raising capital, or explain why the whole national income, as opposed to that derived from industry only, has grown faster. Neither is the simple fact that communism can raise more capital in general a wholly sufficient explanation of its superior growth in general; so that we need have no recourse to the various institutional explanations also offered. For the growth rate is more than double that of a free economy, while the proportion of national income invested is much less than double, and there are diminishing returns to ever greater investment.

Eighth and last is the whole ideology of the movement. Second only to class war, material progress is the criterion of value and the content of history. "Full communism," its last stage, is a state of productivity so great that out of the ensuing plenty, all men's desires can be satisfied according to need, without money or accounting. Yet this fantastic utopia is taken very seriously: It is official dogma that the U.S.S.R. is even now moving toward "full communism," and the speeches of party bigwigs often end in a peroration on this theme. As Christian medieval Europe was building the City of God, so is the U.S.S.R. building material progress.

The economic growth thus attained is, in the eyes of one adhering to the "western," "humanist," or "liberal" tradition, the sole redeeming feature of Soviet society—sole, that is, if he troubles to study the facts and perceives that all other communist claims to what he considers virtue are lies. But if the observer be suffering from extreme poverty, from old-style western imperialism, or from the plain stagnation of his own society, self-deception is not required to sway him in favor of communism. He counts all other "western" values well lost for the sake of economic growth, thus making a choice *within* that system of values which may be unusual but is not irrational.

Arbitrary imprisonment, national subjugation, murder, torture, inequality, corruption, obscurantism: Suppose him never so perfectly informed as to the extent of these, he may all the same prefer a radio and a full stomach. The countrymen of Gandhi and Maharishi are greater materialists, and with reason, than those of Archdeacon Paley and John Bright. The truth about the greater rate of Soviet economic growth is pro-communist propaganda hard to counter.

Moreover, we have not, of course, to deal with rational, albeit undernourished, men. Free men are not now, and are never likely to be, perfectly informed about life under communism; and their own minor quarrels, inertia, and shortness of sight will blunt the sharpness of their reaction to whatever information they do receive. Yet again, there is danger in a much more simple way: Rich countries—as the communist countries will be—have more strategic and diplomatic strength than poor ones —as the NATO countries will one day be, relatively speaking. They can keep more men under arms and stock more hydrogen bombs. They can offer better terms of trade. They can bribe more politicians, finance more spies, entertain more delegations. And since their society is controlled while their opponents' is free, they can use their wealth in yet other ways. They can use nominees to buy shares in armament companies or politically sensitive sectors of the capitalist economy. They can dump in the export markets of countries they particularly dislike. Above all, they can support the local communist parties and press ever more lavishly.

The communist threat is thus partly one of economic growth. In reply to it, neither virtuous conduct, nor rearmament, nor reason, nor psychological warfare, nor cultural freedom are altogether enough. The western rate of economic growth must also be stepped up. Perhaps in view of our other advantages, we can afford to fall a little short, but surely not so far short as we do now. Besides, economic growth is a *very good thing in itself*: There are many very poor people in the U.S., for instance, and even a perfectly just and very wealthy society has the duty to help develop backward areas.

But how can we grow faster economically while remaining more or less what we are in other respects? Can some other economic system produce the required results, or must we adopt the "eightfold way" outlined above? May not many of the evils of communism be directly attributed to that "eightfold way"? The presumption must be forgiven of trying to answer these questions in a thousand words. I am convinced, first, that in manufacturing industry, no other system can generate such growth, whereas in agriculture and commerce the system is a demonstrated failure. Communist agriculture and commerce do not therefore concern us. Now, there are, practically speaking, two alternative ways of encouraging growth in manufacturing industry that bear no resemblance to the communist method. The first is by perfect freedom for entrepreneurs, coupled with the strict enforcement of "capitalist competition" through trust busting and free importation. The second is by full employment and moderate inflation, which means restrictions on imports and possibly other controls as well—though there is no reason why trust busting should be abandoned. To my mind, the second of these methods is much superior to the first; and certainly a crude view of the statistics bears me out, if we compare countries or periods in which the one or the other policy was used. But neither approaches the results of communism, so we are forced to consider adopting some or all of the "eightfold way."

Clearly, it is no threat to political freedom or private morality if earned income is subjected to less steeply progressive rates of tax, or if a general ideology of economic expansion is preached, and the best workers are rewarded with medals or publicity. But it is a much more serious matter to suppress trade-unions or the private ownership of the means of production. Yet these institutions are not good in themselves. They contribute nothing—the former less than nothing—to economic progress. They have no particular moral beauty, since both represent only selfishness, albeit the group selfishness of a trade-union is confused by some with altruism. Their work is as political counter-weights to the overmighty state, and to each other.

Past political thought is hagridden by counter-weights, checks and balances, the separation of powers, etc.; and by the quasi-Marxist notion that there must be institutional as well as constitutional checks to power, such as, indeed, private property and trade-unions. Where manners are unsoftened by education or tradition, where national minorities, sects, or social classes are oppressed, such brakes upon political action are necessary. Power in such countries is dangerous in anyone's hands, and for them the dilemma of economic growth *or* political freedom may indeed be absolute. But for many countries—the Protestant lands of northwestern Europe, the white dominions of the British Commonwealth, and possibly the U.S., there need be no such dilemma. Here, parliamentary democracy itself, and a few other quite ordinary legal safeguards, are check enough upon an omnipotent state machine. The electorate would always vote to check an incipient dictatorship; and as for an unconstitutional seizure of power, no checks or balances would stop that, anyway. We attribute, as Lord Radcliffe has well said, too many of our blessings to our institutions, too few to our character.[1] Given the perfectly simple conditions that general elections are compulsory and an opposition exists,

[1] *The Listener*, December 6, 1951.

freedom could only be killed in, say, Scandinavia by foreign conquest. It would itself kill its internal enemies—easily. Freedom was indeed built up, even in these countries, on the strict limitation of existing power—in England, for instance, by centuries-long insistence on the inviolability of property, the immunity of deputies, and the independence of judges. But once freedom is secure, not every weapon by which it was won remains necessary to guard it. In particular, the institutional guarantees of our social structure are unnecessary; the sword of inviolable private property may well be beaten into the ploughshare of nationalization, if on any non-political ground that seems a good thing.

Moreover, the communists have gone much too far, and we do not need to imitate them very precisely. Their governments have much more power than is required for economic growth. It is not nationalization we need, but state power to rationalize: i.e., to amalgamate enterprises, to enforce specialization upon branch factories, to standardize products, to dissolve restrictive cartels and trade associations, etc. Most of these things occur under private enterprise, only much too rarely and slowly. The whole formal and legal structure of private ownership can and, in my view, should be maintained beneath occasional changes, imposed from above, of management and organization. In planning, again, what matters is that certain standards of efficiency be enforced, not that this or that particular product be produced or price charged. Indeed, on the contrary, such things should, almost all economists agree, be left to the market and the profit motive. A central efficiency audit is a much more practical and less threatening proposition than a 100 per cent central plan; yet, for economic growth, it is much more desirable. Even with trade-unionism, some aspects are less deleterious than others. The cherished right to strike for higher wages is a very minor nuisance on the whole; it might possibly suffice to do away with the major evils—restrictive practices, apprenticeship conditions, and craft demarcations. For while the former affects merely the value of money, the latter affects the quantity of output. Indeed, many American and German trade-unions have reached already this comparatively harmless state.

To compel the sharing of technical secrets, and to finance large investment projects out of taxes if need be, are the remaining items in the "eightfold way." Clearly less serious than planning and nationalization, they are only a political threat insofar as they, too, violate private property rights. The state need not be very powerful to adopt such measures as these. There are, too, various quite libertarian devices, unknown to communism, for making an economy grow: for instance, the relaxation of business taxes.

Fas est et ab hoste doceri [It is right to be taught even by an enemy]. Yet the imitation of communism is a very dangerous thing. If I have been too optimistic above about its compatibility with freedom, the following points must also be considered. Agriculture and commerce should remain capitalistically free because—broadly speaking and for reasons we have not space to give here—they are more efficient that way. This is a very great institutional check upon state power. Moreover, it is a sort of Marxism to believe that interference with the economy entails encroachment upon political liberty. Many politically totalitarian governments have abandoned economic non-intervention (e.g., the Jacobins and the Nazis), but I cannot recall a single democratic or libertarian government which believed in economic planning and was led by that to the curtailment of political freedom. The lesson of history is long and reassuring on this point. It is not merely, as we saw above, that democratic governments *ex hypothesi* submit themselves to the electorate. It is also that planning is not particularly popular, and the excess of it leads to early electoral defeat. Planning does not kill freedom, but freedom planning. Moreover, the clash of economic interest is by no means stilled—it may well be exacerbated—by planning; and this will find expression in electoral controversy about the allocation of government funds, etc. Again, the kind of planning that most threatens liberty is not that which nationalizes property or breaks up the monopolies of labor and capital, but that which interferes with the free play of supply and demand: licensing, rationing, price control, etc. And we have seen all this to be unnecessary.

Finally, if we do not take this risk with our freedom, we shall surely lose it by conquest. The cold war is still with us, and war demands of any society that it take risks. The duty to take these risks, moreover, rests quite as much upon the major industrial countries of NATO as upon the backward countries in the direct line of fire. For the benefit to the free world from the centralized planning of industry is greatest, of course, where there is most industry to plan, and where traditions and constitutions reduce the danger to freedom itself.

PLANNING AS A FORM OF POLICY

The policy followed in a planned economy depends on the purpose of planning. If the purpose is to increase total income, divide it equitably, eliminate private monopoly, and the like, the policy is similar to that in a liberal, or capitalist, economy. The difference between such planning and liberalism is only one of methods and sometimes just a difference in the extent to which the same methods are used. The democratic socialists of Britain, for example, propose policies that usually are an extension of the policies of advocates of free enterprise. What the socialists say is that their planning serves the purpose of liberalism better than the market does or that only socialism can do the job capitalism is supposed to do. There can be, and is, important disagreement between liberals and democratic socialists over the extent to which particular methods of policy should be used and how they should be combined—that is the controversy over the "mixed economy"—but there can be no disagreement over political values. The most important is the idea that all behavior—of individuals, groups, and government—must have the consent of those affected by it. It is the idea that social policy is made by discussion and agreement.

The other form of planning has a quite different purpose. It is to make the economy serve the objectives which society seeks; and that means in practice the objectives laid down by the government, since it states what the objectives are. They are not what men want them to be but are in the nature of things—in history, a divine directive, a social organism, a racial spirit—and cannot be altered by human choice. To the communists the objectives of society are determined by its material means and the attendant social relations. Specifically, the economic policy of the Soviet Union is dictated by historical forces that are transforming the economies of the world and will eventually make them into classless societies. As the objectives of the Soviet Union are historically determined, so is its economic policy. It is not made by the free choice of individuals. Indeed, in Marxian philosophy, free choice is an illusion. Engels said that freedom is the recognition of necessity. Categorically different is Spinoza's conception that the free man is one who lives by reason.

Socialists of both kinds no longer believe in as much centralized planning as they once did. Each group still adheres to its separate aims, and each still believes in comprehensive planning. But they now believe planning should employ less explicit direction by the state and should rely more on the initiative of individuals. The most important changes have been (*a*) to use a price mechanism of some kind to distribute output and to determine what it should be and (*b*) to allow more private ownership of the means of production. Most of the democratic socialists of all countries are convinced of the merit of a price system and, when in power, use it extensively, although in each party there are opponents of it. One of its first proponents was Oskar Lange, who is that country's leading economist. He now sees that policy as a means of making comprehensive planning more effective. The democratic socialists, on the other hand, propose it for that reason and also because a price system reports the free choices of the population. In recent years, they have re-examined the nationalization of industry, another fundamental tenet of socialism, and some have proposed the policy be modified. It may be that the communist countries in time will re-examine nationalization just as they have re-examined the price mechanism. They then will come closer to the democratic socialists in their methods, and both will have come nearer to the methods of capitalism, which itself continues to move toward more comprehensive policy making.

The methods of all three have become less distinctive—a fact which may turn out to be the most important of our time—and their converging upon each other raises the question of whether or not their aims can remain distinct.

The Policy of Democratic Socialism

H. D. Dickinson presents the case for democratic socialism. He defines it as the social ownership of the means of production, their use according to a general plan based on individual preferences, and a distribution of the product on the basis of equal rights. He argues:

a) The purpose of an economic system is to use its resources in a way that will satisfy as many wants as possible.

b)Under capitalism the price mechanism cannot direct resources to their best uses because of the inequality of income and wealth, monopoly, consumer ignorance and deception, and the discrepancy between private and social costs.

c) The cause of these obstructions is private property. It makes incomes unequal, is an inducement to monopoly and exploitation of the consumer, prevents the equalizing of private and social costs, and, beyond economic disadvantages, is the cause of rigid classes and inequality of opportunity.

d) In order that resources be used efficiently, the state should own the means of production and operate them according to a general plan which incorporates individual preferences in an equitable way.

e) Although logically conceivable, unplanned socialism is improbable. The fact that all enterprises are under public scrutiny and must coordinate their decision would lead to planning.

f) Comprehensive planning is possible under capitalism but is likely to lead to dictatorship in order to enforce the distribution of a part of the national product to property owners.

g) Hence, planned socialism is the only feasible form of democratic economic organization.

h) In order to use resources efficiently (i.e., according to individual preferences), it would have to measure demand and costs, and distribute the product.

i) It can use the price system to perform all of the functions, some, or none of them.

It will be noticed that statements (*a*), (*b*), (*c*), and (*f*) are Dickinson's case against capitalism, of which (*c*) is the most important; and of the remainder, which are his case for socialism, the most important are (*d*) and (*e*). That is, he argues that private property is the root of our economic problems, that they can be solved by socializing property and using it according to a comprehensive plan. He does not argue that the price system is at fault or that self-interest, or individual preference, is wrong. It will be noted also that two of the obstructions to the price mechanism—inequality and monopoly—are considered major problems by liberal economists. Finally, it will be noticed that Dickinson, like them, believes that efficiency means using resources in order to satisfy individual preferences.

The Nationalization Issue

Today, democratic socialists are not as sure about nationalization as Dickinson was when he wrote. Crosland states that the industries that were nationalized in Britain after 1945 have not increased their efficiency as much as was expected. The economies of large scale production have been offset in part by the difficulty of managing very large enterprises, whether privately or publicly owned. Another reason is that labor morale has fallen, and that in itself was a disappointment. Nor has nationalization facilitated comprehensive planning, because the ministers in charge have been unclear about what they wanted to do, and because some have believed the nationalized industries should be independent. It also has been found that if a government does wish to plan an industry, it does not always have to own it. It may be controlled by regulation of its investment and output and by other means.

Moreover, nationalization has not reduced the inequality of wealth as much as was hoped, and may actually have increased the proportion of total saving and investment done in the private sector. That is because prices in the nationalized industries were set too low to allow them to save. It has been found that monopoly, even when publicly owned, has grave disadvantages, and that competition has merits that were not hitherto recognized.

Nationalization in the future needs to be guided by different principles, Crosland says. The state no longer should want to own an industry just because it is a monopoly or is big or for some other of the older reasons given by socialists. There are not many private monopolies left in Britain, and the oligopolies and competitive firms are reasonably efficient. Some are multi-product firms and operate in several markets. To nationalize them in one and not in another is a complex and dubious undertaking. Managerial problems in all of them are more difficult than they were in the industries previously taken over. Another consideration is the increase in the productivity of the entire economy, weakening still more the efficiency argument for public ownership. Crosland proposes that the state undertake additional nationalization only if increased efficiency is certain and is obtainable in no other way. He also proposes that firms, rather than industries, be nationalized and operated in competition with private enterprises.

The Historic Guides to Communist Planning

Crosland's conception of planning is much influenced by liberal ideas of policy. It is altogether different from that of the Soviet Union during the rule of Stalin. That form is explained by Baran. He also explains why, in his view, no economic doctrines, liberal or Marxian, can supply a general theory of planning. Marxism cannot, because a communist state cannot predict all of the conditions it will encounter, some of which are of its own making. What the Soviet government did was to use Marxism as a guide to managing the specific economic and political problems of Russia. Those problems, and the guide to them, determined the long run goals of the state.

The central problem of planning after 1917 was to secure a command over the economy's resources in order that the national product could be divided properly between the government's share for defense, investment, administration, social services, etc., on the one hand, and, on the other, the share going to consumption. The government's share is called the "economic surplus." There is no principle by which the necessary amount of the "economic surplus" can be determined as, for example, there is a principle in the market economy for determining what should be the total value of consumer goods.

Guided by the objectives of communism and an appraisal of the problems confronting it, the state decides how the national product should be divided. It fixes total consumer income equal to the value of consumer goods, and the remainder is the profit of state enterprises, most of which the government collects by the turnover tax (approximately, a sales tax levied each time goods change hands). Tax proceeds are used for defense, investment, administration, and the like; and the government decides (a) how to allocate the total among different industries and (b) what shall be the technical form of each outlay. The object of the former decision is to eliminate severe scarcities (like transportation before the war) and of the latter to secure the largest possible increase in productivity. The planning authority summarizes the factual basis of its decision in three sets of national balance sheets, showing what in the west would be called (*a*) the input-output relations of plants and farms, (*b*) a national budget of the income and expenditure of individuals and government, and (*c*) an estimate of the quantity demanded of labor and the sources of additional workers. The efficiency of planning depends on the accuracy of the estimates made in the balance sheets and on the power of government to execute the plans.

The New Forms of Communist Planning

Since the death of Stalin, there have been changes in the Russian planning. Nevertheless, Baran's essay still is important, because not all of the methods he describes have changed. Most of them still seem to be used in China; and in their entirety, they constitute a policy against which changes of recent years are to be understood, measured, and judged. The principal change has been to decentralize to some extent, and by one method or another, the power of the state over the economy, and to increase the power of industries and firms to make decisions and to execute them. Accompanying the change has been some economic writing of exceptional interest, such as that by Oskar Lange.

The methods of planning are determined, Lange states, by the stage of socialism, using that word in its Marxian sense, which makes it synonymous with communism. In the first stage, shortly after the socialists come to power, planning must be centralized. Not all of the economy has yet been socialized, and so not every part can be relied on to follow socialist directives. The state must set the long run goals of development and execute them. In undeveloped countries, there is another reason for centralization: the need to industrialize rapidly, which only the state can satisfy. At all stages the state relies on economic incentives and political power, the former being monetary rewards that induce individuals to act consistently with the central plan, and the latter being force to make them. At the early stage, political power is the more important. As socialism matures, economic incentives are more practical. A working class is formed, and a "socialist intelligentsia" (individuals who accept the purposes of the state and are skilled in promoting them). Some decisions can be delegated to subordinate units like the firm, and detailed supervision then is not necessary. Nevertheless, the state retains ultimate power over the economy. This kind of change is occurring in almost all communist countries in different ways and degrees. Lange proposes a form that decentralized planning should take.

The state should determine, by its long run goals, the division of the national output between consumption and investment. It must coordinate the physical and the value aspects of production separately and together. But that does not require the state's deciding the kind and amount of every single commodity to be produced. It should fix the output of basic commodities only, leaving others to be decided by the state-owned firms so long as the total output of each reaches a certain money value. The firms also should have the power to make subsidiary investments and to make any other decisions which, if left to the state, would not be made in time.

To assure that the proper goods are produced and distributed to the people who want them most, Lange proposes that each commodity have two prices: the market price, which equalizes quantities supplied and demanded, and the normal price, which measures the cost of production. The latter is computed by a variant of the marginal cost principle. It is equal to the average of the average variable costs of the highest cost firms plus the sum of average fixed costs for the industry and the cost of additional investment of the economy and of its collective consumption (free goods), the last three being allocated to keep prices proportional to variable costs. If the market price exceeds the normal price, too little of a commodity is being produced, and vice versa. The inequality reports to the state and the firms that particular outputs and investment should be increased or decreased.

A Policy for Confronting Communism

The west is less interested in the forms of planning than its results. The result of Russian planning has alarmed many. In the opinion of western economists who have made it their special study, the Russian rate of growth is more than twice that of the United States. What is the explanation? Peter Wiles believes it is communist economic policy in eight of its aspects: planning, especially in its centralized form, because that was the form during most of the period of Russian growth; the absence of progressive taxes or anything else that discourages people from being industrious; nationalization, which gives the state complete control of industry; the fact that unions are powerless and cannot restrict output; competition in a form that only increases output and never diverts a part from one person or firm to another; the fact that the state does not rely on people to save but taxes them in order to limit their consumption; the encouragement to invention and innovation; and the zeal of the Russian people to improve their economic position and their pride at succeeding.

The rapid growth of the Soviet Union has impressed the undeveloped areas of the world; and they believe, Wiles states, that to grow rapidly, they too must use communist methods. Most of the people of those areas are not well informed about the dictatorial features of the Soviet economy. But if they were, they would in some way (Wiles continues) believe that they could have the growth without the dictatorship; and if they were pressed to choose between capitalism with its low growth rate and communism with its high rate, they would choose communism. That is one threat of communist efficiency. Another is the military and political power that their high growth rate gives the communist countries. For these reasons the western growth rate must be increased, and also because the people of the west need more goods.

How can the west do it? Wiles proposes that it adapt the "eightfold way" of communism to its purposes. It should maintain full employment even at the cost of moderate inflation; should make income taxes less progressive; instill an enthusiasm for economic expansion; prohibit unions from restricting output; empower the state to rationalize industries by forcing them to use efficient methods and prohibiting any other; compelling them to share technical secrets; establishing a "central efficiency audit"; and if necessary, finance large scale investment with taxes.

The west is reluctant to give its governments all of the power needed for such a policy, because the power may be abused. But, Wiles states, the fear is exaggerated. Popular liberty can be safeguarded by the parliamentary system, by an enlightened and knowledgeable electorate, by trade and agriculture being outside state control, and finally by the fact that planning is unpopular and excesses would provoke resistance to it.

Planning and Policy: A Summary Statement

The principal forms of planning today are democratic socialism and communism, and the policy of each is determined by what it tries to do. Socialism tries to serve the individual; and its policy tries to maintain full employment, promote growth, reduce inequality, limit monopoly, allocate resources efficiently, and do other things that enlarge the economic welfare of the individual. Communism seeks to put the economy on the high road of history so that it will be carried along by forces that lead to higher forms of social institutions. Some of its specific economic goals are the same as those of socialism, and of capitalism as well. It too wants allocational efficiency, full employment, rapid growth, and unwasteful distribution. What distinguishes it is the way the goals are defined and the methods of realizing them. The government of a communist state decides what efficiency is, how rapid growth should be, and the like, while in a socialist or capitalist economy the decisions are made by the people acting directly on the market or indirectly through their elected representatives. Once the decisions are made, they are carried out by more centralized methods under communism.

But there is a notable lessening of the differences in the methods of the three systems. The communists believe in much less centralization than they once did, and the socialists have softened their opposition to private property. Capitalism, meanwhile, is moving toward a more comprehensive view of policy and is conceiving it as a set of decisions about what the government should do or not do in all of the important parts of the economy.

*This book has been set on the Linotype in 10
point Janson, leaded 2 points, and 9 point
Janson, leaded 1 point. Part numbers and titles
are in 18 point Spartan Medium; selection
numbers and titles are in 14 point Spartan
Medium. The size of the type page is 27 by
47 picas.*